INTERPRETING MYANMAR

A DECADE OF ANALYSIS

INTERPRETING MYANMAR

A DECADE OF ANALYSIS

ANDREW SELTH

Australian
National
University

PRESS

ANU PRESS

Published by ANU Press
The Australian National University
Acton ACT 2601, Australia
Email: anupress@anu.edu.au

Available to download for free at press.anu.edu.au

ISBN (print): 9781760464042
ISBN (online): 9781760464059

WorldCat (print): 1224563457
WorldCat (online): 1224563308

DOI: 10.22459/IM.2020

Cover design and layout by ANU Press. Cover photograph: Yangon, Myanmar by mathes on Bigstock.

CONTENTS

Acronyms and abbreviations. xi

Glossary. xv

Acknowledgements xvii

About the author xix

Protocols and politics. xxi

Introduction 1

THE INTERPRETER POSTS, 2008–2019

2008

1. Burma: The limits of international action
    (12:48 AEDT, 7 April 2008) 13

2. A storm of protest over Burma (14:47 AEDT, 9 May 2008). 17

3. Burma's continuing fear of invasion (11:09 AEDT, 28 May 2008) . .21

4. Burma's armed forces: How loyal? (11:08 AEDT, 6 June 2008) . . .25

5. The Rambo approach to Burma (10:37 AEDT, 20 June 2008) . . .29

6. Burma and the Bush White House
    (10:11 AEDT, 26 August 2008) 33

7. Burma's opposition movement: A house divided
    (07:43 AEDT, 25 November 2008). 37

2009

8. Is there a Burma–North Korea–Iran nuclear conspiracy?
    (07:26 AEDT, 25 February 2009) 43

9. US–Burma: Where to from here? (14:09 AEDT, 28 April 2009). . .47

10. US–Burma relations: Told you so (15:37 AEDT, 18 May 2009) . . .51

11. Conspiracies and cockups in Burma
    (11:13 AEDT, 26 May 2009). 53

12. Burma: 'Nationalism is not rationalism'
   (10:23 AEDT, 10 June 2009) 57

13. Burma–North Korea: Rumour and reality
   (12:33 AEDT, 29 June 2009) 61

14. Burma's unanswered nuclear question
   (11:40 AEDT, 3 August 2009) 65

15. Burma's nuclear status: Not the last word, but ...
   (09:24 AEDT, 29 September 2009) 69

16. Burma's 'superstitious' leaders (10:25 AEDT, 22 October 2009) . .73

17. Burma: Obama's 'pragmatic engagement'
   (11:17 AEDT, 18 November 2009). 79

2010

18. Burma: If not nukes, what about missiles?
   (10:53 AEDT, 11 January 2010). 87

19. Burma's new election laws (14:41 AEDT, 19 March 2010) 91

20. Burma: Of arms and the man (17:16 AEDT, 6 April 2010) 95

21. Burma, North Korea and US policy
   (14:59 AEDT, 18 May 2010). 99

22. Does Burma have a WMD program?
   (11:02 AEDT, 7 June 2010) 103

23. Burma, North Korea and WMD: A postscript
   (11:01 AEDT, 10 June 2010) 107

24. Burma and the politics of names (13:51 AEDT, 12 July 2010) . .109

25. Burma: The beast in its entirety (12:08 AEDT, 27 July 2010) . . .113

26. Burma: After the elections, what?
   (10:07 AEDT, 31 August 2010) 115

27. Burma's elections: Thirteen reasons
   (10:57 AEDT, 2 November 2010). 119

28. Burma-watching on film (13:37 AEDT, 30 November 2010). . . .123

2011

29. Burma: Thanks for the memoirs
   (15:45 AEDT, 11 January 2011). 129

30. Burma and North Korea: Reality checks
   (15:00 AEDT, 27 April 2011) 133

31. Burma and WMD: Lost in translation
   (11:57 AEDT, 19 May 2011). 137

32. Burma and Libya: The politics of inconsistency
    (11:06 AEDT, 17 June 2011) 141

33. Burma and ASEAN's seat of yearning
    (11:26 AEDT, 14 September 2011) 145

34. Burma–China: Another dam puzzle (Part 1)
    (12:46 AEDT, 1 November 2011) 149

35. Burma–China: Another dam puzzle (Part 2)
    (16:51 AEDT, 1 November 2011) 151

36. Aung San Suu Kyi's choice (10:30 AEDT, 23 November 2011). . .155

37. Clinton in Burma: The WMD dimension
    (16:52 AEDT, 6 December 2011) 159

2012

38. Assessing Burma's reform program
    (15:04 AEDT, 24 January 2012) 165

39. Burma's reforms: Foreigners can't take much credit
    (16:00 AEDT, 30 January 2012) 169

40. Burma and WMD: Nothing to report?
    (08:23 AEDT, 29 March 2012) 173

41. Kurt Campbell on US–Burma relations
    (12:08 AEDT, 27 April 2012) 177

42. The Rangoon bombing: A historical footnote
    (10:11 AEDT, 16 May 2012) 181

43. Burma and WMD: In the news again
    (15:48 AEDT, 1 August 2012) 185

44. Burma, the Rohingyas and Australia
    (10:23 AEDT, 8 October 2012) 189

45. Burma: The Man has met The Lady
    (09:57 AEDT, 23 November 2012) 193

46. Burma's police: The long road to reform
    (13:45 AEDT, 13 December 2012) 197

47. Burma: Eyes on the prize (10:14 AEDT, 18 December 2012). . . .201

2013

48. Defence relations with Burma: Our future past
    (12:08 AEDT, 4 March 2013) 207

49. Burma's fractious polity: The price of democracy?
    (11:32 AEDT, 14 March 2013) 211

50. Burma's Muslims: A primer (09:17 AEDT, 27 March 2013).....215

51. Aung San Suu Kyi: A pilgrim's progress
    (15:34 AEDT, 7 May 2013)..............................221

52. Will Aung San Suu Kyi be President of Burma?
    (11:20 AEDT, 16 May 2013)............................227

53. Burma: Conspiracies and other theories
    (15:28 AEDT, 5 June 2013)...........................231

54. Burma and North Korea: Again? Still
    (12:58 AEDT, 10 July 2013)..........................237

55. West reaches out to Burma's security sector
    (10:13 AEDT, 26 July 2013)..........................243

56. Risk and reward with Burma's security sector
    (13:26 AEDT, 26 July 2013)..........................247

57. Burma: What chance another coup?
    (13:47 AEDT, 9 September 2013).......................251

58. Burma: Two WMD developments
    (16:41 AEDT, 8 October 2013)........................257

59. Aung San Suu Kyi's risky strategy
    (15:07 AEDT, 30 October 2013).......................261

60. Bombings in Burma: The long view
    (12:33 AEDT, 11 November 2013)......................265

61. Australia and the Burma/Myanmar name debate
    (10:08 AEDT, 27 November 2013)......................271

62. When Aung San Suu Kyi comes to call
    (10:24 AEDT, 3 December 2013).......................275

2014

63. Burma puts its stamp on the world: Philately and foreign policy
    (09:02 AEDT, 7 January 2014).........................281

64. Myanmar becomes Burma, again
    (08:32 AEDT, 14 January 2014).......................287

65. Is Burma really buying submarines?
    (11:50 AEDT, 29 January 2014).......................291

66. Burma: A critical look at those chemical weapons claims
    (14:36 AEDT, 25 February 2014)......................297

67. Should Burma participate in UN peacekeeping?
    (10:19 AEDT, 13 May 2014)...........................303

68. Will Aung San Suu Kyi be president? Odds are lengthening
    (09:05 AEDT, 30 June 2014)..........................309

69. Burma and the Biological Weapons Convention
(08:40 AEDT, 15 October 2014). 315

70. Aung San Suu Kyi and Kipling's Burma
(10:00 AEDT, 31 October 2014). 319

71. Aung San Suu Kyi's aura is fading
(15:10 AEDT, 18 November 2014). 325

72. Myanmar Police Force needs more foreign help to reform
(15:07 AEDT, 3 December 2014). 331

73. Surveying public opinion in Burma
(08:01 AEDT, 18 December 2014). 337

2015

74. Second thoughts on the civil unrest in Burma
(16:28 AEDT, 14 April 2015) 343

75. Burma: The return of the 'vigilantes'
(08:01 AEDT, 22 April 2015) 349

76. Burma: Police reforms expand women's roles
(08:49 AEDT, 1 May 2015). 355

77. Burma: Beware of unrealistic expectations
(10:03 AEDT, 18 June 2015) 361

78. Is Naypyidaw setting the agenda in US–China–Burma relations?
(10:15 AEDT, 18 September 2015) 367

79. Burma's *Tatmadaw*: A force to be reckoned with
(11:32 AEDT, 22 October 2015). 373

80. All change: Election result may see another round of the Burma/
Myanmar name game (08:35 AEDT, 18 November 2015) 379

2016

81. The potential for army–police rivalry in Myanmar
(10:40 AEDT, 2 February 2016) 385

82. Democracy in Myanmar: Who can claim victory?
(08:45 AEDT, 29 March 2016) 389

83. Old Burma hands write on the 'odd man out in Asia'
(12:40 AEDT, 6 June 2016) 395

84. More name games in Burma/Myanmar
(13:34 AEDT, 10 August 2016) 399

85. Aung San Suu Kyi's fall from grace
(08:48 AEDT, 8 December 2016). 405

2017

86. Myanmar and Aung San: The resurrection of an icon
(09:12 AEDT, 31 March 2017) 413

87. Suu Kyi's Myanmar, one year on (09:10 AEDT, 27 April 2017) . . .419

88. Incident at Three Pagodas Pass (13:09 AEDT, 31 May 2017) . . .425

89. A big step back for Myanmar
(07:17 AEDT, 13 September 2017) 431

90. The Rohingya crisis and Myanmar's military responses
(14:00 AEDT, 24 November 2017) 437

2018

91. The Rohingya question: Determining whom to hold to account
(09:30 AEDT, 20 April 2018) 445

92. The Rohingyas: A new terrorist threat?
(06:00 AEDT, 6 September 2018) 449

2019

93. Myanmar's intelligence apparatus under Aung San Suu Kyi
(10:00 AEDT, 12 April 2019) 457

94. Myanmar: Pariah status no bar to defence modernisation
(15:00 AEDT, 7 May 2019) 461

95. With new coastguard, Myanmar looks to improve maritime
security (06:00 AEDT, 9 September 2019) 467

96. Myanmar: Postage stamps and political signals
(06:00 AEDT, 30 September 2019) 471

97. Aung San Suu Kyi: Why defend the indefensible?
(14:00 AEDT, 12 December 2019) 475

Epilogue 479
Sam Roggeveen, Director, International Security Program,
Lowy Institute, and founding editor of *The Interpreter*

Index 483

Acronyms and abbreviations

ABC	Australian Broadcasting Corporation
AFP	Australian Federal Police
ANU	The Australian National University
ARSA	Arakan Rohingya Salvation Army
ASEAN	Association of Southeast Asian Nations
BBC	British Broadcasting Corporation
BSI	Bureau of Special Investigations
BW	biological weapons
C-in-C	commander-in-chief
CSAAR	Centre for the Study of Australia–Asia Relations
CSI	Christian Solidarity International
CSIS	Center for Strategic and International Studies
CW	chemical weapons
CWC	Chemical Weapons Convention
DA	defence attaché
DDI	Directorate of Defence Industries
DFAT	Department of Foreign Affairs and Trade
DIO	Defence Intelligence Organisation
DVB	Democratic Voice of Burma
EU	European Union
GDP	gross domestic product
HIV/AIDS	human immunodeficiency virus and acquired immune deficiency syndrome

HMAS	Her Majesty's Australian Ship
IAEA	International Atomic Energy Agency
ICG	International Crisis Group
ICJ	International Court of Justice
IISS	International Institute for Strategic Studies
IMDb	*Internet Movie Database*
IRI	International Republican Institute
ISIS	Islamic State of Iraq and Syria
JADE Act	*Tom Lantos Block Burmese JADE (Junta's Anti-Democratic Efforts) Act*
JDW	*Jane's Defence Weekly*
KIA	Kachin Independence Army
KNLA	Karen National Liberation Army
MA	Myanmar Army
MI	Military Intelligence
MIS	Military Intelligence Service
MP	Member of Parliament
MPF	Myanmar Police Force
MW/MWt	megawatt
NGO	nongovernmental organisation
NLA	National Library of Australia
NLD	National League for Democracy
NMSP	New Mon State Party
OCMSA	Office of the Chief of Military Security Affairs
PKO	peacekeeping operations
PPF	People's Police Force
R2P	responsibility to protect
ROK	Republic of Korea
RTA	Royal Thai Army
SAM	surface-to-air missile
SAS	Swan Ah Shin/Swan Arshin
SB	Special Branch

SBS	Special Broadcasting Service
SLORC	State Law and Order Restoration Council
SOF	*Soldier of Fortune* magazine
SPDC	State Peace and Development Council
SRBM	short-range ballistic missile
UK	United Kingdom
UMP	Union Military Police
UN	United Nations
UNHCR	United Nations High Commissioner for Refugees
UNICEF	United Nations Children's Fund
UNODC	United Nations Office on Drugs and Crime
UNSC	United Nations Security Council
US	United States (of America)
USDA	Union Solidarity Development Association
USDP	Union Solidarity and Development Party
WMD	weapon of mass destruction

Glossary

Amyotha Hluttaw	House of Nationalities
chinthe	leogryph
dacoit	armed bandit
Daw	female term of respect (literally, 'aunt')
feng shui	Chinese geomancy (literally, 'wind water')
hpoun	spiritual power
Ko	title of a young male or close male friend (literally, 'brother')
Lon Htein	riot police (abbreviation of 'security preservation battalion')
Ma	title of a young female or close female friend (literally, 'sister')
Maung	title given to young males (also adopted by older men to display modesty)
Pyidaungsu Hluttaw	Union Assembly
Pyitthu Hluttaw	House of Representatives
sangha	Buddhist 'clergy'
Sayagyi	male term of respect (literally, 'great teacher')
Swan Arshin/ Swan Ah Shin	Masters of Force (militia)
Tatmadaw	armed forces (literally, 'royal force')
U	male term of respect (literally, 'uncle')
yadaya	magic rituals performed to delay or prevent misfortune

Acknowledgements

Researching and writing about Myanmar for *The Interpreter* over the past 12 years, I have incurred many debts, both in Australia and overseas. My thinking has been enriched by countless discussions and exchanges of emails with fellow Myanmar-watchers and others. Drafts of posts were often shared with people who were more expert than me on various subjects. Given this fact, and the wideranging nature of the subjects covered in this book, it is difficult to single out anyone for special mention. Some of those living in Myanmar and subject to its continuing societal constraints may prefer not to be named. However, there are some people to whom special mention is due.

First of all, I should like to thank the Executive Director of the Lowy Institute, Michael Fullilove, for permitting me to reproduce these articles, which first appeared on *The Interpreter* between 2008 and 2019. Thanks are also due to Sam Roggeveen, the founding editor, and the current editor, Dan Flitton, for productive and enjoyable working relationships that stretch back for more than the life of the blog. Without them, *The Interpreter* would not be the internationally respected institution that it has become and I would not have had the opportunity to share my thoughts about so many aspects of Myanmar with its wide readership.

Thanks are also due to Allan Gyngell, the first executive director of the Lowy Institute and another old Burma hand. I can still remember the briefing he gave me before I was posted to the Australian Embassy in Rangoon in 1974. I have also greatly appreciated the generous support given to me by Michael Wesley, the first director of the Griffith Asia Institute and the second executive director of the Lowy Institute, since our paths first crossed in the Australian intelligence community more than 15 years ago.

Over the years, I have been blessed with a number of exceptional guides and mentors, all of whom helped immeasurably to develop my research, analytical and writing skills, such as they are, and my appreciation of objective, balanced, evidence-based reporting. They include Geoffrey Fairbairn, Garry Woodard, John Hartley and Peter Varghese. Special thanks are due to *Sayagyi* David Steinberg, formerly of Georgetown University and for decades the doyen of modern Myanmar studies. In so many ways, he has supported and encouraged my work ever since our memorable first meeting in Bangkok in 1995.

I should also like to record my appreciation for all the help I have received from the members and staff of the Griffith Asia Institute at Griffith University in Brisbane, which became my academic home after I retired from government service in 2006. Since its formation under Nicholas Farrelly in 2015, the Myanmar Research Centre at The Australian National University in Canberra has also provided me with inspiration, information and opportunities, particularly through its biennial Burma/Myanmar Update conferences, which date back to 1999.

Last, but by no means least, I want to thank my wife, Pattie. For nearly 40 years, she has not only tolerated my abiding interest in everything to do with Myanmar, large and small, but also been a constant source of encouragement, support and advice. I owe her much more than I can record here.

Needless to say, I take full responsibility for any errors of commission or omission in this book. Also, for the record, everything in it is drawn from open sources. It has no official status or endorsement.

About the author

Andrew Selth is an Adjunct Professor at the Griffith Asia Institute, Griffith University, in Brisbane, Australia. He has been studying international security issues and Asian affairs for 45 years, as a diplomat, strategic intelligence analyst and research scholar. Between 1973 and 1986, he was posted to the Australian diplomatic missions in Rangoon, Seoul and Wellington. He later held senior positions in the Defence Intelligence Organisation and the Office of National Assessments. He has also been an Adjunct Associate Professor in the Coral Bell School of Asia Pacific Affairs at The Australian National University (ANU), a Visiting Fellow at the ANU Strategic and Defence Studies Centre, a Chevening Scholar at St Antony's College, Oxford University, an Australian Research Council Fellow at Griffith University and a Harold White Fellow at the National Library of Australia. Dr Selth has published nine other books and more than 50 peer-reviewed works, most of them about Myanmar (Burma) and related subjects. He has also contributed to the public debate on Myanmar through numerous articles and commentaries in magazines, newspapers and online forums, including *The Interpreter*.

Other books by Andrew Selth

1986   *The Terrorist Threat to Diplomacy: An Australian Perspective*

1988   *Against Every Human Law: The Terrorist Threat to Diplomacy*

1996   *Transforming the Tatmadaw: The Burmese Armed Forces Since 1988*

2002   *Burma's Armed Forces: Power Without Glory*

2012   *Burma (Myanmar) Since the 1988 Uprising: A Select Bibliography*

2015	*Burma (Myanmar) Since the 1988 Uprising: A Select Bibliography* (2nd edition)
2017	*Burma, Kipling and Western Music: The Riff from Mandalay*
2018	*Burma (Myanmar) Since the 1988 Uprising: A Select Bibliography* (3rd edition)
2019	*Secrets and Power in Myanmar: Intelligence and the Fall of General Khin Nyunt*

Protocols and politics

After Myanmar's armed forces crushed a nationwide prodemocracy uprising in September 1988, the country's official name (in English) was changed from its post-1974 form, the Socialist Republic of the Union of Burma, back to the Union of Burma, which had been adopted when Myanmar regained its independence from the United Kingdom in January 1948. In July 1989, the new military government changed the country's name once again, this time to the Union of Myanmar, which had long been the vernacular version (in the literary register, at least). In the formal declaration of the country's independence from the UK in 1948, for example, it was called the Union of Burma in the English version and the Union of Myanmar (or 'Myanma') in the Burmese version. In 2011, after formal promulgation of the 2008 national constitution, the country's official name was changed yet again, this time to the Republic of the Union of Myanmar.

Also in July 1989, a number of other placenames were changed by the military government to conform more closely to their original pronunciation in the Burmese language. For example, Arakan State became Rakhine State and Tenasserim Division became Tanintharyi Division (later Tanintharyi Region). The Mergui Archipelago became the Myeik Archipelago, the Irrawaddy River became the Ayeyarwady River and the Salween River became the Thanlwin River. The city of Rangoon became Yangon, Moulmein became Mawlamyine, Akyab became Sittwe and Maymyo became Pyin Oo Lwin. The ethnolinguistic groups formerly known as the Burmans and the Karen are now called the Bamar and the Kayin, respectively.[1]

---

1   'Writing Systems: Romanization—Government of the Union of Myanmar Notification 5/89', Eighth United Nations Conference on the Standardization of Geographical Names, Berlin, 27 August 2002, Doc. E/CONF.94/INF75, unstats.un.org/unsd/geoinfo/UNGEGN/docs/8th-uncsgn-docs/inf/8th_UNCSGN_econf.94_INF.75.pdf.

The new names were accepted by most countries, the United Nations and other major international organisations. A few governments, activist groups and news media outlets, however, still clung to 'Burma' as the name of the country, apparently as a protest against the former military regime's refusal to put the question of a change to the people of Myanmar.[2] The old name was also believed to be the preference of then opposition leader Aung San Suu Kyi, who was held under house arrest by the military regime for periods totalling almost 15 years.[3] Questioned about the official name of the country soon after her party took office in 2016, Aung San Suu Kyi stated her continuing preference for the colonial-era term 'Burma', but said both names were now acceptable.[4]

The chapters of this book reflect the changing attitudes to this question, which are themselves the subject of several *Interpreter* posts. 'Burma' was the name I preferred to use until around 2016, when Aung San Suu Kyi's government took office in Naypyidaw and the widespread use of Myanmar by the international community prompted greater recognition of the official change of name, including by the Australian Government. Even then, however, 'Burma' and 'Burmese' were retained in *Interpreter* articles for formal titles used before 1989 and the citation of institutions and works that used that name. 'Burmese' was also used to describe the dominant language of the country. Such usage did not, and does not, carry any political connotations.

After the UK dispatched troops to the royal capital of Mandalay and completed its three-stage conquest of Burma (as it was then called) in December 1885, Yangon (then known as Rangoon) was confirmed as the administrative capital of the country. It remains the commercial capital but, in November 2005, the ruling military council formally designated the newly built city of Naypyidaw (or Nay Pyi Taw), 327 kilometres (203 miles) north of Yangon, as the seat of Myanmar's government.[5] Where they appear in this book, the terms 'Rangoon regime', 'Yangon regime' or, in some cases, simply 'Rangoon' or 'Yangon' are used as shorthand terms

---

2   Andrew Selth and Adam Gallagher, 'What's In a Name: Burma or Myanmar?', *The Olive Branch*, 21 June 2018, www.usip.org/blog/2018/06/whats-name-burma-or-myanmar.

3   Aung San Suu Kyi's incarceration occurred, with a number of breaks, between July 1989 and November 2010.

4   Andrew Selth, 'More Name Games in Burma/Myanmar', *The Interpreter*, 10 August 2016, www.lowyinstitute.org/the-interpreter/more-name-games-burmamyanmar.

5   Occasionally, it is stated that Naypyidaw is 367 kilometres north of Yangon, but that calculation is based on the distance by road between the two cities.

for the central government, including the military government that was created in 1962 and reinvented in 1974, 1988 and 1997. The government after 2005 is referred to as the 'Naypyidaw regime' or 'Naypyidaw' to reflect the administrative change that took place that year.

Another term used in this book is *Tatmadaw*. It is usually translated as 'royal force', but the honorific '*daw*' no longer refers to the monarchy. Since 1948, the name has been the vernacular term for Myanmar's tri-service (army, navy and air force) armed forces. In recent years, it has gained wide currency in English-language publications on Myanmar. Sometimes, the *Tatmadaw* is referred to simply as 'the army', reflecting that service arm's overwhelming size and influence, compared with the other two. While the term 'defence services' usually refers only to the armed forces, it is sometimes used in a wider context to refer collectively to the armed forces, the Myanmar Police Force, the 'people's militia' and sundry other state-endorsed paramilitary forces. On occasion, the Myanmar Fire Services Department and Myanmar Red Cross have also been included in this category. As the 2008 constitution decrees that 'all the armed forces in the Union shall be under the command of the Defence Services', the formal title of the *Tatmadaw*'s most senior officer is Commander-in-Chief of Defence Services.[6]

Over the years, some components of Myanmar's intelligence apparatus have changed their formal titles several times. The military intelligence organisation, for example, has periodically been renamed, usually to coincide with structural changes in the armed forces. These adjustments have not always been known to, or recognised by, foreign observers. Also, Burmese-language titles have been translated into English in different ways. The use of popular names has added another complication. For example, ever since 1948, the *Tatmadaw*'s intelligence arm has been widely known as the Military Intelligence Service (MIS), or simply the 'MI' ('em-eye'). Similarly, the Police Force's Special Intelligence Department (or, strictly translated, the 'Information Police') has long been known as Special Branch, or 'SB'. All this has meant that in the literature some agencies have been called by several different names, and not always accurately.[7]

---

6   *Constitution of the Republic of the Union of Myanmar (2008)* (Nay Pyi Taw: Ministry of Information, 2008), Ch.7, Clause 338.
7   This issue is discussed in Andrew Selth, *Secrets and Power in Myanmar: Intelligence and the Fall of General Khin Nyunt* (Singapore: ISEAS Publishing, 2019), doi.org/10.1355/9789814843799.

In Myanmar, all personal names are particular. Most people do not have surnames or forenames.[8] Names may be one to four syllables long and are usually chosen depending on the day of the week on which a child is born (which is why many people in Myanmar share the same name). Also, among the majority Bamar ethnic group, names are usually preceded by an honorific, such as '*U*', meaning 'uncle', or '*Daw*', meaning 'aunt'. *U* can also form a part of a man's name, as in U Tin U. The titles '*Maung*', '*Ko*' ('brother') and '*Ma*' ('sister')—usually given to young men and women— are also found in personal names, as in Maung Maung Aye, Ko Ko Gyi and Ma Ma Lay. To all such rules, however, there are exceptions. Some of Myanmar's ethnic minorities, such as the Kachin, have family or clan names, which are placed before their given names, as in cases like Maran Brang Seng, where 'Maran' is the name of a clan.[9] Ethnic minorities— such as the Shan, Kachin, Karen and Chin—also have their own systems of honorifics.

In Myanmar, names can be changed easily, without official permission or registration. This situation is further complicated by the frequent use of nicknames and other sobriquets as identifiers, such as 'Myanaung' (the town) U Tin, 'Tekkatho' (university) Phone Naing or 'Guardian' (the magazine) Sein Win. Pen-names, *noms de guerre* and pseudonyms also have a long history in Myanmar.[10] For example, the birth name of General Ne Win, who effectively ruled the country from 1962 to 1988, was Shu Maung. 'Ne Win' was a *nom de guerre* he adopted in 1941. Some Myanmar citizens were given or have adopted Western names, including those who attended Christian missionary schools in their youth. Others use only one part of their name for convenience—for example, when travelling abroad or dealing with foreigners. It is not uncommon for an obituary to list more than one name by which the deceased was known.

It may also be helpful to sketch out recent political developments and note the changes in the names of some key institutions and positions.

---

8   See David I. Steinberg, *Burma/Myanmar: What Everyone Needs to Know*, 2nd edn (Oxford: Oxford University Press, 2013), pp.xix–xx.
9   See 'A Note on Burmese Names', in Thant Myint U, *The Hidden History of Burma: Race, Capitalism, and the Crisis of Democracy in the 21st Century* (New York: W.W. Norton & Company, 2020), p.xii.
10   See Andrew Selth, 'Burma and the Politics of Names', *The Interpreter*, 12 July 2010, archive.lowy institute.org/the-interpreter/burma-and-politics-names.

The armed forces effectively ruled Myanmar for half a century, after General Ne Win's military coup in March 1962, when they formed the Revolutionary Council. From 1974 to 1988, they exercised power through an ostensibly elected 'civilian' parliament dominated by the Burma Socialist Programme Party—the country's only legal political organisation. On taking back direct control in September 1988, the armed forces created the State Law and Order Restoration Council (SLORC), which ruled by decree. In November 1997, apparently on the advice of a US-based public relations firm, the regime changed its name to the State Peace and Development Council (SPDC), but continued to rule through executive fiat.[11] In May 2008, the SPDC held a constitutional referendum, with predictable results.[12] This was followed by carefully managed elections on 7 November 2010. The resulting national parliament, consisting of 75 per cent elected officials and 25 per cent non-elected military officers, met in January 2011. A new government was installed under president Thein Sein in March that year.

Continuing this process, by-elections were staged on 1 April 2012 to fill 48 seats left vacant after recently elected Members of Parliament had resigned to take up ministerial appointments or had died. The opposition National League for Democracy (NLD), which was re-registered for the elections in December 2011, claimed that fraud and rules violations were widespread, but the party still won 43 of the 45 seats available on the day. One successful candidate was the party's leader, Daw Aung San Suu Kyi.

On 8 November 2015, a new general election was held, which, by most accounts, was reasonably free and fair.[13] The NLD received about 65.6 per cent of all votes cast, while the promilitary Union Solidarity and Development Party (USDP) received 27.5 per cent. Under Myanmar's 'first past the post' electoral system, this gave the NLD 79.4 per cent of all

---

11   David Scott Mathieson, 'The Burma Road to Nowhere: The Failure of the Developmental State in Myanmar', *Policy, Organisation and Society*, Vol.17, No.7, 1999, p.108, doi.org/10.1080/103499 52.1999.11876703. See also 'A SLORC By Any Other Name', *The Washington Post*, 6 March 1998, www.washingtonpost.com/archive/opinions/1998/03/06/a-slorc-by-any-other-name/84bdf222-1eb8-417c-97ee-032cd9535e91/?noredirect=on.

12   The SPDC claimed that 92.48 per cent of eligible voters endorsed the new constitution. *Constitution of the Republic of the Union of Myanmar (2008)*, p.iv.

13   The Carter Centre, *Observing Myanmar's 2015 General Elections: Final Report* (Atlanta: Carter Centre, 2016), www.cartercenter.org/resources/pdfs/news/peace_publications/election_reports/myanmar-2015-final.pdf.

the available seats.[14] It secured 255 of the 440 seats in the lower house (*Pyitthu Hluttaw* or House of Representatives) and 135 in the 224-seat upper house (*Amyotha Hluttaw* or House of Nationalities)—a total of 390 of the 491 seats contested at the union level.[15] The armed forces are allocated 25 per cent of the seats in both houses, but this gave the NLD a clear majority in the combined Union Assembly (*Pyidaungsu Hluttaw*). As a result, it was able to elect a new president in 2016 and pass a law creating the position of state counsellor for Aung San Suu Kyi (who, under the 2008 constitution, is unable to become president, as her children are the citizens of foreign countries).[16]

The national charter clearly states that the President 'takes precedence over all other persons' in Myanmar. However, even before the elections, Aung San Suu Kyi had made it clear that she intended to be 'above the President' and act as the country's de facto leader.[17] Under the NLD, the President acts essentially as a ceremonial head of state. For practical purposes, Aung San Suu Kyi acts as head of the government, within the limits of the constitution, which ensures that considerable power is retained by the armed forces. This position has been accepted by most world leaders, as evidenced by her attendance at various Association of Southeast Asian Nations (ASEAN) meetings and the enthronement in October 2019 of the new Japanese emperor. She is also Myanmar's Minister for Foreign Affairs and, formally at least, attends some international meetings in this capacity.

---

14   Kyaw Kyaw, 'Analysis of Myanmar's NLD Landslide', *New Mandala*, 1 May 2012, www.new mandala.org/analysis-of-myanmars-nld-landslide/.
15   *The Myanmar Elections: Results and Implications*, Asia Briefing No.147 (Yangon/Brussels: International Crisis Group, 9 December 2015).
16   'Myanmar's 2015 Landmark Elections Explained', *BBC News*, 3 December 2015, www.bbc.com/news/world-asia-33547036.
17   *Constitution of the Republic of the Union of Myanmar (2008)*, Ch.3, Clause 58. See also 'Myanmar Election: Aung San Suu Kyi Will Be "Above President"', *BBC News*, 5 November 2015, www.bbc.com/news/av/world-asia-34729691/myanmar-election-aung-san-suu-kyi-will-be-above-president.

Introduction

When Sam Roggeveen invited me to contribute an article to the Lowy Institute's new digital magazine in late 2007, I had no idea that it would be the first step in a long and mutually profitable association. *The Interpreter* soon established itself as a consistently timely, thoughtful and innovative forum for the discussion of a wide range of subjects covering domestic and international politics and economics, foreign policy issues and developments in the broader security sphere. It was not long before it had acquired a global audience and was influencing senior policymakers, both in Australia and abroad. It was thus an ideal outlet for my research and comments on contemporary Myanmar.

The main focus of my articles for the blog was on developments in Myanmar's politics, security and foreign affairs. However, they occasionally ranged more broadly and delved into historical, social and economic matters. Some were purely descriptive, such as my 2013 primer on Myanmar's Muslim communities, but most surveyed current views on breaking stories, including my own observations. A couple of posts, such as the one about Major General John Hartley's 1994 visit to Three Pagodas Pass on the Thailand–Myanmar border, were based on personal experiences.[1] Most pieces stood alone, but a number of issues remained topical throughout the period under review and were the subject of several posts, written as events unfolded and situations developed.

Looking back through all these articles, I have been struck by the way in which they trace the history of Myanmar from the days of the military regime, through president Thein Sein's civilian–military administration, to Aung San Suu Kyi's current coalition government. Indeed, it could be claimed that, during the 12 years covered by this book, Myanmar

---

1   Although not identified in the article, I was the civilian intelligence analyst in the general's party who had a diplomatic posting to the Australian Embassy in Rangoon.

experienced more momentous changes than at any time since the 1962 coup, when the armed forces (known as the *Tatmadaw*) first seized power and established the modern world's most durable military dictatorship. The wider strategic environment also underwent a dramatic transformation, affecting not only internal developments, but also Myanmar's place in international affairs.

For example, during this period, Myanmar made the difficult transition from an authoritarian military regime to a hybrid government consisting of both elected civilians and appointed military officers. This process, which began with the announcement on 30 August 2003 of a 'seven-point roadmap to a discipline-flourishing democracy', broadly unfolded according to the armed forces' stated blueprint.[2] One critical step was the drafting of a new constitution, which was adopted after a nationwide referendum in 2008.[3] This carefully crafted charter allowed the armed forces to step back from direct power in 2011 and paved the way for the election of a National League for Democracy (NLD) government under opposition leader Aung San Suu Kyi in 2015.

Aung San Suu Kyi's personal road to power was another subject of continuing interest. For years an internationally admired symbol of democratic change (she was awarded the Nobel Peace Prize in 1991), she went from being a political prisoner to de facto leader of a government in partnership with the same institution that had kept her under house arrest for nearly 15 years. She was never going to meet all the expectations of her followers, which were quite unrealistic, but, as State Counsellor (she was denied the presidency by the 2008 constitution), her reputation suffered as she proved unable to rise to the challenges of her new position. More shocking to international observers, however, was her failure to maintain the high moral and ethical principles she had espoused as a prisoner of conscience.[4]

During Aung San Suu Kyi's early days in office, there was growing disquiet in many circles about her apparent lack of support for the universal human rights that were once her mantra. Some observers even claimed that her

---

2   Prime Minister General Khin Nyunt, Press conference, Naypyidaw, 30 August 2003. See also Andrew Selth, 'All Going According to Plan? The Armed Forces and Government in Myanmar', *Contemporary Southeast Asia*, Vol.40, No.1, April 2018, pp.1–26, doi.org/10.1355/cs40-1a.

3   *Constitution of the Republic of the Union of Myanmar (2008)*.

4   See, for example, Andrew Selth, *Aung San Suu Kyi and the Politics of Personality*, Griffith Asia Institute Regional Outlook Paper No.55 (Brisbane: Griffith University, 2017).

government was just as repressive as the former military regime.[5] Even then, no one was prepared for her refusal to condemn the excesses of the armed forces, particularly following their brutal 'clearance operations' against the Muslim Rohingyas in Rakhine State in 2016 and 2017. The final straw for her foreign admirers was her clumsy attempt in December 2019 to defend Myanmar against charges of genocide in the International Court of Justice.[6] If it had not been obvious before, Aung San Suu Kyi's appearance at The Hague demonstrated that she was, as she had always claimed to be, a politician, rather than an icon of democracy.

Another issue that continued to attract the attention of foreign observers between 2008 and 2019 was Myanmar's internal security. There were several outbreaks of civil and religious unrest, fanned by political repression, economic hardship, religious extremism and racial prejudice. Also, Myanmar was home to some of the world's longest-running civil wars, as ethnic minority groups struggled to carve out a place in Myanmar's ethnic Bamar Buddhist–dominated society. Aung San Suu Kyi's promise before taking office to give the highest priority to a nationwide ceasefire and peace settlement was never likely to be fulfilled. In any case, these conflicts remained hostage to the armed forces, which strongly resisted the creation of any kind of federal state and always had the power to disrupt negotiations.

Indeed, the *Tatmadaw* remained central to all these questions. Despite Myanmar's transition to a 'disciplined democracy' in 2011, the *Tatmadaw* arguably remained the country's most powerful political institution and, in various ways, its leadership was able to exercise considerable influence over the central government. In military affairs, including operations, it operated completely independently.[7] Also, over the past decade, the *Tatmadaw*'s order of battle has benefited from a series of major arms acquisitions. Despite some notable intelligence failures in recent years, it now appears more capable of fighting both conventional and

---

5   See, for example, Jonathan T. Chow and Leif-Eric Easley, 'Myanmar's Democratic Backsliding in the Struggle for National Identity and Independence', *The ASAN Forum*, 25 June 2019, www.theasanforum.org/myanmars-democratic-backsliding-in-the-struggle-for-national-identity-and-independence/.

6   'Transcript: Aung San Suu Kyi's Speech at the ICJ in Full', *Online Burma/Myanmar Library*, 13 December 2019, www.burmalibrary.org/en/transcript-aung-san-suu-kyis-speech-at-the-icj-in-full.

7   See, for example, Andrew Selth, *Myanmar's Armed Forces and the Rohingya Crisis*, Peaceworks Paper No.140 (Washington, DC: United States Institute of Peace, 2018).

unconventional wars. At one stage there were even fears—later proven unfounded—that Myanmar was developing a nuclear weapon, with North Korean help.[8]

Myanmar's international relations were a source of perennial interest. There were heated debates in the news media and academic literature over the military regime's ties with countries such as North Korea and China. Relations with the West were strained until US president Barack Obama cautiously introduced a policy of 'practical engagement'. This, and the NLD's assumption of office under Aung San Suu Kyi in 2016, led to the removal of most political and economic sanctions. Following the *Tatmadaw*'s operations against the Rohingyas—described by the UN as 'ethnic cleansing'—foreign contacts were once again reviewed.[9] However, this did not seem to worry the Naypyidaw government, which enjoyed close ties with its larger neighbours and the members of the Association of Southeast Asian Nations (ASEAN). More importantly, China and Russia continued to protect Myanmar on the UN Security Council (UNSC).

All these and other issues periodically prompted short updates, comments and, at times, deeper analyses on *The Interpreter*. If there was one thing that tied them all together, however, it was the dearth of reliable information. Little scholarly attention had been paid to Myanmar before 1988 and most of the writings that followed the prodemocracy uprising that year were by politicians, journalists and activists with agendas to pursue. Adding to this problem were the efforts of successive military regimes to hide what was really happening in the country and the opposition movement's attempts to win international support for their cause. There was the constant danger of foreign observers falling victim to what Jean Baudrillard once termed 'a vertigo of interpretations'.[10]

The Interpreter proved an excellent vehicle through which to tackle such problems and to raise subjects for wider discussion. Inevitably, some articles have since been overtaken by events and now have value mainly as part of the historical record. However, others have retained their salience and

---

8   See, for example, Andrew Selth, *Burma and North Korea: Conventional Allies or Nuclear Partners?*, Griffith Asia Institute Regional Outlook Paper No.22 (Brisbane: Griffith University, 2009).
9   United Nations Human Rights Office, Office of the High Commissioner, 'Myanmar: Senior UN Human Rights Official Decries Continued Ethnic Cleansing in Rakhine State', 6 March 2018, ohchr.org/EN/NewsEvents/Pages/DisplayNews.aspx?NewsID=22761&LangID=E.
10   Jean Baudrillard, *Selected Writings*, edited by Mark Poster (Stanford, CA: Stanford University Press, 2001), p.178.

can still help inform the public debate on a range of contemporary issues. Either way, it is hoped that the blog posts reproduced herein will interest, inform and, perhaps in a few cases, amuse anyone who is interested in modern Myanmar and, for one reason or another, is following the long and difficult journey being taken by the members of its diverse population to reach their respective goals.

With hindsight, the blogs hold up reasonably well. My dismissal of claims by journalists, academics and others that China had established military bases in Myanmar was later vindicated by the Indian Government's admission that there was no evidence of any such facilities.[11] My scepticism about repeated reports of clandestine nuclear, chemical and biological weapons programs, submarine purchases and a number of other security matters was justified by subsequent developments.[12] My doubts about the scope and level of North Korea's activities in Myanmar still seem reasonable. Like many others, I expected that the country's many civil wars would continue and I held out little hope for a nationwide ceasefire and peace agreement under the NLD Government. As expected, the international community found it very difficult to influence official thinking in Myanmar.

However, I underestimated both the pace and the extent of president Thein Sein's reform program after 2011 and the size of Aung San Suu Kyi's electoral victory in 2015. The creation of the position of state counsellor was as much of a surprise to me as it appears to have been to the generals. Also, I did not fully appreciate how much the armed forces would continue to influence Aung San Suu Kyi's government after 2016, nor did I anticipate the extent of the NLD's inability, or unwillingness, to overcome the legacies of 50 years of military rule. Like everyone else, I failed to foresee the Rohingya crisis of 2016–17. I was surprised not only by the scale of the *Tatmadaw*'s response, but also by the refusal of Aung

---

11   This was after the Indian foreign minister had himself made such claims. See Andrew Selth, 'Burma, China and the Myth of Military Bases', *Asian Security*, Vol.3, No.3, 2007, pp.279–307, doi.org/10.1080/14799850701568929.

12   The Myanmar Navy did eventually acquire a secondhand Russian submarine from India, but only five years after my article recommending caution about reports of such a purchase. See Andrew Selth, 'Is Burma Really Buying Submarines?', *The Interpreter*, 29 January 2014, www.lowyinstitute. org/the-interpreter/burma-really-buying-submarines; and Anthony Davis, 'Ships Ahoy for Myanmar's New Blue-Water Navy', *Asia Times*, [Hong Kong], 23 December 2019, www.asiatimes.com/2019/12/ article/ships-ahoy-for-myanmars-new-blue-water-navy/.

San Suu Kyi and her government to publicly acknowledge the human rights abuses that occurred, including in forums such as the International Court of Justice.

Over the past 12 years, I wrote articles for the blog with three main aims in mind. First, I wanted to provide background information on, and insights into, developments in Myanmar—a country that even now is little known and poorly understood. In the words of two well-known observers, it has long been considered an 'exotic unknowable'[13] with 'fiendishly complex'[14] problems. Second, I was keen to correct various reports by politicians, officials, journalists, activists and others that I felt were factually inaccurate, incomplete or in other ways misleading.[15] My third aim was to provide objective, evidence-based analyses of developments, public assessments of which were often clouded by political, moral and emotional considerations.

My goal was always to contribute to an informed and balanced public debate on a country that was increasingly capturing the headlines, often in rather sensational ways. This work has been produced with the same intentions.

The book collects 97 articles written for *The Interpreter* between 2008 and 2019 that relate primarily to Myanmar (a post relating to the possibility of a new war on the Korean Peninsula has not been included).[16] Each one is introduced by a short note outlining the circumstances in which the piece was written or the key developments that prompted me to put pen to paper. They have been reproduced almost exactly as they appeared online. No attempt has been made to further edit them or update them in the light of subsequent information and more recent events.

---

13   Chao-Tzang Yawnghwe, 'The Political Economy of the Opium Trade: Implications for Shan State', *Journal of Contemporary Asia*, Vol.23, No.3, 1993, pp.306–326, doi.org/10.1080/00472339380000181.

14   Timothy Garton-Ash, 'Beauty and the Beast in Burma', *The New York Times*, 25 May 2000, www.nybooks.com/articles/2000/05/25/beauty-and-the-beast-in-burma/.

15   For some of the 'political myths' about Myanmar current at the time, see, for example, Derek Tonkin, 'Political Myths', *Network Myanmar*, 2016, web.archive.org/web/20160825030911/http://www.networkmyanmar.org/89-Political-Myths.

16   Andrew Selth, 'Australia and Korea's Wars', *The Interpreter*, 29 November 2010, [Reposted on 14 August 2017], www.lowyinstitute.org/the-interpreter/australia-and-koreas-wars.

That said, I have made a few minor changes.

1. Occasionally, I have restored my original paragraph breaks, which seemed better suited to reproduction of the articles in a book.

2. In a few places, I have restored my original wording, where minor editorial amendments inadvertently changed my precise meaning or slightly altered the nuance of the original text.

3. Where any typographical errors or ambiguities survived the original editing process, they have been removed and the text corrected.

4. As far as possible, all the electronic links given in the original articles have been included as footnotes, even if the relevant web pages have since disappeared. In a couple of cases, where that was not possible, I have given new references.

5. I have added a small number of new references, usually to books, to help identify quotations used in the blogs, where no electronic source was available at the time of writing.

6. I have removed a number of electronic links to my own publications, which in the early days of the blog were given at the head of articles to help readers identify the author and outline his/her qualifications to write about certain matters.

As explained in the 'Protocols and Politics' section above, and discussed in several *Interpreter* articles, the name 'Burma' was officially changed to 'Myanmar' in 1989. Like many other Western commentators, I continued to use the old name until around 2016, by which time the new name had become widely accepted and the perceived benefits of using the old name had largely passed. Aung San Suu Kyi had lifted her objection to the new name, 'Myanmar' had become much better known and ways had been found around the problem posed by the fact that 'Myanmar' had no adjective in the way that 'Burma' had 'Burmese'.[17]

---

17   Another reason I continued to use 'Burma' was that I lived there in the 1970s and had become accustomed to the old name. I explained this once to a senior member of Myanmar's Directorate of Defence Services Intelligence. He said he understood but could not say so in public, as the military regime was firmly attached to the new name and disliked the continued use of the old name, particularly by governments and international organisations.

After appearing on *The Interpreter*, several of the articles reproduced in this book were published (usually with the editor's permission) in various media outlets in Myanmar, such as the *Myanmar Times*, *The Irrawaddy* and *Mizzima News*. They were occasionally picked up by other websites and cited by news services. Later versions of these articles were often given different titles, and in a few cases were subject to further editing.[18]

Canberra
February 2020

---

18   For example, blog 65 (originally posted on 29 January 2014) was republished as 'Myanmar's Aquatic Ambitions', in the *Myanmar Times*, 29 January 2014, www.mmtimes.com/in-depth/9397-myanmar-s-aquatic-ambitions.html.

THE INTERPRETER
POSTS, 2008–2019

2008

1

Burma: The limits of international action

(12:48 AEDT, 7 April 2008)

After nationwide prodemocracy demonstrations in 1988, Myanmar's military government was the target of wideranging international political and economic sanctions. Despite the repeated claims of officials, activists and exile groups, however, there was no evidence that any of these measures prompted significant changes in the regime's thinking or its core policies. The international community's limited ability to influence the generals was again demonstrated after another major outbreak of civil unrest in 2007, which foreign journalists dubbed the 'Saffron Revolution'.

The demonstrations in Burma last August and September—dubbed the 'Saffron Revolution' due to the participation of many Buddhist monks—were initially spontaneous reactions to unexpected fuel price increases and the military government's mistreatment of a few dissident monks. The demonstrations quickly developed, however, into an organised national protest against the regime's brutal and inept rule. Since then, however, the international effort to resolve the crisis in Burma has run into the sand. Indeed, the unprecedented level of attention given to this issue last year, while clearly warranted at the time, may have in fact achieved precisely the opposite of what was intended.

Activist groups claim, with some justification, that the widespread publicity given to the demonstrations last year was the result of their past efforts to arm dissidents with the technology to make the outside world more aware of developments inside Burma. Using satellite phones and the internet, activists were able to send images of the demonstrations (and the regime's harsh response) out to the foreign news media, which then broadcast the dramatic footage around the world. The enormous public response to the 2007 unrest was in stark contrast to that seen in 1988, when a massive prodemocracy uprising received relatively little international attention, due largely to the lack of news and images available from inside Burma.

The publicity given to the 2007 demonstrations and their aftermath resulted in an unprecedented level of diplomatic activity and widespread expressions of concern about the military regime's continued violation of human rights. Strong statements were issued by many governments and international organisations, including Burma's usual supporters, such as China. As the Association of Southeast Asian Nations (ASEAN) chair, Singapore expressed its 'revulsion' at the regime's actions. This rare consensus permitted the UN Human Rights Council to pass a unanimous resolution on the subject and the UN Security Council (UNSC) to issue a presidential statement. Both bodies deplored the violence in Burma, demanded the release of political prisoners and called for a dialogue on national reconciliation among all parties.

Since October 2007, however, relatively few countries have taken any specific measures to demonstrate their outrage over developments in Burma. The United States (US) and European Union (EU) have tightened their sanctions against the regime—a move followed on a much smaller scale by Australia. Most other countries, however, have been content with diplomatically worded statements of concern. ASEAN has specifically ruled out the imposition of sanctions. China, India and Russia have welcomed the military government's February 2008 announcement that it would hold a constitutional referendum this May and general elections in 2010. These steps along the regime's promised seven-step 'roadmap' to a 'discipline-flourishing democracy' have permitted its friends and neighbours to point to 'progress' in Burma and to argue against further punitive measures, including in the UN. The consensus that briefly emerged last year has disappeared.

The UN's Special Representative has been permitted to visit Burma on three occasions, and even to speak to detained opposition leader Aung San Suu Kyi. He has achieved very little in practical terms, however, and has himself acknowledged that the chances of any real progress are slight.

Since last September, the regime has made a number of tactical moves to quieten internal unrest, settle international concerns and reduce the embarrassment felt by Burma's friends in multilateral forums. Yet, there are no signs that Burma's military leadership has been persuaded to modify its core policies, such as a strong central government dominated by the armed forces. Nor has it shown any inclination to seek a substantive dialogue with the opposition movement or to respond differently should Burma's people once again take to the streets. Indeed, some well-informed observers believe that, over the past six months, the regime has become even more obdurate and determined to resist external pressures.

According to this argument, the sudden eruption of protests throughout Burma and the unprecedented international condemnation of the regime have encouraged the country's generals to set aside their differences and stand united against a renewed threat to military rule—both from within and outside the country. At the same time, the failure of the international community to make any progress on political reforms in Burma, despite the rare consensus on the need for change, can only have emboldened the regime. For the international community has once again demonstrated its inability to agree on a policy approach towards Burma and its lack of effective options against a regime that is prepared to put its survival before the welfare of its people and widely accepted norms of behaviour.

Reports by activist groups of serious breakdowns in military discipline last September remain unconfirmed, but the use of force against demonstrating monks clearly unsettled many in the largely Buddhist army. It would be unusual if there was not also a range of personal and policy differences within the armed forces leadership, particularly as Senior General Than Shwe approaches the end of his rule and the regime prepares for a transition to a 'parliamentary' system. Yet, the factors that unite the members of Burma's ruling council still seem to be greater than those which divide them. The former includes a shared determination to keep the country independent, united and stable—qualities the generals feel can only be achieved by continued military rule.

There may be occasional reshuffles of senior military personnel but, as long as the armed forces remain loyal and cohesive and are prepared to maintain their rule with force of arms, it is difficult to see how any domestic opposition group, foreign government or international organisation can loosen their grip on power.

2

A storm of protest over Burma

(14:47 AEDT, 9 May 2008)

On 2 May 2008, Extremely Severe Cyclonic Storm Nargis made landfall in Myanmar, sending a storm surge 40 kilometres up the densely populated Irrawaddy River delta. Causing more than 138,000 fatalities and damage estimated at more than US$10 billion (A$16.6 billion), it was the worst recorded natural disaster in Myanmar's history. The military regime's slow and largely ineffectual response to the crisis, and its clear reluctance to accept any foreign aid, prompted a fresh wave of criticism from the international community and even suggestions that it should unilaterally intervene under the 'responsibility to protect' doctrine.

When Tropical Cyclone Nargis cut a swathe through Lower Burma last week, it left more than death and destruction in its wake. The military government's slow response to the disaster, including its reluctance to accept international assistance, has further blackened its name. Yet it can be argued that the international community has also failed to fully appreciate the dire situation in Burma and has unrealistic expectations of what can be achieved in the current circumstances.

Despite its rich natural resources, Burma is in many ways an undeveloped country. Before the cyclone struck, the military government had made an effort to improve the country's civil infrastructure, but it still suffers from woefully inadequate transport and communications systems, unreliable power supplies, very poor health and educational facilities and an inefficient and corrupt bureaucracy. Thanks to the regime's economic mismanagement and distorted national priorities (since 1988, around 35 per cent of the official budget has been allocated to defence), large numbers of people suffer from poverty, malnutrition and epidemic diseases. Also, 75 per cent of the population lives in small rural villages, with most relying on homegrown agricultural produce to survive. Given this situation, a natural disaster of any magnitude was bound to hit the Burmese population hard and make a rapid national response very difficult.

Also, governments and international agencies calling for immediate action in Burma seem to be overestimating the regime's capacity to respond. It exercises enormous power, but is not quite the efficient, well-organised and well-resourced military machine that some activists claim. All major decisions are referred to the senior leadership in Naypyidaw, which is often shielded from real conditions in the country. Even during periods of relative peace and stability, the regime finds it hard to manage unexpected developments—and this disaster has no precedent in living memory in Burma. Despite their highly privileged position in Burmese society, the armed forces, too, face serious problems. One only has to live in Burma for a few months to realise that, at all levels, there is a lack of modern management systems, administrative expertise, skilled labour and spare parts. The regime has attempted to overcome such problems, but even it finds it difficult to get many things done.

In these circumstances, it is curious that greater allowance has not been made for the enormous problems the military government faces in responding to this disaster. For obvious reasons, Burma has long been one of the West's favourite targets, but if analyses of the situation are to be helpful, they must be objective. It is worth remembering that in 2005 the richest, most powerful and technologically advanced country in the world was unable to respond in a timely and efficient manner after Hurricane Katrina caused widespread flooding around New Orleans. And that disaster was on a smaller scale than the one now facing the Burmese authorities. Also, as the Australian Strategic Policy Institute has recently pointed out, even a country as wealthy, organised and socially cohesive as Australia is still ill-prepared to respond to a large-scale natural disaster entailing mass casualties.[1]

---

1   David Templeman and Anthony Bergin, *Taking a Punch: Building a More Resilient Australia*, Strategic Insights No.39 (Canberra: Australian Strategic Policy Institute, May 2008), s3-ap-southeast-2. amazonaws.com/ad-aspi/import/SI39_Taking_a_punch.pdf?vcIJUhU3L9HG1gmbj04jrpjQFW3 YIOUj.

It is at the level of the military regime's decision-making that it deserves most criticism. It apparently failed to warn the communities in the cyclone's path.[2] Given the choice between conspiracy and cockup, it is usually safer to choose the latter, and in any case there are limits to what small rural communities can do to reduce the impact of a cyclone. Even so, if advance notice had been given, better preparations could have been made. There also seems to have been a deliberate slowness in responding with aid after the cyclone struck. Granted, access is very difficult and Burma does not have sufficient supplies to meet everyone's immediate needs, but the regime could have made a much greater effort. For example, it could have mobilised its large army and put soldiers to work administering first aid, providing food and shelter, clearing roads and drains and helping to restore basic services. Indeed, the armed forces is the only organisation in Burma with the command structure, internal communications, expertise and resources able to undertake such a massive task. Yet to date relatively few servicepeople seem to have been called out.

Even more seriously, there seems to be a real reluctance on the part of the Burmese leadership to open up the country to foreign scrutiny and assistance. It is difficult to know exactly what lies behind the regime's thinking on this, as on so many other issues, but it is doubtless concerned that its grip on the population will be loosened. The presence of large numbers of foreign aid workers and officials would be difficult to monitor. Aided by the international news media, they would undermine the regime's efforts to strictly control what Burma's citizens see, hear and, as far as possible, think. Millions could be exposed to what the regime calls 'alien cultural influences', leading in turn to social instability. In addition, the provision of clearly identifiable foreign aid packages would emphasise the regime's own failure to provide assistance and the country's relative lack of development. To the regime's way of thinking, such factors have the potential to encourage renewed political unrest—something that is already threatened by increases in the prices of fuel, food and other staples.

Burma's generals may have even more serious concerns. They have long been aware that the US and its allies wish to see the military regime replaced with an elected civilian government led by someone like opposition leader Aung San Suu Kyi. After the armed forces crushed a massive prodemocracy uprising and took back direct political power in 1988, the

---

2   Anna Salleh, 'Burma Could Have Had 72h Warning', *ABC Science*, 8 May 2008, www.abc.net. au/science/articles/2008/05/08/2238754.htm?site=science&topic=latest.

regime feared the US might militarily intervene to restore democracy—as it has done in other countries. At the time, a US fleet deployed off the Burmese coast, in case US citizens needed to be evacuated, was viewed as a possible invasion force. Since then, the regime has been subject to tough economic sanctions and repeated public criticism. These days, it seems more confident that it can resist any pressures applied by the international community, but it remains highly sensitive to any possibility of foreign interference in Burma's internal affairs. This is probably another reason the regime is nervous about letting US military forces and other large foreign contingents into Burma.

The military regime has much to answer for, and its reluctance to permit desperately needed aid and expertise into the country at this critical time cannot be justified. However, any government in Burma, including a democratically elected civilian administration, would face the same challenges in responding to the devastation left by Cyclone Nargis. Even countries far more developed and better resourced to manage such crises have failed to meet the standards that many—both inside and outside Burma—expect of the regime. International aid is now trickling into Burma, but the 2004 Indian Ocean tsunami is a useful reminder of how long it takes affected communities to recover.

It remains to be seen whether the international community and the regime can agree on the level of assistance required, and a way to provide it. Burma will need substantial help for years to come, without either side imposing onerous or unrealistic conditions.

3

Burma's continuing fear of invasion

(11:09 AEDT, 28 May 2008)

In the wake of Cyclone Nargis, the international community struggled to give practical effect to its perceived 'responsibility to protect' the victims of the natural disaster. Its efforts were made even more difficult by the military regime's abiding fears of foreign intervention and the generals' determination to resist any attempts by the outside world to interfere in Myanmar's internal affairs.

Even before 1988, when the armed forces crushed a massive prodemocracy uprising and took back direct political power, Burma's military government feared an invasion of the country. In those days, the greatest danger was seen to emanate from China, but over the past 20 years, the US and EU countries have been seen as Burma's greatest military threats. Even the UN is distrusted.

In the wake of the 1988 crackdown, the regime feared that the US, or a coalition of countries led by the US or the UN, planned to invade Burma and restore democratic rule. A US fleet stationed offshore to evacuate US nationals was seen as a possible invasion force. This fear was renewed by the strong international reaction to the regime's refusal to hand over power to the government elected in 1990. Perceptions of an external threat were strengthened by the measures taken by the US, EU and a range of other countries in the years that followed. The various economic sanctions levelled against Burma, for example, were seen as part of an effort to weaken the regime and prepare the ground for forcible regime change. In response, the regime implemented a range of countermeasures, including an ambitious program to expand and modernise Burma's armed forces.

Around 2000, fears of direct military action against Burma seemed to fade, but the regime remained convinced—with some justification—that powerful members of the international community were determined to bring it down. Continued criticism of the military government in multilateral forums like the UN, and links made with rogue regimes like those in Iraq and North Korea in speeches by US President George W. Bush, seemed to presage external intervention.[1] US Secretary of State Condoleezza Rice labelled Burma, along with these countries, 'an outpost of tyranny', to which the US must help bring freedom.[2] Attempts in the UNSC to declare Burma a threat to regional security, public praise for Aung San Suu Kyi and the opposition movement and aid to Burmese dissident groups have all been interpreted as part of a concerted campaign to subvert the military government. If it could not be brought down by the direct application of military force, it was believed, the US and others were trying to cause its collapse by fomenting internal unrest. The 'Saffron Revolution' in September 2007 was apparently seen in this light.

Thus, when the US, UK and France positioned warships off the Burmese coast in May 2008, after Cyclone Nargis, the regime was immediately suspicious of those countries' motives. There were clearly other factors, but fears of military intervention helped persuade it to rule out accepting direct assistance from such countries to the cyclone victims. The regime's fears were greatly strengthened by bellicose statements made by the French Government and others about the international community's overriding 'responsibility to protect' those in need in Burma. There were also calls for an invasion of Burma to provide aid to the cyclone victims, regardless of Burma's national sovereignty and the regime's wishes. Such statements can only have hardened the military leadership's conviction that it, and thus the country itself, remains under threat of armed intervention, against which it must prepare.

---

1   Stephen Lee Myers and Christine Hauser, 'Bush Announces Tighter Sanctions on Myanmar', *The New York Times*, 25 September 2007, www.nytimes.com/2007/09/25/world/25cnd-bush.html.
2   'Rice Names "Outposts of Tyranny"', *BBC News*, 19 January 2005, news.bbc.co.uk/2/hi/americas/4186241.stm.

There has never been any likelihood since 1988 that Burma would actually be invaded, by the US or anyone else, but in international relations, perceptions are often more important than reality. Fears of armed intervention, and of more subtle forms of external interference in Burma's affairs, remain strong influences on Burma's strategic thinking. These fears must be taken into account in the consideration of any future policies towards the military government. Failure to do so will make the delivery of desperately needed aid to the cyclone victims, and the search for viable long-term solutions to Burma's many complex problems, infinitely more difficult.

4

Burma's armed forces: How loyal?

(11:08 AEDT, 6 June 2008)

In the wake of the 'Saffron Revolution' in 2007, and Cyclone Nargis in 2008, there were persistent rumours, mainly among foreign activists and Myanmar's exile community, that, because of the military government's brutality, indifference and incompetence, the loyalty of the country's armed forces could no longer be relied upon. Some commentators even raised the possibility of a mutiny in the ranks, but that was always a remote prospect.

It is always difficult to know what is happening inside Burma and, in particular, inside the armed forces (known locally as the *Tatmadaw*). There are signs, however, that the military government's power base is weakening. The regime is not likely to fall any time soon, but this development has implications for Burma's future stability and possibly even the regime's long-term survival.

It is widely accepted that the ruling State Peace and Development Council (SPDC) depends upon the continued loyalty and cohesion of the armed forces. Military strength and the ability to enforce its rule across the country are the only basis on which the regime, lacking any popular mandate, remains in power. It was partly with this in mind that, after taking back direct political power in 1988, the SPDC's predecessor, the State Law and Order Restoration Council (SLORC), launched an ambitious program to expand and modernise the *Tatmadaw*.

Over the next 15 years, Burma's armed forces doubled in size to around 400,000 personnel, making it the second-largest force in Southeast Asia (after Vietnam's) and, by some counts, the fifteenth-largest in the world. The *Tatmadaw* also acquired a wide range of modern arms and equipment, mainly from China, but also from Russia, the Ukraine, Poland, India, North Korea and several other countries. At the same time, a major effort was put into improving the *Tatmadaw's* command, control and communications systems, intelligence capabilities and logistics, training and support infrastructure. During this period, at least 35 per cent of Burma's national budget was devoted to defence—more than twice the combined allocations made to health and education.

The *Tatmadaw* still faced many difficult problems, but it gradually changed from a lightly armed infantry force geared to counterinsurgency campaigning and regime protection to a much larger, better armed and more balanced force capable of a wider range of military operations, including limited territorial defence. It also constituted a formidable instrument to counter Burma's armed insurgencies and enforce military rule over the civilian population.

From its peak around 2002, however, the *Tatmadaw's* size and capabilities began to decline. It became increasingly difficult to find new recruits, leading to a greater reliance on conscripts and young men pressganged into service. The number of child soldiers in the ranks seems to have increased. According to anecdotal evidence, the rate of desertions has also grown. Overall numbers may have slipped to around 350,000, or possibly even fewer. Also, in terms of living conditions, the gap between the senior officers and other ranks has grown markedly, causing considerable resentment. These and other developments have reportedly led to a serious deterioration in morale and a weakening of commitment to the regime's political objectives.

Reports of tensions among senior officers surface periodically, usually reflecting professional or personal rivalries. Inevitably, there are also policy differences, as occurs in any large organisation. A palace coup within the ruling hierarchy would be significant and could see a change in approach towards Burma's current problems, but it would not mean the end of military rule. The regime is likely to be more threatened by widespread unrest among the rank and file (including junior officers) on whom the daily enforcement of military rule actually depends. Yet, it is at this level that it seems to be losing most support.

The 'Saffron Revolution' in September 2007—and, in particular, the regime's use of force against demonstrating monks—appears to have shaken many in the armed forces. Reports of serious breakdowns in military discipline last year cannot be confirmed, but there is little doubt that many soldiers were very unhappy about the tough action taken by the police and army. Some soldiers were beaten by their officers for refusing to manhandle the revered *sangha*, or Buddhist 'clergy'. And it can be assumed that the violence meted out to the monks upset many other soldiers and their families—almost all of whom are devoutly Buddhist.

What might at other times be dismissed simply as grumbling in the ranks has now been exacerbated by a deep concern—even anger—among many in the armed forces over the regime's ineptitude and wilful obstructionism in response to Cyclone Nargis. Increasingly, reports are filtering out of Burma that many in the *Tatmadaw* believe the armed forces could have done much more to help those affected by the cyclone, in keeping with the regime's oft-repeated claims that the *Tatmadaw* is the protector of the Burmese people. Those most unhappy with the regime are naturally those with family and friends in the Irrawaddy Delta.

In ordinary circumstances, these problems may not have greatly troubled the regime. It faces no real threat from the country's few remaining armed insurgent groups. Nor does it need 400,000 men and women in uniform, armed with the latest military hardware, to crush popular dissent and enforce the SPDC's idiosyncratic policies. It could easily do that with 200,000—the number in the *Tatmadaw* before 1988—armed only with the basic infantry weapons manufactured in Burma. Also, as seen during the disturbances last September, there are still professional army units willing and able to use force against civilian protesters, including Buddhist monks, if ordered to do so.

A serious weakening of morale and commitment among the rank and file, however, is likely to be of greater concern to the SPDC in the light of recent calls for an invasion of Burma—or at least 'coercive humanitarian intervention'[1]—to deliver aid to the cyclone victims. Any attempt to 'bash Burma's doors down', as suggested by the Australian Prime Minister early last month,[2] would be strongly resisted by the regime, probably using

---

1   Romesh Ratnesar, 'Is It Time to Invade Burma?', *TIME*, 10 May 2008, content.time.com/time/world/article/0,8599,1739053,00.html.
2   Jonathan Pearlman, 'Rudd Says Donors Must Bash in Doors', *Sydney Morning Herald*, 10 May 2008, www.smh.com.au/world/rudd-says-donors-must-bash-in-doors-20080510-gdsd3w.html.

armed force. In such circumstances, it would need to rely on the loyalty and cohesion of the Burmese armed forces more than ever before. Such external intervention was never likely, but if the threat had become real, the regime could have had a major problem on its hands.

Discontent among Burma's military rank and file has not yet reached a point at which the regime needs to fear for its survival. It has faced internal problems before and gone on to become the world's most resilient and durable military dictatorship. In any case, there are many well-established mechanisms to identify and root out any potential centres of unrest in the armed forces before they can become a serious challenge to the leadership. It is worth noting, however, that serious cracks are appearing in the *Tatmadaw's* normally solid support for the regime and all it stands for. Depending on how the political situation in Burma develops, and how economic and social conditions evolve in the wake of the cyclone, this development could become much more important.

5

The Rambo approach to Burma

(10:37 AEDT, 20 June 2008)

The fourth instalment in the Rambo *movie series, starring American actor Sylvester Stallone, depicted appalling human rights abuses against Western missionaries and Karen villagers in Myanmar by the country's armed forces. The movie's graphic content and clear political message attracted a wide range of comments from film critics, activists and members of the military government, as was no doubt intended.*

Sylvester Stallone has claimed that his movie *Rambo 4*,[1] released internationally in February and available to Australians on DVD next month, has a serious purpose: to draw attention to the Burmese Government's long record of human rights abuses and to mobilise action against the military regime. Yet, its dubious entertainment value aside, this movie in fact has the potential to do Burma's opposition movement considerable harm.

When deciding where to set his movie, Stallone reportedly asked both the UN and *Soldier of Fortune* (*SOF*) magazine to name the world's worst current war zones. *SOF* nominated the 60-year-old civil war between Burma's central government and the ethnic Karens, most of whom live along the Thailand–Burma border. The cinematic result is an almost cosmic battle between good and evil, as the invincible US Special Forces

---

1   Sylvester Stallone (dir.), *Rambo*, 2008, www.imdb.com/title/tt0462499/.

soldier John Rambo once again comes out of retirement, to rescue a group of Christian missionaries held captive by the evil Burmese army. As the movie's tagline goes: 'Old heroes never die, they just reload.'

The brooding, disaffected antihero of *First Blood* (1982), *Rambo: First Blood Part 2* (1985) and *Rambo 3* (1988) is now in his sixties and less prone to leaping about the landscape, but he can still mow down the bad guys with the best of them. According to the *Internet Movie Database* (*IMDb*),[2] the film averages 2.59 killings per minute. As one US reviewer has noted, the final body count of 236 dead in just 91 minutes makes it 'possibly the most violent movie ever to get an R rating and a wide release in America'.

Rambo's sizeable contribution to this nonstop slaughter is justified on the grounds that Burma's military government has absolutely no redeeming features and its wicked servants thus deserve everything they get. During the course of the movie, the Burmese army is found guilty of genocide, homicide, infanticide, torture, rape, paedophilia, arson, theft, environmental degradation and cruelty to animals, among other crimes. This gives the avenging Rambo a licence for guilt-free mayhem on a grand scale. Nothing is left to the imagination in this digitally enhanced festival of blood, viscera and severed limbs.

Stallone, who cowrote and directed the latest *Rambo* epic, wanted his movie to reflect real world events and to influence international perceptions of the situation in Burma. He has spoken publicly about Burma's terrible human rights record—the suffering of its ethnic minorities, in particular—and challenged the military regime to let him into the country, so he can tell them where they are going wrong. In the movie, the hero suggests by his words and actions—particularly actions—that violent resistance to such oppression is not only justified, but also necessary. Efforts at humanitarian intervention are dismissed as well intentioned but essentially naive. The only way to improve matters, this film clearly says, is to overthrow the regime by force.

Rambo 4 is such a gross caricature of the violence being perpetrated against the civilian population by the regime that few will see it as a convincing picture of contemporary Burma. Even so, its crude political message has been welcomed by activists and members of Burma's scattered exile

---

2 'Rambo (2008): Trivia', *IMDb*, www.imdb.com/title/tt0462499/trivia.

community as a vivid and timely reminder of the military government's brutal rule. It is already popular with Karen insurgents based along the Thailand–Burma border, many of whom idolised Rambo even before the release of Stallone's latest film. In addition to sporting Rambo tattoos and wearing Rambo T-shirts, they have apparently taken to repeating the hero's mumbled line, 'Live for nothing, die for something'.

Not only has *Rambo 4* been denied permission to be screened publicly in Burma but, after it was released, the regime's Press Scrutiny and Registration Board ordered all journals and newspapers in the country to publish a government article criticising the movie. Titled 'Speaking Seriously, It Is Hilarious', the article lampooned the movie, describing the lead character as a fat lunatic with sagging breasts. Despite the efforts of the authorities to prevent its unlicensed distribution, however, DVDs of *Rambo 4* can still be obtained from street sellers and many people are prepared to risk jail to watch it, either at home or in underground theatres. Stallone has said that 'it is flattering to be part of a movie that is giving the Burmese people hope'. He also feels 'it is cool to say "I'm banned in Burma"'.[3]

For all its appeal as a revenge fantasy, however, *Rambo 4* ignores the enormous complexity of Burma's current problems. As Brian McCartan has persuasively argued,[4] the extreme level of violence shown in *Rambo 4* 'trivializes the actual conflict situation in war-torn Karen State'. The regime's long history of atrocities has been well documented, but some of the more horrific scenes in the film are 'complete fiction', according to human rights groups. More children die from a lack of medicines to treat diseases than are shot by the Burmese army. Also, there is no mention in the film of the hundreds of dedicated Burmese who daily risk their lives to assist their countrymen and women along the Thailand–Burma border.

Indeed, by grossly oversimplifying difficult issues and painting the protagonists in such stark colours, *Rambo 4* may actually hinder resolution of Burma's problems. For, if taken to heart, let alone seen as reflecting reality, the movie supports equally simplistic political views and encourages the advocacy of short-term, black-and-white solutions where more carefully calibrated, long-term approaches are necessary. As David

3   Richard C. Paddock, 'Stars Publicize Myanmar Issues', *Los Angeles Times*, 23 May 2008, www.latimes.com/archives/la-xpm-2008-may-23-et-myanmar23-story.html.
4   Brian McCartan, 'Unreal Rambo Finds an Army of Fans', *Asia Times*, [Hong Kong], 27 March 2008, www.atimes.com/atimes/Southeast_Asia/JC27Ae02.html [page discontinued].

Steinberg has written: '[E]ven more problematic, and far more dangerous, is the implication that the regime may be overthrown by US public or private military action.'[5] In the current circumstances, an attempt by prodemocracy groups to seize power by force would inevitably result in a bloodbath, and any encouragement given to such a plan—covertly or otherwise—would be very irresponsible.

Also, ever since the 1988 uprising there have been calls by activists for an invasion of Burma to restore democratic rule. This issue resurfaced in public debates about the international community's overriding 'responsibility to protect' the victims of Cyclone Nargis, after the military regime refused to allow foreign countries to deliver aid to devastated areas of the country. For all the rhetoric heard from world leaders, forcible external intervention has never been on the cards. Yet, even public discussion of such an option increases the regime's paranoia and hardens its resolve to resist what it considers to be a gross violation of Burmese sovereignty and unacceptable foreign interference in Burma's internal affairs.

Thus, while it may give Sylvester Stallone a warm inner glow, and bring temporary comfort to the activist community, *Rambo 4* risks delaying the resolution of Burma's complex problems and prolonging the suffering of the Burmese people.

---

5   David I. Steinberg, 'On Rambo and Burmese Politics', *PacNet*, No.14, 21 February 2008, csis.org/files/media/csis/pubs/pac0814.pdf.

6

Burma and the Bush White House

(10:11 AEDT, 26 August 2008)

The visit of then US president George W. Bush and his wife to Thailand in 2008, and their public gestures in support of Myanmar's prodemocracy movement, gave heart to many activists, both inside and outside the country. However, the president's actions also served to underline the US's inability to significantly affect the course of events in Myanmar. Even to diehard human rights campaigners, it was becoming clear that real and lasting change could only come from the Myanmar people themselves, and from within the country.

When George W. Bush and his wife visited Thailand earlier this month, they took pains to draw attention to their continuing commitment to democracy in Burma. Publicly, their statements of support and gestures of solidarity were welcomed by Burma's opposition movement. Privately, however, most Burmese now accept that the US is not able to remove the generals in Naypyidaw. Indeed, some activists have come to share the view that the US's uncompromising approach to Burma since the ill-fated 1988 prodemocracy uprising may in fact have been counterproductive.

Although President Bush finds it hard to pronounce her name, he has been a strong supporter of opposition leader Aung San Suu Kyi, and the movement for democratic change in Burma. Under his administration, the US has led those countries that have taken a hard line against the military government, mainly through repeated public condemnation of the regime and the imposition of tough economic sanctions, including blocks on international financial assistance. In July 2003, the US

President signed into law the *Burmese Freedom and Democracy Act*, which was designed to strengthen Burma's 'democratic forces'. It explicitly recognised the opposition National League for Democracy (NLD) as the 'legitimate representative of the Burmese people'.

A consistent element in the US approach has been a strong demand for regime change. In 2003, for example, then secretary of state Colin Powell referred to 'the thugs who now rule Burma', and in 2005 his successor labelled Burma 'an outpost of tyranny', to which the US must help bring freedom. In President Bush's 2006 State of the Union speech, immediately after references to the US invasions of Iraq and Afghanistan, Burma was ranked alongside Syria, Iran, Zimbabwe and North Korea as places where 'the demands of justice, and the peace of the world, require their freedom'.[1]

The Bush administration has also attempted to paint Burma under military rule as a strategic problem, due in large part to its failure to address transnational issues, including the outflow of refugees. In 2005 and 2006, the US tried to persuade the UN Security Council to label Burma a threat to regional stability—despite the fact that none of Burma's five neighbours supported the motion. On each occasion that the President has renewed economic and other sanctions, as he is required to do annually, he has formally stated that Burma is 'a continuing unusual and extraordinary threat to the national security and foreign policy of the United States'.[2]

During his two-day stopover in Thailand in early August, President Bush met a select group of Burmese 'freedom activists'—significantly, at the US Ambassador's residence, and thus technically not on Thai soil. He also held a 'roundtable interview' on Burma with radio journalists. In a keynote speech on the US's relations with Asia, he said that 'we seek an end to tyranny in Burma'.[3] He described his wife as a 'devoted champion' of this 'noble cause'. For her part, Mrs Bush made a well-publicised visit to a refugee camp near the Thailand–Burma border, to meet people who had fled oppression and economic hardship in Burma.[4]

---

1   The White House, 'President Bush Delivers State of the Union Address', Press release, Washington, DC, 31 January 2006, georgewbush-whitehouse.archives.gov/stateoftheunion/2006/.
2   The White House, 'Message to the Congress of the United States', Press release, Washington, DC, 17 May 2007, www.whitehouse.gov/news/releases/2007/05/print/20070517-8.html [page discontinued].
3   The White House, 'Bush Visits Bangkok, Thailand', Press release, 7 August 2008, www.white house.gov/news/releases/2008/08/20080807-8.html [page discontinued].
4   The White House, 'Statement by Mrs Laura Bush After a Visit to Mae Tao Clinic', Press release, 7 August 2008, www.whitehouse.gov/news/releases/2008/08/20080807-13.html [page discontinued].

While dismissed by some as a cynical attempt to burnish the Bush administration's tarnished reputation, these gestures were welcomed by many Burmese, both within and outside the country. The fact remains, however, that over the past 20 years, US policy has demonstrably failed to shift the generals from any of their core positions. Indeed, it has been persuasively argued—and not just by Burma's friends and neighbours— that economic sanctions have made life more difficult for the Burmese people. More to the point, the strong rhetoric and punitive measures employed by the US appear to have increased Naypyidaw's sense of threat and made the regime even more determined to resist external pressures.

The risks inherent in current US policy were demonstrated in early May, when the Burmese Government refused to permit US warships to unload aid supplies intended for the victims of Cyclone Nargis. Naypyidaw apparently feared that the US might use the relief effort as cover for an invasion, or at least to provide support for a popular uprising.

At the time, Secretary of State Condoleezza Rice said: 'It is not a matter of politics, it's a matter of a humanitarian crisis.' Yet, on 1 May, the day before the cyclone struck, President Bush had renewed sanctions for another year and expanded the authorities that allowed the US to target those supporting a regime 'that exploits and oppresses the people of Burma'. The President also condemned the regime's new constitution as 'dangerously flawed' and restated his commitment to help the Burmese people 'in their struggle to free themselves from the regime's tyranny'.[5] On 5 May, Mrs Bush made an unprecedented public statement highly critical of the regime and its response to the cyclone. Also, it would not have escaped Naypyidaw's attention that, on 6 May, the day the President called for access to the cyclone-affected areas, he signed a law awarding Aung San Suu Kyi the Congressional Gold Medal, the US's highest civilian honour.

In these circumstances, there was very little chance that Burma's generals would feel inclined to divorce politics from other factors. As Georgetown University's David Steinberg has pointed out, in trying to win the regime's trust after the cyclone, Washington had to overcome the accumulated effects of two decades of aggressive rhetoric, an increasingly harsh sanctions regime and long-term support for the military government's opponents,

---

5   The White House, 'Statement by the President on Burma', Press release, 1 May 2008, www.white house.gov/news/releases/2008/05/20080501-8.html [page discontinued].

most of whom were dedicated to its overthrow. This problem will remain for the foreseeable future, as US policy towards Burma is unlikely to change markedly whoever wins the presidential election later this year.

After 20 years in the political wilderness, there are now few exiled dissidents who imagine themselves returning to Burma at the head of a conquering army or who expect the Burmese armed forces simply to hand over government to the opposition movement and return to their barracks. Since the 1988 uprising, however, Burmese exiles and activist organisations, and many people inside Burma, have nurtured the hope that strong support from the US and other key Western countries, together with concerted action in the UN, might result in a return to democracy in Burma. If they remain at all, these hopes are now fading.

It is gradually, and often reluctantly, becoming more widely accepted by Burmese dissidents and other activists that economic sanctions and public statements, even by some influential members of the international community, are not going to change the government in Burma. A similar sense of disillusionment has been felt by many Burmese over the repeated failure of UN efforts to persuade the generals to free all political prisoners and open a genuine dialogue with Aung San Suu Kyi. Nor, despite the hopes of some activists—and the generals' recurring fears—is the US or UN going to take any direct military action against the regime.

For many idealistic Burmese, outraged at the military regime's brutal behaviour and hopeful for the return of a democratic government, this has been a hard lesson in the harsh realities of international politics, which has left deep disappointment and, at times, even bitterness. External support for the opposition cause in Burma is still being sought and, when provided, is welcomed by the activist community. The gestures made by the US President and First Lady in Thailand were appreciated by many Burmese. Increasingly, however, it is understood that foreign powers are likely to have only limited influence in Burma. Real and lasting change will have to come from the Burmese themselves, and from within the country.

7

Burma's opposition movement: A house divided

(07:43 AEDT, 25 November 2008)

There were always divisions within Myanmar's opposition, which was always a very diverse and broad-based movement. However, during 2008, it was increasingly obvious that these rifts were becoming worse. Not only were there personality clashes and differences over specific policies, but even the leadership of Aung San Suu Kyi and her advocacy of 'active pacifism' were being questioned. These developments could only weaken the opposition and work to the advantage of the military regime.

Burma's opposition movement has always been strong, but never united. After 20 years of struggle, with no sign that the military government is weakening, the fissures in the movement seem to be more pronounced and the divisions more obvious. This could have far-reaching consequences.

Burmese politics has long been known for its fissiparous tendencies. Institutional structures and processes have been weak. Ideological, ethnic and religious loyalties have been strong. Parties and pressure groups have formed around key personalities, rather than durable policy platforms. Patron–client relationships have been the norm, including in the armed forces. And power has been seen as an absolute, making political contests zero-sum games. All this has led to factionalism and instability. Such traits can also be found in the opposition movement.

After Burma's armed forces crushed the 1988 prodemocracy uprising and took back direct political power, the opposition movement divided into two broad camps. One was made up largely of students and other activists who fled to Burma's rugged border areas and formed armed insurgent groups. They forged loose alliances with ethnic guerillas and dedicated themselves to the violent overthrow of the military regime. Some political exiles even advocated a campaign of terrorist attacks inside Burma.

Most prodemocracy campaigners, however, sought a peaceful transfer of power. Even after the regime ignored the results of the 1990 elections and clamped down hard on dissident groups, Aung San Suu Kyi and the NLD continued to advocate a negotiated solution to Burma's political crisis. Others, like the 88 Generation Students Group, have staged peaceful protests against the regime's human rights abuses and economic mismanagement.[1] With foreign help, exiled groups in Thailand have provided training courses in the techniques of civil disobedience and nonviolent resistance.

Within these two broad camps there have been deep divisions. In 1992, for example, the militant All Burma Students' Democratic Front split into two. In 1996, one faction executed 15 of its own members, who were accused of being government spies but were more likely the victims of an internal power struggle.[2] Outside Burma, the opposition movement fragmented into numerous groups, holding a wide range of views. Since 1988, there have been public disagreements over critical issues like the merits of a dialogue with the regime, the impact of foreign aid and the efficacy of economic sanctions.

The NLD has not escaped internal tensions. For example, in 1997 and again in 1999, the party expelled a number of Members of Parliament (MPs) (elected in 1990) for being 'lackeys of the regime'. Contrary to Aung San Suu Kyi's views at the time, they had advocated more broad-ranging discussions with the military government.[3] Also, many younger members of the party have been frustrated with the cautious approach

---

1   'Profile: 88 Generation Students', *BBC News*, 22 August 2007, news.bbc.co.uk/2/hi/asia-pacific/6958363.stm.
2   David O'Hanlon, 'Whatever Happened to the ABSDF?', *The Irrawaddy*, 8 April 2004, www.irrawaddy.org/article.php?art_id=37&page=1 [page discontinued] [now at www2.irrawaddy.com/article.php?art_id=37].
3   Simon Ingram, 'Burma's Opposition Shows Split', *BBC News*, 3 May 1999, news.bbc.co.uk/1/hi/world/asia-pacific/334020.stm.

of the NLD's elderly Executive Committee. Last October, more than 100 NLD youth leaders resigned in protest over their exclusion from the party's decision-making processes.[4]

It is to be expected that, after 20 years in the political wilderness and faced with continuing repression in Burma, there will be personality clashes and squabbles over policy issues. Also, some in the opposition movement have held unrealistic expectations about the extent to which developments within Burma can be influenced by external actors. However, there are now deep rifts between some anti-regime groups, an intense competition for recognition and resources and bitter recriminations over policies and practices. Over the past year, these and other problems seem to have become more pronounced, and potentially more damaging.

After the regime crushed the 'Saffron Revolution' in September 2007, many young Burmese questioned the effectiveness of Aung San Suu Kyi's 'active pacifism' and called for bolder measures. Some Buddhist monks even asked the international community for weapons to defend themselves against the security forces.[5] There was another important development last August, when a prominent activist group formally requested the UN Secretary-General to declare Burma's seat in the General Assembly vacant. This submission was not coordinated with other opposition groups, however, and there was disagreement over which group should inherit Burma's UN seat if it became available.

Even Aung San Suu Kyi has not been immune to criticism. Last month, a leading British newspaper accused her of a lack of leadership.[6] Several Burmese activists were cited as saying that she was too inflexible in her approach to political reform and had failed to give adequate direction, both to the NLD and to the broader opposition movement. Given that she has been under house arrest since 2003 and not allowed any visitors, it is difficult to see what more she could have done. But her strong personal views and highly principled stand against the regime have been viewed by some Burmese (and others) as obstacles to progress.

---

4   Saw Yan Naing, 'Former Youth Members Urge NLD to Prepare for 2010', *The Irrawaddy*, 17 October 2008, www.irrawaddy.org/article.php?art_id=14468 [page discontinued] [now at www2. irrawaddy.com/article.php?art_id=14468].

5   'Monks with Guns? Burma's Younger Activists Get Bolder', *Christian Science Monitor*, 18 September 2008, www.csmonitor.com/2008/0919/p01s01-wosc.html.

6   Cathy Scott-Clark and Adrian Levy, 'Not Such A Hero After All', *The Guardian*, [London], 11 November 2008 [Correction and clarification published as 'Can Aung San Suu Kyi Lead While Captive?', 2 December 2008], www.guardian.co.uk/world/2008/nov/11/burma-aung-san-suu-kyi.

For 20 years, opposition parties and activist groups have kept alive the hopes of many Burmese. Despite numerous challenges, both inside and outside the country, they have not only survived but also won considerable support. All such campaigns attract a wide range of interest groups, with different goals and priorities. And constructive debate over strategies and tactics is both useful and healthy. Burma's opposition movement does itself no favours, however, by public displays of disharmony, inflexibility and intolerance. At best, they are distractions from the main game. At worst, they raise doubts about the movement itself.

Internecine disputes also help the regime to justify continued military rule. For the armed forces claim that only they have the sense of common purpose, internal discipline and staying power needed to keep Burma stable, united and independent. Having introduced a new constitution last May, the regime now plans to create a military-dominated parliament in 2010, as the centrepiece of its 'discipline-flourishing democracy'. Divisions within and between Burma's many opposition groups can only make that process easier.

2009

8

Is there a Burma–
North Korea–Iran
nuclear conspiracy?

(07:26 AEDT, 25 February 2009)

After the leak of a report describing the visit to North Korea by an official Myanmar delegation in 2008, there was widespread unease about the military ties apparently being forged between the two pariah states. These concerns were encouraged by the testimony of Myanmar 'defectors' and the visit to Myanmar of several North Korean cargo vessels. Despite the lack of hard evidence, it was claimed that North Korea was secretly helping Myanmar to manufacture missiles and possibly even develop a nuclear weapon.

If the Obama administration was looking for another foreign policy challenge, all it would have to do is to take seriously the rumours circulating in Thailand that Burma is pursuing a secret nuclear weapons program, with help from North Korea and Iran. These stories have all the ingredients of a real security nightmare. The question is, though, are any of them true?

In 2000, when Burma's military government announced that it was going to purchase a 10 MW light water reactor from Russia, activist groups immediately warned that the generals were not to be trusted. They accused the regime of secretly planning to develop a nuclear weapon, to threaten the international community and resist pressures to reform. The activists cited the regime's long record of duplicity, its abiding fear of external intervention (particularly from the US) and its customary disregard for international norms of behaviour. They dismissed assurances that the reactor was for peaceful research and would be placed under International Atomic Energy Agency (IAEA) safeguards.

Also, well before Naypyidaw and Pyongyang restored diplomatic relations in 2007, some observers (including a few high-profile figures in Washington) expressed concern about Burma's growing ties with North Korea—a known proliferator of nuclear weapons technology.[1]

At the time, these suspicions were greeted with scepticism. Burma had a long record of opposition to nuclear weapons proliferation. Also, Burma's financial reserves and its level of technological development were so low that many doubted its ability to build and manage a nuclear reactor, even with Russian assistance. However, Burma's military leadership was highly unpredictable and prone to bizarre behaviour. Also, some generals clearly envied North Korea's ability to use its nuclear weapons status to resist international pressure and wring concessions out of the US. Still, no reliable evidence could be produced of a clandestine Burmese weapon of mass destruction (WMD) program.[2]

As years passed, the Burma rumour mill ground on, prompting further accusations of the generals' perfidy. There were reports in the news media and on the internet that thousands of Burmese were attending technical training courses in Russia and that Burma was secretly receiving shipments of equipment from North Korea. There were sightings of foreigners at defence establishments all around Burma. At the same time, there were increasingly strident claims by some activist groups to the effect that Burma had constructed a reactor, developed uranium enrichment plants and was exporting yellowcake to North Korea and Iran. A few even said that Burma already possessed nuclear weapons.

Yet the official view of Burma's status remained unchanged. Throughout this period, the US issued numerous warnings about clandestine North Korean, Iranian and Syrian WMD programs but, as far as Burma was concerned, the Bush administration remained conspicuously silent. In 2005 and 2006, for example, during its efforts to have Burma cited

---

1   Norman Robespierre, 'Nuclear Bond for North Korea and Myanmar', *Asia Times Online*, [Hong Kong], 4 October 2008, www.atimes.com/atimes/Southeast_Asia/JJ04Ae01.html [page discontinued].
2   Andrew Selth, *Burma and Nuclear Proliferation: Policies and Perceptions*, Griffith Asia Institute Regional Outlook Paper No.12 (Brisbane: Griffith University, 2007), www.griffith.edu.au/__data/assets/pdf_file/0015/18240/regional-outlook-volume-12.pdf [page discontinued].

by the UN Security Council as 'a threat to international peace and security', the US pointedly made no reference to a Burmese nuclear weapons program. In 2007, the State Department reminded Burma of its obligations under the nuclear Non-Proliferation Treaty, but only referred to the proposed Russian reactor.[3]

For its part, the UK Government stated in 2006 that it was 'not able to corroborate' reports about the alleged transfer of nuclear technology from North Korea to Burma. The UK also put on record its view that no uranium was being processed in Burma and that Burma did not have any operational enrichment facilities. Nor was the UK aware of any Burmese uranium exports. In 2007, Singapore's foreign minister stated that Burma was 'unlikely' to develop a nuclear program, given its many other problems. A new memorandum of understanding signed by Burma and Russia that year revealed that construction of the research reactor had not even begun. The most likely cause was a lack of funds.

Over the past year or so, however, a number of governments have given this issue a higher priority. The increased level of interest seems to have been prompted by the appearance in Thailand of several Burmese officials (both civilian and military) who claimed to have direct knowledge, or even firsthand experience, of a secret nuclear weapons program. According to these 'defectors', in 2002, Burma's military government began building a reactor near Maymyo, with the aim of developing a nuclear device by 2020. The reactor and some related nuclear fuel processing plants were said to be hidden underground. The expertise for this project reportedly came from North Korea, with help from Iran and possibly Pakistan.

These claims are still to be verified. Some may in fact relate not to a secret WMD program, but to the regime's efforts over the past 20 years to upgrade its military infrastructure. Particularly since the Iraq wars, Burma has felt vulnerable to attack from the air. It has reportedly constructed underground command-and-control bunkers, hardened its communications nodes and built protective shelters for a range of new conventional weapon systems. The North Koreans have considerable expertise in constructing such facilities.[4]

---

3   'US Criticises Burma Nuclear Plan', *BBC News*, 17 May 2007, news.bbc.co.uk/2/hi/asia-pacific/6664421.stm.

4   Bertil Lintner, 'Myanmar and North Korea Share a Tunnel Vision', *Asia Times Online*, [Hong Kong], 19 July 2006, www.atimes.com/atimes/Southeast_Asia/HG19Ae01.html [page discontinued].

Even so, both Western and regional governments now seem keen to find out whether the defectors' claims are accurate. Any suggestions of a secret WMD program, let alone one conducted by a pariah state like Burma, must be of concern. Some of the information provided by the defectors appears credible and there are numerous defence facilities in Burma that have not been identified. Also, no one underestimates the lengths to which the generals will go to stay in power, and to protect Burma from perceived external threats.

Understandably, however, foreign officials looking at this issue are being very cautious. No one wants a repetition of the mistakes that preceded the last Iraq war, either in underestimating a country's capabilities or by giving too much credibility to a few untested intelligence sources. Particularly in the highly charged political environment that surrounds consideration of Burma's many complex problems, no government is going to accept claims of a secret nuclear weapons program without investigating them thoroughly first.

There has always been a lot of smoke surrounding Burma's nuclear ambitions. Over the past year or so, the amount of smoke has increased, but still no one seems to know whether or not it hides a real fire. With this in mind, strategic analysts in many countries are looking to the Obama administration for an authoritative statement on Burma's nuclear status. This may come sooner rather than later. The *Tom Lantos Block Burmese JADE (Junta's Anti-Democratic Efforts)* (*JADE Act*) enacted by the US Congress last July stipulates that, within 180 days, the Secretary of State must issue a statement describing 'the provision of weapons of mass destruction and related materials, capabilities, and technology, including nuclear, chemical, and dual use capabilities'.[5] That deadline has already passed.

---

5   *HR 3890 [110th]: Tom Lantos Block Burmese JADE (Junta's Anti-Democratic Efforts) Act of 2008* (Public Law 110-286), United States Congress, enacted 29 July 2008, www.govtrack.us/congress/billtext.xpd?bill=h110-3890.

9

US–Burma: Where to from here?

(14:09 AEDT, 28 April 2009)

After president Barack Obama took office in January 2009, secretary of state Hillary Clinton announced that the US would undertake a comprehensive review of its policy towards the military government in Myanmar, which for the previous 20 years had been marked by strong rhetoric and political and economic sanctions. This readiness to consider a fresh and potentially more productive approach prompted a fierce debate in the US and elsewhere between those wedded to a strong line against the regime and those who were willing to consider other options.

Hillary Clinton's announcement in January that the Obama administration was reviewing US policy towards Burma has raised hopes that the impasse between these two countries might finally be broken.[1] But there are major obstacles in the way of any new initiative. And even if the international community can exert greater influence in Naypyidaw, real and lasting change in Burma can only come from within the country itself.

For some years, pressure had been mounting for a fundamental review of US–Burma relations. The Bush administration's hardline policies had clearly failed to achieve their key objectives. Burma's ruling SPDC was still firmly entrenched in power and was taking steps to perpetuate military rule. Not only had the generals refused to release all political prisoners

---

1   Glen Kessler, 'Shift Possible on Burma Policy', *The Washington Post*, 19 February 2009, www.washingtonpost.com/wp-dyn/content/story/2009/02/17/ST2009021700968.html.

(including opposition leader Aung San Suu Kyi), but also the number of prisoners had increased. And, as demonstrated by the regime's harsh reaction to the 2007 'Saffron Revolution', Burma's human rights record had not improved.

Indeed, it has been argued that the Bush administration's policies were quite counterproductive.[2] In the face of continued diplomatic pressure, the SPDC had become even more obdurate and resistant to calls for political and economic reform. Some US sanctions were specifically targeted against the generals and their cronies, but other economic measures hurt the Burmese people more than the regime. The forces for change in Burmese society were weakened, not strengthened.

In addition, the undisguised hostility shown towards the SPDC by the US—which labelled Burma an 'outpost of tyranny'—has sown a deep distrust of the West among Burma's generals, who even now worry about an invasion of the country by the US and its allies.[3] This fear lay behind Naypyidaw's refusal to let the US, UK and France unload aid supplies from their warships after Cyclone Nargis hit Burma in May 2008. It has also encouraged Burma to develop closer ties with China, Russia and North Korea. Some activists claim that it has even prompted a secret nuclear weapons program.

Hillary Clinton has acknowledged that sanctions have failed to influence Burma's military leaders, while noting that ASEAN's softer policy of 'constructive engagement' has also been unsuccessful. She has said that the US is prepared to consider new options. The Bush administration's policies cannot suddenly be abandoned, but Barack Obama's election has given the US space in which to consider fresh approaches towards pariah states like Burma—approaches that do not sacrifice US core principles and enduring strategic interests, but are less confrontational, more flexible and have more realistic goals.

Deputy Secretary of State Jim Steinberg has revealed that the US is looking for 'collaborative and constructive' solutions to the Burma problem. It plans to discuss a common approach with ASEAN, China, India and

2   Morten Pedersen, 'Limitations of the Global Human Rights Paradigm', *Mizzima News*, [Yangon], 12 March 2009, www.mizzima.com/edop/commentary/1832-limitations-of-the-global-human-rights-paradigm-.html [page discontinued].

3   Andrew Selth, *Burma and the Threat of Invasion: Regime Fantasy or Strategic Reality?*, Griffith Asia Institute Regional Outlook Paper No.17 (Brisbane: Griffith University, 2008), www.griffith.edu.au/business/griffith-asia-institute/pdf/Andrew-Selth-Regional-Outlook-17.pdf [page discontinued].

Japan, 'to find a policy that will improve the lives of the people of Burma and promote stability in the region'.[4] This may be code for humanitarian aid, 'intelligent sanctions' and greater incentives for reforms. The US has also reopened direct links to the regime. In April, the Director of the State Department's Office for Mainland Southeast Asia held discussions with senior SPDC officials in Naypyidaw—the first such visit in seven years.

In a separate move, the US Senate Foreign Relations Committee has announced its own review of Burma policy.[5] This seems designed mainly to ensure that the Obama administration takes account of Congress's concerns. These were expressed last year in the *Tom Lantos Block Burmese Junta's Anti-Democratic Efforts (JADE) Act*, which strongly condemned the regime and increased economic sanctions. It also included provisions for a special envoy to advance US interests (such as the coordination of sanctions and release of political prisoners) and called for increased support to nongovernmental organisations (NGOs) conducting humanitarian projects in Burma.

The Obama administration's more openminded approach has been widely welcomed. However, it will face strong opposition from human rights campaigners and Burmese expatriate groups, who remain convinced that diplomatic pressure and economic sanctions are still the only ways to make the SPDC surrender power. They also claim that this is the only morally defensible position to hold. Already, 17 members of the US Congress have written to Hillary Clinton urging her not to lift sanctions against Burma, and activists around the world are preparing to oppose any apparent 'weakening' of the US position.

These groups have long claimed that any concessions offered by the international community will simply be pocketed by the regime, without substantive movement towards political and economic reforms. They are also concerned that a perceived retreat from the US's current tough stance will encourage other states—notably, members of the EU, but also countries like Australia and Japan—to soften their own policies. To the activist community, this would simply reward the regime for its bad behaviour and encourage even greater repression.

---

4   'US Wants Common Myanmar Strategy with Asia', *Agence France-Presse*, 1 April 2009, news. yahoo.com/s/afp/20090401/pl_afp/usmyanmardiplomacy/print [page discontinued].

5   'Senate to Review Burma Policy', *Radio Free Asia*, [Washington, DC], 8 April 2009, www.rfa.org/ english/news/burma/burmapolicy-04072009123741.html.

It may turn out that the opposition movement is worrying for no reason. For, without a significant gesture on the part of the SPDC, such as the release of Aung San Suu Kyi, any new US policy or international initiative is not likely to get very far. And even if such a gesture was forthcoming, the bilateral relationship would always be hostage to the regime's behaviour. In this regard, the historical record does not promote confidence.

Ever since the abortive prodemocracy uprising in 1988, which saw more than 3,000 people killed, the generals have demonstrated their intolerance of dissent and readiness to crush any civil unrest. As economic conditions in Burma deteriorate—as they are expected to do over the next year—and as the elections for a new military-dominated parliament get closer, more demonstrations seem inevitable. Some observers have even predicted instability within the armed forces. Protests of any kind are likely to trigger a strong reaction, as seen in 2007.

Further instances of human rights violations in Burma would severely undercut attempts by the US to adopt a more nuanced approach towards the regime and strengthen the hand of those (including in Congress) calling for a continuation of the old hardline policies.

Even if Naypyidaw can be persuaded to conduct a genuine dialogue with Washington, there remains the problem that the generals are fiercely nationalistic and intensely protective of Burma's independence and national sovereignty. Attempts by foreign countries or multilateral organisations to involve themselves in Burma's internal affairs will continue to be resisted. Meetings to discuss such issues (along the lines of the six-party talks involving North Korea, for example) are unlikely to be seen as useful, or even legitimate.

The Obama administration's willingness to explore new and more constructive approaches towards Burma is a very positive step, but it has some powerful opponents. Also, no one is under any illusions as to the nature of the military regime and its resistance to change. As always, the key to Burma's future lies in the country itself. The international community can do more to improve the lot of the Burmese people but, barring an unforeseen change of government in Burma, its ability to promote much needed reforms will remain limited.

10

US–Burma relations: Told you so

(15:37 AEDT, 18 May 2009)

After Aung San Suu Kyi allowed an uninvited American visitor to stay at her home for a couple of days, and did not report his presence, Myanmar's military government announced that she would be prosecuted for violating the conditions of her house arrest. This made it impossible for president Obama to relax US sanctions against the regime, for the time being at least.

President Obama has just renewed US sanctions against Burma.[1] This follows a strong statement by Secretary of State Clinton condemning the military regime for its latest moves against Aung San Suu Kyi (that is, sending her to trial for breaking the conditions of her house arrest, after receiving an uninvited visitor).[2]

In my last Lowy blog post, I said that, if the regime did not change its behaviour and there was another incident in which it demonstrated its contempt for human rights and international concerns, it would undercut Obama's moves to review US policy towards Burma and strengthen the hand of those wanting to keep the hard line pursued by the Bush White House.[3]

1   Demetri Sevastopulo, 'Obama Renews Sanctions Against Burma', *Financial Times*, [London], 16 May 2009, www.ft.com/content/60cce76e-41a1-11de-bdb7-00144feabdc0.
2   'Clinton Joins in Condemnation of "Baseless Charges"', *Brisbane Times*, 16 May 2009, www.brisbanetimes.com.au/world/clinton-joins-in-condemnation-of-baseless-charges-20090515-b63g.html.
3   Andrew Selth, 'US–Burma: Where to From Here?', *The Interpreter*, 28 April 2009, archive.lowyinstitute.org/the-interpreter/us-burma-where-here.

US sanctions were due for formal renewal this month. In the circumstances, Obama had no choice but to extend them for another year. Once again, the regime has shot itself in the foot, by making it politically impossible for the US (or any other country) to reconsider sanctions and other punitive policies (which they have acknowledged are achieving very little).

11

Conspiracies and cockups in Burma

(11:13 AEDT, 26 May 2009)

The claims made by the military government and the activist community about the bizarre behaviour of an American tourist in Yangon in 2009 were outlandish and at times even extreme. However, they conformed to Myanmar's long tradition of wild speculation and conspiracy theories about developments in the country.

Major political developments in Burma have always encouraged conspiracy theories, and the bizarre case of an American tourist's unauthorised visit to Aung San Suu Kyi's house earlier this month has proved no exception. In a familiar refrain, both the opposition movement and the military government are now accusing each other of hatching Machiavellian plots.

Soon after it became known that John Yettaw had swum across a lake to Aung San Suu Kyi's Rangoon home, activist groups began claiming that something was amiss.[1] It seemed inconceivable to them that a foreigner could penetrate the security cordon around Aung San Suu Kyi's compound, let alone remain there for two nights, without the authorities finding out. Surely, they claimed, there were guards posted along the lake shore and possibly even listening devices inside her house, which would have ensured Yettaw's immediate arrest.

---

1   'Was Yettaw a Pawn of Burma's Generals?', *The Irrawaddy*, 15 May 2009, www.irrawaddy.org/article. php?art_id=15650 [page discontinued] [now at www2.irrawaddy.com/article.php?art_id=15650].

The only explanation, these activists have suggested, was that Yettaw was a dupe, if not a willing accomplice of the regime, who was permitted to enter Aung San Suu Kyi's compound specifically to compromise her. Feigning illness and exhaustion, he asked to stay for a few days. The idealistic opposition leader could hardly refuse or report the intruder to the authorities. According to this theory, the visit thus gave the regime the excuse it was seeking to keep her incarcerated after her current detention order expires—some say later this month, others say November.

Naypyidaw doubtless expected some reaction after it charged Aung San Suu Kyi with breaking the terms of her house arrest and sent her to trial. Yet it seems to have been taken aback by the tsunami of outrage that has washed over Burma in recent weeks. World leaders, international organisations, Nobel laureates and other prominent figures have all condemned the regime's actions and called for the charges against Aung San Suu Kyi to be dropped. They have also demanded her immediate release from house arrest.[2]

In response, the regime has developed a conspiracy theory of its own. The Burmese foreign minister has been reported as saying that Yettaw's visit to Aung San Suu Kyi's lakeside home was part of a cunning plot by the opposition movement to intensify international pressure on Naypyidaw. The culprits were 'internal and external anti-government elements', trying to discredit the regime at a time when the US and several other countries were reviewing their hardline policies against the military government.[3]

In another sadly familiar tactic, one senior Burmese official has even suggested that Yettaw was either a 'secret agent' or Aung San Suu Kyi's foreign 'boyfriend'.[4] Opposition spokespeople have accused the regime of trying to humiliate Aung San Suu Kyi and undermine her standing with the Burmese people by suggesting that the widowed democracy icon had allowed 'a man' to stay at her house overnight.[5]

---

2   'Western Outcry Over Suu Kyi Case', *BBC News*, 14 May 2009, news.bbc.co.uk/2/hi/asia-pacific/8050545.stm.
3   Yeni, 'Burmese FM Says Yettaw Visit Part of Opposition Plot', *The Irrawaddy*, 22 May 2009, www.irrawaddy.org/article.php?art_id=15715 [page discontinued] [now at www2.irrawaddy.com/opinion_story.php?art_id=15715].
4   Yeni, 'Burmese Diplomat Suggests That Yettaw Could Be Suu Kyi's "Boyfriend"', *The Irrawaddy*, 22 May 2009, www.irrawaddy.org/article.php?art_id=15709 [page discontinued] [now at www2.irrawaddy.com/opinion_story.php?art_id=15709].
5   Wai Moe, 'Regime Accused of Trying to Humiliate Suu Kyi', *The Irrawaddy*, 22 May 2009, www.irrawaddy.org/article.php?art_id=15713 [page discontinued] [now at www2.irrawaddy.com/article.php?art_id=15713].

The details of this incident are still unclear. There is a suggestion, for example, that Yettaw had pulled this stunt once before and been reported by Aung San Suu Kyi's staff. If true, that would certainly strengthen the theory that the authorities allowed him to make a second visit. But the facts of the matter are likely to be far more prosaic.

The likelihood of someone trying to swim across Inya Lake, in the heart of Rangoon, to visit Aung San Suu Kyi was always very remote. No supporter would knowingly endanger the opposition leader in that way. As a consequence, the rear of her compound was never heavily guarded. Also, after 13 years without significant incident—at least on the lake side of the house—it is unlikely that Aung San Suu Kyi's guards gave the possibility of an aquatic intruder any thought. Their attention was focused elsewhere, allowing Yettaw simply to wade ashore.

In looking for explanations of developments in Burma and given the choice between conspiracy and cockup, it is always safer to opt for the cockup. In this case, it appears that there were two. A rather foolish and naive man simply failed to think through the dire consequences of his actions. The regime's mistake was in not being more vigilant in their patrols around Aung San Suu Kyi's compound. The result of these cockups has been a major international incident.

In one sense, however, none of this makes any difference. There is little doubt that the regime always intended to extend the term of Aung San Suu Kyi's house arrest, probably until after the 2010 general elections. It did not need an excuse to do so. Yettaw's misguided exploit has given the regime an opportunity to dress up its decision in formal legal terms, but it has not changed Aung San Suu Kyi's fate.

12

Burma: 'Nationalism is not rationalism'

(10:23 AEDT, 10 June 2009)

The burial of India's last king in Myanmar in 1862, and of Myanmar's last king in India in 1916, opened the way for a swap of earthly remains that would be highly symbolic and satisfying for nationalists on both sides. It could also appeal to Myanmar's military regime, which was always keen to shore up its populist credentials.

British journalist Dennis Bloodworth once wrote that 'nationalism is not rationalism'.[1] This aphorism came to mind when I was in Burma recently and visited the mausoleum of the last Mughal emperor of India, Bahadur Shah II.

Also known as Zafar (the pen-name he used when writing poetry), the emperor was exiled to Rangoon in 1858 for his small part in the uprising that became known to the British as the Great Mutiny and to Indians as the First War of Independence. He died in Rangoon in 1862, aged 87, and was buried in an unmarked grave. Early last century, a shrine was built close to his presumed burial place. It is now a modest mosque and mausoleum housing the emperor's remains, which were accidentally discovered close to the site in 1991.

---

1   Dennis Bloodworth, *An Eye for the Dragon: Southeast Asia Observed: 1954–1970* (New York: Farrar, Straus & Giroux, 1970), p.31.

The mausoleum is a popular place of pilgrimage for Burma's Muslim community, which considers Zafar a Sufi saint. He is also honoured by many Hindus, who recognise his efforts to reconcile religious differences in India, both before and during the 1857 uprising (his mother was a Hindu). And he still has some resonance in political circles. As William Dalrymple (author of *The Last Mughal*) has written: '[D]ignitaries from India, Pakistan and Bangladesh now compete to shower the grave with presents.'[2]

In India, too, Zafar remains 'the focus of much nostalgic sympathy'. Interest in the late emperor peaked in 2007—the 150th anniversary of the uprising. However, there are still intermittent calls by nationalists, Muslims and Zafar's descendants for the return of his remains to India.[3] There is no sign of this happening just yet, but it does raise the intriguing possibility of a swap. For India has something it can offer Burma in return.

In 1885, after the fall of Mandalay, the British Government exiled the young Burmese king Thibaw Min to India. He died there in 1916, aged 58, and was buried in a mausoleum in the grounds of his house at Ratnagiri, near Bombay. Thibaw's queen, Supayalat, was permitted to return to Burma in 1919. When she died in 1925, she was buried at the foot of the revered Shwedagon Pagoda in Rangoon. The colonial authorities feared the king's remains might become a focus for anti-British sentiment in Burma, so they were left in India.

Thibaw has not been treated kindly by historians. He is usually portrayed either as a tyrant or as a weakling manipulated by his wife. Certainly, his reputation does not stand comparison with Burma's three most prominent warrior kings, Anawratha, Bayinnaung and Alaungpaya, who are held up as national heroes by the current regime. Their 10-metre-high statues tower over the main parade ground in the new capital of Naypyidaw.[4] Even so, Thibaw was the last king of Burma and the chief patron of the Buddhist monastic order. In both political and religious terms, the return of his remains from India would be symbolically important.

---

2   Geoffrey Moorhouse, 'Zafar the Ditherer', *The Guardian*, [London], 11 November 2006, www.guardian.co.uk/books/2006/nov/11/featuresreviews.guardianreview6.
3   Dean Nelson, 'Last Mughal Emperor's Descendants to Be Traced', *The Telegraph*, [London], 6 April 2009, www.telegraph.co.uk/news/worldnews/asia/india/5114995/The-Last-Mughals-descendants-to-be-traced.html?hc_location=ufi.
4   Bertil Lintner, 'Burma's Warrior Kings and the Generation of 8.8.88', *Global Asia*, Vol.2, No.2 (Fall 2007), globalasia.org/articles/issue3/iss3_10.html [site discontinued].

Burma's military rulers are ardent nationalists and look back to the time when Burma was an independent monarchy. In state propaganda, precolonial Burma is described as a political, economic and cultural force in the region—denied its true greatness only by the three-stage British conquest of the country between 1824 and 1885. The 60 or so years Burma spent under colonial rule are characterised as a period of unrelieved oppression during which the British imperialists shamelessly exploited Burma's rich natural resources. The king's exile to India is cited by the regime as the beginning of modern Burma's suffering.

More to the point, perhaps, both leaders of the military council that has ruled Burma since 1988 have displayed monarchical pretensions. When Senior General Saw Maung suffered a 'nervous breakdown' in late 1991, he startled diplomats at a golf tournament by screaming: 'I am the great king Kyansittha.' In early 1992, he was quietly replaced with Senior General Than Shwe. Despite his humble origins, Than Shwe, too, has begun to see himself as a kingly figure, dedicated to founding a new Burmese dynasty based on military strength.[5] In some translations, Naypyidaw means 'abode of kings'.

Than Shwe is a former psychological warfare officer and, as such, is well aware of the power of popular symbols. He has already presided over a series of high-profile projects designed to shore up the regime's credentials. These have included an officially sponsored tour of Burma of the Buddha's tooth relic (on loan from China) and the construction of a near-exact replica of the Shwedagon Pagoda in Naypyidaw. The return of Thibaw's remains to Burma for ceremonial reburial, perhaps in the new capital, would enhance the status of both the regime and Than Shwe himself.

Mix together the regime's extreme nationalism, its exploitation of Burmese history for propaganda purposes, its need for popular legitimacy and Than Shwe's royal ambitions and the result is a potent combination. In these circumstances, it is not beyond the realms of possibility that the Burmese Government will one day suggest to its Indian counterpart that, in return for Shah Bahadur Zafar's remains, Burma's last king be permitted to come home. To nationalists on both sides of the border, this might seem like a good idea.

---

5   Richard Ehrlich and Shawn W. Crispin, 'The Man Behind the Myanmar Madness', *Asia Times Online*, [Hong Kong], 28 September 2007, www.atimes.com/atimes/Southeast_Asia/II28Ae02.html [page discontinued].

13

Burma–North Korea: Rumour and reality

(12:33 AEDT, 29 June 2009)

Myanmar had long encouraged wild stories and unsubstantiated rumours. Few modern developments illustrated this problem more than the shadowy relationship that existed between Myanmar and North Korea, which prompted many unreliable and often colourful claims relating to secret military deals and clandestine weapons programs.

On security-related issues, Burma and North Korea are well known as information black holes. Also, both are at the centre of emotive and highly politicised debates about human rights, nuclear weapons and regional security. It is particularly important, therefore, that reports of developments involving these two countries are carefully researched, intellectually rigorous and analytically objective. At times, however, these requirements seem to be overlooked in all the excitement generated by current events.

At present, there are three issues that tie Burma and North Korea together in the news media and the public imagination. All have the potential to create much more heat than light.

The first issue is the recent publication of a series of photographs showing tunnels and other underground facilities in Burma, apparently built by North Korea or with North Korean expertise (see *Al Jazeera*'s report on the photos below).[1] Activist groups have cited these photos as evidence of nefarious dealings between the military governments in Naypyidaw and Pyongyang.

The second issue is the departure from North Korea of a cargo ship reportedly carrying missiles and nuclear components to Burma, despite UN embargoes on such exports.[2] This vessel, the *Kang Nam 1*, is being shadowed by a US Navy destroyer. There is the likelihood that it will resist inspection when it stops to refuel, probably in Singapore.

The third issue is the claim repeatedly made by Burmese exile groups, activists and others that Pyongyang is helping Naypyidaw to secretly build a nuclear reactor with the aim of developing a nuclear weapon.[3] According to this theory, Burma's generals believe that possession of such a weapon will help them resist international pressure to introduce political, economic and social reforms.

The main problem with all of these stories is that there is very little hard, independently verifiable information available, either about Pyongyang's relationship with Naypyidaw or about North Korea's activities in Burma. Inevitably, perhaps, the information gap has been filled with rumours, speculation and possibly even deliberate misinformation. Once it appears in print, this material tends to assume the status of established fact, further muddying the waters.

So, what do we know, or think we know?

In 1983, Burma severed diplomatic relations with Pyongyang after North Korean agents tried to assassinate the South Korean President in Rangoon. Formal ties were restored in 2007, but even before then there were unconfirmed reports that Burma—denied access to its usual arms suppliers—had turned to North Korea for small arms, artillery

1   'Myanmar's Secret Tunnels Revealed', *Al Jazeera*, 25 June 2009, english.aljazeera.net/news/asia-pacific/2009/06/20096255353936689.html [page discontinued].
2   Jae-soon Chang, 'North Korea Ship Suspected of Carrying Missiles to Burma', *The Huffington Post*, 21 June 2009, www.huffingtonpost.com/2009/06/21/north-korea-ship-suspecte_n_218599.html [page discontinued].
3   Andrew Selth, 'Is There a Burma–North Korea–Iran Nuclear Conspiracy?', *The Interpreter*, 25 February 2009, www.lowyinterpreter.org/post/2009/02/25/Is-there-a-Burma-North-Korea-Iran-nuclear-conspiracy.aspx [page discontinued] [now at archive.lowyinstitute.org/the-interpreter/there-burma-north-korea-iran-nuclear-conspiracy].

and other conventional weapons. In 2004, it was revealed that Burma had also considered the purchase of surface-to-surface missiles and possibly a small submarine.[4]

Since then, there have been further (again, unconfirmed) reports that North Korea has sold Burma arms, including anti-ship missiles and multiple-launch rocket systems. In recent years, however, these possible sales have been overshadowed by accusations that Pyongyang is helping Burma's government to expand and modernise its military infrastructure and is aiding in the construction of clandestine nuclear weapons facilities.

It is true that, over the past 20 years, Burma has made a major effort to strengthen its military capabilities and this has included the construction of underground facilities—up to 800 of them, according to exile groups. It would be logical for Naypyidaw to ask Pyongyang to assist in this program. Both are secretive and isolated military regimes fearful of external intervention, particularly by the US. The North Koreans need Burmese primary products. They also manufacture arms and have considerable experience in subterranean engineering projects.

However, from the recently released photos—both published and unpublished—it is not clear what all these underground facilities are for. Many of those shown are quite modest and, despite efforts at concealment, appear vulnerable to attack by a modern air force equipped with the latest weapons. Some may be connected to communications upgrades or other civil engineering projects. None of the photos supports activist claims of a secret nuclear plant.

Similarly, the *Kang Nam 1* seems to be another case of public commentary running ahead of the known facts. It is not clear what the ship is carrying or where it is going. This particular vessel has visited Burma before, possibly to deliver conventional arms or heavy machinery, but that does not automatically mean it is going there again. Reports that it is carrying missiles, let alone nuclear weapon components, simply cannot be justified on the basis of the information currently available.[5]

---

4   Paul Kerr, 'US Accuses Burma of Seeking Weapons Technology', *Arms Control Association*, May 2004, www.armscontrol.org/act/2004_05/Burma.

5   'Navy Positions Destroyer for Possible Intercept of North Korean Ship Suspected of Proliferating Missiles, Nukes', *Fox News*, 19 June 2009, www.foxnews.com/politics/2009/06/19/military-set-intercept-north-korean-ship-suspected-proliferatin-missiles-nukes/ [page discontinued].

As regards the third issue, it can be argued that, of all Southeast Asian countries, Burma has the strongest strategic rationale to develop nuclear weapons.[6] Also, in the past few years, some of the previous obstacles to such a program appear to have been overcome. Yet Burma's nuclear ambitions have never been clear. Work on a Russian research reactor— first announced in 2002—has still not begun. And North Korea's possible involvement in a second, clandestine nuclear reactor has never been verified.

Indeed, it is noteworthy that no government or international organisation (including the IAEA) has ever commented publicly on these claims. This includes the Bush administration, which had no love for the Naypyidaw regime and was quick to denounce suspected nuclear programs elsewhere. The relevant agencies seem to be keeping an open mind but, speaking off the record last month, a senior US official dismissed reports of a secret Burmese nuclear weapons project as an 'unsubstantiated rumour'.[7]

Burma and North Korea both have such poor international reputations that they are easy targets for criticism. Also, given their highly provocative and often bizarre behaviour, they lend themselves easily to conspiracy theories and sensationalist stories in the news media and on blogs. This is not to say that, whenever the names of these two pariah states are linked, there are no grounds for concern, but the links have to be real. And care needs to be taken to distinguish between what is actually known and what is assumed or claimed by special interest groups. For only then will we know what to be concerned about.

---

6   Andrew Selth, *Burma and the Threat of Invasion: Regime Fantasy or Strategic Reality?*, Griffith Asia Institute Regional Outlook Paper No.17 (Brisbane: Griffith University, 2008), www.griffith.edu.au/business/griffith-asia-institute/pdf/Andrew-Selth-Regional-Outlook-17v2.pdf [page discontinued].
7   'Nelson Report: About That Pesky Burma/NK Nuke Rumor', *The Agonist*, 5 June 2009, agonist.org/tina/20090605/nelson_report_about_that_pesky_burma_nk_nuke_rumor [page discontinued].

14

Burma's unanswered nuclear question

(11:40 AEDT, 3 August 2009)

On 1 August 2009, a number of sensational reports in Australian newspapers drew attention to claims that Myanmar was developing nuclear weapons. The stories were based on the testimony of so-called defectors, but they still failed to provide any hard evidence of a secret weapons program. More to the point, none of the claims were confirmed by the US Government, which was probably the external observer best placed to determine the real situation.

Burma's suspected WMD program is in the news once again. This time, the focus is on a couple of Burmese nationals who 'defected' two years ago, claiming firsthand knowledge of Naypyidaw's secret nuclear plans. As I noted in *The Interpreter* in February, however, the picture is still far from clear.[1]

Saturday's *Sydney Morning Herald* led with the dramatic headline 'Revealed: Burma's Nuclear Bombshell', followed by 'Atomic Weapons in Five Years' and 'North Korea Helping Build Secret Reactor'.[2] *The Age* carried a version of the story headed 'Burma "Building Secret N-Plant"'. Both papers balanced these stories with a thoughtful op-ed by *The Age*'s

---

1   Andrew Selth, 'Is There a Burma–North Korea–Iran Nuclear Conspiracy?', *The Interpreter*, 25 February 2009, www.lowyinterpreter.org/post/2009/02/25/Is-there-a-Burma-North-Korea-Iran-nuclear-conspiracy.aspx [page discontinued] [now at archive.lowyinstitute.org/the-interpreter/there-burma-north-korea-iran-nuclear-conspiracy].
2   Hamish McDonald, 'Revealed: Burma's Nuclear Bombshell', *Sydney Morning Herald*, 1–2 August 2009, www.smh.com.au:80/world/revealed-burmax2019s-nuclear-bombshell-20090731-e4fw.html.

diplomatic editor, reminding readers that, despite the defectors' startling claims, the issue was still the subject of considerable debate among scholars and officials.[3]

This is not the first time local newspapers have made such claims. In 2006, for example, *The Australian* published a story under the headline 'Burma Seeks Nuclear Weapons Alliance with N. Korea'.[4] No evidence was provided to justify this statement, but it was followed in 2007 by a report in the same paper entitled 'Unconventional Wisdom on Burma'. The report claimed that 'US intelligence believes that Burma is seeking to develop nuclear weapons from technology provided by North Korea'.[5]

There are many unanswered questions about Burma's nuclear aspirations and its ties with North Korea. As might be expected, given the isolated and secretive nature of both military regimes, details of their relationship are very hard to discover. The most pressing question for many analysts, however, is why no government or international organisation has made any official statement on this issue, despite all the articles and blogs published since 2002, when Burma was first accused of wanting a nuclear weapon.

For eight years, the Bush administration took every opportunity to criticise Burma's military regime, loudly and publicly. The US also made numerous statements condemning those countries—like Iraq, Iran, Syria and North Korea—that it believed were pursuing clandestine nuclear weapons programs or proliferating sensitive nuclear technologies. At no time, however, did the US Government ever accuse the Naypyidaw regime of trying to build a secret reactor or develop nuclear weapons, with or without North Korean assistance.

Throughout this period, Washington was watching developments in Burma closely. It beggars belief that the US Government did not know about the two Burmese 'defectors' on whose testimony the *Sydney Morning Herald* and *The Age* have based their latest stories. Indeed, both papers have suggested that a third Burmese defector was 'picked up' by US intelligence agencies last year, presumably to be interviewed on this

---

3   Daniel Flitton, 'Burma and the Bomb', *The Age*, [Melbourne], 1 August 2009, www.theage.com. au:80/world/burma-and-the-bomb-20090731-e4h6.html?page=-1.

4   Greg Sheridan, 'Burma Seeks Nuclear Weapons Alliance with N. Korea', *The Australian*, 5 July 2006, www.tai4freedom.info/articles/nuke2.html [page discontinued].

5   Greg Sheridan, 'Unconventional Wisdom on Burma', *The Australian*, 3 November 2007, www. theaustralian.news.com.au/story/0,25197,22693077-5013460,00.html [page discontinued].

issue. Yet, even when armed with the apparent revelations of all these defectors, the Bush administration remained conspicuously silent about Burma's nuclear status.

This is not to say that there were no suspicions of a possible nuclear weapons program. In 2007, for example, *The Australian* based its story on a statement by a former White House staffer to the effect that 'Western intelligence officials have suspected for several years that the regime has had an interest in following the model of North Korea and achieving military autarky by developing ballistic missiles and nuclear weapons'. Yet suspicions of an interest in following a model are a far cry from hard evidence of a secret nuclear weapons program.

As rumours of a secret WMD program grew in frequency and scope, the Bush administration came under increasing pressure from activists, exile groups and certain members of Congress to openly accuse Burma's military regime of developing nuclear weapons, with North Korea's help. Yet it steadfastly refused to do so, even when the US conducted a concerted campaign in the UN Security Council to have Burma branded a threat to regional security.

It is difficult to escape the conclusion that the Bush administration felt obliged to remain silent on this issue largely because there was insufficient reliable evidence on which to make a public case against Naypyidaw and Pyongyang.[6]

Since taking office, the Obama administration has conducted a thorough investigation of this matter, as part of its comprehensive review of US Burma policy. Yet, it too has been very cautious in its comments about Burma's nuclear ambitions. For example, Naypyidaw's suspected WMD program was not raised during Senate hearings to confirm the appointments of Secretary of State Clinton or UN Representative Susan Rice. Nor has it been raised by the US in other public forums (including the IAEA) where nuclear weapons proliferation has been discussed.

---

6   Denis D. Gray, 'Is Myanmar Going Nuclear with North Korea's Help', *The San Diego Union-Tribune*, 21 July 2009, www.washingtonpost.com/wp-dyn/content/article/2009/07/21/AR20090721 00256_pf.html [page discontinued] [now at www.sandiegouniontribune.com/sdut-myanmar-nuclear-ambitions-072109-2009jul21-story.html].

In her comments at the ASEAN summit last month, Hillary Clinton finally broke the US's official silence on the subject.[7] Yet it is instructive to examine what was actually said. She expressed concern over military links between Burma and North Korea, including 'the transfer of nuclear technology and other dangerous weapons'. She later modified her position, however, referring only to 'dealings' between Pyongyang and Naypyidaw that were 'perhaps' taking place.

Despite having the perfect opportunity to do so, the Secretary of State did not say that Burma was secretly building a nuclear reactor or trying to develop a nuclear weapon. She did not even specify that North Korea was passing Burma nuclear *weapons* technology. This continuing official reticence strongly suggests that, while the US is clearly concerned about Naypyidaw's growing relationship with Pyongyang, it still does not have clear evidence of a secret Burmese WMD program.

As noted in *The Interpreter* in February, the Burma *JADE Act* passed by the US Congress in July 2008 stipulated that, within 180 days, the Secretary of State must issue a statement describing the provision of WMD and related technologies to Burma.[8] Reports filtering out of Washington suggest there have been a number of confidential briefings to senior officials on this subject. However, the world is still waiting for an authoritative public statement from the US that will put all the rumours and newspaper stories into their proper perspective.

---

7   Julian Borger, 'Burma Suspected of Forming Nuclear Link with North Korea', *The Guardian*, [London], 21 July 2009, www.guardian.co.uk/world/2009/jul/21/burma-north-korea-nuclear-clinton.
8   Selth, 'Is There a Burma–North Korea–Iran Nuclear Conspiracy?'.

15

Burma's nuclear status: Not the last word, but …

(09:24 AEDT, 29 September 2009)

A comprehensive report in 2009 by the London-based International Institute for Strategic Studies concisely and very usefully put into context all the rumours and speculation that had been circulating about Myanmar's reported clandestine nuclear weapons program.

It is indicative of the uncertainty surrounding Burma's nuclear status that the issue has attracted as many true believers as devoted sceptics.[1] In the absence of enough hard information to settle the argument either way, Burma-watchers and other observers are left waiting for an authoritative statement from an institution like the IAEA or the US Government.[2]

It may not be quite the same thing, but a comprehensive study just completed by the London-based International Institute for Strategic Studies (IISS) comes close. The IISS strategic dossier, entitled *Preventing Nuclear Dangers in Southeast Asia and Australasia*, was published

1   Andrew Selth, *Burma and North Korea: Smoke or Fire?*, Policy Analysis No.47 (Canberra: Australian Strategic Policy Institute, 24 August 2009), www.aspi.org.au/publications/publicationlist. aspx?pubtype=9 [page discontinued] [now at www.aspi.org.au/report/burma-and-north-korea-smoke-or-fire].

2   Andrew Selth, 'Burma Unanswered Nuclear Question', *The Interpreter*, 3 August 2009, www.lowy interpreter.org/post/2009/08/03/Burmas-unanswered-nuclear-question.aspx [page discontinued] [now at archive.lowyinstitute.org/the-interpreter/burma-unanswered-nuclear-question].

yesterday.[3] It is based on extensive research over several months and draws on information provided by a wide range of officials, academics, scientists and journalists.

On Burma, its key findings include:

1. Of all the Southeast Asian countries, Burma is the only one that might be considered to have a strategic motivation to develop nuclear weapons.

2. To date, no firm evidence of a secret nuclear weapons program has been produced and no government or international organisation has confirmed any of the claims put forward by regime opponents. Yet suspicions remain.

3. As of September, the contract covering the proposed construction of a Russian 10 MW research reactor in Burma had still not been finalised. If agreement can be reached, the research centre would take about five years to build.

4. A light water reactor of this size would produce no more than 1 kilogram of weapons-usable plutonium a year, even if operated for this purpose (considerably less than the 8 kg defined by the IAEA as a significant quantity).

5. In mid 2007, 203 Burmese students were studying in Russia. It was expected that about 1,000 Burmese students would go there within the next few years, including 300 experts who would eventually work in the Russian-built nuclear research centre in Burma.

6. Apart from the Russian reactor project, which will be under IAEA safeguards, Burma is not known to have any significant nuclear facilities or to have conducted any work in any area of the nuclear fuel cycle.

7. Burma is not known to have broken any international laws or commitments. However, in addition to persistent claims about transfers of missiles and other sensitive technology from North Korea, questions have been raised about Burma's importation of some dual-use equipment.

---

3   *Preventing Nuclear Dangers in Southeast Asia and Australasia* (London: International Institute for Strategic Studies, 2009), www.iiss.org/publications/strategic-dossiers/preventing-nuclear-dangers-in-southeast-asia-and-australasia/ [page discontinued] [now at epdf.pub/preventing-nuclear-dangers-in-southeast-asia-and-australasia-an-iiss-strategic-d.html].

8. While North Korea has a history of proliferation activities, there is only circumstantial evidence of a North Korea–Burma nuclear connection. Indeed, less appears to be known about North Korean activity in Burma than was known about North Korean activity in Syria.

9. Recent claims of a secret nuclear weapons program in Burma—none of which has yet been verified—should be assessed with a high degree of caution. Many claims made by the Burmese defectors do not stand up to scrutiny.

The strategic dossier's chapter on Burma (which the IISS calls Myanmar, the country's official name) concludes:

> Myanmar has no known capabilities that would lend themselves to a nuclear weapons program, apart from limited uranium deposits and some personnel who have received nuclear training overseas. If it is built, a 10MWt research reactor and associated training from Russia could provide the basis for an eventual civilian nuclear power program, but few of the skills required for such a program are readily transferrable to nuclear weapons development. Specialised reprocessing or enrichment facilities would be necessary to produce weapons-usable fissile material, and any attempt to divert plutonium from the reactor is likely to be detected by IAEA inspectors.

> The concern is whether Myanmar might take the road Syria appears to have taken by building secret facilities. With sufficient foreign help in the complex technologies and equipment required for plutonium implosion weapons, lack of indigenous technical capabilities would not be an insurmountable hurdle. Nor, despite the huge investment required for nuclear weapons, would Myanmar's relative poverty be a deal-breaker ... the regime is no longer short of funds for such ambitious projects. The question hinges more on political decisions. In this regard, there is insufficient information to make a well-founded judgement about Myanmar's nuclear intentions and the North Korean connection.

> Concerned governments have therefore erred on the side of caution, refraining from committing themselves. Until recently, this approach reflected scepticism about a secret nuclear program. Since 2008, however, concerned governments and international organisations appear to be giving this matter a higher priority and making greater efforts to test the claims of defectors. There is

a growing international determination to be alert to signals about nuclear-weapons programs that in countries such as Israel and Pakistan were overlooked until it was too late.[4]

The IISS's chapter is necessarily based on open sources and thus lacks some data that might be available to others. However, until the US Government or the IAEA reveals the results of their own investigations, the IISS strategic dossier constitutes the most comprehensive and detailed examination of Burma's nuclear status currently available.

---

4   ibid., p.115.

16

Burma's 'superstitious' leaders

(10:25 AEDT, 22 October 2009)

To a greater or lesser extent, most people in Myanmar, including the country's military leaders, put their faith in superstitions, magic and the occult. However, it would be a mistake simply to blame such beliefs for the regime's more bizarre and apparently self-defeating policies and practices. Allowances must always be made for 'irrational actors', but, seen from the generals' point of view, their decisions usually make sense.

Whenever critics of Burma's military government run out of explanations for the regime's apparently self-defeating policies, they tend to fall back on the fact that regime leader Senior General Than Shwe is very superstitious. He has been accused of making decisions not on the basis of rational calculations, but on the advice of astrologers, numerologists and magicians.

There is probably some truth to such claims. However, they can also reflect weak analysis and a failure to delve more deeply into the government's mindset. Indeed, some of these stories seem designed simply to promote anti-regime sentiment by exciting cultural and religious biases in Western countries.

Burma is predominantly Theravada Buddhist, which is a tolerant philosophy that easily accommodates older animist traditions as well as esoteric schools such as astrology and numerology. It is not unusual for statues of mythical beings to be found alongside Buddha images in

Burma, and pagodas are often encircled by guardian animals representing the days of the week. Most Burmese have an astrological chart drawn up at birth and many consult fortune tellers to guide their daily lives. Natural phenomena such as earthquakes and cyclones, or the collapse of a pagoda, are interpreted as omens or signs of celestial disfavour.

For centuries, such beliefs have been deeply embedded in Burmese society and have influenced attitudes and behaviour at almost every level.[1]

All Burma's modern rulers have consulted soothsayers and propitiated supernatural forces. For example, the country's independence from Britain on 4 January 1948 was formally declared at 4:20 am—the time considered most favourable by local astrologers. In 1961, prime minister U Nu ordered the construction of 60,000 sand pagodas all over Burma to avert impending dangers and bring peace to the war-ravaged country. The government's instructions for the construction and consecration of the pagodas were based on the auspicious number nine.

After seizing power in 1962, General Ne Win relied heavily on astrologers and numerologists for policy advice. The decision in 1970 for Burma to change from driving on the left-hand side of the road to the right-hand side was reportedly taken because the general's astrologer felt that Burma had moved too far to the left in political terms. In 1987, Ne Win introduced 45-kyat and 90-kyat currency notes, as the face values added up to nine—his lucky number. It was said that he walked backwards over bridges to ward off evil spirits and bathed in dolphins' blood to extend his life to the age of 90.

Many of the military officers who have exercised power since the abortive 1988 prodemocracy uprising have personal astrologers. Like most Burmese, they believe that personal names and dates of birth carry special significance and, being equated with particular planets, can influence events on Earth. The generals are also known to practise *yadaya*, a mystical technique for manipulating the results of astrology or portents. Such beliefs have reportedly influenced a number of important military appointments and policy decisions over the past 20 years.

---

1   Joseph A. Allchin, 'Numbers of the Beast: The Politics of Superstition', *Democratic Voice of Burma*, 31 March 2009, english.dvb.no/news.php?id=2401 [site discontinued].

Than Shwe is reputed to be even more superstitious than his predecessors. For example, the decision to build a new capital in Naypyidaw and the precise time in 2005 for the government's transfer from Rangoon were reportedly based on advice from his astrologers.[2] Other decisions (such as the 65-year prison sentences given to some dissidents last year) are said to deliberately reflect 11—Than Shwe's lucky number.[3] He has also been accused of engaging in occult practices, including human sacrifices and cannibalistic rites, to consolidate his rule over Burma.

Anti-regime activists, too, have used magic to pursue political ends. For example, in 2007, one Thailand-based group launched a global 'panties for peace' campaign, in which supporters were encouraged to send women's underwear to Burmese embassies, in the hope that contact with such garments would weaken the regime's *hpoun*, or spiritual power.[4] The generals may indeed subscribe to this belief. It is rumoured that, before a foreign envoy visits Burma, an article of female underwear or a piece of a pregnant woman's sarong is hidden in the ceiling of the visitor's hotel suite, to weaken their *hpoun* and thus their negotiating position.

These days, Burma is awash with such stories. In themselves, they are no basis for serious analysis. They are important, however, in that they tap into popular belief systems, and this gives them considerable currency in Burma. The official Board of Astrologers, created by Ne Win to advise on the timing of major state events, is now used to help manage local soothsayers. This reflects the military regime's awareness of the influence exercised by such figures, their ability to sway public sentiment and their potential to encourage social unrest through pronouncements unfavourable to the regime.

Burma is not alone in having leaders who observe such practices. Indira Gandhi secretly consulted astrologers. Indonesian presidents Sukarno and Suharto both allowed superstitions to influence the nature and timing of certain policy decisions. Current Sri Lankan President Mahinda Rajapaksa recently declared his belief in astrology. Other Asian cultures

---

2   Richard C. Paddock, 'Abrupt Relocation of Burma Capital Linked to Astrology', *Boston Globe*, 1 January 2006, www.boston.com/news/world/asia/articles/2006/01/01/abrupt_relocation_of_burma _capital_linked_to_astrology/.

3   Aung Zaw, 'Than Shwe, Voodoo and the Number 11', *The Irrawaddy*, 25 December 2008, www. irrawaddy.org/opinion_story.php?art_id=14844 [page discontinued] [now at www2.irrawaddy.com/ opinion_story.php?art_id=14844].

4   Martin Hodgson, 'Activists Send Female Underwear to Burmese Embassies', *The Guardian*, [London], 19 October 2007, www.guardian.co.uk/world/2007/oct/19/burma.martinhodgson.

give an important place to esoteric belief systems, including the occult. Even in resolutely secular commercial centres like Singapore and Hong Kong, lucky numbers are highly prized and *feng shui* plays an important part in urban planning.

Nor are such beliefs confined to Asia. Western leaders as diverse as Adolf Hitler, Winston Churchill, Franklin Delano Roosevelt, Charles de Gaulle, François Mitterrand and Leonid Brezhnev were all known to have consulted astrologers.[5] In 1988, it was revealed that US president Ronald Reagan was superstitious and allowed his daily schedule to be dictated by his wife's personal astrologer.

Arguably, astrology, numerology and magic are as valid as faith-based belief systems as sources of political guidance and inspiration. In the Western news media, however, these practices are usually cited as evidence of the ignorance and irrationality of Burma's leaders and, by implication, their unfitness to rule. Ironically, even Burmese activists—themselves imbued with many traditional beliefs—have emphasised such characteristics to garner support from Western constituencies, such as conservative Christians in the US.

In such reports, democratically elected U Nu tends to be described simply as quixotic or eccentric. Burma's military leaders, however, are painted in much harsher colours. It is implied that their attachment to 'primitive' and 'dangerous' superstitions has been a major factor in the country's ruin, and thus the terrible plight of the Burmese people. The generals are implicitly contrasted with refined, Oxford-educated and devoutly Buddhist opposition leader Aung San Suu Kyi, who is not known to share her compatriots' belief in such matters.[6]

In any study of political culture and the behaviour of national leaders, some allowance must be made for 'irrational actors' and idiosyncratic decisions made by powerful individuals like Than Shwe.[7] His personal beliefs and those of other generals—not to forget key opposition figures—need to

---

5   Ben Macintyre, 'I Foresee a Troubled Future for Burmese Generals', *The Times Online*, [London], 28 September 2007, www.timesonline.co.uk/tol/comment/columnists/ben_macintyre/article2547120. ece [page discontinued].

6   Sudha Ramachandran and Swe Win, 'Instant Karma in Myanmar', *Asia Times Online*, [Hong Kong], 18 June 2009, www.atimes.com/atimes/Southeast_Asia/KF18Ae02.html [page discontinued].

7   Andrew Marshall, 'The Soldier and The State', *TIME*, 19 October 2009, www.time.com/time/magazine/article/0,9171,1929130,00.html [page discontinued] [now at andrewmarshall.com/articles/reporting-for-time-on-burmese-dictator-than-shwe/].

be considered in analyses of contemporary Burma. However, they are certainly not the whole story. The regime's foreign and domestic policies are dictated by a wide range of complex factors, many of which would be familiar to other governments.

The superstitions of Burma's leaders will doubtless continue to provoke public comment. However, greater foreign influence in Naypyidaw will depend on an understanding of all the elements that make up the regime's worldview and prompt its policy settings, not just one.

17

Burma: Obama's 'pragmatic engagement'

(11:17 AEDT, 18 November 2009)

US President Obama's cautious policy of 'pragmatic engagement' with Myanmar inevitably attracted criticism, particularly from diehard activists, but many observers felt that it was more likely to break the deadlock in bilateral relations and improve conditions for people in the country than a continuation of George W. Bush's discredited hardline approach.

I recently returned from Washington, DC, where I was able to hear Kurt Campbell, Assistant Secretary of State for East Asian and Pacific Affairs, and Scot Marciel, US Ambassador to ASEAN, speak about the Obama administration's review of US policy towards Burma.[1] Earlier this month, these two officials made a short 'exploratory' visit to Burma, where they explained the context of the review to members of the military government, Aung San Suu Kyi and other political figures.

Most observers have welcomed the end of the Bush administration's hardline Burma policy, but there is still widespread scepticism that President Obama's more nuanced approach involving closer engagement

---

1   'SAIS Hosted Conference on Political and Economic Development in Myanmar/Burma on October 30', *News and Events* (Washington, DC: Paul H. Nitze School of Advanced International Studies, Johns Hopkins University), www.sais-jhu.edu/news-and-events/index.htm [page discontinued].

and dialogue with Naypyidaw will be any more successful. One seasoned Burma-watcher has described it as 'naive'.[2] A Republican congressman labelled the new policy 'alarming' and even 'immoral'.[3]

Given such reactions, it might be helpful to look at the thinking behind the Obama administration's approach, what it is actually trying to do and how its policies differ from those of the previous administration.

The Naypyidaw government is notoriously opaque. Even when official statements are issued, the reasons behind certain policies are difficult to discern. To many observers, some positions adopted by the military regime have been not only illogical, but also self-defeating. Popular pundits have put this down to the ruling hierarchy's superstitions, but on important issues, it is unlikely that such factors outweigh careful consideration of the country's—and the regime's—perceived interests.[4]

Understanding those perceptions, and the way decisions are made in Burma, is made even harder by the regime's isolation. Almost all foreign diplomats in Burma are based in Rangoon, yet the seat of government is in Naypyidaw, hundreds of kilometres away. Foreigners find it hard to meet Burmese officials outside a strictly controlled environment, and the country's pervasive security apparatus makes it difficult to gain accurate insights into the regime's inner workings.

Paradoxically, attempts since the abortive 1988 prodemocracy uprising to isolate Burma diplomatically have resulted in an expansion of the regime's foreign relations. It has established closer ties with its regional neighbours and countries like China, Russia and North Korea. Indeed, by imposing economic sanctions, travel bans and other punitive measures on Burma, the US and members of the EU effectively isolated themselves. This complicated communications with the regime, added to its mistrust of foreign powers and reduced the ability of countries like the US to affect thinking in Naypyidaw.

---

2   Bertil Lintner, 'Reaching Out to Burma', *The Wall Street Journal*, 3 November 2009, online.wsj. com/article/SB10001424052748703740004574512231868995674.html.
3   Lalit K. Jha, 'Key Republicans Oppose Engagement with Burma', *The Irrawaddy*, 22 October 2009, www.irrawaddy.org/article.php?art_id=17041 [page discontinued] [now at www2.irrawaddy. com/article.php?art_id=17041].
4   Andrew Selth, 'Burma's "Superstitious" Leaders', *The Interpreter*, 22 October 2009, www.lowy interpreter.org/post/2009/10/22/Burmas-superstitious-leaders.aspx [page discontinued] [now at archive. lowyinstitute.org/the-interpreter/burma-uperstitious-leaders].

Misreading the nature of the regime, the Bush administration tried to force the generals to abandon policies they considered essential for regime survival and for Burma's unity, stability and independence. Not only was this approach demonstrably unsuccessful, it was also counterproductive. According to Kurt Campbell, sanctions have been no more than 'modest inconveniences' to the military leadership.[5] Yet such measures hardened the generals' resolve to resist external pressures and made them even more determined to remain the arbiters of Burma's future.

The Obama administration seems to understand that there are few practical ways for the international community to influence a government that is deeply committed to its self-appointed role in national affairs, does not care for the welfare of its own people, does not observe international norms and is protected by powerful friends and allies. President Obama's new approach acknowledges these harsh realities. It also takes full account of the regime's intensely nationalistic mindset and posits more achievable short-term goals.

Kurt Campbell and other officials have stressed that the fundamental US aims have not changed. It still wants a unified, peaceful, prosperous and democratic Burma. Washington is still calling for the release of all political prisoners.[6] The best way of pursuing these aims, however, is now seen to be through a direct senior-level dialogue. Recognising the political realities—in Washington as well as in Naypyidaw—sanctions will remain in place, pending concrete steps by the regime towards addressing core US concerns.

Administration officials recognise the challenges in formulating an effective engagement policy that remains focused on democratic reforms but is also sustainable and convincing to a regime that has long perceived such concerns as a means to remove it from power. Clearly, much work lies ahead in crafting inducements that will lead to real change in Burma. The regime has expressed an interest in developing closer ties with the US, however, and presumably recognises it will have to give up something in return—possibly even the release of Aung San Suu Kyi.

5   Dan Robinson, 'US Diplomat Outlines Obama Approach on Burma', *Voice of America*, 1 October 2009, www.voanews.com/english/2009-10-01-voa32.cfm [page discontinued] [now at newsvideo.su/video/3437016].

6   Scot Marciel, Bureau of East Asian and Pacific Affairs, 'Burma: Policy Review', Remarks, Chulalongkorn University, Bangkok, Thailand, 5 November 2009, www.state.gov/p/eap/rls/rm/2009/11/131536.htm [page discontinued] [now at 2009-2017.state.gov/p/eap/rls/rm/2009/11/131536.htm].

Listening to senior US officials speak on this subject recently, and surveying their public statements, three other aspects of the new US policy struck me as noteworthy.

First, it is apparent that the new approach is founded on a very hardheaded and realistic appreciation of the current situation in Burma. The US administration expects engagement with Burma to be a long, slow and step-by-step process. It is under no illusions about the nature of the military government and the difficulty of shifting it from its firmly held positions on issues such as Burma's constitution, the proposed elections and political freedoms. As Kurt Campbell said last month: '[A]chieving meaningful change in Burma will take time.'[7]

Second, the new approach lacks the hubris that characterised the Bush administration. For eight years, the US seemed to feel that it could resolve Burma's complex problems by actively intervening in the country's affairs through a range of direct and indirect measures. By contrast, the Obama policy, while not losing sight of US principles and national interests, places much greater emphasis on the Burmese people themselves deciding their political future and attempts to encourage positive steps in that direction.[8]

Third, the Obama administration has openly embraced ASEAN as a partner in its attempts to bring about reforms in Burma. In July, the US signed the Treaty of Amity and Cooperation—a step the Bush administration refused to take, partly because of Burma's ASEAN membership. ASEAN's own policy of 'constructive engagement' has made few substantive gains. The US hopes, however, that by coordinating their Burma policies, it and regional countries can make greater progress towards their shared objectives.[9]

Not surprisingly, the US's new Burma policy is unpopular in some quarters, and critics of both governments will seize on inevitable setbacks to denounce it further. Given the continuing terrible problems in Burma,

---

7   Kurt M. Campbell, Assistant Secretary of State, Bureau of East Asian and Pacific Affairs, 'US Policy Towards Burma', Testimony Statement Before the House Committee on Foreign Affairs, Washington, DC, 21 October 2009, www.internationalrelations.house.gov/111/cam102109.pdf [page discontinued] [now at 2009-2017.state.gov/p/eap/rls/rm/2009/10/130769.htm].

8   'Playing "Wait and See" in Myanmar', *Myanmar Times*, [Yangon], 2–8 November 2009, www.mm times.com/no495/n012.htm [page discontinued].

9   'Myanmar Will No Longer Dictate ASEAN Ties: White House', *Agence France-Presse*, November 2009, www.google.com/hostednews/afp/article/ALeqM5gxpnxh413mGqW7eZ_5LzyUVI7aZw [page discontinued].

their frustration is understandable. Yet the Obama administration's critics seem only to be offering a continuation of the discredited policies of the Bush era and a perpetuation of the diplomatic impasse that has characterised the past 20 years.

As Hillary Clinton stated in Singapore earlier this month, there are no quick or easy solutions to Burma's many problems.[10] However, President Obama's fresh approach seems to hold out some hope for breaking the current deadlock and achieving gradual progress on a number of pressing issues.

10   'Clinton Says No New Conditions for Myanmar', *CBS News*, 11 November 2009, widgets-cbsn. cbsnews.com/news/clinton-says-no-new-conditions-for-myanmar/.

2010

18

Burma: If not nukes, what about missiles?

(10:53 AEDT, 11 January 2010)

Although overshadowed by claims of a secret nuclear weapons program, there had long been persistent rumours that Myanmar planned to acquire or build short-range ballistic missiles—also with North Korean help.

Fears that Burma's military government is secretly building a nuclear weapon, with North Korean help, seem to have subsided—at least for the time being.

There is wide agreement that the issue needs to be monitored closely, but at this stage most informed observers feel there is insufficient reliable information on which to base any firm judgements.[1] After consulting the IAEA—which apparently said there was nothing new in the 2009 media stories—the Australian Government has joined the US and UK in referring only to 'unconfirmed' reports of a Burmese nuclear weapons program.[2]

---

1   Andrew Selth, 'Burma's Nuclear Status: Not the Last Word, But …', *The Interpreter*, 29 September 2009, www.lowyinterpreter.org/post/2009/09/29/Burmas-nuclear-status-Not-the-last-word-but.aspx [page discontinued] [now at archive.lowyinstitute.org/the-interpreter/burma-nuclear-status-not-last-word].
2   'Burma's Nuclear Program', The Greens, Canberra, 10 September 2009, greensmps.org.au/content/question/burma's-nuclear-program [page discontinued].

Curiously, given all the publicity surrounding Burma's possible nuclear ambitions, much less attention has been paid to the regime's interest in acquiring some Scud-type short-range ballistic missiles (SRBMs) from North Korea. Yet the evidence for Naypyidaw's interest in SRBMs is at least as strong as that for nuclear weapons, if not stronger.

Any SRBM sales to Burma would have implications for regional security. Despite an operational range of only about 700 kilometres, such missiles could give Burma a power projection capability for the first time. More to the point, perhaps, they would constitute a potent psychological weapon and have a significant political impact, not only on Burma's regional neighbours, but also in the US and Europe, where Burma remains a sensitive issue.

Activists have long claimed that Burma's generals want to get their hands on some SRBMs. Few reports on this subject have been based on hard evidence, however, and news stories have often failed to distinguish clearly between SRBMs and other kinds of missiles. For example, the regime's reported efforts to buy or manufacture anti-ship, tactical surface-to-surface, surface-to-air and air-to-air missiles have frequently been confused with its interest in acquiring ballistic weapon systems.

The picture has been further clouded by unsubstantiated claims that Burma already possesses SRBMs, and possibly even medium-range ballistic missiles. An anonymous *Wikipedia* entry states that Naypyidaw took delivery of 11 North Korean Hwasong-6 (Scud C–type) SRBMs in 2009.[3] The regime has been accused of paying for such missiles with heroin. One activist website has referred to four 'bases' along the Burma–Thailand border where SRBMs have supposedly been deployed. Such reports have been dismissed by serious Burma-watchers.

Similarly, when the North Korean cargo ship *Kang Nam 1* was heading to Rangoon last June, it was widely speculated that the vessel was carrying 'missile parts', as well as nuclear components. If this was so, it would probably have been boarded under UNSC Resolution 1874, which prohibits North Korean arms exports. After the ship turned back, the commander of US Pacific forces admitted that no one knew what cargo it was carrying.

---

3   'Hwasong-6', *Wikipedia*, en.wikipedia.org/wiki/Hwasong-6.

There is no evidence that Burma has acquired any ballistic missiles. Yet the regime does seem interested in doing so and, at one stage, it may have even begun negotiations with the North Koreans. In 2004, the US State Department revealed that it had made robust representations to the military government to forestall the possible purchase of surface-to-surface missiles from Pyongyang. This was later acknowledged to be a reference to SRBMs. The US undertook to respond 'vigorously and rapidly' to any such sales.[4]

North Korean military expert Joseph Bermudez believes the issue of ballistic missile sales has arisen in all major meetings between the North Koreans and Burmese since bilateral relations warmed in the early 2000s.[5] However, he thinks Naypyidaw is not yet ready for such weapons. It needs to train personnel, form units and build specialised support facilities (including some underground). Bermudez has also suggested that premature acquisition of SRBMs might complicate the purchase of other foreign arms and equipment sought by the regime.

Another possibility is that Naypyidaw plans to build its own SRBMs, with Pyongyang's help. Senior Burmese officials visiting North Korea have inspected ballistic missile production plants. Some of the sophisticated machine tools and dual-use equipment imported from Europe and Japan in recent years may not be for a secret nuclear weapons program, as often claimed, but for an indigenous SRBM factory. While not very economical, such a scheme would be in keeping with the regime's wish for defence self-sufficiency.

If this is the regime's aim, such a development is likely to be some years away. Still, the question needs to be asked: what could Burma do with such weapons? Given their relatively short range, questionable accuracy and small conventional warhead, SRBMs are of limited military utility. Inevitably, this has prompted speculation that Naypyidaw plans to arm them with chemical or nuclear warheads, either made in Burma or acquired from North Korea.

---

4   'US Will Persevere on Democracy in Burma, State's Daley Says', *America.gov*, 25 March 2004, www.america.gov/st/washfile-english/2004/March/20040325181911ASesuarK0.3054773.html [page discontinued].

5   Joseph S. Bermudez Jr, *The Armed Forces of North Korea* (London: I.B. Taurus, 2001), www. amazon.com/Armed-Forces-North-Korea/dp/1860644864.

Even so, SRBMs would be ineffective against a seaborne threat and they are unlikely to be aimed at China or India, both of which currently support Burma's military regime.

One theory is that Naypyidaw wants a weapon that can pose a threat to Bangkok, to help deter Thailand from allowing the US to launch an invasion of Burma from Thai territory. The US has never contemplated such an invasion and is unlikely ever to do so, but the prospect of military intervention has worried Burma's generals since they crushed the 1988 prodemocracy uprising.[6] Even the Thai king has expressed his concerns about Thailand being used by the US in this way.

Other reasons for Naypyidaw's interest in SRBMs probably include the regime's desire for status and prestige, its perceptions of what 'modern' armed forces should have in their weapons inventories and its wish for Burma to be taken seriously as an international actor.

As with so many aspects of Burma's security, there is very little hard evidence on which to base assessments. And analysis of this problem is complicated, as always, by rumours, unsubstantiated claims, speculative news reports and political propaganda. Even so, the chances of Burma one day acquiring or manufacturing SRBMs seem to be greater than those of Naypyidaw producing a nuclear weapon.

That makes another reason to monitor security developments in Burma closely.

---

6   Andrew Selth, *Burma and the Threat of Invasion: Regime Fantasy or Strategic Reality?*, Griffith Asia Institute Regional Outlook Paper No.17 (Brisbane: Griffith University, 2008), www.griffith.edu.au/business/griffith-asia-institute/pdf/Andrew-Selth-Regional-Outlook-17v2.pdf [page discontinued].

19

Burma's new election laws

(14:41 AEDT, 19 March 2010)

At the beginning of March 2010, Myanmar's military government enacted five laws that were designed to pave the way for the national elections to be held at the end of the year. The new election laws were immediately criticised by the opposition NLD, the US and the UK, among other countries, and a wide range of activist organisations.

The international outcry over Burma's new election laws was inevitable and justified. More surprising was the apparent expectation on the part of some commentators that these laws would be anything other than repressive and unjust. This raises an intriguing question: was some of the public outrage expressed last week designed to put pressure on governments other than the military regime in Naypyidaw?

Given the regime's behaviour since 1988, not to mention the provisions of the 2008 constitution, it has long been clear that the proposed transition to a 'genuine multiparty discipline-flourishing democracy' in Burma is simply a legalistic device to disguise continuing military rule, behind the facade of an 'elected' parliament. This being the case, few observers seriously expected the new laws to be other than, in the words of one US official, 'a mockery of the electoral process'.[1]

---

1   David Gollust, 'US: Burma Election Law "Mockery" of Democratic Process', *Voice of America*, 10 March 2010, www1.voanews.com/english/news/US--Burma-Election-Law-Mockery-of-Democratic-Process-87269337.html [page discontinued].

There is still some uncertainty over what the laws actually mean, but it appears that political parties cannot list any members who have criminal convictions. This means the NLD, which won the 1990 elections by a landslide, must expel opposition leader Aung San Suu Kyi—and other political prisoners—or be declared illegal.[2] The laws also require allegiance to the new constitution, which, among other provisions, sets aside 25 per cent of all parliamentary seats for members of the armed forces.

The fact that everyone's worst fears have been realised is no reason to passively accept the new electoral laws, but it does make some of the comments heard about them seem a little disingenuous. There are good reasons to decry the failure of the military government to observe widely accepted democratic principles and to acknowledge the clear wishes of the Burmese people. But no one should act surprised that the laws are as restrictive as they are.

Indeed, given the tenor of a few of the comments heard over the past week, it is worth considering whether there might be some other reason this issue has attracted so much attention, particularly from hardline opponents of the regime.

It is self-evident that, over the past 20 years, economic sanctions and other punitive measures levelled against Burma have failed to remove the military regime or persuade it to abandon any of its core policies. It has refused to transfer power to a democratically elected civilian government or to engage in a substantive dialogue with the opposition movement and ethnic communities. Nor has the regime taken steps to improve its human rights record, release political prisoners (including Aung San Suu Kyi) or introduce major economic reforms.

The harsh reality is that, despite all the pressures it has faced over the past 20 years, from both internal opposition forces and hardline foreign states, the military regime has become progressively stronger. It still faces some serious problems but, measured objectively against several criteria, the regime is now better off and more firmly entrenched in power than at any time since the abortive 1988 prodemocracy uprising. It would not be risking the transition to a new system of government if it was not confident of being able to control the process.

---

2   'PM Calls Election Terms in Burma "Restrictive and Unfair"', *Number 10.gov.uk*, 15 March 2010, www.number10.gov.uk/Page22826 [page discontinued].

There are still some politicians and activist groups, however, who remain convinced that even stronger rhetoric and tougher sanctions will eventually bring down Burma's military regime, or at least persuade it to mend its ways. These advocates have strongly criticised the Obama administration and others, like the ASEAN member states, for engaging with the military regime in an effort to ameliorate political, economic and social conditions in Burma. Critics of this approach have characterised it as naive, while some have even branded it immoral.[3]

In these circumstances, it is worth asking whether some of the criticisms heard about Burma's new election laws—characterised by US Senator Mitch McConnell as 'a farce'—represent at least in part an attempt to discredit the Obama administration's policy of 'practical engagement'.[4] By highlighting Naypyidaw's apparent indifference to US wishes, opponents of the administration's more nuanced approach are able to press their case for a return to the hardline policies of the Bush era.

When it introduced its new Burma policy last September, the Obama administration stated that political change in that country was going to be a long, slow and difficult process. It knew that there were going to be setbacks. It also accepted that, at times, President Obama would face accusations from his political opponents that Burma's generals were treating the US with contempt. And, indeed, over the past six months, all this has proven to be the case. Yet this does not mean that the policy was misguided or will be easily abandoned.

The US Government has publicly expressed its deep disappointment over the new election laws. It has stated plainly that Washington has no hope that the elections due to be held later this year, given their nature, will be credible.[5] However, officials have also said that the US is not surprised by the regime's failure so far to open up the political process.

---

3   Andrew Selth, 'Burma: Obama's "Practical Engagement"', *The Interpreter*, 18 November 2009, www. lowyinterpreter.org/post/2009/11/18/Burma-Obamas-pragmatic-engagement.aspx [page discontinued] [now at archive.lowyinstitute.org/the-interpreter/burma-obama-pragmatic-engagement].

4   Senator Mitch McConnell, 'Statement of Senator McConnell on Burma's Election Laws', Press release, 10 March 2010, mcconnell.senate.gov/public/index.cfm?p=PressReleases&ContentRecord_id=791027b0-1f0b-489c-9022-4105a85fc37c&ContentType_id=c19bc7a5-2bb9-4a73-b2ab-3c1b5191a72b&Group_id=0fd6ddca-6a05-4b26-8710-a0b7b59a8f1f&MonthDisplay=3&YearDisplay=2010.

5   Philip J. Crowley, Assistant Secretary, 'Daily Press Briefing', US Department of State, Washington, DC, 10 March 2010, www.state.gov/r/pa/prs/dpb/2010/03/138195.htm [page discontinued] [now at 2009-2017.state.gov/r/pa/prs/dpb/2010/03/138195.htm].

They have emphasised the continuing need for a strategic approach, taken in collaboration with likeminded countries, based on commitment, consistency and patience.[6]

After all is said and done, perhaps the most obvious lesson to be drawn from the regime's new electoral laws is that meaningful political change can only come from within Burma and from the Burmese people themselves. Whatever their policies, the ability of foreign countries and international organisations to influence internal developments will remain limited.

6   Aye Chan Naing, 'Kurt Campbell: "No Change in Burma"', *Democratic Voice of Burma*, 8 March 2010, www.dvb.no/interview/kurt-campbell-no-change-in-burma/ [page discontinued].

20

Burma: Of arms and the man

(17:16 AEDT, 6 April 2010)

There was widespread international support for an arms embargo against Myanmar, but such a measure was never going to have much of an impact, either on the Tatmadaw*'s combat capabilities or on domestic political developments. Not only were Myanmar's friends and neighbours still prepared to sell arms to the military government, but also the regime's defence industries already manufactured what it needed to fight armed ethnic groups and maintain a firm grip on the population.*

In their continuing search for policies that might have an impact on the Naypyidaw regime, nearly 30 countries have called for a global arms embargo against Burma.[1] Foreign Minister Stephen Smith expressed Australia's support for such a measure last August and Gordon Brown recently stated that an arms embargo remained a 'high priority' for the UK Government.[2]

Organisations like Amnesty International and Human Rights Watch have thrown their support behind the proposal, as have Burmese exile groups, human rights campaigners and Nobel laureates, among others.

---

1   Stephen Smith MP, 'Questions Without Notice: Burma', *House Hansard*, Australia, House of Representatives, 12 August 2009, www.foreignminister.gov.au/transcripts/2009/090812_AungSan SuuKyi.html [page discontinued] [now at parlinfo.aph.gov.au/parlInfo/search/display/display.w3p;db= CHAMBER;id=chamber%2Fhansardr%2F2009-08-12%2F0079;query=Id%3A%22chamber%2 Fhansardr%2F2009-08-12%2F0182%22].
2   'UK Government: Burma Global Arms Embargo "Remains a Priority"', Burma Campaign UK, London, 15 February 2010, www.burmacampaign.org.uk/index.php/news-and-reports/news-stories/ uk-government-burma-global-arms-embargo-remains-a-priority/111.

An arms embargo, mandated or at least endorsed by the UN Security Council, would have considerable symbolic importance. It would send a strong diplomatic signal to the generals in Naypyidaw. It would also complicate the maintenance and further development of the regime's coercive apparatus. However, the chances of such an initiative receiving widespread support must be considered slight. And, even if an arms embargo was implemented, it would have little practical effect on the situation in Burma.

There are always formidable obstacles in the way of an effective arms embargo, but in Burma's case these are perhaps even greater than usual.

Burma's major arms suppliers include China and Russia, both of which are unlikely to support moves in the Security Council to formally declare an embargo. They have already ignored bans on defence exports to Burma imposed by the US, the EU member states, the Nordic countries, Japan and Australia. Indeed, over the past 20 years, China has been largely responsible for the re-arming of Burma's armed forces. According to recent news reports, Beijing and Moscow are currently negotiating additional arms contracts with Naypyidaw.[3]

Also, since the abortive prodemocracy uprising in 1988 and the subsequent imposition of unilateral embargoes by Burma's traditional arms suppliers, a wide range of other countries have provided weapons and defence equipment to the military government. These have reportedly included India, Pakistan, North Korea, South Korea, Israel, Italy, Poland, Bulgaria, Ukraine, Serbia and Slovakia.[4] It is unlikely that all these—and several other—countries would support, let alone observe, a global arms embargo.

Notwithstanding the criticisms recently levelled against Burma by regional countries over Naypyidaw's draconian new election laws, it is also unlikely that ASEAN would endorse a global arms embargo. Such a move would be seen by some states at least as offending the principle of non-interference in the internal affairs of association members. This is quite apart from the vexed question of whether or not a few ASEAN countries have themselves provided arms, equipment and training to the Burmese armed forces.

---

3   Mungpi, 'Russia, Burma Sign Arms Deal', *Mizzima News*, [Yangon], 23 December 2009, www. mizzima.com/news/world/3200-russia-burma-sign-arms-deal.html [page discontinued].
4   'SPDC Arms Suppliers', ALTSEAN-Burma, Bangkok, www.altsean.org/Research/SPDC%20 Whos%20Who/Armssuppliers.htm#China [page discontinued].

Even if there was wide support for a global arms embargo, there are still many independent arms dealers who would be more than happy to step in and fill the gap—either directly or indirectly—by providing Naypyidaw with the weapons it wants. Burma has probably already received several shipments of arms and ammunition through third countries and other intermediaries.

These sorts of deals would be made easier by the fact that the kinds of arms purchased by Naypyidaw over the past 20 years tend to be readily available. Indeed, most major weapon systems in Burma's order of battle are widely considered to be obsolete and are being phased out elsewhere. This makes replacements and spare parts relatively easy to find, not only from other countries modernising their armed forces and keen to dispose of their old inventory, but also from private arms dealers and black marketeers.

This is quite apart from the fact that a wide range of equipment designed for civilian use—and thus readily available on the open market—can be used or adapted for military use. Only last year, for example, an Australian firm was accused of selling frequency-hopping radios to Burma, which the regime reportedly employed in its campaigns against ethnic insurgents.[5] Whether or not these particular radios were adapted after delivery, Burma is widely recognised for its ingenuity in modifying civilian designs for military use.

Another factor to be considered is that, ever since the 1962 coup d'état, the military government has made an effort to develop Burma's own defence industries, specifically to reduce its reliance on overseas arms suppliers. Since 1988, this program has been greatly expanded and stockpiles of strategic materiel have been increased. Burma now manufactures a wide range of its own arms, ammunition and military equipment. Some are made under licence, but it has also developed a number of indigenous designs, ranging from small arms to armoured vehicles.

Burma's armed forces will always need some imported parts to keep their major weapon systems operational. Yet, despite the fears of some generals, Naypyidaw does not face any serious external threats that would make such purchases a pressing issue. More importantly, the military government does not rely on foreign arms to maintain its tight grip on

---

5   'Australia Breaches Burma Arms Embargo', *Green Left*, 12 February 2010, www.greenleft.org. au/2010/826/42468 [page discontinued].

the country. This is done almost exclusively with locally made weapons and ammunition, rendering a global arms embargo largely ineffective as a tool for political change.

Thus, the international community faces another conundrum over Burma. A global arms embargo would help register the widespread concern felt over Naypyidaw's behaviour, but is unlikely to have any real impact on the situation in the country. In fact, to launch a major initiative of this kind and have it fail—as seems most likely—would risk reminding the generals of the world's limited ability to influence developments in Burma.

21

Burma, North Korea and US policy

(14:59 AEDT, 18 May 2010)

Naypyidaw's continued violations of human rights and apparent pursuit of a military relationship with North Korea left US president Obama very little room to implement his more nuanced policy of 'pragmatic engagement' with the military regime.

The Obama administration's policy of 'practical engagement' with Burma is running into serious trouble. The military government in Naypyidaw has shown no inclination to respond to the US's overtures and, although the policy is barely nine months old, pressure is mounting for a return to the hardline approach of the Bush era.

Ironically, the new policy may eventually be undone not by the regime's recalcitrance or the efforts of Obama's political opponents and anti-regime activists, but by Burma's continuing shadowy links with North Korea.

During a visit to Naypyidaw earlier this month, US Assistant Secretary of State Kurt Campbell expressed the administration's 'profound disappointment' over recent developments in Burma. These included the promulgation of election laws that effectively excluded Aung San Suu Kyi from the political process and forced the dissolution of her party.[1] He also referred to increased ethnic tensions.

---

1   Andrew Selth, 'Burma New Election Laws', *The Interpreter*, 19 March 2010, www.lowy interpreter.org/post/2010/03/19/Burmas-new-election-laws.aspx [page discontinued] [now at archive. lowyinstitute.org/the-interpreter/burma-new-election-laws].

For his trouble, Campbell was told by the Burmese foreign minister that 'guests who criticise the host again and again are unwelcome'.

The new policy has also been facing problems at home. In March, nine Senators signed an open letter calling for increased sanctions against Burma. On 7 May, the US Senate unanimously passed a resolution calling on the administration to reconsider its approach, on the grounds that it had failed to shift the Burmese regime.[2] The US House of Representatives introduced a similar measure the following week, with bipartisan support.

Establishing a productive dialogue with Naypyidaw was always going to be very difficult. As senior US officials repeatedly warned when the new policy was announced last September, there are no quick or easy solutions to Burma's many complex problems. Despite rhetorical flourishes from some activists, no one realistically expected that the regime would suddenly release all its political prisoners, introduce democratic reforms and return to the barracks.

The administration was still hopeful, however, that Naypyidaw would offer something to help justify Washington's more subtle and nuanced approach. This has not occurred, strengthening the hand of Obama's critics. Even so, the US may find that the greatest problem it faces in pursuing engagement with Burma is not the regime's continuing commitment to military rule or its human rights abuses, but its contacts with North Korea.

When the North Korean ship *Kang Nam 1* was sailing towards Burma last June—possibly with weapons on board—Burma gave an undertaking to the US that it would observe UNSC Resolutions 1718 and 1874.[3] Inter alia, these instruments prohibit the export of arms from North Korea, including missile and nuclear components. At Burma's request, the *Kang Nam 1* returned to North Korea.

---

2   United States Senate, Senate Resolution 480, 'A Resolution Condemning the Continued Detention of Burmese Democracy Leader Daw Aung San Suu Kyi and Calling on the Military Regime in Burma to Permit a Credible and Fair Election Process and the Transition to Civilian, Democratic Rule', Passed Senate amended 7 May 2010, *Congress.Gov*, www.congress.gov/bill/111th-congress/senate-resolution/480.

3   *Resolution 1718: Non-proliferation/Democratic People's Republic of Korea*, United Nations Security Council Resolution 1718 (2006), 14 October 2006, daccess-dds-ny.un.org/doc/UNDOC/GEN/N06/572/07/PDF/N0657207.pdf?OpenElement [page discontinued] [now at unscr.com/en/resolutions/1718]; and *Resolution 1874: Non-proliferation/Democratic People's Republic of Korea*, United Nations Security Council Resolution 1874 (2009), 12 June 2009, ods-dds-ny.un.org/doc/UNDOC/GEN/N09/368/49/PDF/N0936849.pdf?OpenElement [page discontinued] [now at unscr.com/en/resolutions/1874].

Yet, it appears that another North Korean cargo vessel has arrived at the port of Thilawa, near Rangoon. Naypyidaw claims that the ship is simply taking on board a shipment of rice, but there are suspicions it may have delivered arms, possibly even components of a nuclear or ballistic missile program.[4] If so, this would be in direct violation of the UNSC. These suspicions have been strengthened by recent US and Burmese statements.

Following his visit to Burma, Kurt Campbell said: '[W]e have urged Burma's senior leadership to abide by its own commitment to fully comply with UN Security Council Resolution 1874. Recent developments call into question that commitment.'[5] In reply, the Burmese said that Naypyidaw would observe UNSC Resolutions 1718 and 1874, but the military government had 'the duty to maintain and protect national sovereignty'.

Over the past 10 years, Naypyidaw has developed close defence links with Pyongyang, including the importation of conventional arms. There have also been claims that North Korea is helping Burma to acquire ballistic missiles and possibly even develop a nuclear weapon. Washington has never commented directly on the latter claims, but it has admitted that the US is discussing a range of 'broad proliferation issues' with Naypyidaw.

When he was in Burma earlier this month, Campbell called for a transparent process that would permit the international community to verify Naypyidaw's compliance with the relevant UNSC resolutions. In its absence, he said, the US maintained the right 'to take independent action within the relevant frameworks established by the international community'.

This seems to be a reference to UN instruments permitting the interdiction of North Korean arms shipments, by land, sea and air. However, Naypyidaw is likely to interpret these remarks more broadly. It doubtless remembers that, in 2004, before UNSC Resolutions 1718 and 1874 were passed, Washington said it would respond 'vigorously and rapidly' to any evidence of North Korean ballistic missile sales to Burma.[6]

---

4   Wai Moe, 'Arms Imported Over New Year?', *The Irrawaddy*, 10 May 2010, irrawaddy.org/article. php?art_id=18439 [page discontinued] [now at www2.irrawaddy.com/article.php?art_id=18439].
5   'Assistant Secretary Campbell's Remarks on Visit to Burma', *America.gov*, 10 May 2010, www.america. gov/st/texttrans-english/2010/May/20100510143632eaifas0.8452417.html [page discontinued].
6   Paul Tighe, 'North Korea, Myanmar See Missile Trade, State Department Says', *Bloomberg.com*, 26 March 2004, www.bloomberg.com/apps/news?pid=newsarchive&sid=a9t_L4U1Avmw&refer= asia%3C%2Fa%3E-redirectoldpage [page discontinued].

Also, the military regime would be aware of the February 2010 Quadrennial Defence Review, which stated that the US would develop its capacities to 'contain WMD threats emanating from fragile states' and increase its ability to intervene in states where 'responsible state control' of WMD materials was not guaranteed.[7]

Whether or not Burma is trying to acquire strategic weapons, such statements are bound to heighten Naypyidaw's threat perceptions. The regime has never shaken off its fear of external intervention, including an invasion by the US and its allies. Comments by other world leaders— including Kevin Rudd, who once threatened to 'bash Burma's doors down'—have strengthened these concerns.[8]

If the US continues to press the regime about its relationship with Pyongyang, as seems highly likely, tensions between Washington and Naypyidaw are bound to grow, making a constructive dialogue on other issues even more difficult. Should it be discovered that Burma is indeed violating one or more UNSC resolutions, President Obama would have no option but to revert to a much tougher line.

This outcome may satisfy critics of the administration's current policy, but it will not bring the resolution of Burma's domestic problems any closer.

---

7   *Quadrennial Defense Review: Report* (Washington, DC: US Department of Defense, February 2010), www.defense.gov/qdr/images/QDR_as_of_12Feb10_1000.pdf [page discontinued] [now at archive.defense.gov/qdr/QDR%20as%20of%2029JAN10%201600.pdf].

8   Jonathan Pearlman, 'Rudd Says Donors Must Bash in Doors', *Sydney Morning Herald*, 10 May 2010, www.smh.com.au/news/world/rudd-says-donors-must-bash-in-doors/2008/05/09/1210131275004.html.

22

Does Burma have
a WMD program?

(11:02 AEDT, 7 June 2010)

At the beginning of June 2010, the Norway-based activist group and radio broadcaster known as the Democratic Voice of Burma released a documentary film and written report on Myanmar's suspected nuclear weapons program and apparent interest in acquiring ballistic missiles. Both the film and the report appeared to offer rare insights into the military regime's ambitions to secretly develop strategic weapons.

Reports produced by activist organisations always need to be treated with caution, particularly if they rely heavily on a single source. However, a documentary film and written report just released by the Oslo-based Democratic Voice of Burma (DVB) appear to offer a rare insight into Burma's secret nuclear ambitions.[1]

Over the past 10 years, this issue has attracted some sensational claims. For example, activist websites have stated that, with North Korean help, the Naypyidaw regime has secretly constructed an underground nuclear

---

1   'Myanmar "Nuclear Plans" Exposed', *Al Jazeera*, 4 June 2010, english.aljazeera.net/news/asia-pacific/2010/06/2010642542469132.html [page discontinued] [now at www.aljazeera.com/news/asia-pacific/2010/06/2010642542469132.html]; and Robert Kelley, 'Expert Says Burma "Planning Nuclear Bomb"', *Democratic Voice of Burma*, 3 June 2010, www.dvb.no/news/expert-says-burma-%e2%80%98planning-nuclear-bomb%e2%80%99/9527 [page discontinued].

reactor. Last August, there was a spate of news stories suggesting that Burma could have a nuclear weapon by 2014 and 'a handful' of such devices by 2020.[2]

The DVB dismisses these kinds of claims as 'technically incredible'. In their place, it offers the detailed testimony of a well-placed Burmese army officer, supported by a large number of photographs and leaked documents. Drawing mainly on these sources, the DVB film and report describe the very early stages of what might be called an aspirational WMD program.

The DVB shares the view that Burma's generals feel threatened and are convinced that possession of a nuclear weapon would provide an effective deterrent against external intervention.[3] The regime apparently sees North Korea as a useful model to follow—despite the clear differences in strategic circumstances between the two countries.

With this external threat in mind, Naypyidaw has reportedly charged elements of Burma's armed forces with constructing a nuclear reactor, enriching uranium and developing a nuclear weapon. To this end, the DVB claims, the regime has built a number of specialised facilities, acquired dual-use equipment from abroad and begun a range of nuclear-related experiments.

As described by the DVB's main source, however, such activity as has occurred has been rather disjointed and marked by a lack of resources and expertise. There are also suggestions of poor management and a lack of coordination, if not incompetence. For example, some of the sophisticated machine tools imported from Europe have been so poorly maintained they are now useless.

If the DVB's material is accurate, Burma's WMD program—if it can be called that—does not seem to have progressed much beyond crude experiments. It is certainly a very long way from posing a credible threat to regional security. Indeed, one of the co-authors of the DVB report, a former IAEA official, believes that on the available evidence Naypyidaw has little chance of succeeding in its quest for a nuclear weapons capability.

---

2   Hamish McDonald, 'Revealed: Burma's Nuclear Bombshell', *Sydney Morning Herald*, 1 August 2009, www.smh.com.au/world/revealed-burmax2019s-nuclear-bombshell-20090731-e4fw.html.
3   Andrew Selth, *Burma and the Threat of Invasion: Regime Fantasy or Strategic Reality?*, Griffith Asia Institute Regional Outlook Paper No.17 (Brisbane: Griffith University, 2008), www.griffith.edu.au/business/griffith-asia-institute/pdf/Andrew-Selth-Regional-Outlook-17v2.pdf [page discontinued].

Part of the DVB's documentary film is devoted to an examination of the many underground facilities in Burma. As previously reported, these 'tunnels' appear to have been built with North Korean assistance—most with military purposes in mind.[4] Their inclusion in the documentary is curious, as no evidence has yet been put forward to support claims that they are in some way connected to a secret nuclear program.

The DVB also refers to ballistic missiles. Short-range, medium-range and even intercontinental weapons are mentioned—almost interchangeably. There are occasional references to a reported agreement with North Korea for the provision of a ballistic missile production line and allusions to the beginnings of a Burmese research program.[5] It would appear, however, that indigenous production of such weapons is still a long way off.

Both the film and the written report cite North Korea's involvement in the development of Burma's defence infrastructure and arms industries. Yet, there is almost no discussion of foreign participation in Burma's nascent nuclear program. This is strange, given that activist groups and others routinely portray Naypyidaw's secret WMD program almost as a joint venture with Pyongyang. Pakistan and Iran have also been mentioned in this context.[6]

One explanation for this omission might simply be that the DVB's informant was not privy to all aspects of the program. It is also possible, however, that the regime's obsession with secrecy, its distrust of foreigners and its commitment to self-reliance extend even to its nuclear ambitions. If so, the result would seem to be that the Burmese are now facing challenges well beyond their technological capabilities.

---

4   Andrew Selth, *Burma and North Korea: Conventional Allies or Nuclear Partners?*, Griffith Asia Institute Regional Outlook Paper No.22 (Brisbane: Griffith University, 2009), www.griffith.edu. au/__data/assets/pdf_file/0004/172579/burma-and-north-korea-conventional-allies-or-nuclear-partners.pdf [page discontinued].
5   Andrew Selth, 'Burma: If Not Nukes, What About Missiles?', *The Interpreter*, 11 January 2010, www.lowyinterpreter.org/post/2010/01/11/Burma-If-not-nukes-what-about-missiles.aspx [page discontinued] [now at archive.lowyinstitute.org/the-interpreter/burma-if-not-nukes-what-about-missiles].
6   Andrew Selth, 'Is there a Burma–North Korea–Iran Nuclear Conspiracy?', *The Interpreter*, 25 February 2009, www.lowyinterpreter.org/post/2009/02/25/Is-there-a-Burma-North-Korea-Iran-nuclear-conspiracy.aspx [page discontinued] [now at archive.lowyinstitute.org/the-interpreter/there-burma-north-korea-iran-nuclear-conspiracy].

The DVB film and report do not pretend to be comprehensive surveys of Burma's interest in strategic weapons. They rely heavily on the data provided by one mid-ranking officer whose access, while good, was nevertheless limited. In the written report, there are some notable gaps. In places, the language is quite loose and the analysis shallow. The technical issues raised have yet to be verified by other experts. Inevitably, there is a host of unanswered questions.

Even so, the DVB's film and report are more credible and convincing than most treatments of these matters. They help put the fragmentary, anecdotal and often exaggerated claims of the past 10 years into a more sensible perspective. The potential dangers of even an aspirational WMD program should not be underestimated, but it would appear that the world's first Buddhist bomb is still a distant prospect.

The DVB's apparent revelations raise a number of other important strategic issues. These relate, for example, to Burma's observance—or otherwise—of several international agreements, its relations with its near neighbours, its continuing membership of ASEAN and the reaction of the broader international community—in particular, the US (which is already worried about Burma's relations with North Korea).[7]

Three months ago, US Assistant Secretary of State Kurt Campbell was asked to comment on persistent reports about nuclear proliferation by Burma. He replied that 'there are some signs that there has been some flirtation around these matters, and perhaps even more'.[8] Washington has yet to explain what this 'flirtation' actually entails. Perhaps the release of the DVB's film and report will be the trigger that finally prompts an authoritative official statement on this issue.

---

7   Andrew Selth, 'Burma, North Korea and US Policy', *The Interpreter*, 18 May 2010, www. lowyinterpreter.org/post/2010/05/18/Burma-North-Korea-and-US-policy.aspx [page discontinued] [now at archive.lowyinstitute.org/the-interpreter/burma-north-korea-and-us-policy].
8   Aye Chan Naing, 'Kurt Campbell: "No Change in Burma"', *Democratic Voice of Burma*, 8 March 2010, www.dvb.no/interview/kurt-campbell-no-change-in-burma/7984 [page discontinued].

23

Burma, North Korea and WMD: A postscript

(11:01 AEDT, 10 June 2010)

Two Western researchers responsible for the film and associated report by the Democratic Voice of Burma (DVB) about Myanmar's suspected nuclear weapons program later clarified a key issue. They both emphasised the lack of hard evidence relating to North Korea's direct involvement.

Since the release of the DVB's compelling documentary film on Burma's military ambitions and the written report on nuclear-related activities in that country,[1] the report's co-authors have given a number of interviews to the news media. They have both made statements about North Korea's possible role in Burma's nascent nuclear weapons program:

- Robert Kelley, a former senior IAEA inspector, is quoted on the DVB's website as saying: '[North Korea's] role in the nuclear program is only anecdotal.'[2]

- Ali Fowle, a DVB researcher, told the *Voice of America*: 'None of our evidence implies that North Korea has anything to do directly with evidence that we think points to a nuclear program.'[3]

---

1   Andrew Selth, 'Does Burma Have a WMD Program?', *The Interpreter*, 7 June 2010, archive.lowy institute.org/the-interpreter/does-burma-have-wmd-program.
2   'Expert Says Burma "Planning Nuclear Bomb"', *Democratic Voice of Burma*, 9 June 2010, www. dvb.no:80/news/expert-says-burma-'planning-nuclear-bomb'/9527 [page discontinued].
3   Kate Woodsome, 'Expert Accuses Burma of Trying to Build Nuclear Bomb', *Voice of America*, 4 June 2010, www1.voanews.com/english/news/asia/Expert-Accuses-Burma-of-Trying-to-Build-Nuclear-Bomb-95607209.html [page discontinued].

These comments are more specific and go further than anything in the DVB's written report. They are particularly interesting in light of the claims made by a wide range of commentators over the years that North Korea is directly involved in the construction of a secret nuclear reactor in Burma and is actively helping the Naypyidaw regime to develop a nuclear weapon.

They are also relevant to recently stated US concerns about Burma's relationship with North Korea and Naypyidaw's possible violation of UNSC resolutions banning the export of both conventional and WMD-related arms by Pyongyang.[4]

Clearly, despite the DVB's revelations, there is still a wide range of views about Burma's nuclear ambitions, which seem destined to remain the subject of speculation and controversy.

---

4   Andrew Selth, 'Burma, North Korea and US Policy', *The Interpreter*, 18 May 2010, www.lowy interpreter.org/post/2010/05/18/Burma-North-Korea-and-US-policy.aspx [page discontinued] [now at archive.lowyinstitute.org/the-interpreter/burma-north-korea-and-us-policy].

24

Burma and the politics of names

(13:51 AEDT, 12 July 2010)

Foreigners are often confused by personal names in Myanmar. There has also been a long tradition of pseudonyms, both inside the country and among Myanmar-watchers outside it. There are thus many traps for the unwary. In the interests of transparency, it should be noted that 'William Ashton' and 'Kay Merrill', both listed in the article below, are pen-names used at different times by the author.

The use of pseudonyms in international relations, public commentary and literature has a long and sometimes distinguished history.

An example of the former that springs to mind is George Kennan's influential article 'The Sources of Soviet Conduct', which was published in the US journal *Foreign Policy* in 1947 under the pen-name 'X'.[1] In 1976, noted Australian Sinologist Pierre Ryckmans published *Chinese Shadows*, his trenchant critique of Maoist China, under the name 'Simon Leys'.

The use of *noms de plume*, *noms de guerre*, stage names and the like has also been common in Asia. Burma, for example, has a well-established tradition of pseudonyms and other kinds of assumed names. This derives in part from Burmese society and culture, but it has also been encouraged by the country's chequered political history.

---

1   'X' [George F. Kennan], 'The Sources of Soviet Conduct', *Foreign Affairs*, July 1947, www.foreign affairs.com/articles/russian-federation/1947-07-01/sources-soviet-conduct.

There are a limited number of name elements in use by the Burmese.[2] Also, names are usually based on astrological portents and the day of the week on which a child is born. As a result, many Burmese bear the same name. Hence the widespread use of nicknames and other sobriquets, even in professional life, to distinguish individuals from their namesakes.

Some public figures have added the name of their hometown, like former health minister 'Myanaung' U Tin, or their profession, like 'Tekkatho' ('university') Phone Naing. It is also common for Burmese journalists and authors to be tagged with the names of their host publications, such as 'Guardian' U Sein Win and 'Journal Kyaw' Ma Ma Lay.

The developing use of *noms de plume* was an integral part of the evolution of modern Burmese literature, particularly since the final British conquest of the country in 1885. A 'sampling survey' of Burmese pen-names compiled by Cornell University in 1975 listed the titles of 650 pseudonymous works under 320 personal names.

Some British colonial authors also used pseudonyms. J.G. Scott's classic work *The Burman* (1882) was published under the name 'Shway Yoe'. Eric Blair, author of *Burmese Days* (1934), adopted the *nom de plume* 'George Orwell'. He was inspired by another member of the Indian Imperial Police, Burma-born Hector Munro, who wrote short stories as 'Saki'.

The reasons for adopting pseudonyms are many and varied. Some authors simply want to remain anonymous for personal or professional reasons. Others have considered it fashionable to publish under a pen-name. In the 1920s and 1930s, critics of colonial rule wished to avoid detection and arrest by the British authorities.

Burma's famed Thirty Comrades, who allied themselves with Japan in 1942, all adopted *noms de guerre*. Nationalist leader Aung San was known as Bo Tayza ('General Flames'). Another in the group was Ne Win ('Radiant Sun'), who went on to rule Burma from 1962 to 1988. He was born Shu Maung—a name he was happy to discard as it betrayed his mixed Chinese–Burmese ancestry.

---

2   'Burmese Names', *Wikipedia*, en.wikipedia.org/wiki/Burmese_name.

After Ne Win's coup d'état, many independent journalists, commentators and literary figures sought to hide their identities from the military regime. Despite heavy censorship, some were still able to become quite influential.[3] This prompted the regime to ban the use of certain *noms de plume*—a practice it repeated after the 2007 'Saffron Revolution'.

During and after the 1988 prodemocracy uprising, many activists adopted pseudonyms. For example, Min Ko Naing ('Conqueror of Kings') is the *nom de guerre* of a key figure in the opposition movement. Many members of the militant All Burma Students' Democratic Front took new names, both for security reasons and to reflect their commitment to armed struggle.[4]

Some anti-regime figures have become well known under stage names. One is the satirist Zarganar ('Tweezers'), who in 2008 was sentenced to 35 years in prison for 'public order offences'. The undercover reporters who covered the 2007 civil unrest and later appeared in the docudrama *Burma VJ* used pseudonyms to avoid official retribution.[5]

Even exiled Burmese have felt the need to hide their identities, mainly to protect friends and relatives still living in Burma. Most journalists working for expatriate news services, such as *The Irrawaddy* magazine, publish their stories under pen-names.[6] Burmese working illegally outside the country have used false names to avoid being identified and sent home.

Foreign authors and journalists covering Burma have also used pseudonyms, mainly to ensure they are not denied entry to the country. A rollcall of such *noms de plume* includes many that are familiar to Burma-watchers, such as Emma Larkin, William Ashton, Michael Black, Norman Robespierre, Clive Parker, Arnold Corso, Edmond Dantes, Kay Merrill and William Boot.[7]

---

3   Anna J. Allott, *Inked Over, Ripped Out: Burmese Storytellers and the Censors* (New York: PEN America, 1993), burmalibrary.org/docs/inked-over-ripped%20-out.htm [page discontinued].
4   Aung Naing Oo, 'Nom de Guerre', *The Irrawaddy*, 23 February 2008, www.irrawaddy.org/article.php?art_id=10524 [page discontinued].
5   *Burma VJ*, burmavjmovie.com/ [site discontinued].
6   *The Irrawaddy*, www.irrawaddy.com/.
7   See, for example, 'Emma Larkin: Writing about Burma', www.emmalarkin.com/test/ [site discontinued].

All these people have good reason to be wary of the Naypyidaw regime. Over the years, it has been highly sensitive to public criticism and quite ruthless in hunting down the relatives of exiles and 'defectors' opposed to military rule. Several prominent foreign journalists and academics have been banned from Burma for writing frankly about the regime's failings.

That said, the use of pseudonyms can pose problems. Given the dearth of reliable information about developments in Burma, it is often necessary to know who is speaking to make informed judgements about the reliability of their sources and the value of their analysis.

Also, if an author's identity is concealed it can be difficult to take into account any possible political bias or personal agenda. In the highly charged atmosphere that characterises the public debate on Burma, this is an important consideration. Even the military government has published propaganda and disinformation under pseudonyms.

Another problem is that, hiding behind false names, some activists have launched ad hominem attacks against scholars and commentators who have expressed unfashionable views about Burma or advocated unpopular policy positions. Not knowing the identity of their accusers, the targets of these attacks have found it difficult to defend themselves.

Given the wide range of views heard about most aspects of contemporary Burma, it should come as no surprise that even names can be controversial. After all, more than 20 years after the military government changed the country's official name, argument still rages over the relative merits of 'Burma' and 'Myanmar'.[8]

8   'Should It Be Burma or Myanmar?', *BBC News*, 8 May 2008, news.bbc.co.uk/2/hi/uk_news/ magazine/7389525.stm.

25

Burma: The beast in its entirety

(12:08 AEDT, 27 July 2010)

In her book Everything is Broken, *noted Myanmar-watcher Emma Larkin succinctly summed up the difficulty of really knowing what is going on in the country and, even when some reliable information is available, learning its secrets.*

In considering approaches to Burma, and management of the many complex challenges it poses, senior policymakers necessarily rely on objective, evidence-based analyses that take into account issues like Burma's critical geostrategic position in a changing regional environment and the protection of vital national interests in the face of competing imperatives.

Yet, in tackling all these weighty issues, it is important that governments and international organisations do not lose sight of the harsh realities on the ground. In that regard, Burma-watchers at all levels of analysis and commentary would do well to read *Everything is Broken*, a book just published by Emma Larkin.[1]

Larkin (the pseudonym of an American journalist based in Thailand) combines extensive firsthand observation with careful research to produce an informative and insightful overview of recent developments in Burma.

---

1   Emma Larkin, *Everything is Broken: The Untold Story of Disaster Under Burma's Military Regime* (London: Granta, 2010).

She closely examines the 'Saffron Revolution' in 2007, the devastation caused by Cyclone Nargis in 2008 and the military regime's responses to both.

While clearly sympathetic to the plight of the Burmese people, she rises above sensationalist reporting and partisan political commentary to describe, in elegant and often moving prose, the impact of these events at the grassroots level. In so doing, she gives an immediate, human perspective to government statements and official reports.

Larkin is also refreshingly self-aware and candid about the many traps that lie in wait for those who try to write about modern Burma. Having followed developments in that deeply troubled country for nearly 40 years, in various capacities, I found the following passage from the book struck a particular chord:

> Given the regime's restrictions on information and association, it is difficult to form any public consensus or verifiable version of the truth. While certain events can be accounted for with certainty, there is much that remains unknown. Like those blind men in the parable [trying to describe an elephant from different vantage points], it has become impossible for anyone to see or fathom the beast in its entirety.
>
> In a society where nothing can be taken for granted, distorted truths, half stories, and private visions are, by necessity, woven into the popular narrative of events. Burma is a place where the government hides behind convoluted smoke screens. It is a place where those who sacrifice themselves for their country must go unrecognised and can only be lauded or remembered in secret. It is a place where natural disasters don't happen, at least not officially, and where the gaping misery that follows any catastrophe must be covered up and silenced. In such an environment, almost anything becomes believable.[2]

---

2   ibid., pp.251–252.

26

Burma: After the elections, what?

(10:07 AEDT, 31 August 2010)

There were widespread predictions that Myanmar's 2008 constitution and 2010 elections would result in the emergence of essentially sham parliaments, at both the national and the provincial levels, and a puppet government still controlled by the armed forces. However, some experienced Myanmar-watchers were prepared to entertain the possibility that the new institutions being created could gradually allow for the expression of a wider range of views and possibly even independent decision-making.

If all goes according to plan, on 7 November, Burma's ruling council will hold nationwide elections for what it is calling a 'genuine multiparty discipline-flourishing democracy'.

The creation of an elaborate, multilayered parliamentary system is clearly aimed at consolidating and perpetuating military rule. However, as the French political thinker Alexis de Tocqueville noted more than 150 years ago, once they are begun, such transitions can have unintended consequences.

The post-2010 scenario favoured by most commentators and activists is that, after its sham elections are held and its faux parliamentary structure is in place, the Naypyidaw regime will continue to pursue its militarisation of Burmese society, leading to an even wider gulf between the armed forces leadership and the civilian population.

According to this thesis, the controlled engagement of selected civilians in the new national and provincial assemblies is designed to reduce social pressures while confirming the current power position of the armed forces in state and society. It is also aimed at eliminating—or at least neutralising—alternative sources of power and influence, including opposition political movements and ethnic minority organisations.

Based on the regime's behaviour over the past 20 years, the obvious aims of the 2008 constitution and the restrictive electoral regulations promulgated in recent months, such an outcome is quite possible—even likely.[1] Yet, in a number of ways, the implementation of the new constitution will significantly alter Burma's political landscape.

The change from direct to indirect rule will mark an important shift in the way the armed forces approach the business of government. Some allowance must be made, therefore, for the possibility that not everything will proceed quite as the regime envisages. As The Australian National University's Morten Pedersen has observed, Burma's generals would not be the first to underestimate the processes set in train by what began as reforms closely managed from above.[2]

After 2010, there will be many more centres of formal decision-making. In addition to the national parliament in Naypyidaw, there will be seven regional assemblies, seven state assemblies, five self-administered ethnically designated zones and one self-administered ethnically designated division.

The relationships between all these entities are unclear. Despite its length, Burma's new constitution is either incomplete or ambiguous on many matters. Naypyidaw will always be able to exercise its overriding authority, but practical arrangements for interaction between the assemblies and the boundaries of their respective areas of responsibility are still to be worked out.

---

1   'Myanmar Announces Strict Election Campaign Laws', *The Star Online*, [Malaysia], 19 August 2010, thestar.com.my/news/story.asp?file=/2010/8/19/worldupdates/2010-08-19T180751Z_01_NO OTR_RTRMDNC_0_-509434-1&sec=Worldupdates [page discontinued].

2   Morten B. Pedersen, *Prospects for Political Change in Burma*, Issues Paper No.13 (Canberra: Centre for International Governance and Justice, The Australian National University, November 2009), cigj.anu.edu.au/cigj/link_documents/IssuesPapers/IssuesPaperNo.13.pdf [page discontinued].

Similarly, it is not clear how the provincial assemblies and ethnic zones will coexist with the country's 13 regional military commanders. While due to relinquish their civil responsibilities after 7 November, these senior officers will retain considerable independence and power.

Also, with 21 new governing bodies, there will be many more participants in the formal political process, representing a much wider range of interests. Twenty-five per cent of seats at all levels are reserved for military personnel, but there is still scope for the election of a large number of genuine candidates. The bicameral national parliament, for example, has 498 popularly elected seats, with another 665 allocated to the provincial assemblies.[3]

The voting patterns of the personnel occupying the reserved seats will be managed by the government, but there will be others who could act more independently. Some former military officers and even members of the regime's own party may not be quite as pliant as everyone now imagines. Also, there are bound to be some MPs, including representatives of the ethnic communities, who will make a real effort to represent their constituents.

Bear in mind, too, that the armed forces will be going through a number of major changes. Regime leader Than Shwe is reportedly unwell and preparing to retire, possibly to become president or an 'advisor' to the new government. Over the next few years, several more senior generals will pass from the scene. Also, thousands of other officers are due to 'retire', to provide a cadre of loyal 'civilian' candidates for the new national and regional assemblies.

In such a fluid environment, one cannot rule out a gradual diffusion of power between members of the armed forces and civilians and between the central government and provincial assemblies. While powerless at first, some ceremonial and administrative positions may slowly accrete some real influence. To have any credibility, the provincial assemblies will need to be seen to exercise a degree of sovereign authority, if only over parochial issues.

---

3   Richard Horsey, *Countdown to the Myanmar Elections: Prepared for the Conflict Prevention and Peace Forum* (New York: Social Science Research Council, 25 August 2010), www.boell.de/sites/default/files/assets/boell.de/images/download_de/weltweit/Elections_Report_25Aug.pdf.

A few analysts have gone so far as to suggest that such trends could slowly open up political space that will permit the evolution of a more effective and democratic government.[4] Others, like David Steinberg of Georgetown University, have raised the possibility that there may eventually develop greater scope for debate and compromise, and even some independent decision-making.

There is unlikely to be much movement in that direction while Than Shwe and senior officers of that ilk remain influential—whether or not these older generals remain in uniform, retire or assume new civilian positions. They are too hard line and set in their ways to allow any weakening of the current controls. It is conceivable, however, that after they pass from the scene a new generation of military leaders may gradually relax their grip.

These younger officers are still unlikely to permit a truly representative civilian government to emerge in Burma, but they may allow the national and provincial assemblies a little more latitude. If there is the prospect of increased national prosperity and less civil unrest, they may be more open to arguments for the introduction of economic reforms, and possibly even the gradual development of civil society.

If this occurs, however, it is likely to be a very slow process and one that will be carefully monitored. There is no chance that the military leadership would knowingly allow control of the government, or the armed forces, to slip from its grasp. In the event of any challenges to these institutions, or perceived threats to Burma's unity, stability and independence, there is little doubt that the generals would swiftly reassert their domination of Burmese society.

---

4   Graham Reilly, 'Ray of Hope in Burma's Sham Elections', *The Age*, [Melbourne], 18 March 2010, www.theage.com.au/opinion/society-and-culture/ray-of-hope-in-burmas-sham-election-20100317-qfj1.html.

27

Burma's elections:
Thirteen reasons

(10:57 AEDT, 2 November 2010)

On 7 November 2010, elections were held in Myanmar for the bicameral national parliament and 14 unicameral provincial assemblies. About 30 million registered voters were asked to choose between more than 3,000 candidates for over 1,100 seats. If, as the regime's critics claimed at the time, the entire exercise was simply a charade—albeit a very elaborate one—the question had to be asked, why bother? There were at least 13 reasons to do so.

Burma's first national elections in 20 years are due to be held this Sunday. They have already attracted a great deal of official attention and public commentary—almost all of it negative.[1] That is to be expected. No one believes the polls will be free or fair. The only debate has been whether the proposed new arrangements for governing Burma can yield any positive outcomes. On this question, opinion remains strongly divided.[2]

Curiously, few commentators have questioned why the regime is bothering to hold elections. After all, it clearly has no intention of surrendering real power, which will remain firmly in the hands of the armed forces, regardless of the election results. So, why the charade?

---

1   'Rudd Concerned about Burma Elections', *Sydney Morning Herald*, 31 October 2010, www.smh.com.au/national/rudd-concerned-about-burma-elections-20101031-178os.html.

2   *The Myanmar Elections*, Asia Briefing No.105 (Brussels: International Crisis Group, 27 May 2010), www.crisisgroup.org/en/regions/asia/south-east-asia/burma-myanmar/B105-the-myanmar-elections.aspx [page discontinued] [now at www.crisisgroup.org/asia/south-east-asia/myanmar/myanmar-elections].

The military government does not face any serious challenges, either from the opposition movement inside the country or from its supporters outside it. Nor does any insurgent group have the armed strength or popular support to overthrow the generals—now firmly ensconced in their new capital of Naypyidaw.

For its part, the international community has repeatedly demonstrated that it cannot agree on a common policy approach to Burma and, in any case, it has few effective means of influencing the generals. Despite the generals' fears, and the hopes of some activists, no country is going to try to change the regime by force.

Indeed, the military government is probably stronger now than it has been since the 1962 coup. Provided that the armed forces remain cohesive and loyal, they could quite easily continue to rule Burma as they have done for the past 22 years, by decree and force of arms.

The regime has stated that it is holding elections to install a 'genuine multiparty, discipline-flourishing democracy' that is better suited to Burma's changing circumstances. Yet, it is patently clear that no one is fooled by the rhetoric emanating from Naypyidaw—not the international community and certainly not the Burmese people.

If that is the case, why are the generals going to all the trouble of staging elections and creating an elaborate multilayered parliamentary structure that can only complicate life for them, and possibly even weaken their grip on the country? In recent months, numerous theories have been advanced to answer this question. They include the following:

1. The regime hopes that, by creating an 'elected' national parliament, 14 regional parliaments, five self-administered ethnically designated zones and one self-administered ethnically designated division, it will let the steam out of the opposition movement and reduce the likelihood of further civil unrest.
2. By allowing the election of selected popular candidates, the regime hopes to reduce the influence of prominent opposition leader Aung San Suu Kyi. The regime can claim that it needs to listen to the people's 'true' representatives, not a private citizen who holds no elected office.

3. Through the pre-election process, the regime has effectively eliminated the NLD, which decided not to contest the polls and has since been dissolved. In fact, the regime has split the opposition movement, some elements of which have decided to field candidates for the new national parliament.[3]

4. By introducing restrictive election laws and favouring the government's own political party, the generals have ensured the election of a large number of people sympathetic to military rule. This will permit the regime to claim popular endorsement in a way not possible before the elections.

5. After Sunday, the elections can be cited by the regime as the most recent national poll, based on a constitution endorsed by more than 90 per cent of the population. This counters the opposition's argument that only the NLD can provide a legitimate government, having won the 1990 elections by a landslide.

6. The new political arrangements will give Burma's ethnic minorities a voice in government for the first time since 1988. This will help direct their demands through official channels, where they can be more easily managed, and permit the regime to bypass other ethnic leaders who can be branded as 'unrepresentative'.

7. The 2008 constitution, the switch from direct to indirect military rule and the creation of a wide range of new government institutions are all part of a master plan by ageing regime leader Senior General Than Shwe to protect himself and his family and to safeguard his legacy after he dies.[4]

8. The professionals in Burma's armed forces want to divest themselves of direct responsibility for running the country and return to soldiering, while retaining the option of taking back political control if necessary.

---

3   'UN Expert: Genuine Change from Burma's Elections are "Limited"', *Voice of America*, 20 October 2010, www.voanews.com/english/news/UN-Expert--Burma-Conditions-for-Genuine-Elections-Limited-105470653.html [page discontinued] [now at www.voanews.com/east-asia-pacific/un-expert-genuine-change-burmas-elections-are-limited].

4   Ba Kaung, 'Than Shwe's Post-Election Plans', *The Irrawaddy*, 15 July 2010, www.irrawaddy.org/highlight.php?art_id=18974 [page discontinued] [now at www2.irrawaddy.com/article.php?art_id=18974].

9. As a modern, 'progressive' country, Burma needs to have a modern-style parliament to meet in its new capital. This will bring it into line with other countries in the region, which also have parliamentary systems of various kinds.

10. The regime hopes that having a parliamentary system will reduce the level of international criticism levelled against Burma since 1988. The generals anticipate that the new government will eventually win the same kind of recognition that is given to other 'guided' democracies.

11. Once Burma has an 'elected' parliament, it will be easier for countries like China to justify their continuing support for the regime, including in multilateral forums.[5] This is critical, given Burma's need for continued diplomatic cover in the UN, not to mention its dependence on China and other countries for arms, technology, aid and markets.

12. The regime calculates that the facade of an elected parliament will help ease Burma's diplomatic relations with its fellow members of ASEAN, which have been embarrassed by the regime's periodic resort to military force to suppress popular dissent and stay in power.

13. The regime hopes that an elected parliament of sorts will pave the way to an easing of international sanctions and greater access to international finance, such as that provided by the World Bank and Asian Development Bank.

All these theories are quite plausible. More than likely, the regime has considered most, if not all, of them at one time or another and sees the elections as serving a wide range of purposes. If so, the 7 November polls are much more than just a device to consolidate and perpetuate military rule. Indeed, they may be part of a quite sophisticated attempt by the regime to change the way that Burma is governed and interacts with the outside world.

---

5   *China's Myanmar Strategy: Elections, Ethnic Politics and Economics*, Asia Briefing No.112 (Brussels: International Crisis Group, 20 September 2010), www.crisisgroup.org/en/regions/asia/south-east-asia/burma-myanmar/B112-chinas-myanmar-strategy-elections-ethnic-politics-and-economics.aspx [page discontinued] [now at www.crisisgroup.org/asia/south-east-asia/myanmar/china-s-myanmar-strategy-elections-ethnic-politics-and-economics].

28

Burma-watching on film

(13:37 AEDT, 30 November 2010)

Since the 1988 prodemocracy uprising, Myanmar has increasingly attracted the attention of documentary filmmakers. To varying degrees, they have not only recorded developments in the country, but also played an important part in informing international audiences about the dire situation in the country and the opposition movement's efforts to replace the military regime with a more democratic government.

Before 1988, when a nationwide prodemocracy uprising thrust it into the headlines, Burma was studied only by a small circle of officials and academics. With some notable exceptions, journalists and members of the public tended to pay it little attention. Since then, however, official, scholarly and popular interest in Burma has grown markedly, with a commensurate increase in the output of published works.[1]

This year alone, there has been an outpouring of news, analysis and comment—of all kinds—on topical issues such as Burma's alleged nuclear weapons program, its apparent links with North Korea, the elections for a new national government, the release from house arrest of opposition leader Aung San Suu Kyi and the dangers of a renewed civil war with the country's ethnic minorities.

---

1   Andrew Selth, *Modern Burma Studies: A View from the Edge*, Working Paper No.96 (Hong Kong: Southeast Asia Research Centre, City University of Hong Kong, 2007), www6.cityu.edu.hk/searc/ Data/FileUpload/289/WP96_07_ASelth.pdf [page discontinued] [now at www.cityu.edu.hk/searc/ Resources/Paper/WP100_08_ASelth.pdf].

Most of this output has been in written form. A vast amount of material is now posted online. Over the years, however, Burma has also attracted a growing number of documentary filmmakers. Some efforts have been better than others, but together they have increased public awareness about certain developments in Burma and helped form popular perceptions about the main actors.

Among the best documentaries on Burma are three reports made between 1966 and 1978 by the British filmmaker Adrian Cowell, which remain unsurpassed as accounts of the narcotics trade in the Golden Triangle.[2] But the 1988 uprising and events following the military takeover were what attracted the attention of most contemporary filmmakers.

A number have been Australian. For example, in 1995, Sophie and Lyndal Barry made a film entitled *Barefoot Student Army* about anti-regime activists on the Thailand–Burma border. The following year, John Pilger released *Inside Burma: Land of Fear*, in which he took his trademark approach to the question of human rights abuses in Burma under the generals.[3]

Former ABC foreign correspondent Evan Williams has made several highly regarded films, including *Burma's Secret War* (2006) and, with the DVB, *Orphans of the Storm* (2008). In June this year—again in collaboration with the DVB—he directed *Burma's Nuclear Ambitions*.[4] Most recently, he made 'Burma's Betrayal', a report on the elections for SBS TV's *Dateline* program.[5]

Other documentaries on Burma have included *Lines of Fire* (1991) by Brian Beker, *Burma Diary* (1997) by Jeanne Hallacy, *Burma: Anatomy of Terror* (2003) by Isabel Hegner, *Don't Fence Me In* (2004) by Ruth Gumnit and *Breaking the Silence: Burma's Resistance* (2009) by Pierre Mignault and Helene Magny.

---

2   'Adrian Cowell: Biography', *PBS Frontline*, www.pbs.org/wgbh/pages/frontline/shows/heroin/ interviews/cowellbio.html.

3   John Pilger (dir.), *Inside Burma: Land of Fear* (Network First, Central Independent Television/ Carlton UK), *ITV*, 14 May 1996, video.google.com/videoplay?docid=253734287578732261# [page discontinued] [now at johnpilger.com/videos/inside-burma-land-of-fear].

4   Evan Williams for the Democratic Voice of Burma (dir.), *Dispatches: Burma's Nuclear Ambitions* (Evan Williams Productions for Channel 4 'Dispatches', 2010), www.dvb.no/dvb-tv/burmas-nuclear-ambitions/10073 [page discontinued] [now at ewpl.tv/dispatches-burma%E2%80%99s-nuclear-ambitions.html?devicelock=desktop].

5   Evan Williams (dir.), 'Burma's Betrayal', *Dateline*, [SBS TV], 31 October 2010, www.sbs.com. au/dateline/story/about/id/600861/n/Burma-s-Betrayal [page discontinued] [now at www.enhancetv. com.au/video/dateline-burma-s-betrayal/4105].

Last year, Anders Ostergaard released *Burma VJ*, a dramatised documentary about the 2007 'Saffron Revolution'. It highlighted the role of the 'citizen journalists' inside Burma who managed to send out footage of the civil unrest for further dissemination by the international news media.[6] The film was later nominated for an Academy Award in the 'Best Documentary Feature' category.

With varying degrees of success, all these films aimed to reveal and explain what was happening inside Burma—for decades, one of the world's most isolated and secretive countries. This was often done by juxtaposing the country's physical beauty and the gentleness of its traditional culture with the brutality and ineptitude of the military regime. Most of these films are now available online.

The latest contribution to this body of work is an outstanding film by Nic Dunlop, Annie Sundberg and Ricki Stern entitled *Burma Soldier*. It looks at—and, more importantly, tries to understand—not just the oppressed in Burma, but also their oppressors. Of the latter, the directors ask: 'Who are they, and where do they come from?' Their answers to these questions are given through the story of a disabled Burmese veteran turned peace activist.[7]

Dunlop and his team look behind the propaganda of both sides to underscore the human tragedy that is modern Burma. Using some remarkable footage, including rare film of the army on operations, they show how nearly 50 years of military rule have not only blighted the lives of Burma's civilian population, but also deeply corrupted its armed forces. The film is well complemented by Dunlop's still photographs.

The resulting documentary is informative, visually stimulating and in places very moving. It pulls no punches but is a nuanced and thoughtful portrayal of Burma and its complex problems. *Burma Soldier* has just been released in the UK and wider distribution is planned. It is a film that promises to swell the ranks of Burma-watchers even further.

---

6   Anders Ostergaard (dir.), *Burma VJ: Reporting from a Closed Country*, burmavjmovie.com/ [page discontinued] [now at www.imdb.com/title/tt1333634/].
7   Nic Dunlop, Annie Sundberg and Ricki Stern (dirs), *Burma Soldier* (HBO Enterprises, Buddhist Broadcasting Foundation, Panorama, Ireland, 2010), www.panos.co.uk/blog/?p=2799&archive=news& dateopen=1286807022 [page discontinued] [now at www.idfa.nl/en/film/e30d4114-d670-4893-ba0b-d38777d057a8/burma-soldier].

2011

29

Burma: Thanks for the memoirs

(15:45 AEDT, 11 January 2011)

Despite numerous expressions of concern about Myanmar and its people when they were in office, few public officials were inclined to devote any space to Myanmar or its problems when they came to write their memoirs.

Graeme Dobell's recent post about the legacy of foreign policymakers has set me thinking about the nature of political memoirs and their value to Burma-watchers.[1]

Such works are rarely reliable guides to the real issues that have preoccupied governments or particular statesmen and women. Individual egos aside, most seem to be written with an eye to the historical record and usually include ex post facto justifications for policies and actions that it is feared may reflect badly on them.

Even so, political memoirs can offer insights into issues that were considered important at one time, and for the handling of which the authors would like to be remembered.

---

1   Graeme Dobell, 'Foreign Policy: From Practice to Theory', *The Interpreter*, 10 January 2011, www.lowyinterpreter.org/post/2011/01/10/Foreign-policy-From-practice-to-theory.aspx [page discontinued] [now at archive.lowyinstitute.org/the-interpreter/foreign-policy-practice-theory].

In this regard, it can be just as interesting to note the subjects that are not broached in these publications as it is to see which ones are given most attention. Why are some issues, once claimed by national leaders to be of major importance, simply not addressed or only briefly passed over when they come to reflect on their terms in office?

Over the past year or so, memoirs have been released by a number of prominent Western politicians. George W. Bush has published an account of his time in the White House, as has his wife. Several other senior US officials have ventured into print, including Condoleezza Rice and Donald Rumsfeld. Elsewhere, Tony Blair, John Howard and Malcolm Fraser have recounted their political careers. There are doubtless others.

Following the 1988 prodemocracy uprising in Burma and a number of important developments since, the US, UK and Australian governments stated that the sorry state of affairs in Burma was a critical issue that demanded the world's attention. Albeit in different ways, they called for international action to replace the military government, end its human rights violations and assist the Burmese people to make the transition to a fairer and more prosperous society.

Yet, a quick survey of the latest batch of political memoirs reveals that Burma has been addressed by very few of them, and none in any detail.

Although he constantly railed against Burma's leaders when in office, George Bush does not even touch on the subject in his recent book *Decision Points*.[2] Tony Blair, too, is silent about Burma and its challenges in *A Journey: My Political Life*.[3] The only mention of Burma in John Howard's memoir, *Lazarus Rising*, is when he lists the membership of ASEAN.[4]

Unsurprisingly, given her largely domestic focus, Condoleezza Rice does not mention Burma in *Extraordinary, Ordinary People: A Memoir of Family*.[5] And, given the period it covers, Malcolm Fraser can be forgiven for not raising Burma in his *Political Memoirs*.[6]

---

2   George W. Bush, *Decision Points* (New York: Broadway Books, 2010).
3   Tony Blair, *A Journey: My Political Life* (New York: Knopf Doubleday Publishing Group, 2010).
4   John Howard, *Lazarus Rising* (Sydney: HarperCollins Australia, 2010).
5   Condoleezza Rice, *Extraordinary, Ordinary People: A Memoir of Family* (New York: Penguin Random House, 2010).
6   Malcolm Fraser and Margaret Simons, *Malcolm Fraser: The Political Memoirs* (Melbourne: The Miegunyah Press, 2010).

It has not been released yet, but it would be very surprising if Burma is discussed in former US defence secretary Donald Rumsfeld's memoir, *Known and Unknown*.[7]

In omitting any reference to Burma, all these public figures follow a well-established pattern. For example, neither Bill Clinton in *My Life* nor former US Central Intelligence Agency (CIA) chief George Tenet in *At the Centre of the Storm* make any mention of Burma, despite well-publicised US concerns about that country during their terms of office.[8]

Two exceptions to this rule spring to mind. In her aptly titled memoir, *Spoken From the Heart*, former first lady Laura Bush mentions Burma several times.[9] As in her past public pronouncements on this subject, however, her comments reflect her personal feelings about the country and its people more than any real understanding of their complex problems.

The other exception is *Madam Secretary: A Memoir*, written by former secretary of state Madeleine Albright.[10] In this book, Albright describes an official visit to Burma in 1995 (as the US ambassador to the UN) and expresses her admiration for Burmese opposition leader Aung San Suu Kyi.

Granted, over the past 20 years, Burma has not been high on the list of national priorities for most countries. Its problems, while serious and continuing, would have always found it hard to compete for space in a tightly edited account of important and controversial issues like the wars in Iraq and Afghanistan, Islamic extremism, the rise of China, nuclear proliferation, the Global Financial Crisis and global warming.

And, of course, not everyone shares my specialist interest in Burma.

Even so, given all the political rhetoric that has been heard about Burma since 1988 and the space devoted to its problems by the news media, it is curious that it has been accorded so little attention. One might have thought that Burma would receive at least a brief mention in these memoirs, perhaps in the context of China's growing strategic weight, ASEAN's internal tensions, fears of nuclear and missile proliferation, human rights violations, transnational crime or the challenges posed by rogue regimes.

---

7   Donald Rumsfeld, *Known and Unknown: A Memoir* (New York: Penguin Group, 2011).
8   Bill Clinton, *My Life* (New York: Vintage Books, 2005).
9   Laura Bush, *Spoken From the Heart* (New York: Scribner, 2010).
10   Madeleine Albright, *Madam Secretary: A Memoir* (Los Angeles: Miramax Books, 2005).

It is interesting to speculate whether greater attention might be paid to Burma should more Asian statesmen turn their hand to writing political memoirs. In *From Third World to First: The Singapore Story*[11]—as in more recent conversations[12]—that country's Minister Mentor, Lee Kuan Yew, has already demonstrated that regional politicians can offer interesting and useful perspectives on the situation in Burma.

As the Canadian academic George Egerton noted some years ago, political memoirs 'have but a brief flowering in the attention of the public and popular media, finding resurrection, if ever, only as sources in the hands of curious historians'.[13] Yet, for a period at least, the reminiscences of public figures can be influential in shaping perceptions of topical issues and in raising options for future consideration.

Burma is certainly one subject area for which informed reflections and fresh policy ideas from experienced senior officials could make a difference.

11   Lee Kuan Yew, *From Third World to First: The Singapore Story, 1965–2000* (New York: HarperCollins, 2000).
12   'Wikileaks: Singapore's Lee Says Burma "Stupid"', *Asian Correspondent*, 15 December 2010, asiancorrespondent.com/43697/wikileaks-singapore-lee-says-burma-stupid/# [page discontinued].
13   George Egerton, 'Politics and Autobiography: Political Memoir as Polygenre', *Biography*, Vol.15, No.3 (Summer), 1992, pp.221–242, at p.239. doi.org/10.1353/bio.2010.0368.

30

Burma and North Korea: Reality checks

(15:00 AEDT, 27 April 2011)

It looked like the continuing and often heated debate over the nature of Myanmar's links with North Korea and Naypyidaw's possible nuclear weapons program could see some resolution in 2011, when the US Government appointed a special envoy for Burma and started providing Congress with official statements on key aspects of the problem.

Earlier this month, a conference was held in Washington to look at Burma's relationships with the two Koreas. Inevitably, the issue that attracted most attention was Pyongyang's purported assistance to Naypyidaw in the nuclear field and the possibility that this extends to collaboration on a secret weapons program.

Unsurprisingly, the conference did not produce any dramatic new insights on this subject. Indeed, its greatest value was to provide an opportunity for some of the main participants in the current, rather heated, public debate to lay out for scrutiny and discussion the key elements of their arguments.

One of the speakers was Robert Kelley, a former IAEA inspector and the principal author of a March 2010 report on Burma's nuclear ambitions, which was sponsored by the opposition DVB.[1] Another speaker was David Albright, also a nuclear physicist and president of the respected Institute for Science and International Security.[2]

Kelley reiterated his firm belief that Burma has a nascent nuclear program. He acknowledged that it does not seem to have advanced very far, nor is it being managed very competently by the local authorities. It is therefore not an immediate military threat. Drawing mainly on information provided by a Burmese army defector, however, Kelley remains convinced that the sole purpose of this secret program is to produce nuclear weapons.[3]

This view was strongly challenged by Albright. He allowed for the possibility that Burma was interested in acquiring nuclear technology—in itself a matter for concern—but he argued that there was still insufficient hard, verifiable evidence to claim the existence of a nuclear weapons program.[4] To his mind, the data provided so far have been fragmentary and ambiguous and often tainted by association with Burmese opposition groups.

On one critical issue, Kelley and Albright were in agreement. They both pointed out that, despite clear signs of a growing defence relationship between the two countries, there was still no reliable evidence of direct North Korean assistance to Burma in the nuclear field. These comments were in stark contrast to the claims made by some activist groups and misleading headlines in a number of prominent news outlets.[5]

---

1   'Burma's Nuclear Ambitions', *Democratic Voice of Burma*, March 2010, www.dvb.no/burmas-nuclear-ambitions/burmas-nuclear-ambitions-nuclear/expert-analysis/9297 [page discontinued].

2   Institute for Science and International Security, Washington, DC, www.isis-online.org/.

3   Robert E. Kelley, 'Nuclear Proliferation in Southeast Asia: Is Burma a Problem?', Presentation at a conference on Myanmar and the Two Koreas, School of Advanced International Studies, Johns Hopkins University, Washington, DC, 11 April 2011, www.sais-jhu.edu/bin/s/i/robert-kelley-myanmar-and-the-two-koreas-conference-paper-april-2011.pdf [page discontinued].

4   David Albright and Christina Walrond, *Technical Note: Revisiting Bomb Reactors in Burma and an Alleged Burmese Nuclear Weapons Program*, ISIS Report (Washington, DC: Institute for Science and International Security, 11 April 2011), pp.1–7, www.isis-online.org/uploads/isis-reports/documents/Burma_Analysis_Bomb_Reactors_11April2011.pdf.

5   Cameron Stewart, 'Burma's Nuclear Plans Exposed by Wikileaks', *The Australian*, 11 December 2010, www.theaustralian.com.au/in-depth/wikileaks/burmas-nuclear-plans-exposed-by-wikileaks/story-fn775xjq-1225969238522 [page discontinued].

The two scientists also agreed, however, that any technical assistance provided by Pyongyang would be critical to Naypyidaw's ability to pursue a nuclear program, peaceful or otherwise.

One of the reasons this debate continues to arouse strong feelings, and why some unlikely scenarios still get an airing in the news media, is that there have been almost no authoritative statements by the IAEA or reputable government sources to clarify the picture or to put all the competing claims into a sensible context.

The strongest official statement issued so far has been by the US State Department, which reported in July 2010: 'At this time, the United States lacks evidence to support a conclusion that Burma has violated its NPT [Non-Proliferation Treaty] obligations or IAEA safeguards.'[6] Yet this report appears to have been discounted by some observers, who prefer to cite the US's oft-stated concerns about the possible implications of Burma's links with North Korea.

There are a number of developments on the horizon, however, that could see some of these uncertainties resolved, or that will at least give the public debate some perspective.

The first is the likely Senate confirmation later this year of President Obama's special envoy for Burma, Derek Mitchell.[7] Such an appointment is required under the 2008 Burmese *JADE Act*, through which Congress sought to pressure the Bush administration into taking tougher measures against Naypyidaw. The envoy's stated role includes a range of activities designed to 'restore civilian democratic rule to Burma', but he will also be responsible for coordinating US policy and consulting other countries on the issue.

Second, it was revealed at the Washington conference that one of the special envoy's first tasks will be to address the longstanding requirement—also stemming from the *JADE Act*—for the US Government to issue a formal statement listing all those countries and entities that provide Burma

---

6   *2010 Adherence to and Compliance with Arms Control, Non-Proliferation and Disarmament Agreements and Commitments* (Washington, DC: US Department of State, July 2010), p.59, www.state. gov/documents/organization/145181.pdf [page discontinued] [now at 2009-2017.state.gov/t/avc/rls/rpt/170924.htm].

7   'US Appoints Burma Special Envoy Derek Mitchell', *BBC News*, 15 April 2011, www.bbc.co.uk/news/world-asia-pacific-13090242.

with 'military or intelligence aid'. Specifically covered by this clause is any provision of WMD and related materials, technologies, training and equipment.[8]

Third, a resolution has just been introduced into the US Senate by Foreign Relations Committee Chairman Dick Lugar.[9] It carefully notes (but does not confirm) 'reports that the Governments of North Korea and Burma are collaborating on matters relating to the development of Burma's nuclear program'. The resolution calls upon the US Government to provide Congress with an unclassified report on the volume of ships and planes from North Korea that have visited Burma since 2009.

Taken together, these three developments hold out the promise of more reliable data and greater clarity about the US Government's views regarding Burma's relationship with North Korea, including the complex problem of Naypyidaw's nuclear ambitions. This is to be welcomed, for the public debate sorely needs an informed and objective official view to balance the more sensationalist stories that have already appeared on this subject.

Even so, as the conference attendees were reminded earlier this month, Burma and North Korea are challenging intelligence targets and reliable information on both countries is still very difficult to obtain. Regardless of any public statements by the US, a number of critical questions are likely to remain unanswered. Also, Burma's interest in nuclear technology and its relationship with North Korea will remain emotive and highly politicised issues.[10]

These factors alone will ensure that a wide range of claims and counterclaims will continue to be heard on this vexed issue for the foreseeable future.

8   'HR 3890 (110th): Tom Lantos Block Burmese JADE (Junta's Anti-Democratic Efforts) Act of 2008', Introduced 18 October 2007, Enacted 29 July 2008, US Congress, www.govtrack.us/congress/bill.xpd?bill=h110-3890.

9   'Lugar Seeks Investigation into Military Ties between North Korea and Burma', *Senatus*, 8 April 2011, senatus.wordpress.com/2011/04/08/lugar-seeks-investigation-into-military-ties-between-north-korea-and-burma/.

10   Stephen Engelberg, 'Experts, Intelligence Agencies Question a Defector's Claims about Burma's Nuclear Ambitions', *ProPublica*, 12 November 2010, www.propublica.org/article/experts-intel-agencies-question-a-defectors-claims-about-burmas-nuclear.

31

Burma and WMD: Lost in translation

(11:57 AEDT, 19 May 2011)

If there was greater familiarity with a range of technical terms and a more considered use of the language used by participants, the public debate over Myanmar and its reported WMD programs would most likely be clearer and more productive.

Over the past 10 years, the public debate about Burma's nuclear ambitions and possible missile purchases has generated more heat than light. This is perhaps to be expected, given the dearth of reliable information on these issues, the emotive nature of the subject matter and the fact that, since the abortive 1988 prodemocracy uprising, Burma-watching has become highly politicised.

Yet there may be another reason the debate has at times been unproductive—even misleading—and that is the nature of the language employed.

Academics and other professional analysts are under considerable pressure to write deliberately and to choose their words with great care. They are encouraged to pay almost forensic attention to questions of terminology, for whatever they say will be scrutinised by other subject experts ready and able to test their data and weigh every nuance of their argument. Reputations and important decisions can hang on questions of accuracy and balance.

This emphasis on precision, however, is not usually characteristic of journalists and activists. There are exceptions, of course, but generally speaking the interests of these groups lie more in telling a good story or promoting a political line. Also, some of those engaged in the Burma debate are not familiar with the relevant technical issues, leading them, in the words of one former IAEA inspector, to be 'very loose with terminology'.[1]

The result has been numerous articles and blogs that make casual references to quite specific issues. To a certain extent, this is inevitable and understandable. As Lindsay Tanner has recently pointed out—albeit rather trenchantly—the news media demands concise stories written in simple prose that can be easily understood by non-specialists.[2] Advocacy groups appeal to a mass audience that is more likely to respond to short, catchy phrases and dramatic claims.

And, to be fair, even professionals resort to familiar terms and common phrases to refer economically to complex issues or to convey subtle arguments, particularly when writing for a public audience. Often this practice is harmless. It can in fact aid popular understanding and advance the debate. At other times, however, it can cause confusion and take the discussion in unhelpful directions.

For example, surveying the literature on Burma since 2000, there are numerous references to its 'nuclear program'. Yet it is not always clear whether the author is referring to the peaceful nuclear research program that has been subject to prolonged negotiations between Burma and Russia or a secret military program that some observers claim has already been launched by the Burmese regime, with North Korean help.

Indeed, the term 'program' itself means different things to different people. To specialists, a program is a systematic plan to reach a specific goal, accompanied by the full panoply of political endorsement, bureaucratic oversight, budgetary allocations, dedicated infrastructure, assigned personnel and technical support. As the Institute for Science and

---

1   Robert Kelley and Ali Fowle for the Democratic Voice of Burma, *Nuclear Related Activities in Burma* (Oslo and Bangkok: Democratic Voice of Burma, 25 May 2010), www.dvb.no/burmas-nuclear-ambitions/burmas-nuclear-ambitions-nuclear/expert-analysis/9297 [page discontinued] [now at www.washingtonpost.com/wp-srv/world/documents/060410.pdf].

2   Lindsay Tanner, *Sideshow: Dumbing Down Democracy* (Melbourne: Scribe, 2011).

International Security has recently stated, based on the fragmentary and ambiguous evidence available so far, it would be premature to apply this term to Burma's possible interest in nuclear weapons.[3]

To take another example, there have been a large number of reports about Burma's wish to acquire 'missiles'.[4] Yet it is rarely stated what kinds of missiles are being referred to. Burma has long had an interest in buying or manufacturing a wide range of such weapons, including surface-to-surface missiles, surface-to-air missiles, air-to-air missiles, anti-ship missiles and anti-tank missiles. Some activist websites even include artillery rockets in this category.[5]

Even when a reference is made, specifically or by implication, to ballistic missiles, a clear distinction needs to be made between tactical, short-range, medium-range, long-range and intercontinental weapons. Each kind has different technical characteristics and requires different levels of supporting infrastructure and expertise.[6] Their purchase prices, too, are different. More to the point, they have quite different values as military and political weapons.

Another term used very loosely in discussions about missiles in Burma is 'Scud'. This name can be applied to several ballistic missile variants, with widely differing capabilities. Used in the right context, the broad phrase 'Scud-type missiles' can be more useful, but it still needs to be understood by the author and the reader that this term covers an entire family of weapons, made by several countries, with ranges estimated to vary from 180 to 1,500 kilometres.[7]

Similar confusion surrounds the phrase 'weapons of mass destruction', or WMD. It is used as either a synonym for nuclear weapons or, as in the title of this post, shorthand for a wide range of exotic weapons from

3   David Albright and Christina Walrond, *Technical Note: Revisiting Bomb Reactors in Burma and an Alleged Burmese Nuclear Weapons Program*, ISIS Report (Washington, DC: Institute for Science and International Security, 11 April 2011), www.isis-online.org/uploads/isis-reports/documents/Burma_Analysis_Bomb_Reactors_11April2011.pdf.
4   Andrew Selth, 'If Not Nukes, What About Missiles?', *The Interpreter*, 11 January 2010, www.lowyinterpreter.org/post/2010/01/11/Burma-If-not-nukes-what-about-missiles.aspx [page discontinued] [now at archive.lowyinstitute.org/the-interpreter/burma-if-not-nukes-what-about-missiles].
5   'N. Korea Missiles at Burma Base', *Democratic Voice of Burma*, 24 June 2010, www.dvb.no/news/n-korea-missiles-at-burma-base/10425 [page discontinued].
6   'Ballistic Missile', *Wikipedia*, en.wikipedia.org/wiki/Ballistic_missile.
7   'Scud', *Wikipedia*, en.wikipedia.org/wiki/Scud.

ballistic missiles through to chemical, biological and nuclear weapons. At times it has been applied to certain conventional weapons. There is no agreed definition of the phrase, even among experts.[8]

Raising issues of this kind will doubtless strike some as nothing more than academic pedantry or a futile attempt to impose specialist criteria on the wider public discourse. But it would not take much to raise the level of an important debate that demands accuracy and mutual understanding. And it is worth bearing in mind that discussions of this kind influence not only popular perceptions, but also consideration of official policy.

So, everyone concerned about Burma has an interest in ensuring they are speaking the same language and talking about the same things.

---

8   'Weapon of Mass Destruction', *Wikipedia*, en.wikipedia.org/wiki/Weapon_of_mass_destruction.

32

Burma and Libya: The politics of inconsistency

(11:06 AEDT, 17 June 2011)

The Libyan crisis in early 2011 prompted an uncharacteristically swift and concerted response from the international community. Activists immediately asked why Myanmar did not qualify for such attention, given that the language used to describe Libya and its problems could also apply to Myanmar. However, there were factors that made Myanmar's case different. In any case, one always looked in vain for consistency in international affairs.

Lord Palmerston said nearly 200 years ago that countries have no eternal allies or perpetual enemies, only eternal and perpetual interests. Whether or not this is true, one always looks in vain for consistency in the conduct of international relations. Burma-watchers have recently been reminded of this fact by the world's dramatic response to developments in Libya.

In February, the UN Security Council effectively invoked the 'responsibility to protect' (R2P) doctrine to justify military intervention in Libya. The UNSC referred the Libyan case to the International Criminal Court and the UN Human Rights Council endorsed an International Commission of Inquiry. President Obama later stated that 'left unchecked, we have every reason to believe that [Libyan President Muammar] Gaddafi would commit atrocities against his own people. Many thousands could die.'[1]

---

1   'Obama Endorses Military Action to Stop Gaddafi', *Yahoo News*, 18 March 2011, news.yahoo.com/s/ap/20110318/ap_on_re_us/us_us_libya [page discontinued].

Burma activists were quick to ask why similar actions could not be taken against that country. After all, almost every criticism made of the Libyan regime could be levelled equally strongly at the military-dominated government in Naypyidaw. Indeed, as one observer pointed out: '[M]uch of the language used in the [Libya] resolution has for many years featured almost word for word in UN General Assembly resolutions on Burma, and reports from the UN Special Rapporteur on Burma.'[2]

According to opposition websites, people inside Burma watched in disbelief at how quickly UN Secretary-General Ban Ki-moon and the Security Council acted after Gaddafi's attacks on Libyan civilians. They contrasted this response with the consistent lack of international action to prevent military operations against unarmed demonstrators and ethnic minorities in Burma, which, since the 1988 prodemocracy uprising, have probably resulted in tens of thousands of deaths and forced hundreds of thousands of refugees into neighbouring countries.[3]

Several commentators have since pointed out that the rare consensus in the UNSC supporting international action against Libya was most unlikely to be repeated in the event of a similar proposal to intervene in Burma. The political and strategic circumstances—China's national interests, in particular—are quite different. Nor would ASEAN endorse an armed attack against a fellow member. There are also questions over the feasibility of an extended multinational military operation against a country like Burma, particularly if it were opposed by regional countries.

Another critical difference between Libya and Burma—one that has been noted by opposition leader Aung San Suu Kyi—is that the Libyan armed forces are divided in their loyalties.[4] Despite regime fears that the Middle Eastern 'contagion' might spread to Burma—prompting censorship of the protests in the local news media—there have been no signs that significant

---

2   Mark Farmaner, 'UN Resolution on Libya Exposes German Hypocrisy on Burma', *The Irrawaddy*, 4 March 2011, www.irrawaddy.org/article.php?art_id=20874&page=1 [page discontinued].
3   Nant Bwa Bwa Phan, 'UN's Libya Action Must Be Reproduced', *Democratic Voice of Burma*, 1 March 2011, www.dvb.no/analysis/un%E2%80%99s-libya-action-must-be-reproduced/14506 [page discontinued] [now at english.dvb.no/analysis/un%E2%80%99s-libya-action-must-be-reproduced/14506].
4   Luke Hunt, 'Aung San Suu Kyi Notes Parallels Between Middle East and Burma', *Voice of America*, 24 February 2011, www.voanews.com/english/news/asia/Aung-San-Suu-Kyi-Notes-Parallels-Between-Middle-East-and-Burma-116860863.html [page discontinued] [now at www.voanews.com/east-asia/aung-san-suu-kyi-notes-parallels-between-middle-east-and-burma].

elements in the Burmese armed forces are ready to back the opposition movement and bring down the hybrid military/civilian government that was installed earlier this year.

Some Burma activist groups have condemned the uneven application of the R2P doctrine as blatant hypocrisy by Western countries devoted to their own narrow interests. Yet, there have always been inconsistencies in the Burma policies of both national governments and international organisations. For example, Burma is currently the target of wideranging sanctions that are aimed at few other countries, despite the fact that many—including a number in Asia—also have authoritarian regimes and long records of human rights abuses.

Such anomalies have rarely been questioned—at least not openly. In a recent Nelson Report, however, Georgetown University's David Steinberg asked why US sanctions against Burma are far harsher and more extensive than those levelled against North Korea.[5] Pyongyang poses a much greater strategic threat to the US, and the wider world, than Naypyidaw. And the situation inside North Korea—in terms of undemocratic governance, human rights abuses, political prisoners, restrictions on civil society and economic mismanagement—is far worse than in Burma.

There are good reasons for the US to be concerned about Burma, but singling it out for exemplary punishment seems to disprove Palmerston's dictum. For, as US Senator Jim Webb in particular has argued, Burma still engages the US's national interests.[6] It occupies a sensitive geostrategic position between the nuclear-armed giants of India and China. It is a member of ASEAN and plays an important role in the management of several transnational problems. Burma has also developed a defence relationship with North Korea that probably includes ballistic missile sales and possibly even illicit transfers of nuclear technology.

Senior US officials have privately conceded that the main reason for the inconsistency in approach is Aung San Suu Kyi, whose influence on US policymakers has been profound.[7] As Steinberg has also observed, had Suu

---

5   David Steinberg, 'Disparate Sanctions', *The Nelson Report*, 15 June 2011.
6   'Senator Webb Holds a Hearing on Burma Policy', *YouTube*, 6 October 2009, www.youtube.com/watch?v=SGPbhJzJDBQ.
7   David Steinberg, 'Aung San Suu Kyi and US Policy Toward Burma/Myanmar', *Journal of Current Southeast Asian Affairs*, Vol.29, No.3, 2010, pp.35–59, doi.org/10.1177/186810341002900302.

Kyi not risen to global prominence and captured the popular imagination, it is likely that the US and other Western countries would have felt less constrained in considering a wider range of policy options towards Burma. As things currently stand, Washington is unlikely to make any significant changes to its Burma policy without first considering The Lady's views.

All other considerations aside, this fact alone—that one, albeit remarkable, person can have such an effect on the foreign policy of the world's most powerful country—underlines the futility of looking for consistency in the conduct of international relations.

33

Burma and ASEAN's seat of yearning

(11:26 AEDT, 14 September 2011)

Myanmar's chairmanship of ASEAN in 2014 depended on a number of factors, including the Thein Sein Government's approach to human rights issues. Two of the most critical factors, however, were Myanmar's military relationship with North Korea in violation of UNSC resolutions and Naypyidaw's reported interest in acquiring nuclear weapons.

As *The Interpreter* noted last week,[1] there has been a spate of articles and op-eds in recent months looking at the apparently more openminded and conciliatory approach being taken by Burma's President Thein Sein.[2] Inevitably, given the opaqueness of Burmese politics and the highly polarised nature of the Burma-watching community, opinion on this development is divided, sometimes bitterly so.

A number of respected commentators have taken a strategic view and, with the usual caveats, sought to highlight what may prove to be the first signs of a gradual process of political reconciliation and incremental reform.[3]

---

1   Andrew Carr, 'Monday Linkage', *The Interpreter*, 5 September 2011, www.lowyinterpreter.org/post/2011/09/05/Monday-linkage-110905.aspx [page discontinued] [now at archive.lowyinstitute.org/the-interpreter/monday-linkage-82].

2   Andrew Marshall, 'The Slow Thaw of Burma's Notorious Military Junta', *TIME*, 31 August 2011, www.time.com/time/world/article/0,8599,2091229,00.html [page discontinued] [now at content.time.com/time/world/article/0,8599,2091229,00.html].

3   David Steinberg, 'The Folly of More Burma Sanctions', *The Diplomat*, [Washington, DC], 2 August 2011, the-diplomat.com/2011/08/02/the-folly-of-more-burma-sanctions/ [page discontinued] [now at thediplomat.com/2011/08/the-folly-of-more-burma-sanctions/].

A hard core of activists and their supporters, however, have dismissed the latest developments as part of a massive confidence trick by an entrenched military regime.[4] Focusing on more immediate issues, some have even called for harsher sanctions against Naypyidaw.

It is always difficult to discern what is in the minds of Burma's leaders, but few of their decisions lend themselves to simple explanations. Most seem to reflect consideration of a range of complex issues. One possible reason for the more nuanced policies emanating from Naypyidaw that has not received much attention to date is that Burma is seeking to satisfy certain expectations expressed by ASEAN to assume the chairmanship of the association in 2014.

In 2005, when Burma gave up its turn to assume the chair, citing the 'ongoing national reconciliation and democratisation process', it was on the understanding that it could reclaim the position when it was ready to do so. Naypyidaw has now made its wish for the position abundantly clear and it would lose considerable face if its bid was unsuccessful. As the current chair, Indonesia plans to send a review team to Burma shortly and will make a recommendation on the matter at this November's summit meeting in Bali.

Despite strong reservations on the part of a few member states, and opposition from the US and EU, there is a reasonable chance that Burma will get its wish. It will ultimately be a political decision, not an objective one, but arguably the measures being taken by Thein Sein help Burma demonstrate its commitment to the ASEAN charter. Remarkably, given the organisation's rather mixed membership, this requires states to adhere to 'the principles of democracy and constitutional government' and to promote and protect human rights.

As Singapore-based Burma scholar Tin Maung Maung Than has noted, there are no formal benchmarks to measure these commitments.[5] However, if ASEAN was keen to find signs of Burmese compliance, it could cite the 2008 constitution, the 2010 elections and the hybrid civilian–military government that was inaugurated in January. All three are gravely flawed,

4   Bertil Lintner, 'Could Burma Finally be Poised for Reform?', *Global Asia*, 22 December 2010, www.globalasia.org/V5N4_Winter_2010/Bertil_Lintner.html [page discontinued].
5   Tin Maung Maung Than, 'ASEAN Chair for Myanmar: Musical Chairs?', *News* (Singapore: Institute of South East Asian Studies, 30 July 2011), asc.iseas.edu.sg/images/stories/pdf/TinOp-ed MyanmarASEANchairAug11.pdf [page discontinued].

but Burma's new 'disciplined democracy' has been described positively by some ASEAN members and accepted by others as at least a step in the right direction.

Two other issues that are bound to be considered by ASEAN members are Naypyidaw's treatment of opposition leader Aung San Suu Kyi and the plight of the 2,200 political prisoners currently believed to be held in Burmese prisons.[6] Here, too, if ASEAN was looking for reasons to justify Burma's elevation to the chairmanship, its members may be able to claim that there has been some progress.

Not only has Aung San Suu Kyi been released from house arrest, she also has been invited to Naypyidaw for discussions with Thein Sein about political reconciliation and other matters. She has expressed herself 'happy and satisfied' with the discussions to date, going so far as to describe them as 'a positive beginning'.[7] More importantly, for ASEAN's purposes, she has reportedly stated that 'the president wants to achieve real positive change'.[8] Among other things, this suggests that a release of political prisoners is imminent.

The Burmese Government has already declared one amnesty this year, releasing around 14,000 people from the country's jails, but few were counted as political prisoners.[9] It is now rumoured that the release of around 500 in this category will be announced soon. Nothing short of an amnesty for all 2,200 will satisfy Naypyidaw's strongest critics, but a tranche of 500 may be large enough for ASEAN members to claim that, in this respect too, the regime's record is improving and it is making an effort to meet the criteria for the chairmanship.

Even so, until ASEAN makes its final decision, nothing can be taken for granted. Another mass protest in Burma, for example, prompting yet another military crackdown, would be hard for the association to ignore. An escalation of the current counterinsurgency campaigns against armed

6   Larry Jagan, 'Burma's New Political Dynamics', *Radio Free Asia*, [Washington, DC], 9 September 2011, www.rfa.org/english/commentaries/burma-09092011132605.html?searchterm=None.

7   'Positive Beginning', *Radio Free Asia*, [Washington, DC], 1 September 2011, www.rfa.org/english/women/conversation-aungSanSuuKyi/conversation-09012011174918.html.

8   'Suu Kyi Says Burma President Wants "Real Change"', *Bangkok Post*, 24 August 2011, www.bangkokpost.com/news/asia/253296/suu-kyi-says-burma-president-wants-real-change [page discontinued].

9   'Myanmar Prisoner Release Fails to Impress', *Al Jazeera*, 17 May 2011, english.aljazeera.net/news/asia-pacific/2011/05/2011517181542379456.html [page discontinued] [now at www.aljazeera.com/news/asia-pacific/2011/05/2011517181542379456.html].

ethnic groups and a renewed flood of refugees across Burma's borders would also be major obstacles. And there is still Naypyidaw's problematic relationship with Pyongyang, with its associated claims of ballistic missile and nuclear weapons cooperation.

ASEAN seems unpersuaded by these claims.[10] Yet, if it could be shown that Burma was violating UNSC resolutions against defence links with North Korea, Naypyidaw's chances of international rehabilitation would plummet. And if hard evidence could be produced of an active WMD program, Burma's relations with ASEAN would be seriously jeopardised. As Washington's new Burma envoy recently said of such a development, with regard to relations with the US, it would be a 'game-changer'.[11]

Any questions of UNSC violations aside, ASEAN might be able to wear Burmese acquisition of short-range ballistic missiles (which have long been held by Vietnam, for example). However, the association simply could not ignore firm evidence that one of its members had blatantly disregarded the 1995 Bangkok Treaty, which declared Southeast Asia a nuclear weapon–free zone. Already, one ASEAN Secretary-General has stated that discovery of a secret nuclear weapons program would mean Burma's expulsion from the organisation.[12]

---

10   Mustaqim Adamrah, 'Myanmar Developing Nukes? We Don't Think So, ASEAN Says', *The Jakarta Post*, 21 July 2011, www.thejakartapost.com/news/2011/07/21/myanmar-developing-nukes-we-don%E2%80%99t-think-so-asean-says.html [page discontinued].

11   'The Straits Times (Singapore): On Myanmar Chairing ASEAN and Its North Korean Ties', *Burmanet News*, 6 September 2011, www.burmanet.org/news/2011/09/06/the-straits-times-singapore-on-myanmar-chairing-asean-and-its-n-korean-ties/ [page discontinued].

12   'No US Confirmation of Myanmar Nuclear Report', *Global Security Newswire*, 10 August 2009, www.globalsecuritynewswire.org/gsn/nw_20090810_9726.php [page discontinued].

34

Burma–China: Another dam puzzle (Part 1)

(12:46 AEDT, 1 November 2011)

On 30 September 2011, president Thein Sein shocked everyone—both inside Myanmar and outside it—by announcing the suspension of work on the massive Myitsone Dam and associated hydroelectric power project. These facilities were being developed in Kachin State by a consortium of Chinese and Myanmar companies, but China stood to benefit the most from the power produced.

Over the past 20 years, Burma has developed a close relationship with China. It thus came as a shock when President Thein Sein announced in September that he had suspended construction of the massive Myitsone Dam in northern Burma.[1]

China's public response was low key, but the decision clearly upset Beijing, which had already invested heavily in the project and stood to benefit most from it. The Burmese President claimed that he was responding to the popular mood in Burma, where there is reportedly widespread concern about the dam and its consequences.[2]

---

1   Francis Wade, 'China-Backed Myitsone Dam "Suspended"', *Democratic Voice of Burma*, 30 September 2011, www.dvb.no/news/china-backed-myitsone-dam-%E2%80%98suspended%E2%80%99/17887 [page discontinued].

2   Aung Zaw, 'Is the Myitsone Dam Burma's WMD?', *The Irrawaddy*, 26 September 2010, www.irrawaddy.org/article.php?art_id=22143 [page discontinued] [now at www2.irrawaddy.com/opinion_story.php?art_id=22143].

Given Naypyidaw's record, however, this explanation was unconvincing, leading to widespread speculation about the real reasons for the decision and the future of the bilateral relationship. After the failure of the 1988 uprising, Burma was ostracised by the West, which imposed economic and other sanctions against the new military government. Largely as a result, the generals turned to China, which was prepared to provide Burma with loans, technical assistance, arms, trade goods and diplomatic support.

Burma has since balanced this relationship with other foreign policy links—for example, it joined ASEAN in 1997. The unprecedented closeness of the two countries, however, and groundless rumours about a Chinese military presence in Burma have led some observers to label Burma a Chinese client state.[3]

China has never exercised the kind of influence in Burma that has often been claimed. Indeed, it has been careful not to upset its notoriously prickly southern neighbour. It could even be argued that, in some respects, Burma has exercised the whip hand in the relationship, by exploiting its critical geostrategic position and possession of precious natural resources.

Even so, successive Burmese governments have recognised that a close friendship with China serves the country's national interests and they have tried to maintain an amicable relationship. Burma still relies on China's protection in the UN Security Council. This makes Thein Sein's suspension of the Myitsone project even more surprising.

So, what might be the reasons for Thein Sein's decision? A number of possible explanations present themselves, which will be examined in a follow-up post.

---

3   Andrew Selth, *Chinese Military Bases in Burma: The Explosion of a Myth*, Griffith Asia Institute Regional Outlook Paper No.10 (Brisbane: Griffith University, 2007), www.griffith.edu.au/__data/assets/pdf_file/0018/18225/regional-outlook-andrew-selth.pdf [page discontinued].

35

Burma–China: Another dam puzzle (Part 2)

(16:51 AEDT, 1 November 2011)

Several explanations were put forward to explain president Thein Sein's unexpected decision to suspend work on the Myitsone Dam project. However, on this, as in so many other areas of government activity, the thinking of Myanmar's leadership was largely a mystery. Thirteen possible reasons were put forward, but it was difficult to choose those most likely to have persuaded the president to risk the ire of the Chinese.

If past practice is any guide, Burmese President Thein Sein is probably trying to satisfy a number of aims and send signals to several different targets in announcing his decision to suspend construction of the massive Myitsone Dam in northern Burma, in which Beijing had invested heavily and stood to benefit most.[1]

If that is the case, what might the reasons be for his decision? The pundits have offered a range of views, but the bottom line is that no one really knows. As always, the thinking in senior Burmese leadership circles remains a mystery.

---

1   Francis Wade, 'Have Protests Succeeded in Myanmar?', *Al Jazeera*, 9 October 2011, www.aljazeera.com/indepth/opinion/2011/10/201110391126493167.html.

Bearing in mind the danger of mirror-imaging, it is important to try to put ourselves in the place of Burma's policymakers and decision-takers.[2] On the assumption that they are rational actors, with a nuanced understanding of the country's national and international interests, a number of possible explanations present themselves. These include the following:

1. The new 'civilian' president may be keen to demonstrate that he is not beholden to the old military leadership, which signed the 2007 agreement with a Chinese consortium for the construction of seven dams in northern Burma, the largest being Myitsone.

2. By the same token, Thein Sein's decision could be intended to demonstrate that Burma has broken with the past and, despite the questionable means by which it was formed, the new hybrid civilian–military parliament is an independent body that must be taken seriously.

3. While public opinion is unlikely to be the main driver, it cannot harm the president to be seen to be responsive to concerns expressed about the site and manner of the dam's construction, the environmental damage it will cause, its displacement of local communities and its potential downstream impact.[3]

4. Given that the Kachin ethnic minority stands to be hurt most by the dam, Thein Sein may be trying to lay the groundwork for a peace settlement with the Kachin Independence Army, against which the Burmese armed forces are currently fighting a bitter guerilla war.

5. Thein Sein could also be demonstrating that he is aware of the deep unease in Burma over the dramatic growth in the number of Chinese immigrants and businesses—both legal and illegal—over the past 20 years and is prepared to do something about them.

6. It could also be the case, as some have argued, that Thein Sein is trying to protect his own position in the national leadership by meeting the concerns of an anti-China faction in the armed forces.[4]

---

2   'Cognitive Traps for Intelligence Analysis', *Wikipedia*, en.wikipedia.org/wiki/Cognitive_traps_for_intelligence_analysis.

3   Supalak Ganjanakhundee, 'Is Myitsone a Landmark for Reform in Burma?', *The Nation*, [Bangkok], 5 October 2011, www.nationmultimedia.com/new/opinion/Is-Myitsone-a-landmark-for-reform-in-Burma-30166832.html [page discontinued].

4   Bertil Lintner, 'China Behind Myanmar's Course Shift', *Asia Times Online*, [Hong Kong], October 2011, www.atimes.com/atimes/Southeast_Asia/MJ19Ae03.html [page discontinued].

7. The suspension of the dam project—for the duration of his five-year term in office—could be an attempt by Thein Sein to open up political space for the implementation of economic and other reforms, some of which are likely to be unpopular inside Burma.

8. Another possibility is that Thein Sein is manoeuvring to renegotiate the dam contract, either to provide greater protection for the Irrawaddy River—a vital economic resource and emotive cultural icon—or perhaps to get a larger share of the anticipated hydropower. Under the current contract, 90 per cent is reserved for China.[5]

9. At the international level, the president could be making a point with the Chinese—and others—that he, the new government and Burma more generally cannot be taken for granted. They wish to be treated with respect and taken seriously as international players.

10. The Myitsone Dam decision serves as a reminder that, when they are completed, the oil and gas pipelines currently being built from the Bay of Bengal to Yunnan will be under the effective control of Burma. Should relations with Beijing deteriorate, Naypyidaw will have the means to close these critical sources of energy to southern China.

11. The suspension of such a large joint project (it is valued at US$3.6 billion [A$5.9 billion]) lets the international community know that Burma is not, and never has been, a client state of China. This message will not be lost on India, where the relationship has been a cause for concern.

12. A reputation for independence and a willingness to stand its ground, even against a superpower, may strengthen Naypyidaw's negotiating position with the US, with which it is currently engaged in a dialogue over reforms and sanctions. Curiously, China does not seem to have been a major factor in US thinking about Burma, but this is likely to change.[6]

13. The suspension of the dam project suggests to regional countries that, should Naypyidaw be given the ASEAN chair in 2014, it would be prepared to act in the association's best interests, even in the face of opposition from its powerful neighbour and purported 'ally'.

---

5   *Damming the Irrawaddy* (Burma Rivers Network, 2007), www.burmariversnetwork.org/resources/publications/13-publications/95-damming-the-irrawaddy.html [page discontinued] [now at burmariversnetwork.org/title/resources/publications/damming-the-irrawaddy.html].
6   Douglas H. Paal, *Myanmar: Time for a Change*, Asia Pacific Brief (Washington, DC: Carnegie Endowment for International Peace, 28 October 2011), www.carnegieendowment.org/2011/10/28/myanmar-time-for-change/699v.

Any or all of these factors could have been included in Naypyidaw's consideration of the Myitsone issue before Thein Sein made up his mind. There may have been others. We can be sure, however, that the decision would not have been made lightly. That said, it is important to remember that work on the dam has only been suspended. It is possible that, after a period, when the presidency changes or the circumstances are more favourable, the project will be revived, in one form or another. China is still involved in several other dam projects in northern Burma.[7]

Whatever the reasons for Naypyidaw's move, the fact remains that it will always be in Burma's national interests to share a cooperative relationship with China. And, given the geostrategic, economic and other issues at stake, it will always be in China's interests to avoid a major falling out with Burma. Both sides know this.

---

7   *Dam Projects* (Burma Rivers Network, 2018), www.burmariversnetwork.org/dam-projects.html [page discontinued] [now at burmariversnetwork.org/title/dam-projects.html].

36

Aung San Suu Kyi's choice

(10:30 AEDT, 23 November 2011)

When the Thein Sein Government announced that it would hold by-elections for the national parliament on 1 April 2012, Aung San Suu Kyi and the opposition NLD were faced with the choice of whether to continue their boycott of the political process or to join it. Both decisions carried certain risks.

In some ways, it is easier and safer to be a critic on the sidelines than to become an active participant in the formal political process. Yet, to not do so when an opportunity presents itself risks continuing powerlessness, a loss of credibility and possibly even irrelevance. This has been the dilemma faced by Burma's main opposition party and its charismatic leader, Aung San Suu Kyi.

On 18 November, however, the NLD announced it would re-register as a political party and compete in the country's forthcoming by-elections for 48 vacant seats.[1] According to news reports, Aung San Suu Kyi herself is considering standing as a parliamentary candidate.

The decision to re-register was described as unanimous, but clearly there are still deep concerns within the NLD and among its supporters. Aung San Suu Kyi has cautiously welcomed the new and apparently reformist government in Naypyidaw, but formally joining the political process will require the NLD to put the past behind it and embrace an entirely new paradigm.

---

1   'Suu Kyi's NLD Democracy Party to Rejoin Burma Politics', *BBC News*, 18 November 2011, www.bbc.co.uk/news/world-asia-15787605.

This will not be easy. The legacy of 50 years of military misrule is evident for all to see. There are still hundreds of political prisoners in Burma and some ethnic communities are fighting bitter guerilla wars. It will also mean forgetting the 1990 elections, which the NLD won by a landslide but which were shelved by the ruling military council. For more than 20 years, this has been the basis of the NLD's claim to be Burma's legitimate government.

It will mean abiding by and 'respecting' the flawed 2008 constitution, which perpetuates military rule, in part by setting aside 25 per cent of all seats in the national and regional parliaments for members of the armed forces. The charter also provides an amnesty for all past members of the regime guilty of human rights abuses. And, because of her marriage to a British citizen, it prevents Aung San Suu Kyi from becoming president.

Registration as a political party will also require the NLD to accept the current government, which is dominated by the Union Solidarity and Development Party—an organisation made up of former military officers and regime supporters. Thanks to a rigged poll held last year, it currently holds 883 of the 1,154 elected seats in Burma's 15 parliaments.[2]

The decision to re-register only came after the NLD heard Aung San Suu Kyi's own views. Yet, it is by no means certain that she will join the formal political process.[3]

If Aung San Suu Kyi stood for parliament and was successful in winning a seat, she would become only one elected member in the 664-seat national parliament. She would not have any official position and, even if the NLD swept the by-elections, she would lack a strong party base in Naypyidaw. However, she would still be bound to observe all the rules and regulations governing the parliament and its subordinate bodies.

As a private citizen, Aung San Suu Kyi is currently an independent actor, albeit a very influential one. Yet, as an MP, there is a real risk that she would lose her ability to speak and act so freely. If she is appointed to

---

2   *2010 Election Watch: Key Results* (Bangkok: ALTSEAN-Burma, 2010), www.altsean.org/Research/ 2010/Key%20Facts/Results/Overall.php [page discontinued] [now at archive.altsean.org/Research/ 2010/Key%20Facts/Results/Overall.php].

3   'Myanmar Opposition Leader Undecided on Contesting Polls', *M&C*, 22 November 2011, www.monstersandcritics.com/news/asiapacific/news/article_1676737.php/Myanmar-opposition-leader-undecided-on-contesting-polls [page discontinued].

a senior position by President Thein Sein, she may have greater power— in a formal sense—in one area, but this would probably mean losing her ability to play a significant role in others.

Also, as a parliamentarian, Aung San Suu Kyi would be obliged to adopt much more detailed policies and vote on a wide range of domestic issues. To date, she has tended to speak in very broad terms, often referring to Buddhist moral teachings and universal democratic principles. Direct participation in the political process would mean formulating and taking firm positions on a host of contentious issues.

Even if she argues and votes against specific policies, the government is bound to prevail. And, as an MP, she would still have been part of the formal process by which those issues were decided. She will in effect have been coopted by the government and may become associated, at least in some minds, with a range of unpopular laws over which she had no effective control.

More to the point, perhaps, for more than 20 years, Aung San Suu Kyi has been an enormously powerful figure, lauded and consulted by presidents, prime ministers and other world leaders. She has never seen herself simply as another member of Burma's parliament. Her ability to maintain this elevated position and influence events will be greatest if she remains outside the formal political process, at least for the time being.

Burma's opposition 'movement' has never been a tightly knit, well-organised and disciplined force with an agreed policy platform.[4] It has always been a very loose and fractious coalition of groups and individuals in Burma and abroad. The two things it has had most in common have been a shared commitment to regime change and respect for Aung San Suu Kyi.

The NLD's decision to re-register as a party and participate in the formal political process will place even those shared beliefs under considerable strain. Some ethnic groups, for example, distrust the NLD and will follow

---

4   Andrew Selth, 'Burma's Opposition Movement: A House Divided', *The Interpreter*, 25 November 2008, www.lowyinterpreter.org/post/2008/11/25/Burmas-opposition-movement-A-house-divided.aspx [page discontinued] [now at archive.lowyinstitute.org/the-interpreter/burma-opposition-movement-house-divided].

a different path, possibly including armed resistance. If Aung San Suu Kyi stands for parliament, she is bound to alienate some of her supporters. If she does not, it may look as if she lacks faith in the process.

Burma's prodemocracy forces have endured terrible privations over the past 23 years to get to this position. Now that it is here, however, they may find that the real work has only just begun. The existence of an undisguised military dictatorship guilty of appalling human rights abuses offered them a simple choice. The decision of whether or not to trust a hybrid civilian–military government that seems to promise incremental reform and national reconciliation is much more difficult.

It is said that politics is the art of compromise. The NLD seems to have accepted that, albeit reluctantly. However, some others in the opposition movement remain unwilling to abandon their hardline stance against the Naypyidaw government. If Aung San Suu Kyi does not become a part of the formal political process herself, they will doubtless feel more justified in not joining the NLD's bold leap of faith into the future.

37

Clinton in Burma: The WMD dimension

(16:52 AEDT, 6 December 2011)

Hillary Clinton paid a three-day visit to Myanmar in December 2011—the first by a US Secretary of State since John Foster Dulles visited the country in 1955. No one expected any dramatic breakthrough in the diplomatic relationship, but the US made it clear beforehand that it had a number of important issues to raise with president Thein Sein—not least its concerns over Myanmar's reported WMD ambitions.

As expected, Hillary Clinton's historic visit to Burma last week prompted a flurry of reports and op-eds in the news media and on activist websites.

Most of the immediate coverage focused on her discussions with President Thein Sein and opposition leader Aung San Suu Kyi. The perennial issues of democratic reform in Burma, the release of political prisoners, the development of civil society, the plight of ethnic communities and US economic sanctions were all given a good airing.

While some were more cautious than others, most observers acknowledged that something very important is happening in Burma, and the Secretary of State's visit was a turning point in relations with the US.

However, even experienced Burma-watchers were unable to agree on what actually prompted the visit. It was variously described as a calculated move to leave behind the failed policies of the Bush era, an effort to encourage

Thein Sein's reform process, an attempt by the Obama administration to reengage with the Asia-Pacific and a ploy by the US to score points in its strategic competition with China.

To a greater or lesser extent, all these factors probably contributed to the decision to make the visit—the first by a US Secretary of State to Burma in more than 50 years.

Despite a rather forlorn plea for attention by US Senator Richard Lugar, Burma's reported WMD ambitions and shadowy relationship with North Korea received relatively little press coverage.[1] Yet those subjects were clearly high on the US agenda. By examining public statements made during the visit, it is possible to glean some clues about the current thinking on these vexed issues.

In a background briefing given prior to Hillary Clinton's arrival in Burma, a senior State Department official—most likely Assistant Secretary of State for East Asian and Pacific Affairs, Kurt Campbell—said the primary US concerns with regard to Naypyidaw's relations with Pyongyang were 'missiles and other military equipment' that were subject to UNSC sanctions.[2]

Questioned specifically about the possible transfer of nuclear technology to Burma, the same official said that 'there are perhaps other activities, nascent activities'. It was 'an issue of concern' that had been looked at 'very, very closely', but the US did not see signs of a 'substantial effort' in this area 'at this time'. He repeated that, as regards North Korean ties with Burma, the US focus was on missiles—an issue that had been examined 'fairly carefully'.

When Hillary Clinton met President Thein Sein in Naypyidaw, she was frank in stating that improved relations with the US were dependent on 'the entire government' of Burma respecting the international consensus against the spread of nuclear weapons. She looked to Burma to fully

1   Senator Richard G. Lugar, 'Lugar: Burma–North Korea Ties Should be Exposed', Press release, 28 November 2011, lugar.senate.gov/news/record.cfm?id=334974&& [page discontinued].
2   *Background Briefing on Secretary Clinton's Travel to Burma* (Washington, DC: US Department of State, 29 November 2011), www.state.gov/p/eap/rls/rm/2011/11/177896.htm [page discontinued].

implement the UNSC resolutions against certain contacts with Pyongyang and supported the Burmese Government's 'stated determination to sever military ties with North Korea'.[3]

This reference to Burma cutting its defence links with North Korea—described by the US side elsewhere as 'very clear commitments' by Naypyidaw—goes further than past Burmese statements on this issue.[4] Also, the reference to the 'entire government' seems to be a veiled warning to hardline elements in Burma that they should not try to pursue WMD in defiance of Thein Sein's 'strong assurances regarding his country's compliance' with the relevant UNSC resolutions and other nonproliferation commitments.

'Other nonproliferation commitments' appears to be a reference to Burma's stated intention to strongly consider signing the IAEA's additional protocol.[5] Indeed, according to US officials, the Thein Sein Government is already engaged in a dialogue with the IAEA regarding Burma's possible accession to this key instrument. Among other things, it requires comprehensive reporting of nuclear-related activities and—critically—permits IAEA inspections of suspected nuclear facilities.

The overall impression left by all these statements is quite positive. While still of concern, Burma's nuclear research program does not seem to have made much progress and in any case is considered less important than other WMD-related issues. Accession to the additional protocol would be an important confidence-building measure, particularly if it was followed by IAEA inspections.[6] A Burmese ballistic missile program is clearly a major worry for the US, but on that subject, too, Naypyidaw seems prepared to respond to Washington's representations.

3   Hillary Rodham Clinton, Secretary of State, 'Press Availability in Nay Pyi Taw, Burma', 1 December 2011, www.state.gov/secretary/rm/2011/12/177994.htm [page discontinued] [now at 2009-2017.state. gov/secretary/20092013clinton/rm/2011/12/177994.htm].

4   Senior State Department Official, 'Background Briefing on Secretary Clinton's Meeting with Aung San Suu Kyi', Special Briefing, Rangoon, Burma, 2 December 2011, www.state.gov/r/pa/prs/ps/2011/12/178091.htm [page discontinued] [now at 2009-2017.state.gov/r/pa/prs/ps/2011/12/178125.htm].

5   Senior State Department Official, 'Background Briefing on Secretary Clinton's Meeting with Burmese President', Special Briefing, Nay Pyi Taw, Burma, 1 December 2011, www.state.gov/r/pa/prs/ps/2011/12/178025.htm [page discontinued] [now at 2009-2017.state.gov/r/pa/prs/ps/2011/12/178025.htm].

6   IAEA Safeguards Overview: Comprehensive Safeguards Agreements and Additional Protocols (Vienna: International Atomic Energy Agency, 1998–2019), www.iaea.org/Publications/Factsheets/English/sg_overview.html.

Most importantly, the US appears to have accepted a firm assurance by President Thein Sein that Burma will observe the relevant UNSC resolutions and cut all military ties with North Korea. This would have a direct impact on any Burmese WMD programs. It remains to be seen whether and when this actually occurs. Hillary Clinton said in Burma that 'history teaches us to be cautious' but, as she also stated with regard to the democratic reform process, there are 'some grounds for encouragement'.

Of course, it is possible to read too much into these public statements. Not everyone speaks with legalistic precision. The US spokespersons were senior officials, however, with strong track records in international diplomacy, conscious that they were speaking on the record. They were trying to convey specific messages to the public and to other governments, including the one in Naypyidaw. On that basis, their comments deserve serious consideration.

2012

38

Assessing Burma's reform program

(15:04 AEDT, 24 January 2012)

Nine months after president Thein Sein took office on 30 March 2011, it was possible to look back and make an assessment of his unexpected reform program and its chances of success. Was he, as some claimed, 'Myanmar's Gorbachev'? Inevitably, there was a wide range of opinion expressed, but most observers agreed that his relationship with opposition leader Aung San Suu Kyi was critical to achieve his aims, whatever they were.

Burma's hybrid civilian–military government is not yet one year old but already it has been the subject of countless blogs, op-eds and academic articles. These works have covered the full spectrum of political opinion, from enthusiastic plaudits to anti-regime diatribes. In one way or another, however, they have all tried to answer the questions: is President Thein Sein a genuine reformer and, if so, what does this mean for Burma?

Most commentators have highlighted the President's constructive relationship with opposition leader Aung San Suu Kyi, who, with other members of her party, will contest by-elections for the national parliament in April. There have also been promising negotiations with ethnic Karen and Shan insurgents, the release of hundreds of political prisoners, the lifting of restrictions on the press and internet access and other encouraging signs of political, economic and social reform.

More pessimistic observers have noted the promilitary bias of the 2008 constitution, the conflict with Kachin insurgents, continuing human rights abuses, the government's failure to release all dissidents from prison and the lack of substantive progress on many of the promised reforms. They distrust Thein Sein's motives and question Aung San Suu Kyi's judgement in joining the formal political process.[1]

There are also differences of view over the blossoming of relations between Naypyidaw and other governments—notably, the Obama administration. Most analysts have welcomed the increased diplomatic contacts—albeit accompanied by a degree of cynicism over the number of politicians making the pilgrimage to Aung San Suu Kyi's house. A few diehard opponents of the regime, however, have seen the concessions and assistance offered to Burma as dangerously premature.[2]

Despite the more open atmosphere, it is still difficult to know precisely what is happening in Burma and why, so these differences of view are to be expected. Also, so momentous was last year's paradigm shift that it is taking some veteran Burma-watchers a while to absorb.[3] Now that Thein Sein has been in office for nine months, however, it is possible to take stock and see last year's dramatic developments in a broader perspective.

Within self-imposed limits, the reform process appears to be real. Close observers with direct access to key players, including Thein Sein himself, are convinced the President is genuine in his wish to introduce a wide range of new and more enlightened policies and to bring greater peace and prosperity to Burma. Significantly, this view is shared by Aung San Suu Kyi, who perhaps more than anyone else has reason to be cautious about accepting the government's statements at face value.

The changes seen in Burma during 2011 are largely the result of internal developments—notably, Senior General Than Shwe's retirement, the advent of the Thein Sein Government and Aung San Suu Kyi's willingness to work with the new President. Despite the rather unseemly scramble by

---

1   Bertil Lintner, 'The Limits of Reform in Myanmar', *Asia Times*, [Hong Kong], 18 January 2012, www.atimes.com/atimes/Southeast_Asia/NA18Ae03.html [page discontinued].

2   'Ros-Lehtinen Urges Administration to Stop Talks with the Burmese Regime: Says "Any Concession to Dictatorship Would be Grossly Premature"', US House of Representatives, Committee on Foreign Affairs, Washington, DC, 13 January 2012, foreignaffairs.house.gov/press_display.asp?id=2161 [page discontinued].

3   Andrew Selth, 'Thein Sein as Myanmar's Gorbachev', *Asia Times*, [Hong Kong], 19 October 2011, www.atimes.com/atimes/Southeast_Asia/MJ19Ae01.html [page discontinued].

some foreign governments, activist groups and individuals to claim credit for aspects of the reform program, forces outside Burma have contributed only marginally to this outcome.[4]

The task facing Thein Sein is daunting. After more than 50 years of brutal, inept and ideologically distorted military rule, there is hardly a single sector of Burma's government, economy and civil society that is not begging for reform and desperate for financial, technical and other kinds of assistance. Some steps can be taken quickly and relatively painlessly, but the depth and complexity of the challenges faced by Burma are such that fundamental reform will take considerable time, effort and resources.

The most intractable problem confronting Thein Sein is the gulf between Naypyidaw and the country's ethnic minorities. Generations of war, human rights abuses, economic exploitation and broken promises have left the minorities deeply distrustful of the Burman-dominated central government. For their part, the government and armed forces remain determined not to compromise—as they see it—Burma's unity, stability and independence. Some progress has been made but a durable solution to this problem seems a distant prospect.[5]

Another important question is whether Naypyidaw can manage popular expectations. After decades of hardship and disappointment, few Burmese are taking anything for granted, but according to recent visitors to Burma the population is increasingly hopeful of real reforms and an improvement in their standard of living.[6] Having Aung San Suu Kyi on side should help Thein Sein keep these hopes within realistic limits but already there have been demands for faster and more far-reaching changes.

Given Burma's recent history and current problems, Naypyidaw's critics will be able to point to issues of concern for some time yet. In parts of the country, military operations are continuing. Officials used to wielding unbridled authority will not change their behaviour overnight. Corruption, discrimination and the abuse of power have become deeply

---

4   David I. Steinberg, 'Myanmar: On Claiming Success', *The Irrawaddy*, 18 January 2012, www.irra waddy.org/opinion_story.php?art_id=22875 [page discontinued] [now at www2.irrawaddy.com/article. php?art_id=22875].

5   *Myanmar: A New Peace Initiative*, Asia Report No.214 (Brussels: International Crisis Group, 30 November 2011), www.crisisgroup.org/asia/south-east-asia/myanmar/myanmar-new-peace-initiative.

6   Graham Reilly, 'The West Must be Patient as Burma Changes', *Sydney Morning Herald*, 20 January 2012, www.smh.com.au/politics/federal/the-west-must-be-patient-as-burma-changes-20120120-1q8yv.html.

embedded in Burmese society. And in some ways Naypyidaw is being held to a standard higher than that applied to other regional governments. Even if he had a firmer power base and greater resources, Thein Sein would not be able to satisfy everyone.

The reform program has considerable momentum and even if it falters it will be difficult to turn the clock back to 2010. But the President needs to balance competing political pressures while taking account of Burma's limited ability to implement and absorb rapid change. His aim, in the short term at least, seems to be something along Chinese lines—namely, a prosperous and independent country with a measure of individual freedom, exercised within the framework of a restrictive constitution.[7]

For her part, Aung San Suu Kyi is facing the challenge posed to all popular leaders, of making the transition from political icon to effective politician. For the time being, she seems prepared to work with Thein Sein in achieving national reconciliation and incremental reform. This is a pragmatic strategy, but it carries risks. It has already upset some of her supporters. It will also be difficult to sustain. For there will come a time when pressure will build for Burma's 'disciplined democracy' to give way to a genuinely representative system of government. That may prove the real test of the President's reform program.

---

7   Lally Weymouth, 'Burma President Thein Sein: Country is on "Right Track to Democracy"', *The Washington Post*, 19 January 2012, www.washingtonpost.com/opinions/burma-president-thein-sein-country-is-on-right-track-to-democracy/2012/01/19/gIQANeM5BQ_story.html?wprss=rss_economy.

39

Burma's reforms: Foreigners can't take much credit

(16:00 AEDT, 30 January 2012)

Many governments, international organisations and individuals claimed they were responsible for Myanmar opening up under president Thein Sein, but most of the credit belonged to those inside the country. The international community's ability to influence developments was always very limited. The latest developments represented what Aung San Suu Kyi called a rare and precious opportunity for the new government, the opposition movement and the international community to work together.

After the Bay of Pigs fiasco in 1961, John F. Kennedy ruefully observed that success has many fathers, but failure is an orphan.[1] Albeit from the opposite perspective, this old saw can be applied to Burma today. For, despite 20 years of frustrating and unsuccessful diplomacy, there is no shortage of people and organisations now claiming credit for Naypyidaw's welcome but unexpected reform program.

---

1   President Kennedy actually said: 'Victory has a hundred fathers, defeat is an orphan.' Several sources have been given for this comment, or variations thereof, but not all of them are accurate. It was made at a press conference given by the US president at the State Department in Washington, DC, on 21 April 1961. See 'President Kennedy's News Conference No.10, 04/21/1961', *YouTube*, www.youtube.com/watch?v=AYx6MG6NkjU.

As stated in *The Interpreter* recently, the remarkable paradigm shift that took place in Burma last year was due mainly to internal developments and a few key local personalities.[2] External factors played a role, but they were incidental to the main game. This in itself is noteworthy, however, and with the benefit of hindsight prompts a number of observations.

First, Burma demonstrates once again that the international community is limited in its ability to influence the behaviour of states that are determined to go their own way. There were costs, of course, but Burma has shown that, if it is prepared to discount international opinion, forgo rapid economic development and ignore the suffering of its own people, an authoritarian government can withstand considerable external pressure.

Mind you, Burma has a long history of self-reliance, based on a deep commitment to national independence and a strong sense of strategic vulnerability. It has immense natural resources, which reduces its dependence on the outside world. It is also relevant that, when the armed forces took back direct political power in 1988, Burma was in some respects a pre-industrial society. Even now, two-thirds of the population live in rural towns and villages.

Burma also serves as a reminder that economic sanctions are at best a clumsy diplomatic tool and at worst a counterproductive one. They are easy to invoke but difficult to remove. Unless applied carefully, they can miss their intended targets and harm the innocent. Also, unless sanctions have very wide backing, countries can turn elsewhere for trade, capital, arms and diplomatic support.

In Burma's case, the regime responded by developing strong ties with China and improving relations with a wide range of other countries. These steps severely undercut the West's punitive measures. When the Obama administration reviewed US policy towards Burma in 2009, it concluded that sanctions were at best 'modest inconveniences' to the military government.[3]

A third issue is the importance of strategic imperatives. One reason the US, the EU and likeminded countries adopted a policy towards Burma that was much tougher than any directed at other undemocratic countries

---

2   Andrew Selth, 'Assessing Burma Reform Program', *The Interpreter*, 24 January 2012, www.lowy interpreter.org/post/2012/01/24/Assessing-Burmas-reform-program.aspx [page discontinued] [now at archive.lowyinstitute.org/the-interpreter/assessing-burma-reform-program].

3   Derek Tonkin, 'Suu Kyi is Fighting, But for How Long?', *Democratic Voice of Burma*, 11 February 2012, www.dvb.no/analysis/suu-kyi-is-fighting-but-how-long-for/14223 [page discontinued].

in Asia was because they felt there were few critical national interests at stake. After the 1988 uprising, Burma was seen as isolated, weak and of little commercial or strategic value. It was thus deemed a cost-free target.

Yet, as the years went by, Burma's critical geostrategic position and role became clearer.[4] It was able to play China off against India and, by joining ASEAN, became a factor in regional diplomacy. It was a factor in international efforts against transnational crime and its ties to North Korea raised the spectre of nuclear and missile proliferation. Also, Burma possessed vast energy resources, making it critical to its neighbours' economic development.

Fourth, the steady expansion of the regime's power and influence, in the face of constant external pressure, illustrates the danger of formulating foreign policies without objectively assessing their likely impact. The Bush administration's principled stand against Burma's military government was applauded by many but was pursued despite clear evidence that it would not achieve its stated objectives.

Indeed, the punitive measures and harsh rhetoric aimed at Burma after 1988 aroused the generals' nationalist sentiments and made them determined to resist external intervention. They strengthened the armed forces and may have even considered WMD. Foreign pressure also helped justify their bunker mentality and made them even more fearful of political, economic and social change.

Granted, those countries favouring a policy of engagement did not have much success either. China was closest to Burma during this period, but it struggled to influence the attitudes of Senior General Than Shwe and his circle. ASEAN, too, was unable to make much of an impact. The regime put its survival and Burma's stability, unity and independence—as perceived by Naypyidaw—above all other considerations.

It is also worth noting the impact that notable individuals have had on Burma's foreign relations. During the Bush era, for example, Western policy owed a great deal to Aung San Suu Kyi.[5] It has yet to be seen whether

---

4   Andrew Selth, *Burma: A Strategic Perspective*, Working Paper No.13 (San Francisco: The Asia Foundation, May 2001), asiafoundation.org/pdf/wp13.pdf [page discontinued] [now at indianstrategic knowledgeonline.com/web/burma%202001.pdf].
5   David I. Steinberg, 'Aung San Suu Kyi and US Policy Toward Burma/Myanmar', *Journal of Current Southeast Asian Affairs*, Vol.29, No.3, 2010, pp.35–59, doi.org/10.1177/186810341002900302.

Thein Sein deserves the title 'Burma's Gorbachev', but his elevation to the presidency appears to have broken the diplomatic impasse between Burma and Western countries.

Arguably, President Obama could be included in this category. Despite strong opposition, he adopted a more nuanced US approach to Burma that emphasised dialogue and cautious engagement, rather than criticism and punishment. This opened the way for the incremental restoration of bilateral ties, in contrast to the Bush policy, which, for many years, called for nothing less than complete regime change.

In 2010, senior US officials acknowledged that the new policy had failed as far as a constructive dialogue with Naypyidaw was concerned. However, had Obama given up and reverted to Bush's discredited policies, as many members of Congress and activists demanded, Washington would not have been in a position to respond as promptly and positively as it did to the diplomatic openings that emerged last year.[6]

Now that a reform process has begun and there is the possibility of far-reaching changes in Burma, the international community can play a much greater role. Both Naypidaw and other governments will remain wary of each other and proceed cautiously.[7] However, foreign countries and multilateral organisations are in a position to help Burma and it is in everyone's interests that they should do so.

The best way to consolidate recent changes and encourage further reform is to help make the current process successful. There will still be differences of view (for example, over the 2008 constitution) and the provision of large-scale assistance to Burma will pose its own challenges. But for the time being, the aims of the government, the opposition movement and the international community appear to be broadly aligned.

As Aung San Suu Kyi told the World Economic Forum in Davos last week, this offers 'a rare and extremely precious opportunity'.[8]

---

6   'Recent Developments on Burma', US Department of State Special Briefing, Washington, DC, 13 January 2012, www.state.gov/r/pa/prs/ps/2012/01/180710.htm [page discontinued].
7   William Hague and Kevin Rudd, 'Burma: Real and Enduring Change is Not Assured— But the Glimmers of Hope Must Not Be Stifled', *The Huffington Post*, 24 January 2011, www. huffingtonpost.co.uk/william-hague/burma-glimmer-of-hope-must-not-be-stifled_b_1228543.html [page discontinued].
8   'Aung San Suu Kyi: Annual Meeting 2012', World Economic Forum, Davos, Switzerland, www. weforum.org/videos/aung-san-suu-kyi-annual-meeting-2012 [page discontinued].

40

Burma and WMD: Nothing to report?

(08:23 AEDT, 29 March 2012)

On 9 March 2012, the US State Department released two reports in response to the 2008 Tom Lantos Block Burmese JADE (Junta's Anti-Democratic Efforts) Act. *To the disappointment of many, they did not provide the comprehensive and authoritative statement that was expected regarding foreign aid to Myanmar in areas such as intelligence cooperation, arms sales and the provision of nuclear technology.*

For nearly four years, activists, journalists and sundry other Burma-watchers have been waiting with keen anticipation for the US State Department to issue the annual reports on Burma that were formally mandated by an Act of Congress in 2008. It was expected that these reports would provide comprehensive, authoritative public statements on a range of issues that have long been mired in controversy.

As noted on *The Interpreter* last April, the preparation and release of these reports were among the first tasks set for the US's Special Envoy to Burma, who was finally appointed in August 2011 under provisions of the same Act.[1]

---

1   Andrew Selth, 'Burma and North Korea: Reality Checks', *The Interpreter*, 27 April 2011, www.lowy interpreter.org/post/2011/04/27/Burma-and-North-Korea-Reality-Checks.aspx [page discontinued] [now at archive.lowyinstitute.org/the-interpreter/burma-and-north-korea-reality-checks].

The State Department has just released its Burma reports for 2009[2] and 2010.[3] They are helpful, as far as they go, but are likely to raise more questions than they answer. Indeed, they are significant more for what they do not say than for what they do say.

Under the *JADE Act* of 2008, the State Department was required to report annually to the foreign relations committees of both the House of Representatives and the Senate on all military and intelligence aid provided to Burma's ruling SPDC.[4] WMD and related technology, materials and training were singled out for special attention.

The two reports just released are notable for their brevity and their reticence. Each is only one page long, even though half the page is taken up with an introduction and an overview that repeats much of the content. In neither of the reports do the words 'nuclear' or 'missile' appear even once, and 'intelligence' is only referred to as part of the reports' terms of reference, which are set out in the introduction.

Unsurprisingly, the State Department identifies state-controlled arms companies from China, North Korea, Ukraine, Russia, Belarus and Serbia as Burma's main suppliers of weapons and military-related technology during 2009 and 2010. China and North Korea also helped establish unspecified military production plants in Burma.

Interestingly, the reports also state that firms based in Singapore and Taiwan have 'reportedly' assisted Burma's defence industry in acquiring production technology and 'production-related equipment'. It is not clear precisely what is being referred to here, but Singapore has long played down such links. The Taiwanese connection seems to be mainly through sales to North Korea.

On North Korea's direct links with Burma, the two reports are very circumspect. They refer to attempts to deliver 'likely military equipment' and support for Burma's efforts to build and operate military-related

---

2   *Report to Congress per PL 110-286 on Military and Intelligence Aid to Burma for 2009* (Washington, DC: US Department of State, 9 March 2012), www.state.gov/s/inr/rls/burmareport/185615.htm [page discontinued].

3   *Report to Congress per PL 110-286 on Military and Intelligence Aid to Burma for 2010* (Washington, DC: US Department of State, 9 March 2012), www.state.gov/s/inr/rls/burmareport/184851.htm [page discontinued].

4   *H.R. 3890 (110th): Tom Lantos Block Burmese JADE (Junta's Anti-Democratic Efforts) Act of 2008*, Passed 23 July 2008, US Congress, Washington, DC, www.govtrack.us/congress/bills/110/hr3890/text.

production facilities. In this regard, however, the 2010 report alludes only to possible cooperation in the construction of 'underground facilities for military aircraft'. No comment is made on persistent claims that nuclear and ballistic missile plants are being built and operated in Burma with North Korean help.

Nor is any specific reference made to the nuclear-related training that Russia is supposed to have provided to more than 4,000 Burmese military and civilian officers over the past decade.[5] All the 2010 report says in that regard is that 'Russia also continues to train Burmese students in a wide range of fields with military applications'.

The absence of any reference to Burma's reported WMD ambitions is curious, as only last December the US was prepared to speak openly about the subject. In a background briefing to journalists just before Hillary Clinton's historic visit to Burma, a senior State Department official made it clear that the US was concerned about Burma's possible acquisition of ballistic missiles or related technology from North Korea.[6]

The same official said Burma's 'nascent' nuclear research program was much less of a concern but, even so, both issues were raised in the Secretary of State's discussions with President Thein Sein.[7] US representatives later expressed their appreciation of the President's firm undertaking to sever all military contacts with North Korea, the clear implication being that this would stem any clandestine WMD technology transfers.

Neither of the two reports refers to any intelligence links between Burma and foreign countries. If accepted at face value, this suggests that the State Department places little credence on reports in the news media and on activist websites over the past 10 years claiming the existence of Chinese signals intelligence collection stations in Burma.[8] Some of these stories have also stated that China shares its intelligence with Burma.

---

5   'Russia Trained 4,000 Myanmar Nuclear Officers', *Hindustan Times*, [New Delhi], 6 August 2010, www.hindustantimes.com/News-Feed/World/Russia-trained-4-000-Myanmar-nuclear-officers/Article1-583149.aspx [page discontinued] [now at www.hindustantimes.com/world/russia-trained-4-000-myanmar-nuclear-officers/story-AJWaZQtfiBwplTICJCQgIN.html].

6   'Background Briefing on Secretary Clinton's Travel to Burma', US Department of State, Washington, DC, 29 November 2011, 2009-2017.state.gov/p/eap/rls/rm/2011/11/177896.htm.

7   Andrew Selth, 'Clinton in Burma: The WMD Dimension', *The Interpreter*, 6 December 2011, www.lowyinterpreter.org/post/2011/12/06/Clinton-and-Burmese-WMD.aspx [page discontinued] [now at archive.lowyinstitute.org/the-interpreter/clinton-burma-wmd-dimension].

8   Andrew Selth, *Chinese Military Bases in Burma: The Explosion of a Myth*, Griffith Asia Institute Regional Outlook Paper No.10 (Brisbane: Griffith University, 2007), www.griffith.edu.au/__data/assets/pdf_file/0018/18225/regional-outlook-andrew-selth.pdf [page discontinued].

Of course, Burma has long been acknowledged by senior US officials as an extremely hard intelligence target, and it is possible that reliable information about such sensitive matters can only be obtained using sources and methods that cannot be revealed in public statements. This leaves open the question as to what might have been included in the classified and presumably more comprehensive reports delivered to the two congressional committees.

Another factor that may have influenced the State Department's cautious approach is the fragility of the current relationship between Washington and the apparently reform-minded government in Naypyidaw. The two reports cover a period when Burma was under direct military rule but, even so, revelations of nefarious activities involving WMD and North Korea would hardly encourage a closer relationship and stimulate further reforms. After all, President Thein Sein was Burma's prime minister from 2007 to 2011.

The 2008 *JADE Act* refers specifically to Burma under the SPDC's rule. The 2010 report points out that this council was formally dissolved on 30 March 2011, when the new hybrid civilian–military government took power. On that basis, it is unlikely that the State Department will feel bound to provide any further reports of this kind on military and intelligence aid to Burma.

Despite the progress made on several fronts since 2011, the latest US reports will not satisfy diehard critics of the Burmese Government. They were relying on the tough provisions of the 2008 Act to expose what they have long been convinced were secret nuclear weapon and ballistic missile programs. The fact that this has not happened will no doubt disappoint them, but it is unlikely to quieten the rumour mill or prevent similar claims in the future.

41

Kurt Campbell on US–Burma relations

(12:08 AEDT, 27 April 2012)

Testimony to the US Congress by Kurt Campbell, the Assistant Secretary of State for East Asian and Pacific Affairs, offered a fascinating glimpse into the Obama administration's thinking about developments in Myanmar and its relations with the US.

On 25 April, the US House of Representatives Committee on Foreign Affairs examined US policy towards Burma.[1] The Senate Committee on Foreign Relations held similar hearings the following day. Both heard testimony from officials and influential Burma-watchers.[2]

Kurt Campbell, the Assistant Secretary of State for East Asian and Pacific Affairs and, in the minds of many, the chief architect of the Obama administration's current approach to Burma, made a number of key points in his comments to the House Committee. These include the following:

---

1   'Oversight of US Policy Toward Burma', Hearings, Committee on Foreign Affairs, US House of Representatives, Washington, DC, 25 April 2012, foreignaffairs.house.gov/hearings?ID=4B811069-3F87-41BE-A2DB-E08B1EA4E128.

2   'US Policy on Burma', Subcommittee Hearing, Subcommittee on East Asian and Pacific Affairs, Committee on Foreign Relations, US Senate, Washington, DC, 26 April 2012, www.foreign.senate.gov/hearings/us-policy-on-burma.

1. With regard to the reforms made since March 2011 by President Thein Sein, the US believes this 'nascent opening' is real and significant. In contrast to much of the commentary published to date, however, the US believes this process is 'fragile and reversible'. As Hillary Clinton said on 4 April: '[T]he future of Burma is neither clear nor certain.'[3]

2. The US welcomes the progress made in negotiations between Naypyidaw and Burma's various ethnic communities, but Washington remains concerned that 'the impact of Burma's reform efforts has not extended far beyond the capital and major cities'. The continued fighting in Kachin State and human rights violations against the Rohingya minority, for example, remain major concerns.

3. According to Campbell, much work remains to be done in Burma. 'The legacy of five decades of military rule—repressive laws, a pervasive security apparatus, a corrupt judiciary and media censorship—is still all too present.' This has prompted the Obama administration to adopt a 'step-by-step process' towards the easing of economic sanctions. This approach is more measured than that which some other governments appear to be adopting.

4. The by-elections on 1 April, in which Aung San Suu Kyi and 42 other members of the NLD were elected, were considered 'a significant step forward'. Despite some irregularities, the elections 'demonstrated a smooth and peaceful voting process'. Washington is hoping that current differences over the oath can be resolved soon so that the elected NLD members can take their seats and make a contribution to the parliamentary process.[4]

5. The Burmese Government is proceeding with a strong program of economic reforms, including overdue changes to the exchange rate mechanism, but in Washington's view, allocations for the armed forces remained 'grossly disproportionate', at 16.5 per cent of the (formal) budget. At 3.25 per cent and 6.26 per cent, respectively, the allocations for health and education were still very low, but the US acknowledged that they were more than double previous levels.

---

3   Paul Eckert and Arshad Mohammed, 'US Moves to Ease Myanmar Sanctions After Reforms', *Reuters*, 5 April 2012, www.reuters.com/article/us-myanmar-usa-idUSBRE83315U20120405.
4   'In Myanmar, What a Difference an Oath Makes', *CNN*, 26 April 2012, edition.cnn.com/2012/04/26/world/asia/myanmar-politics/index.html.

6. Although Thein Sein has given assurances that Burma will observe the relevant UNSC resolutions, the US remains 'troubled' by Burma's military trade with North Korea. This has the potential to 'impede progress in improving our bilateral ties'. Indeed, despite two rather noncommittal US reports on the subject recently, Campbell described this as 'a top national security priority'.[5]

7. In recent months, the US has appeared less concerned about Burma's 'nascent' nuclear research program.[6] Campbell told the committee that the US welcomed assurances from senior officials that Burma had no intention of pursuing nuclear weapons. However, Washington continues to urge Naypyidaw to display greater transparency on nonproliferation issues and to accede to a range of additional IAEA instruments.

---

5   Andrew Selth, 'Burma and WMD: Nothing to Report?', *The Interpreter*, 29 March 2012, www. lowyinterpreter.org/post/2012/03/29/Burma-and-WMD-Nothing-to-report.aspx [page discontinued] [now at archive.lowyinstitute.org/the-interpreter/burma-and-wmd-nothing-report].

6   Andrew Selth, 'Does Burma Have a WMD Program?', *The Interpreter*, 7 June 2010, archive.lowy institute.org/the-interpreter/does-burma-have-wmd-program [page discontinued] [now at archive. lowyinstitute.org/the-interpreter/does-burma-have-wmd-program].

42

The Rangoon bombing: A historical footnote

(10:11 AEDT, 16 May 2012)

The brief visit to Myanmar by the President of the Republic of Korea (ROK), Lee Myung-bak, in May 2012 prompted numerous references in the news media and elsewhere to the North Korean bomb attack against ROK president Chun Doo-hwan during his state visit to Myanmar in 1983. Not all these historical references were accurate.

President Lee Myung-bak's historic visit to Burma this week has inevitably sparked references in the news media to the bomb attack by North Korea against the last South Korean president to make this trip, 29 years ago.[1] Unfortunately, these stories have breathed new life into some myths about that incident that deserve to be finally put to rest.

In 1983, president Chun Doo-hwan made a state visit to Burma, accompanied by a large delegation of South Korean officials. The morning after his arrival in Rangoon, he was due to lay a wreath at the Martyrs' Mausoleum, a shrine dedicated to nationalist leader Aung San and six other Burmese figures who were assassinated in 1947, just before the country regained its independence.

---

1   'South Korean President Lee Myung-bak in Burma Visit', *BBC News*, 14 May 2012, www.bbc.co.uk/news/world-asia-18055319.

Three North Korean agents secretly entered Burma just before the visit. They planted three remotely controlled bombs in the mausoleum's roof. However, these devices were detonated prematurely, before Chun arrived at the venue. Seventeen South Koreans were killed, including four cabinet ministers. Four Burmese citizens were killed and 32 were injured.[2]

The three North Korean agents were soon hunted down. One was killed and the other two were captured. One was hanged in 1985, but the other (who cooperated with the authorities) survived in a Burmese jail until 2008. Because of the attack, Burma severed its diplomatic ties with North Korea. Contacts were resumed in the late 1990s, but formal bilateral relations between the two pariah states were only restored in 2007.

According to most accounts, Chun was already on his way to the Martyrs' Mausoleum when the bombs exploded, but was late because his motorcade was stuck in traffic.[3] Some recent reports repeat the story that he was late, but say he arrived at the mausoleum 'a few minutes' after the bombs had exploded.[4]

Both these accounts are inaccurate. When interviewed about the incident, both Burmese and Korean officials who were in Burma at the time and directly involved in the state visit told a different story.

The night before the wreath-laying ceremony, just after Chun's arrival in Rangoon, it was realised that the president's departure from the State Guest House the following morning clashed with the arrival of a group of Burmese women who were scheduled to have tea with the Korean First Lady. For reasons of both protocol and efficiency, Korean officials were anxious to separate the two events.

Korean and Burmese protocol officers discussed the problem late into the night. Their solution was for president Chun to deliberately delay his departure for a few minutes, until after all his wife's guests had arrived and been officially welcomed. However, the South Korean Ambassador to Burma would leave the State Guest House at the original time and advise all those waiting at the mausoleum of the altered timings.

---

2   'North Korea Where the Dictator Loves Terrorism', *YouTube*, www.youtube.com/watch?v= khPAWCNnICk.

3   'Rangoon Bombing', *Wikipedia*, en.wikipedia.org/wiki/Rangoon_bombing.

4   'Lee Makes First S. Korean Trip to Myanmar Since Attack', *The Jakarta Post*, 14 May 2012, www.thejakartapost.com/news/2012/05/14/lee-makes-first-s-korean-trip-myanmar-attack.html [page discontinued].

When the ambassador's official car arrived at the mausoleum, with its South Korean flag flying, the watching North Korean agents apparently believed it was Chun Doo-hwan. Some reports state that they heard the Burmese military band at the venue begin playing, as it, too, was under the impression that the president had just arrived (on time). The agents triggered the bombs.

Chun Doo-hwan's motorcade was en route to the mausoleum—through streets cleared of traffic by the local police—when the attack occurred. Informed of the incident by radio, the presidential party immediately returned to the State Guest House. It is true that Chun Doo-hwan was late for the ceremony, but this was by design, not by accident. He was not held up by traffic. Nor did he ever reach the mausoleum. Only in that sense can it be said that the president 'narrowly escape death or injury'.[5]

While this version of the story lacks some of the drama of the news reports, it nevertheless underlines the fact that sometimes even minor events— in this case, a scheduling error that posed protocol problems for status-conscious Korean officials—can have far-reaching historical significance. As it was, war nearly broke out on the Korean Peninsula in 1983, as South Korea seriously contemplated retaliation against the North.

It is unlikely that Lee Myung-bak will need to remind anyone of this incident during his visit this week. Burma's relations with North Korea grew rapidly between 2000 and 2010, but the Burmese have never forgotten what happened nearly 30 years ago. Besides, even if President Thein Sein had not undertaken to sever Burma's military links with North Korea, closer political and economic relations with Seoul promise the reformist government in Naypyidaw much more than ties with Pyongyang ever will.[6]

---

5   Wai Moe, 'A Friend in Need', *The Irrawaddy*, August 2009, www2.irrawaddy.org/article.php? art_id=16425.
6   'US Welcomes Burma's Decision to Cut Military Ties with North Korea', *Mizzima News*, [Yangon], 2 December 2011, www.mizzima.com/news/inside-burma/6247-us-welcomes-burmas-decision-to-cut-military-ties-with-north-korea.html [page discontinued].

43

Burma and WMD: In the news again

(15:48 AEDT, 1 August 2012)

President Thein Sein told US secretary of state Hillary Clinton during her December 2011 visit that Myanmar had no intention of manufacturing or using WMD. He also said that Myanmar would sever its military ties with North Korea. However, reports kept emerging that cast doubt on these promises, not the least a remarkable document issued by the US State Department in July 2012 outlining Myanmar's apparent WMD ambitions.

Despite Burma's promise last year to cut its defence ties with North Korea and to not pursue any WMD programs, these problems simply will not go away. Naypyidaw's relations with the international community have greatly improved over the past year or so, but the potential remains for these issues to bring Burma's diplomatic rapprochement and domestic reform to a grinding halt.

Given North Korea's past sales of conventional arms to Burma and likely involvement in a ballistic missile production program, if not a nuclear weapons development program, it was a relief to all concerned when President Thein Sein told the US Secretary of State in December 2011 that Burma would sever its military links with North Korea.[1]

---

1   'Background Briefing on Secretary Clinton's Travel to Burma', Special Briefing, US Department of State, Washington, DC, 29 November 2011, www.state.gov/p/eap/rls/rm/2011/11/177896.htm [page discontinued].

There have since been statements by other senior Burmese officials assuring the world that Naypyidaw had abandoned its small nuclear research program and that military relations with North Korea had ceased.[2] It was partly with these 'firm assurances' in mind that the US, and most other countries, suspended or lifted a wide range of punitive measures that had been progressively imposed against Burma since the 1988 prodemocracy uprising.

Both the WMD and North Korea issues, however, remain of concern. Indeed, even more than the election of opposition leader Aung San Suu Kyi to Burma's parliament in April,[3] they have the potential to dramatically alter the trajectory of Burma's internal and external affairs. In the parlance of US analysts, they are 'game-changers'.

Last year, there were renewed claims of chemical weapons use by the Burmese armed forces. In June, Shan insurgents told activist groups they had been attacked with artillery shells containing chemical weapons.[4] In November, Kachin insurgents and refugees claimed they had been the victims of 'toxic gas'.[5]

None of these reports could be independently verified and most observers remained wary about accepting them at face value. Similar claims had been made by ethnic insurgent groups on several occasions over the past 30 years, but no hard evidence of chemical weapons use by Burma had ever been produced.

In November 2011, however, the latest claims attracted the attention of at least one member of the US Congress opposed to the Obama administration's policy of 'practical engagement' with Burma—namely,

2   John O'Callaghan, 'Myanmar Abandons Nuclear Research: Defence Minister', *Reuters*, 2 June 2012, in.reuters.com/article/uk-asia-security-myanmar/myanmar-abandons-nuclear-research-defence-minister-idUKBRE85105520120602.

3   Esmer Golluoglu, 'Aung San Suu Kyi Hails "New Era" for Burma After Landslide Victory', *The Guardian*, 3 April 2012, www.theguardian.com/world/2012/apr/02/aung-san-suu-kyi-new-era-burma.

4   'Fears Mount Over Chemical Weapon Use', *Democratic Voice of Burma*, 8 June 2011, www.dvb.no/news/fears-mount-over-chemical-weapons-use/16018 [page discontinued].

5   Zin Linn, 'Kachin Fighters Claim Burma Army Using Chemical Weapons', *Asian Correspondent*, 1 November 2011, asiancorrespondent.com/68545/burma-must-make-a-judgment-to-end-civil-war-immediately/ [page discontinued].

the Chairwoman of the House Foreign Affairs Committee, Ileana Ros-Lehtinen. Being cited by such a prominent figure, and without the usual caveats, these claims were given greater credence.[6]

Ros-Lehtinen stated that North Korea remained active in Burma, deepening her concern that the Burmese Government was still intent on acquiring 'contraband weapons ... including for the possible development of a nuclear program'. No evidence was provided to support these claims, but on 11 July this year, the State Department released a fact sheet that acknowledges that the US remains worried about Burma's links with North Korea.[7]

In the context of revised US sanctions against Burma, a new executive order has been issued by President Obama that imposes a range of measures against Burmese individuals and entities that are engaged in arms trade with North Korea, including the Directorate of Defence Industries (DDI). According to the fact sheet, the DDI 'carries out missile research and development at its facilities in Burma, where North Korean experts are active'.

The State Department also referred to a memorandum of understanding signed by the head of the DDI in 2008, in which North Korea undertook to assist Burma to build medium-range, liquid-fuelled ballistic missiles. The fact sheet added that, 'in the past year, North Korean ships have continued to arrive at Burma's ports carrying goods destined for Burma's defence industries'.

This fact sheet seems to have been barely noticed by international observers, but it is an important document.[8] It confirms reports that, despite Thein Sein's personal undertaking to Hillary Clinton, Burma has still not severed its military ties with North Korea. Indeed, in defiance of UNSC resolutions, it continues to receive shipments of defence-related goods. Also, for the first time, the US describes the extent of Burma's ballistic missile ambitions.

---

6   'Ros-Lehtinen Expresses Concern about Atrocities in Burma, Possible Connections to North Korea and Secretary Clinton Trip', House Committee on Foreign Affairs, US House of Representatives, Washington, DC, 29 November 2011, foreignaffairs.house.gov/news/story/?2103 [page discontinued].
7   'Administration Eases Financial and Investment Sanctions on Burma', *Fact Sheet* (Washington, DC: US Department of State, 11 July 2012), 2009-2017.state.gov/r/pa/prs/ps/2012/07/194868.htm.
8   'Obama Curbs Myanmar Penalties', *Global Security Newswire*, 12 July 2012, www.nti.org/gsn/article/obama-curbs-myanmar-energy-penalties/.

The strategic impact of a Burmese ballistic missile capability is still the subject of debate. Recent revelations that Vietnam has long had such weapons have raised little comment.[9] The political implications of Burma's continued defence links with North Korea, however, are profound. They have the potential to set Burma's foreign relations back years and with it any real hope of the President's domestic reform program achieving its aims.

Thein Sein's reforms have been prompted mainly by internal factors, and only in part by external concerns. Yet, ironically, they depend heavily on foreign assistance to succeed. Almost every sector of Burma's economy and civil society badly needs help and most of the capital, technology and expertise can only come from abroad. Should Burma once again be relegated to the status of an international pariah, either for violating UNSC resolutions or for secretly producing WMD, most key sources of assistance would evaporate.

There are a number of possible explanations for Burma's apparently self-defeating behaviour. The fact that the US has not made more of the continuing defence links with North Korea suggests that, for a period at least, Washington is prepared to give Thein Sein the benefit of the doubt. No one wants to see Burma once again slip back into shadow. Yet, such tolerance has definite limits, and there are many in the activist community, and in Congress, who would be happy to tell the Obama administration that it was always unwise to trust the generals and ex-generals in Naypyidaw.

9   Carlyle A. Thayer, 'Vietnam Bares Scud Missile Force: Missile Brigade 490', *Background Briefing*, 9 July 2012, www.scribd.com/doc/99567766/Thayer-Vietnam-Bares-Scud-Missile-Force.

44

Burma, the Rohingyas and Australia

(10:23 AEDT, 8 October 2012)

The circulation in Myanmar of a speech supposedly made by the Australian Prime Minister, expressing views similar to those held by anti-Muslim extremists in Myanmar, once again drew attention to the bitter racial and religious divisions in that country and the plight of the Rohingya in particular.

Burma faces more than its fair share of complex, sensitive and potentially divisive problems, but it is difficult to imagine one more intractable than the future of the Rohingyas, the estimated 800,000 Muslims of South Asian descent who are currently denied any formal recognition, either by Naypyidaw or by the international community.

Canberra has always been very careful in its responses to this controversial issue. However, through no fault of its own, the Australian Government may now become embroiled in it, and in a way that will not be helpful to anyone.

Over the past decade, the plight of the Rohingyas has attracted increased attention, mainly from Muslim countries and multilateral organisations such as the United Nations High Commissioner for Refugees (UNHCR). Yet, the issue is still little known and poorly understood. Accurate and objective analyses tend to be drowned out by passionate interventions from activists and others, amplified by the internet.[1]

---

1   Tin Maung Maung Than and Moe Thuzar, 'Myanmar's Rohingya Dilemma', *ISEAS Perspective*, 9 July 2012, www.networkmyanmar.org/images/stories/PDF13/iseas-rohingya.pdf [page discontinued].

Since Burma's independence in 1948, several attempts have been made to define the status of the Rohingyas, but they have always suffered discrimination. After 1962, the military government launched a number of pogroms against them, driving hundreds of thousands into squalid refugee camps in Bangladesh. Others have fled further afield and eke out a precarious existence in countries like Malaysia, Thailand, Pakistan and Saudi Arabia.

On 3 June, communal violence erupted in Rakhine (Arakan) State, on the northwest coast, where most of Burma's Rohingyas live. The unrest appears to have been sparked by the rape and murder of a Buddhist woman by three Muslim men in late May, but such was the depth of feeling already dividing the two communities that it rapidly escalated.

On 10 June, the President declared a state of emergency. The armed forces were sent in to restore law and order, although it has been claimed that they only contributed to the violence.[2] According to the UN, about 90 people died in the unrest, an estimated 90,000 were displaced and around 5,300 buildings were damaged or destroyed.

The Rohingya problem is particularly resistant to a negotiated settlement. This is despite, or because of, the fact that many in Burma's government and opposition movement, and most of the population, seem to be in broad agreement. In their eyes, the Rohingyas are not entitled to Burmese citizenship and should be expelled. They also feel that the Rohingyas in refugee camps in Bangladesh or in exile elsewhere should not be permitted to return home.

Asked for her views earlier this year, Aung San Suu Kyi was initially equivocal on this issue, prompting rare criticism from international human rights campaigners.[3] She has since formulated a more nuanced policy position that emphasises 'the rule of law', but continues to shy away from calls for the Rohingyas to be granted the same legal rights as other Burmese.

---

2   'The Government Could Have Stopped This': Sectarian Violence and Ensuing Abuses in Burma's Arakan State (New York: Human Rights Watch, 2012), www.hrw.org/sites/default/files/reports/burma0812web wcover_0.pdf.

3   Anna Maria Tremonti, 'Aung San Suu Kyi's Silence Over the Plight of the Rohingya Muslim Minority', The Current, 23 August 2012, www.cbc.ca/thecurrent/episode/2012/08/23/aung-san-suu-kyis-silence-over-the-plight-of-the-rohingya-muslim-minority/ [page discontinued].

Understandably, Australia has been cautious about expressing any views on this vexed question, which touches on aspects of Burma's history, politics, economy and culture. Also, like everyone else, Canberra is keen to avoid saying or doing anything that might slow the momentum of President Thein Sein's domestic reform program.[4]

In June, Bob Carr advised the Burmese Government of Australia's 'strong concern' at the ethnic and religious violence that had broken out in Rakhine State, and called on all parties involved to seek a negotiated, peaceful outcome that respected all sides.[5] The ambassador in Rangoon was asked to present Australia's concerns directly to the President's office and relevant government ministers.

Last month, the foreign minister announced that Australia would provide humanitarian aid for 14,000 people left homeless in Rakhine State by the recent sectarian violence. Australia is also working with CARE and other agencies 'to identify opportunities for ongoing, long-term support … that will help the victims of violence rebuild their lives, strengthen community resilience to ethnic conflict and restore peace'.[6]

In the circumstances, these responses seem measured and sensible. Australia has expressed its justifiable concerns over the situation in Rakhine State, called on all parties to settle their differences and provided practical assistance to the victims of the violence. It is worth noting, too, that, since 2008, Rohingya refugees in camps in Bangladesh have been included in Australia's humanitarian immigration program.

This carefully considered position, however, may be threatened by a leaflet that appears to be circulating in Burma, claiming that the Australian Prime Minister supports the hardline anti-Muslim stance taken by many Burmese.

---

4   Michelle Nichols, 'UN Chief Urges Careful Handling of Myanmar Rohingyas Issue', *Reuters*, 29 September 2012, www.rohingya.org/un-chief-urges-careful-handling-of-myanmar-rohingyas-issue/.
5   Senator the Hon. Bob Carr, Minister for Foreign Affairs, 'Violence in Rakhine State, Myanmar', Media release, Parliament House, Canberra, 15 June 2012, foreignminister.gov.au/releases/2012/bc_mr_120615.html [page discontinued].
6   'Support for Rakhine State, Myanmar', News release, AusAID, Canberra, 11 September 2012, www.ausaid.gov.au/HotTopics/Pages/Display.aspx?QID=801 [page discontinued].

The document in question purports to be a speech made by Julia Gillard, in which she demands that Muslims in Australia accept the country's predominantly English-speaking Christian culture or leave.[7] The 'speech' seems to have been lifted from the internet and translated into Burmese. At least one copy has been found in Rangoon, but it may have already spread more widely around the country.

The Rangoon copy was given some credibility by being attached to an article on Muslim migration to Rakhine State that was being sold through local bookshops by a member of Burma's Historical Research Department. In an accompanying commentary, Prime Minister Gillard was praised as a resolute world leader, standing up for the rights of Australian citizens in the face of a Muslim threat. The message to Burmese readers was clear.

This kind of scurrilous literature has a long history in Burma. The violence periodically perpetrated against Muslim communities—not just in Rakhine State, but also elsewhere in Burma—has often been sparked, or inflamed, by virulent anti-Muslim propaganda. Peddled by hardline nationalists and religious zealots, such leaflets usually repeat the canards that local Muslims are disrespecting Burmese women and insulting Buddhism.

The Gillard 'speech' is obviously a crude hoax. As with similar reports in the past, it is unlikely to fool anyone who knows anything about Australia's government or political culture.[8] Yet, some in Burma may be inclined to believe it. Quite apart from any lack of familiarity with Australia, the purported remarks by the Prime Minister are likely to find a ready audience among those Burmese who already harbour deep reservations about Muslims in their country—not least the Rohingyas.

---

7   Holte Ender, 'Aussie Prime Minister Julia Gillard to Muslims: Live with Our Beliefs or Get Out', *MadMike'sAmerica.com*, madmikesamerica.com/2011/01/hate-begets-hate-julia-gillard-to-muslims/.
8   David Mikkelson, 'Muslims Out of Australia!', *Snopes.com*, 2005, www.snopes.com/politics/soap box/australia.asp.

45

Burma: The Man has met The Lady

(09:57 AEDT, 23 November 2012)

President Obama's historic visit to Myanmar in November 2012 symbolised not only the dramatic evolution of US–Myanmar relations, but also the changes that were taking place in Myanmar under president Thein Sein. Most of the coverage by journalists and commentators of the visit was balanced and sensible, but there were a number of issues that were not paid the attention they deserved.

To long-time Burma-watchers, and countless others, it was an astonishing sight, enthusiastically conveyed by the international news media: two of the world's most iconographic (not to mention photogenic) figures, both winners of the Nobel Peace Prize, embracing in Rangoon.[1] It was the ultimate hero shot.

To use Nich Farrelly's apt phrase,[2] the international community was for a moment at least transfixed by the image of Barack Obama and Aung San Suu Kyi standing together on the steps of the house where the Burmese opposition leader had spent most of the past 24 years under arrest. More than anything else, perhaps, it demonstrated just how far Burma—and US–Burma relations—had come over the past two and a half years.

---

1 Lindsay Murdoch, 'Obama Courts Burma as US Pivots to Asia', *The Age*, [Melbourne], 19 November 2012, www.theage.com.au/world/obama-courts-burma-as-us-pivots-to-asia-20121119-29m37.html.

2 Nicholas Farrelly, 'Mr Obama Goes to Myanmar', *New Mandala*, 19 November 2012, asiapacific.anu.edu.au/newmandala/2012/11/19/mr-obama-goes-to-myanmar/.

While it only lasted six hours, the Obama visit was highly symbolic. After more than two decades of direct military rule, Burma effectively shed its pariah status. As the US President reminded everyone in his keynote speech at Rangoon University (for generations, the home of political protest in Burma), a host of difficult issues is still to be resolved.[3] However, President Thein Sein's ambitious program of political, economic and social reforms has been endorsed at the highest level.

Before, during and after the Obama visit, there was an avalanche of reporting and commentary from a wide range of academics, journalists and others, covering everything from US global security interests to the colour of Hillary Clinton's pant suits. Most coverage of the visit was balanced and sensible.[4] However, a few of the matters raised—and not raised—in the press are worth a brief comment.

First, there were a few stories that stated that Burma's reform program and readiness to develop its relationship with the US were the result of the Bush administration's earlier hard line.[5] This claim simply cannot be sustained. Not only is there no evidence that external pressures prompted the paradigm shift that occurred in Burma in 2011, but also there is a wide consensus that US sanctions were in fact counterproductive. Without the Obama administration's new policy of 'pragmatic engagement', Washington would not have been in a position to respond to Thein Sein's initiatives in the way it has.

Second, a great deal has been written about how Burma fits into the US 'pivot' towards Asia and now constitutes an important element in the US's strategic competition with China.[6] It would be naive to ignore the implications of closer US–Burma ties for Washington's relations with Beijing, but a fixation on China ignores other imperatives behind the

3   'Remarks by President Obama at the University of Yangon', Office of the Press Secretary, The White House, Washington, DC, 19 November 2012, www.whitehouse.gov/the-press-office/2012/11/19/remarks-president-obama-university-yangon.
4   Evan Osnos, 'Obama to Burma: A "Remarkable Journey"', The New Yorker, 19 November 2012, www.newyorker.com/online/blogs/evanosnos/2012/11/obamas-trip-to-burma-a-remarkable-journey.html.
5   Mary Kissel, 'Bush's Burma Policy, Obama's Victory Lap', The Wall Street Journal, 18 November 2012, online.wsj.com/article/SB10001424127887324439804578115312833763472.html?mod=asia_opinion.
6   Jurgen Haacke, Myanmar: Now a Site for Myanmar–US Geopolitical Competition?, in IDEAS Reports: Special Reports, Nicholas Kitchen (ed.), SR015. LSE IDEAS (London: London School of Economics and Political Science, November 2012), www2.lse.ac.uk/IDEAS/publications/reports/pdf/SR015/SR015-SEAsia-Haacke-.pdf [page discontinued].

Obama visit, not least the US's wish for closer relations with ASEAN. It is also worth remembering that Burma is not a pawn in this game and has already taken steps to balance its growing links with the US with renewed strategic ties to China.

Third, it was noteworthy that the Obama visit produced little comment about Burma's reported nuclear and ballistic missile ambitions or its relationship with North Korea, which was characterised by the US in April as 'a top national security priority'.[7] Yet, during the visit, Thein Sein announced that Burma would sign the additional protocol to the IAEA's Comprehensive Safeguards Agreement and would observe UNSC Resolution 1874 imposing sanctions against North Korea. For his part, Obama hinted at renewed military ties between the US and Burma.

Something else not examined closely was the fact that Obama spent as much time with an opposition member of Burma's parliament as he did with the president of the country hosting his state visit. Given Aung San Suu Kyi's global status as a champion of democracy and a political rock star, this is hardly surprising, but the domestic implications of this meeting attracted little comment. As was the case during her overseas visits earlier this year, few seem to have considered the potential damage that such high-level attention (verging at times on adulation) could do to Aung San Suu Kyi's relationship with Thein Sein, the maintenance of which is essential for continuing stability and progress in Burma.

Finally, it was again apparent that many observers, not just activists and human rights campaigners, but also governments and international organisations, are holding Burma to standards of behaviour and levels of achievement that are rarely applied to other regional countries—even North Korea.[8] There is of course nothing wrong with having high ideals and one always looks in vain for consistency in international relations. However, Burma will struggle to meet all the goals set for it by outsiders, many of which have proven beyond the ability and acceptability of many richer and more developed countries.

---

7   Andrew Selth, 'Kurt Campbell on US–Burma Relations', *The Interpreter*, 27 April 2012, www.lowy interpreter.org/post/2012/04/27/Kurt-Campbell-on-US-Burma-relations.aspx [page discontinued] [now at archive.lowyinstitute.org/the-interpreter/kurt-campbell-us-burma-relations].
8   Andrew Selth, 'Burma and Libya: The Politics of Inconsistency', *The Interpreter*, 17 June 2011, www.lowyinterpreter.org/post/2011/06/17/Burma-and-Libya-The-politics-of-inconsistency.aspx [page discontinued] [now at archive.lowyinstitute.org/the-interpreter/burma-and-libya-politics-inconsistency].

It remains to be seen where US–Burma relations go from here, but the signs are encouraging. Washington warmly welcomed the announcement, made by Thein Sein during the Obama visit, that his government would pursue a range of measures in areas such as human rights, prisoner releases, forced labour, conflict mitigation and reconciliation (including with the country's ethnic minorities), nuclear proliferation and people trafficking.[9] All are issues on which the US has expressed concern over the years, most recently by Obama during his visit.

Despite all the diplomatic handshakes and photo opportunities, however, no one should underestimate the difficulties involved in tackling these issues. There are no easy solutions to Burma's fiendishly complex problems, which will challenge governments in Naypyidaw for many years to come. Some reforms may be easy to introduce into law, but their implementation will prove very difficult. Notwithstanding all the signals given by Obama to the Burmese Government, Washington clearly recognises this fact and seems prepared to cut Naypyidaw considerable slack to maintain the momentum of the reform process.

Given that Burma is only just emerging from the world's most durable military dictatorship, Obama's visit was politically risky. Geostrategic factors aside, however, the President seems to be gambling that the reform process will continue and the country's problems can be managed in a way that will not make his stopover look premature or ill-advised. It is a hope that is widely shared.

---

9   Government of the Republic of the Union of Myanmar, Information Team, Press release No.2/2012, 19 November 2012, www.president-office.gov.mm/en/briefing-room/news/2012/11/19/id-1049 [page discontinued].

46

Burma's police: The long road to reform

(13:45 AEDT, 13 December 2012)

Although it once played a much greater national role, Myanmar's police force had long been overshadowed by the much larger and more powerful armed forces. However, there were signs that, under president Thein Sein, the police were becoming a larger, more professional and more independent part of the state's coercive apparatus.

Last week, television viewers in Burma were treated to a remarkable sight: the police force formally apologising for using excessive force to break up a protest at a mine site and injuring more than 20 Buddhist monks.[1] This unusual event was in response to widespread public criticism of the violence, which will also be the subject of an official inquiry led by Aung San Suu Kyi.[2]

The 'sorry ceremony', in which senior police officers and other officials paid obeisance to Buddhist elders and washed the feet of monks, was prompted in large part by the special place that Buddhism occupies in

---

1   'Burma Apologises for Police Attack on Protesting Monks', *BBC News*, 8 December 2012, www.bbc.co.uk/news/world-asia-20650576.

2   'Suu Kyi Adds Credibility to Burma Mine Probe, Says Academic', *Radio Australia*, 3 December 2012, www.radioaustralia.net.au/international/radio/program/connect-asia/suu-kyi-adds-credibility-to-burma-mine-probe-says-academic/1055212 [page discontinued].

Burmese society.[3] However, it is significant for another reason, for it reflected the Thein Sein Government's wish to reform the police, not only to make this arm of the security forces more effective and to improve its public standing, but also to make it more accountable.

For more than 50 years, whenever reference has been made to Burma's coercive state apparatus, the armed forces (*Tatmadaw*) have always sprung to mind. This is hardly surprising. After all, since General Ne Win's coup in 1962, the country has been governed by the world's most durable military dictatorship. Since the 1990s, Burma has boasted one of the largest armed forces in Southeast Asia.

Throughout this period, troops were not only deployed to combat armed insurgents and narcotics warlords in Burma's countryside, but also routinely used to enforce the law, maintain order and, if deemed necessary, crush civil unrest in urban centres.[4] The *Tatmadaw*'s intelligence apparatus— the dreaded MI—monitored the civilian population and underpinned continued military rule.

Historically speaking, however, another institution was once more important than the armed forces and, arguably, is starting to recover its former role in Burma's internal affairs. This is the country's national police, currently organised as the Myanmar Police Force (MPF).

After the 1962 coup, the police received few resources and little publicity. From time to time, there were references in Burma's state-controlled news media to police campaigns against crime in the cities and police involvement in rural anti-narcotics operations. There were even occasional reports in the press of police corruption and other abuses. Yet the force was viewed merely as the 'younger brother' of the *Tatmadaw* and excited little interest, either in Burma or abroad.

Since the 1988 prodemocracy uprising, international human rights organisations and activist groups have highlighted the activities of the force's 'riot squads' and Special Branch, which in different ways targeted

---

3   'It Is Time for All to Carry Out Purification and Propagation of Sasana Ceremony to Apologise to State Sangha Maha Nayaka Sayadaws for Incidents Stemming from Protest in Letpadaungtaung Copper Mining Project', *New Light of Myanmar*, [Yangon], 8 December 2010, www.networkmyanmar. org/images/stories/PDF13/nlm081212.pdf [page discontinued].

4   Andrew Selth, *Civil–Military Relations in Burma: Portents, Predictions and Possibilities*, Griffith Asia Institute Regional Outlook Paper No.25 (Brisbane: Griffith University, 2010), www.griffith.edu. au/__data/assets/pdf_file/0016/215341/Selth-Regional-Outlook-25.pdf [page discontinued].

anti-regime elements. In 2007, the MPF's blue-helmeted 'combat' battalions initially took the lead role in suppressing the so-called Saffron Revolution.[5] Even then, however, little attention was paid to the police force as a national institution.

That situation is now changing. The MPF is gradually being recognised as a large, increasingly powerful and influential organisation that, in a more modern and civilianised form, seems likely to become a key instrument of state control under the mixed civilian–military government inaugurated in Naypyidaw in March 2011.

Even before President Thein Sein came to power, an effort was being made to expand the MPF's capabilities, improve its performance and reform its culture. The force is now about 80,000 strong, which gives an estimated ratio of one police officer for every 750 Burmese (Australia's national average is about 1:350). This includes 18 battalions of paramilitary police, which are specially equipped to respond to serious outbreaks of civil unrest, such as that seen in Arakan (Rakhine) State earlier this year.

The MPF is grappling with a wide range of problems, with the aim of creating a more professional force. Loyalty to the government is still valued highly, but there is now a greater emphasis in training courses on personal discipline and an increased focus on community policing. Officer recruitment standards have been raised and specialised instruction at all levels has increased. Some steps have been taken to deal with corruption and further measures have been promised.[6]

It remains to be seen how successful this program will be. As developments over the past year demonstrate, such a profound cultural shift will be difficult and will take time. Until that occurs, the force will continue to face accusations of brutality and corruption. Even so, the latest incident suggests not that the reform process is stalling, as some have suggested, but rather that the government is aware of the need for change and is trying to be more responsive to public concerns.[7]

---

5   *Crackdown: Repression of the 2007 Popular Protests in Burma*, Vol.19, No.18(C) (New York: Human Rights Watch, December 2007), www.hrw.org/reports/2007/burma1207/burma1207web.pdf.

6   Aye Nai, 'Corruption Charges Hit Police Chiefs', *Democratic Voice of Burma*, 26 January 2011, www.dvb.no/news/corruption-charges-hit-police-chiefs/13894 [page discontinued].

7   Parameswaran Ponnudurai, 'Is Reform Stalling in Burma?', *Radio Free Asia*, [Washington, DC], 4 December 2010, www.rfa.org/english/east-asia-beat/mine-12042012121852.html.

A particularly thorny issue will be the future relationship between Burma's police and armed forces. If the formal separation of the two institutions in Indonesia in 1999 is any guide, there are bound to be disagreements over their respective roles, areas of jurisdiction and budgets.[8] In Indonesia, the police and army have also (literally) fought over the spoils of corruption.

In Burma's case, much will depend on developments in Naypyidaw—in particular, the success of Thein Sein's ambitious program of political, economic and social reforms. Another critical factor will be the willingness of the *Tatmadaw*'s leadership to further loosen its grip on Burmese society. The process will bear watching closely, though, as it holds out the promise of a more capable and professional police force—something that will be essential if Burma is ever to make an orderly transition to genuine and sustained democratic rule.

---

8   *Indonesia: The Deadly Cost of Poor Policing*, Asia Report No.218 (Jakarta/Brussels: International Crisis Group, 16 February 2012), www.crisisgroup.org/-/media/Files/asia/south-east-asia/indonesia/218%20Indonesia%20--%20The%20Deadly%20Cost%20of%20Poor%20Policing. pdf [page discontinued] [now at www.crisisgroup.org/asia/south-east-asia/indonesia/indonesia-deadly-cost-poor-policing].

47

Burma: Eyes on the prize

(10:14 AEDT, 18 December 2012)

When Myanmar's president Thein Sein was awarded a number of major prizes and stories began to appear suggesting he may even be nominated for the 2012 Nobel Peace Prize, many activists and human rights campaigners were outraged. Yet, judged against the historical record and Thein Sein's achievements, these honours did not seem completely out of place.

Last Friday, *Foreign Policy* magazine named Burma's President Thein Sein and opposition leader Aung San Suu Kyi as the two top global thinkers for 2012.[1] On the same day, Thein Sein was named Asian of the Year by the Singapore-based *Straits Times*.[2]

These days, few people are surprised when Aung San Suu Kyi receives such accolades, but this level of public recognition for Thein Sein has prompted a range of comment, both about the former general and about the current status of Burma's 'disciplined democracy'.

Before the inauguration of its new parliament in March 2011, and the launch of Thein Sein's ambitious reform program, Burma's government was condemned as a brutal military dictatorship, guilty of appalling

---

1   'The FP Top 100 Global Thinkers', *Foreign Policy*, 26 November 2012, www.foreignpolicy.com/2012globalthinkers.
2   'Multimedia: 90 Seconds with Thein Sein', *The Straits Times*, [Singapore], 14 December 2012, www.straitstimes.com/through-the-lens/story/90-seconds-thein-sein [page discontinued].

human rights abuses and nefarious dealings with pariah states like North Korea. The only prize it ever won was to be labelled one of the world's most repressive and corrupt regimes.

For her steadfast and nonviolent opposition to this regime, Aung San Suu Kyi was given the Nobel Peace Prize, the US Congressional Gold Medal of Honour, the Jawaharlal Nehru Award for International Understanding, the Sakharov Prize for Freedom of Thought and numerous other prestigious awards.[3]

Yet Aung San Suu Kyi is now an elected member of Burma's new parliament and its government is winning warm (albeit still guarded) praise from the international community. President Thein Sein is playing host to a stream of world leaders, most recently Barack Obama. He in turn has been invited to make state visits to numerous countries, including the US and the UK, which were once the strongest opponents of Burma's military regime.

In addition to those announced last week, Thein Sein has been considered for several other honours and awards. For example, he is soon to be presented with the In Pursuit of Peace Award by the International Crisis Group (ICG). He has been tipped to be *TIME* magazine's Person of the Year (along with Aung San Suu Kyi). And, in what can only be described as a supreme irony, it appears he was a nominee for the 2012 Nobel Peace Prize.[4]

The mere suggestion of such high-level recognition for the President has provoked protests from human rights campaigners and other activists, who point to Burma's continuing harsh treatment of political prisoners, Muslim Rohingyas, members of the ethnic minorities and civil protesters. One British MP recently queried whether, during Thein Sein's visit to the UK, the President could be arrested and charged with war crimes.[5]

---

3   Mary Hathaway, 'Aung San Suu Kyi Picks up Congressional Gold Medal', *ABC News*, 19 September 2012, abcnews.go.com/blogs/politics/2012/09/aung-san-suu-kyi-picks-up-congressional-gold-medal/.

4   'Nobel Peace Prize 2012: PRIO Director's Speculations', *PRIO* (Oslo: Peace Research Institute Oslo, 2012), www.prio.no/About/PeacePrize/PRIO-Directors-Speculations-2012/.

5   'Thein Sein Prosecution Raised in UK Parliament', *Burma Campaign UK*, 7 December 2012, www.burmacampaign.org.uk/index.php/news-and-reports/news-stories/thein-sein-prosecution-raised-in-uk-parliament/142.

Discussions of honours and awards tend to generate more heat than light. To put the current public debate into perspective, it is worth looking briefly at the nature of these awards, why they are given and, in particular, who has received them in the past.

The ICG has always been forward leaning in its assessments of developments in Burma. While not blind to the former regime's record of abuses and the current government's shortcomings, the ICG has consistently based its policy recommendations on the principle of positive reinforcement. While this has attracted some strong criticism, granting an award to Thein Sein for his 'visionary leadership' is consistent with this broad approach.[6]

Like other media outlets, *TIME*'s interest is in people who have been particularly newsworthy over the past 12 months. The magazine's editors claim to take into account the views of their readers, but they do not apply any test for high ideals, observance of democratic values or contributions to world peace.[7] Past Man (now Person) of the Year covers have featured Adolf Hitler, Joseph Stalin, Chiang Kai-shek, Yuri Andropov, Ayatollah Khomeini and Vladimir Putin.

For its part, the Nobel Peace Prize is no stranger to controversy.[8] While many of the Nobel Committee's decisions have been popular and widely respected—as was the case when Aung San Suu Kyi received the award in 1991—others have been greeted with much less enthusiasm. Past recipients have included several leaders of authoritarian governments, two former terrorists and at least one statesman accused of crimes against humanity.[9]

One of the notable characteristics of the Nobel Peace Prize, however, has been its recognition of world leaders and other public figures who have been prepared to take political risks and embrace bold change, despite their personal histories or official positions. Thus, the committee has

---

6   'In Pursuit of Peace Award Dinner 2013', International Crisis Group, New York, 21 April 2013, www.crisisgroup.org/en/support/event-calendar/annual-award-dinner-2013.aspx [page discontinued].

7   Hannah Beech, 'Who Should Be TIME's Person of the Year 2012?', *TIME*, 26 November 2012, www.time.com/time/specials/packages/article/0,28804,2128881_2128882_2129196,00.html [page discontinued] [now at content.time.com/time/specials/packages/article/0,28804,2128881_212888 2_2129196,00.html].

8   Jamie Frater, 'Top 10 Controversial Nobel Peace Prize Winners', *Listverse*, 17 October 2007 [Updated 27 July 2014], listverse.com/2007/10/17/top-10-controversial-nobel-peace-prize-winners/.

9   Christopher Hitchens, *The Trial of Henry Kissinger* (London: Verso, 2002).

felt able to recognise characters like Menachem Begin, F.W. De Klerk and Yasser Arafat—none of whom enjoyed a reputation as a conciliator or peacemaker.[10]

At times, dramatically changing the political climate and offering hope for real improvements in people's lives seem to have been sufficient grounds for the Nobel Committee to make its choice. Barack Obama was awarded the 2009 Peace Prize less than a year after taking office, more on the basis of his lofty aspirations and more idealistic approach to world affairs than as the result of any specific achievements.[11]

There is no denying that Burma still faces difficult problems and that, measured against widely accepted international standards, its reform program has a long way to go. This would argue for caution in handing out bouquets to the current government or any of its representatives.[12] Yet, given the precedents, the choice of Thein Sein for international recognition—even a prestigious award—does not seem as surprising, or out of place, as it might at first appear.

10   'All Nobel Peace Prizes', The Nobel Prize, www.nobelprize.org/nobel_prizes/peace/laureates/.

11   'The Nobel Peace Prize for 2009: Barack H. Obama', The Nobel Prize, Oslo, 9 October 2009, www.nobelprize.org/nobel_prizes/peace/laureates/2009/press.html.

12   Benedict Rogers, 'Thein Sein and the Nobel Peace Prize', *Democratic Voice of Burma*, 2012, www. dvb.no/analysis/thein-sein-and-the-nobel-peace-prize/24204 [page discontinued].

2013

48

Defence relations with Burma: Our future past

(12:08 AEDT, 4 March 2013)

When president Thein Sein took office in 2011 and began an ambitious program of political, economic and social reforms, Myanmar began to shed its pariah status, making it easier for Western countries to contemplate the development of military relations. Australia had a long history of defence links with Myanmar, and there were suggestions that the resumption of such ties was going to be part of the 2013 Defence White Paper process.

John Blaxland's persuasive piece on the possible renewal of defence cooperation between Australia and Burma (Myanmar) prompts a look at past contacts in this field.[1] For it is a little-known fact that Australia was once an important source of military training and advice for the Burmese armed forces (known as the *Tatmadaw*). It could become so again.[2]

Between 1948, when Burma regained its independence from Britain, and General Ne Win's coup d'état in 1962, Australia provided training for more than 90 Burmese military officers and noncommissioned officers.

---

1   John Blaxland, 'Myanmar: Time for Australian Defence Cooperation', *The Interpreter*, 23 October 2012, www.lowyinterpreter.org/post/2012/10/23/Myanmar-Time-for-Australian-Defence-Cooperation.aspx [page discontinued] [now at archive.lowyinstitute.org/the-interpreter/myanmar-time-australian-defence-cooperation].
2   Lindsay Murdoch, 'PM Raises Prospect of Defence Ties with Burma', *Sydney Morning Herald*, 6 November 2012, www.smh.com.au/opinion/political-news/pm-raises-prospect-of-defence-ties-with-burma-20121105-28u6m.html.

They were drawn from the army and air force as part of a major effort by the fledgling *Tatmadaw* to develop its technical and leadership capabilities (there is no record of any naval trainees).

Australia was also considered a source of expertise in areas relevant to Burma's national security. In 1957, an Australian army officer was chosen over candidates from several other countries to train the Burmese in counterinsurgency warfare, in Burma. In 1960, he was made a strategic advisor to the *Tatmadaw*.[3]

When the xenophobic Ne Win seized power, this assignment was terminated and most foreign military contacts ceased. However, a small number of Burmese officers still attended training courses in Australia, the last in 1987. Despite its alliance with the US, Australia was viewed by Rangoon as a friendly country prepared to provide assistance to Burma, in both military and civil fields, without trying to exert undue political influence or subvert its trainees.[4]

After the *Tatmadaw* crushed a nationwide prodemocracy uprising in 1988, such defence contacts ceased, as Australia joined wider Western efforts to isolate and punish the new military regime. Yet, even then, Australia took a measured approach and kept open important lines of communication. Australia's defence attaché (DA) had been withdrawn from Rangoon in 1979, mainly for financial reasons, but after 1988, the DA in Bangkok remained accredited to Burma and continued to make occasional visits.

It was reported in January that defence relations with Burma will be considered as part of the 2013 White Paper.[5] Given the remarkable changes taking place under President Thein Sein—believed by many to be 'Burma's Gorbachev'—this move is timely.[6] In both practical and symbolic terms, the outcome of those deliberations could have far-reaching implications.

---

3   John Farquharson, 'Serong, Francis Philip (Ted) (1915–2002)', *Obituaries Australia* (Canberra: National Centre of Biography, The Australian National University, 2002), oa.anu.edu.au/obituary/serong-francis-philip-ted-901.

4   Ademola Adeleke, 'The Strings of Neutralism: Burma and the Colombo Plan', *Pacific Affairs*, Vol.76, No.4, Winter 2003–04, pp.593–610, www.pacificaffairs.ubc.ca/files/2011/09/adeleke.pdf [page discontinued] [now at www.jstor.org/stable/i40001464].

5   Cameron Stewart, 'Defence Door to Myanmar Ajar', *The Australian*, 24 January 2013, www.theaustralian.com.au/national-affairs/defence/modest-relations-considered-to-support-reform/story-e6frg8yo-1226560412364 [page discontinued].

6   Joshua Hammer, 'Myanmar's Gorbachev?', *The New Yorker*, 14 January 2012, www.newyorker.com/online/blogs/newsdesk/2012/01/myanmars-gorbachev.html.

Over the past 24 years, activists have successfully painted the *Tatmadaw* as a brutal and corrupt military machine that has not only dominated Burma's political affairs, but has also been guilty of terrible human rights abuses. Some now claim that nothing has changed. They point to the strong military bias in the 2008 constitution, the excessive force used against the Rohingyas in Arakan State in 2012[7] and the bitter civil war in Kachin State.[8]

It is precisely because the *Tatmadaw* remains the most powerful political institution in the country, however, and continues to employ harsh measures against its opponents, that a carefully managed program of external engagement with the armed forces is so important.

Despite continuing scepticism on the part of some commentators, it is clear that Thein Sein's reforms are real and that Burma has entered a new phase of political, economic and social development. The Burmese Government still faces many challenges and, in most areas, reforms will be slow. Old habits on the part of the security forces will die hard, particularly among those with vested interests in the old system. However, the best way to encourage further reform is to strengthen the hand of the reformers and to give the armed forces a larger stake in a more democratic Burma.[9]

There are many officers in the *Tatmadaw* who broadly welcome their government's reforms and share Thein Sein's wish to see Burma become a more modern, prosperous, stable and respected country. By inviting such people to Australia for training in nonlethal disciplines—such as those offered by staff colleges, engineering schools and medical colleges—Australia can expose them to international norms, promote new ways of thinking and encourage them to consider different ways of approaching Burma's complex problems.

As a recent visit to Burma revealed, the *Tatmadaw* is keen to resume contacts with developed Western countries. Not only would this help balance its links with other states—notably, China—but also Burma's military is hungry for the technology, expertise and ideas of the West.

---

7   'Burma: Government Forces Targeting Rohingya Muslims', *News* (New York: Human Rights Watch, 31 July 2012), www.hrw.org/news/2012/07/31/burma-government-forces-targeting-rohingya-muslims.
8   Anthony Davis, 'Pyrrhic Victory in Myanmar', *Asia Times Online*, [Hong Kong], 31 January 2013, www.atimes.com/atimes/Southeast_Asia/OA31Ae03.html [page discontinued].
9   Morten Pedersen, 'The Real Threat to Democracy in Myanmar', *The Fletcher Forum of World Affairs*, 26 February 2012, www.fletcherforum.org/2013/02/26/mortensen/ [page discontinued].

The door is already open. During his December 2012 visit, Barack Obama foreshadowed closer US–Burma defence ties[10] and last month, for the first time, Burma sent a team of observers to Exercise Cobra Gold in Thailand.[11]

No one realistically expects that a six-month staff course will turn Burmese officers into pocket democrats, able to influence national events on their return. Some may even reject the lessons offered to them. Yet, it would seem worth making a modest investment in this area while the need is greatest and the outcomes potentially so beneficial. Also, until the reappointment of a resident DA, these officers can offer points of entry for Australian officials into a system that for decades has been closed to them.[12]

It is perhaps also worth making the point that, due largely to the efforts of Burmese exiles, human rights campaigners and other supporters of opposition leader Aung San Suu Kyi, Burma has long been held to a higher standard than that applied to any of its regional neighbours, even North Korea.[13] Australia already has close defence ties—including exchanges of personnel—with several countries that have less than perfect records when it comes to their systems of government and the conduct of their armed forces.

Notwithstanding Thein Sein's ambitious reform program, the *Tatmadaw* will exert a strong influence on Burma's government, economy and society for the foreseeable future. In considering the question of bilateral defence relations, the Australian Government can look at Burma's dark past and imperfect present or it can look to the future and take the opportunity to assist in the development of a more professional, capable and openminded officer corps. That would be in not only Burma's long-term interests, but also Australia's.

---

10   Aung Zaw, 'Can US–Burma Defense Ties Return Generals to the Barracks?', *The Irrawaddy*, 21 December 2012, www.irrawaddy.org/archives/21815.

11   Donna Miles, 'Exercise Cobra Gold 2013 Kicks Off in Thailand', American Forces Press Service, US Department of Defense, 11 February 2013, www.defense.gov/News/NewsArticle.aspx?ID=119256 [page discontinued].

12   John Blaxland, 'Myanmar: Time for Australian Defence Cooperation', *Security Challenges*, Vol.7, No.4, Summer 2011, pp.63–76, asiancentury.dpmc.gov.au/sites/default/files/public-submissions/dr-john-blaxland_0.pdf [page discontinued] [now at www.jstor.org/stable/26467117?seq=1#metadata_info_tab_contents].

13   David I. Steinberg, 'Disparate Sanctions: US Sanctions, North Korea and Burma', *East Asia Forum*, 23 June 2011, www.eastasiaforum.org/2011/06/23/disparate-sanctions-us-sanctions-north-korea-and-burma/.

49

Burma's fractious polity: The price of democracy?

(11:32 AEDT, 14 March 2013)

While understandable in certain contexts, the use of short descriptive titles for large, diverse and changing groups of people in Myanmar sometimes led to inaccurate or misleading descriptions of internal developments. There was a need for the careful use of language and, as far as possible within the constraints of various reporting mediums, clear recognition of the complexity and dynamism of the country's political scene.

It has often been said that one of the greatest challenges faced by academics, journalists and others who write about international affairs is to describe complex and unfamiliar issues succinctly, and in ways that can be understood by lay readers, while remaining accurate and objective. A recent visit to Burma has brought home the truth of this observation.

It has long been the case that, in speaking about developments in Burma, observers have referred to various institutions and political groupings by using short descriptive titles. Thus, we have read about 'the government', 'the armed forces', 'the opposition', 'the monks' and so on. This is an easy and economical way of referring to large bodies of people who appear to have common backgrounds or share certain characteristics.

There is a real danger, however, that in using such shorthand terms, observers will paint a picture that is inaccurate or misleading. For each of these brief descriptors disguises large, diverse and constantly changing bodies of people with widely differing views. While their members may identify publicly with specific organisations, they are rarely a homogeneous mass, but more a loose collection of groups clustered around particular policies or personalities.

For example, since forming the majority in Burma's national parliament in 2011, the Union Solidarity Development Party (USDP) has revealed a range of attitudes towards President Thein Sein's ambitious reform program and the role of elected MPs. Even the 25 per cent of parliament made up of serving military officers has demonstrated a surprising degree of flexibility.[1] It cannot be taken for granted that these officers will always vote as a bloc in favour of the government.

Indeed, Burma's large armed forces appear to hold views of the government's reforms that range from unconditional support to total rejection. Given the dearth of reliable information, it is not possible to be certain, but most seem to lie somewhere between these two extremes, with members supporting some aspects of Burma's democratisation process, while opposing others.[2] The point is that there is no uniform 'military' view.

The opposition movement is even more diverse, with myriad parties and organisations, each following its own path, and often owing their allegiance to powerful patrons. The NLD, for example, has always been riven by factional disputes, some of which continue to test its cohesion and unity.[3] There are also tensions between the NLD and other groups, including the 88 Generation and some ethnic-based parties.

For its part, the Buddhist clergy—usually described simply as 'the monks'—is also a very mixed bag. During the 2007 'Saffron Revolution', for example, few commentators pointed out that Burma's 400,000 or so monks represented a wide range of views. Most were sympathetic to the

---

1   Rangoon Correspondent, 'Burma's Parliament Emerges from the Shadows', *Inside Story*, 26 March 2012, insidestory.org.au/burmas-parliament-emerges-from-the-shadows/.
2   Andrew R.C. Marshall and Jason Szep, 'Special Report: Myanmar Military's Next Campaign—Shoring Up Power', *Reuters*, 15 November 2012, www.reuters.com/article/2012/11/16/us-myanmar-military-idUSBRE8AF02620121116.
3   Phyo Wai Kyaw and Than Naing Soe, 'NLD Facing More Unrest Over Assembly', *Myanmar Times*, [Yangon], 28 January 2013, www.mmtimes.com/national-news/3936-nld-facing-more-unrest-over-assembly.html.

initial aims of the demonstrators, who sought relief for the country's poor. But many monks declined to join the street marches and others were reportedly unhappy when the protests took on a strong political tone.[4]

Another sector frequently misrepresented is that of Burma's ethnic minorities. According to the government, there are 135 'national races'. Even if this contentious claim is accepted, bald references to 'the Kachin', 'the Karen', 'the Shan' and so on fail to take into account the many different viewpoints and often deep divisions found within these communities.[5] Nor is it necessarily the case that the country's ethnic minorities are faithfully represented by the armed groups that bear their names.

At times, certain political figures and institutions in Burma have been reduced to caricatures. Perhaps the most obvious example of this phenomenon is the treatment routinely accorded to Aung San Suu Kyi and the security forces. Luc Besson's 2011 movie *The Lady*, for example, raised the Nobel Peace Prize winner to the level of a secular saint, while portraying Burma's military leaders as brutal and superstitious oafs, lacking any real concern for the country or its people. The same crude approach has been taken towards Burma's police force.

There is no denying Aung San Suu Kyi's many qualities, but uncritical biographies and adulatory articles in the news media do not assist the public to understand the complexities either of the person or of Burmese politics.[6] She has long been an active player in Burma's power games and, as such, deserves to be judged against the same criteria as those applied to other major political figures.[7]

Similarly, an effort needs to be made to try to understand the mindset of Burma's military leaders. Before 2011, for example, it was easy to question their idiosyncratic notions of internal and external security threats, but

---

4   Kyaw Yin Hlaing, 'Challenging the Authoritarian State: Buddhist Monks and Peaceful Protests in Burma', *The Fletcher Forum of World Affairs*, Vol.32, No.1, Winter 2008, pp.125–144, ui04e.moit. tufts.edu/forum/archives/pdfs/32-1pdfs/Kyaw.pdf [page discontinued] [now at dl.tufts.edu/concern/pdfs/qf85nn79h].

5   Ashley South, 'Karen Nationalist Communities: The "Problem" of Diversity', *Contemporary Southeast Asia*, Vol.29, No.1, April 2007, pp.55–76, www.jstor.org/discover/10.2307/25798814?uid=3737536&uid=2129&uid=2&uid=70&uid=4&sid=21101745551823.

6   Rowan Callick, 'Touched by the Divine, Suu Kyi is Set Apart by Her Goodness', *The Australian*, 14 February 2013, www.theaustralian.com.au/arts/books/touched-by-the-divine-aung-san-suu-kyi-is-set-apart-through-her-goodness/story-e6frg8nf-1226577272972 [page discontinued].

7   Billy Tea, 'Suu Kyi's Fading Glory', *Asia Times Online*, [Hong Kong], 9 February 2013, www.atimes.com/atimes/Southeast_Asia/OB09Ae01.html [page discontinued].

such views appear to have been genuinely held, and probably still inform aspects of state policy. Dismissing the old regime as simply a collection of thugs played well with the activist community at the time, but to continue to do so risks perpetuating some serious misperceptions and, as a consequence, flawed policies.[8]

Arguably, the fractiousness and volatility of modern Burmese politics is evidence of a more democratic system of government, with all its strengths and weaknesses. With the more relaxed atmosphere under President Thein Sein has come increased space for the population to join political parties and civil society organisations and to openly discuss new approaches to the country's future. However, there is a danger that, should the domestic political climate become too heated, it will prompt a backlash from conservative elements. This has happened before.

One of the main reasons why General Ne Win engineered a military 'caretaker government' in 1958, and mounted a coup in 1962, was that Burma's civilian politicians were considered dangerously incompetent and corrupt.[9] The armed forces leadership feared that the politicians' internecine squabbles and pursuit of personal gain would reduce the country to chaos and make it vulnerable to its enemies. Times have changed, but it would not be surprising if some members of the armed forces hierarchy still hold such views.

All these factors argue not only for the careful use of language when speaking about Burma, but also, as far as possible within the constraints of the various reporting mediums, for clear recognition of the complexity and dynamism of the country's political scene.

---

8   Colin Powell, 'It's Time to Turn the Tables on Burma's Thugs', *The Wall Street Journal*, 12 June 2003, 2001-2009.state.gov/secretary/former/powell/remarks/2003/21466.htm.
9   Mary P. Callahan, *Democracy in Burma: The Lessons of History*, NBR Analysis, Vol.9, No.3 (Washington, DC: The National Bureau of Asian Research, May 1998), pp.5–26, www.nbr.org/publications/element.aspx?id=96.

50

Burma's Muslims: A primer

(09:17 AEDT, 27 March 2013)

Another round of anti-Muslim violence in Myanmar prompted a survey of the different Muslim communities in the country, their relations with the central government, popular attitudes towards local Muslims and the likelihood of further outbreaks of civil unrest.

Given the spate of articles in the news media that connect the anti-Muslim riots in Burma last week[1] with the sectarian violence in Rakhine (Arakan) State last year,[2] it may be helpful to sketch out the multifaceted nature of Burma's Muslim communities and some of the underlying issues.

Burma is often left off lists of Southeast Asian countries with sizeable Muslim populations. Yet, at least 4 per cent of Burmese are Muslims or, by most counts, well over 2 million people. A large number of Muslims in Burma are not recognised as citizens, however, and thus do not figure in the official statistics. Some unlikely claims range as high as 20 per cent, or more than 11 million people. A few websites include up to 1.5 million Muslims currently living overseas.

---

1   Thomas Fuller and Wai Moe, 'Sectarian Clashes Are Reported in Central Myanmar', *The New York Times*, 21 March 2013, www.nytimes.com/2013/03/22/world/asia/sectarian-clashes-are-reported-in-central-myanmar.html?_r=0.
2   *'The Government Could Have Stopped This': Sectarian Violence and Ensuing Abuses in Burma's Arakan State* (New York: Human Rights Watch, August 2012), www.hrw.org/sites/default/files/reports/burma0812webwcover_0.pdf.

Most of Burma's Muslims are Sunnis. They are widely dispersed and notable for the diversity of their ethnic backgrounds, socioeconomic status and degrees of social and political integration into mainstream society. There is some correlation between ethnicity and religion, and not all Muslims are from Burma's 135 recognised 'national races', but the picture is not a simple one.[3]

The oldest Muslim group in Burma can trace its origins back to the eighth century, but most look to the thirteenth and fourteenth centuries, when their ancestors arrived in Burma as traders, court servants and mercenaries. Some achieved high office. They were known as Pathi or Zerbadee—a term that usually denoted someone with a Burmese mother and Muslim father. Now known as 'Burmese Muslims', they are linguistically and culturally integrated into Burmese society.

There is a small Chinese Muslim community—found mainly in the northeast—known as the Panthay. Their origins go back to ethnic Chinese who settled in Burma during the thirteenth century, but most are descendants of Chinese Muslims who fled to Burma after the collapse of a sultanate in Yunnan in the nineteenth century. Another group, the Kamans, live in Rakhine State and there are some Malay Muslims, or Pashu, in southern Burma.

Following the British conquests of Burma in 1826, 1852 and 1885, there were major inflows of Muslims from the Subcontinent. They entered as immigrants, businessmen, officials and labourers. Before World War II, more than one-third of all Burmese Muslims were Indian. There were then over one million Indians in Burma, out of a total population of 16 million. Many left during the Japanese invasion in 1942 or after Ne Win's military coup in 1962.

The largest Muslim community in Burma—estimated to be about 800,000 strong—calls itself 'Rohingyas'. Most live in Rakhine State, but there is also a sizeable number in Rangoon. Broadly speaking, they are ethnically South Asian and speak a characteristic Bengali dialect.

---

3   Khin Maung Yin, 'Salience of Ethnicity among Burman Muslims: A Study in Identity Formation', *Intellectual Discourse*, Vol.13, No.2, 2005, pp.161–179, iium.edu.my/intdiscourse/index.php/islam/article/viewFile/108/110 [page discontinued] [now at journals.iium.edu.my/intdiscourse/index.php/islam/article/view/108].

Controversy surrounds almost everything to do with this group—even its name[4]—and the picture has been further clouded by inaccurate and biased commentaries in print and on the internet.

Some Rohingyas trace their ancestry back to Muslim kingdoms in the Arakan area during the fifteenth and sixteenth centuries, but most seem related to Indians who arrived during the British colonial period. There was another influx after 1945, and further inflows followed natural disasters in East Pakistan and Bangladesh's 1971 war of independence. In 1974, the Bangladeshi Ambassador in Rangoon stated that there were about half a million illegal Bengali immigrants in Burma.[5]

Full rights for Muslims were enshrined in the 1947 constitution, but in 1960 Buddhism was made Burma's state religion and, after the 1962 coup, the military regime tended to equate Muslims with colonial rule and the exploitation of Burma by foreigners. Muslims were not permitted to run for public office, join the security forces or work as civil servants. The number of mosques was restricted, some Muslim cemeteries were destroyed and a number of madrassas were closed.

'Burmese Muslims' and 'Chinese Muslims' are now largely assimilated into Burmese society, but some other communities are not. In 1982, the government decreed that all citizens must be able to trace their line to forebears who lived in Burma before 1823—that is, before the first Anglo-Burmese War.[6] As was doubtless intended, the impact of this policy was mainly felt by the Rohingyas.[7]

Religious tensions have never been far from the surface. Since the twelfth century, Burma has been predominantly Buddhist—a philosophy that has become deeply woven into the fabric of the local culture. Islam, however,

---

4   'The Rohingya Question', *Network Myanmar*, www.networkmyanmar.org/component/content/article/106/The-Rohingya-Question [page discontinued].

5   'A Bangladesh View from December 1975: FCO Archives Transcript', *Network Myanmar*, www.networkmyanmar.org/images/stories/PDF13/kaiser-obrien.pdf [page discontinued].

6   Tin Maung Maung Than and Moe Thuzar, 'Myanmar's Rohingya Dilemma', *ISEAS Perspective*, 9 July 2012, www.networkmyanmar.org/images/stories/PDF13/iseas-rohingya.pdf [page discontinued] [now at www.researchgate.net/publication/259625408_Myanmar's_Rohingya_Dilemma].

7   *Myanmar: Storm Clouds on the Horizon*, Asia Report No.238 (Brussels: International Crisis Group, 12 November 2012), www.crisisgroup.org/~/media/Files/asia/south-east-asia/burma-myanmar/238-myanmar-storm-clouds-on-the-horizon.pdf [page discontinued] [now at www.crisisgroup.org/asia/south-east-asia/myanmar/myanmar-storm-clouds-horizon].

grew incrementally through historical accident and natural development. As a result, Muslims became socially and politically marginalised, particularly after Burma regained its independence in 1948.

For example, anti-Indian riots in Rangoon during the 1930s were sparked by economic issues, but they soon became racial and religious in character. More recent unrest has centred on popular fears of economic domination by Muslims and competition for land. There have been disputes over property and marriage laws. Racist literature and smear campaigns have also alleged Muslim insults to Buddhism, Burmese women and the 'Burmese race'.

Few parts of Burma have been unaffected. For example, anti-Muslim riots occurred in Mandalay in 1997, in Toungoo and Sittwe in 2001 and in Meiktila and Yamethin last week. The Rohingyas in Rakhine State, however, have been the most severely treated. In 1978, 200,000 fled to Bangladesh to escape persecution. After another pogrom in 1992, 300,000 followed. Last year, an estimated 52,000 Rohingyas were displaced in the sectarian violence. Many have been killed.

Burma's Muslims have found it difficult to fight back. They are divided among themselves and there has been no single organisation able to represent all their interests. Watched equally closely by the authorities and the local citizenry, most Muslims have been essentially nonpolitical and tried to keep a low profile. There has been little religious proselytising, although some community leaders have referred to the plight of Muslims in Burma and elsewhere.

Before 2011, Burma's Muslims had little outside contact. Trips to Mecca were limited by the regime. There were occasional appeals for foreign help but, some UN aid to refugee camps aside, they produced few practical results. That situation is now changing, as the freedoms enjoyed under President Thein Sein are encouraging Burma's Muslims to speak out more strongly. The Rohingyas, for example, are now more adept at using the internet to present their case.[8]

There have been a few Muslim insurgent groups, but with one exception they have been small and ineffective. Some attempts have been made to link the Rohingyas to international terrorist organisations, citing the

---

8   Sarah Logan, 'The Rohingya and the Viral Ummah', *Circuit: International Relations and Information Technology*, 14 March 2013, ircircuit.com/?p=265 [page discontinued].

obvious triggers for their radicalisation. To date, any such ties appear to have been slight, but such fears have probably been encouraged since the 2012 unrest by expressions of support from prominent Islamic extremists.[9]

It has been suggested by some commentators that the latest outbreaks of anti-Muslim unrest have occurred because, under Thein Sein's reformist government, the Burmese people are now free to vent their deepest feelings.[10] This may have been a contributing factor but, as noted above, religious intolerance is not new to Burma. Indeed, before 2011, the regime reportedly encouraged some anti-Muslim riots to divert attention from its own failings.

The key issue now is not what has happened in the past, but how Naypyidaw will respond to sectarian violence in the future. Even if the government is determined to tackle social tensions in a more sensitive manner—and last year's abuses in Rakhine State showed how difficult that can be—it will still face enormous challenges. For the problem is not just the tactics of the security forces, but also the discriminatory policies and community attitudes in Burma that make anti-Muslim unrest likely to recur. These are issues that few Burmese politicians seem willing to seriously address.

---

9   'Abu Bakar Bashir Threatens War if Burma Harms Muslim Rohingyas', *Herald Sun*, [Melbourne], 3 August 2012, www.heraldsun.com.au/news/world/abu-bakar-bashir-threatens-war-if-myanmar-harms-muslim-rohingyas/story-fnd134gw-1226442628062.
10   'Ashes and Fear in Myanmar Town', *The Australian*, 23 March 2013, www.theaustralian.com.au/news/world/ashes-and-fear-in-myanmar-town/story-e6frg6so-1226603788468 [page discontinued] [now at www.theaustralian.com.au/news/world/ashes-and-fear-in-myanmar-town/news-story/b806 cb0a6c0b8fa1c9857df7dc5effc6].

51

Aung San Suu Kyi: A pilgrim's progress

(15:34 AEDT, 7 May 2013)

For decades, Aung San Suu Kyi was a democratic icon, held to be without fault or peer, floating above the grubby political fray. Once she became an elected politician, however, she was obliged to face the harsh realities of retail politics. She could no longer take refuge in broad principles and Buddhist precepts. This inevitably led to more critical news reports about her and her policies, both within Myanmar and outside it.

There was a time when to criticise Aung San Suu Kyi was to court a firestorm of angry responses from her legion of supporters, who ranged from radical activists to conservative Western officials.[1] She was considered by many to be without fault and without peer.

That situation has now changed, as the Burmese opposition leader has gone from being a democracy icon to a practising politician—a process that has obliged her to adopt public positions on a wide range of contentious issues. Criticisms are now being levelled at Aung San Suu Kyi from many quarters, both within Burma and outside it. Questions have even been raised about her future leadership role—something that would have been unthinkable not long ago.[2]

---

1   Cathy Scott-Clark and Adrian Levy, 'Can Aung San Suu Kyi Lead While Captive?', *The Guardian*, [London], 11 November 2008, www.guardian.co.uk/world/2008/nov/11/burma-aung-san-suu-kyi.
2   Karl-Ludwig Gunsche, 'Icon Under Fire: Burma's Suu Kyi Eyes Presidency Amid Criticism', *Der Spiegel*, [Hamburg], 3 August 2012, www.spiegel.de/international/world/aung-san-suu-kyi-eyes-burmese-presidency-but-faces-growing-criticism-a-887665.html.

For more than 20 years, Aung San Suu Kyi was the living symbol of Burma's nonviolent struggle for democracy and human rights in the face of the world's most durable military dictatorship. Despite being under house arrest for long periods, and denied access to her family, she remained true to her convictions. She inspired millions with her high ideals and dignified resistance to oppression. This earned her the 1991 Nobel Peace Prize and numerous other prestigious international awards.[3]

It did not hurt her global standing that Aung San Suu Kyi was also an intelligent, English-speaking and attractive woman. This stood in stark contrast to Burma's exclusively male military leadership, which was frequently caricatured by activists, the international news media and even some foreign governments as a collection of superstitious and corrupt thugs.[4] The differences between them were made even more obvious by the regime's blatant human rights abuses and seemingly irrational policies.

Being denied a public voice for so long, Aung San Suu Kyi's views on many important issues were unknown. Even when able to speak publicly, she tended to express herself in terms of broad democratic principles and Buddhist moral precepts. This may have reflected her party's lack of a detailed and agreed policy platform, but it encouraged her supporters, both inside Burma and outside it, to project on to her all their hopes and dreams. Even by some experienced observers, she came to be seen as the answer to all of Burma's complex problems.

Indeed, she routinely attracted accolades like 'the bravest and most moral person in the world'—giving her enormous moral authority.[5] This was difficult to exercise inside Burma, but she gained a strong following overseas and had a marked influence on the attitudes of the international community. For years, she effectively determined the parameters of US policy towards Burma.[6] People like UK Prime Minister Gordon

3   'The Nobel Peace Prize 1991', The Nobel Prize, Oslo, www.nobelprize.org/nobel_prizes/peace/laureates/1991/.

4   Colin L. Powell, 'It's Time to Turn the Tables on Burma's Thugs', The Wall Street Journal, 12 June 2003, online.wsj.com/article/0,,SB105537654192139700,00.html.

5   R.L. Parry, 'West Has No Simple Way to Treat the Lady', The Australian, 21 June 2012, www.the australian.com.au/opinion/world-commentary/west-has-no-simple-way-to-treat-the-lady/story-e6frg6ux-1226403411193 [page discontinued].

6   David I. Steinberg, 'Aung San Suu Kyi and US Policy Toward Burma/Myanmar', Journal of Current Southeast Asian Affairs, Vol.29, No.3, 2010, doi.org/10.1177/186810341002900302.

Brown and US First Lady Laura Bush became her champions. Other politicians saw benefits in being publicly associated with the photogenic opposition leader.

However, this widespread admiration—adulation even—had a downside. Some of her policies were challenged but, in public at least, there was little critical examination of Aung San Suu Kyi herself. After some mildly negative commentaries were bitterly attacked, few public figures dared to incur the wrath of her supporters.[7] Others held back for fear of giving the military regime ammunition that could be used in its propaganda campaigns against her. The result was a degree of self-censorship on the part of journalists, biographers and even academics.[8]

Since her release from house arrest in 2010, Aung San Suu Kyi has had to make the difficult transition from political prisoner and democracy icon to party leader and opposition member of parliament. She had always been an active player in Burma's power games—for example, by using her international status to influence the policies of foreign governments and organisations. But she is now expected to have a view on every topical issue—a demand complicated by her interest in running for president (a constitutional amendment permitting) in 2015. Her every action and statement, or lack thereof, is subject to close scrutiny.

This has often placed her in a difficult position. Last year, for example, she was criticised for not speaking out against the sectarian violence in Arakan State[9] and the civil war in Kachin State.[10] Earlier this year, she was heckled by angry villagers at Letpadaung after a commission of inquiry under her leadership failed to produce the expected results.[11] She has had to answer

---

7   'Aung San Suu Kyi and Western Intervention in Burma', [Letters to the Editor], *The Guardian*, [London], 13 November 2008, www.guardian.co.uk/world/2008/nov/13/letter-burma-suu-kyi.

8   Andrew Selth, *Burma Watching: A Retrospective*, Griffith Asia Institute Regional Outlook Paper No.39 (Brisbane: Griffith University, 2012), www.griffith.edu.au/__data/assets/pdf_file/0004/469426/Selth-Regional-Outlook-39.pdf [page discontinued].

9   Edward Loxton, 'Aung San Suu Kyi Loses Her Gloss for Failing to Denounce Killings', *The Week*, [London], 29 October 2013, www.theweek.co.uk/asia-pacific/burma/49788/aung-san-suu-kyi-loses-her-gloss-failing-denounce-killings.

10   Eric Randolph, 'Aung San Suu Kyi Has Abandoned Us, Say Burmese Rebels Being Bombed into Submission', *The Independent*, [London], 29 January 2012, www.independent.co.uk/news/world/asia/aung-san-suu-kyi-has-abandoned-us-say-burmese-rebels-being-bombed-into-submission-8471734.html.

11   Ei Ei Toe Lwin, 'Fury Over Letpadaung Copper Mine Report', *Myanmar Times*, [Yangon], 18 March 2013, www.mmtimes.com/index.php/national-news/5175-fury-at-copper-mine-report.html.

criticisms of her low-key response to anti-Muslim riots in central Burma[12] and she was accused of betraying her principles by attending the annual Armed Forces Day parade in Naypyidaw.[13]

While not given as much exposure in the international news media, there are also other critics of Aung San Suu Kyi in Burma (in addition, that is, to hardline elements in the armed forces). For example, she is perceived by many as a strong Burman centralist, unsympathetic to the aspirations of the ethnic minorities to separate states or a federal system of government. She also has detractors among more radical opposition groups who reject her cautious, conciliatory approach to the current government and apparent support for an amnesty on past human rights abuses.[14] These voices are now becoming louder and more widely reported.

Given the quite unrealistic expectations held by her supporters, it was inevitable that many would be disappointed. Just as Aung San Suu Kyi has had to grapple with the harsh realities of Burmese politics, so have her followers. They are learning the hard way that all politicians have to make compromises and, particularly in Burma's volatile political environment, they are rarely able to satisfy everyone. Also, as Aung San Suu Kyi knows, anyone aspiring to a leadership role in Burma has to work with the armed forces—still the country's most powerful political institution.

In international circles, Aung San Suu Kyi remains a charismatic figure. She has recently attracted some criticism, including from prominent human rights organisations,[15] but she is still highly regarded. Also, few politicians, particularly in the Western democracies, want to be openly critical of such a political rock star. Even if they have reservations about

12 'Suu Kyi Meets with Islamic Leaders Amid Growing Criticism', *GlobalPost*, [Boston], 10 April 2013, www.globalpost.com/dispatch/news/asianet/130410/suu-kyi-meets-islamic-leaders-amid-growing-criticism [page discontinued].

13 Kate Hodal, 'Aung San Suu Kyi Surprise Spectator at Burma Armed Forces Day Parade', *The Guardian*, [London], 27 March 2013, www.guardian.co.uk/world/2013/mar/27/aung-san-suu-kyi-burma-parade.

14 Parameswaran Ponnudurai, 'Holding Rights Abusers Accountable', *Radio Free Asia*, [Washington, DC], 12 January 2012, www.rfa.org/english/commentaries/east-asia-beat/junta-01212012180532.html.

15 Alex Spillius, 'Aung San Suu Kyi Facing Backlash for Silence on Abuses', *The Telegraph*, [London], 26 July 2012, www.telegraph.co.uk/news/worldnews/asia/burmamyanmar/9430518/Aung-San-Suu-Kyi-facing-backlash-for-silence-on-abuses.html.

her reputed inflexibility and strong leadership style, her lack of practical experience or her stance on particular issues, they know that they will have to work with her to achieve their aims in Burma.[16]

Aung San Suu Kyi's many qualities are not in doubt. However, she is now being viewed more as a real person, with many of the strengths and weaknesses of real people, rather than as some kind of ethereal being floating above the rough and tumble of Burmese politics. She is also gradually becoming accepted as a hardheaded politician trying to hold together a fractious party and act strategically in a divided country where politics is dominated by tactics and personalities.

The critical stories about her appearing in the news media and on websites may upset some, but they reflect a more mature and objective appreciation of her important place in modern Burmese history. In one sense, that is to be welcomed as much as her long-awaited entry into the country's political arena.

---

16   Steve Finch, 'Suu Kyi's Party Told It's Too Authoritarian as Burma's Activists Quit', *The Independent*, [London], 12 November 2012, www.independent.co.uk/news/world/asia/suu-kyis-party-told-its-too-authoritarian-as-burmas-activists-quit-8307219.html.

52

Will Aung San Suu Kyi be President of Burma?

(11:20 AEDT, 16 May 2013)

Even two years out from the next national election in Myanmar, there was considerable speculation about the possibility that Aung San Suu Kyi might fulfil her strong wish to become the country's next president. However, there were major obstacles preventing that from happening, not least being the difficulty of changing the 2008 constitution and the armed forces' apparent determination to deny her the top job.

One question uppermost in the minds of many who attended last week's Lowy Institute panel discussion on Burma[1] was whether Aung San Suu Kyi might become president when Thein Sein's five-year term of office expires in 2015. There is no simple answer to this question, but it may be helpful to look at some of the challenges the popular opposition leader would need to overcome to become president.

She is sometimes reluctant to say so, but it is clear that Aung San Suu Kyi wants to become President of Burma.[2] Her own ambition and profound sense of destiny aside, she will turn 70 in 2015 and, if she misses her

---

1   'Lowy Lecture Series: Burma's Transition: Progress and Prospects', The Lowy Institute, Sydney, 8 May 2013, www.lowyinstitute.org/events/lowy-lecture-series-burmas-transition-progress-and-prospects [now at www.lowyinstitute.org/news-and-media/multimedia/video/lowy-lecture-series-burmas-transition-progress-and-prospects].
2   Mizuo Aoki, 'Suu Kyi Hopes to Surmount Obstacles to Presidency', *Japan Times*, 18 April 2013, www.japantimes.co.jp/news/2013/04/18/national/suu-kyi-hopes-to-surmount-obstacles-to-presidency/.

chance, there may not be another. Several legal and procedural steps would need to be taken before she can bid for the top job, but the key factor will be the attitude of the armed forces (*Tatmadaw*).

Predicting Burma's future is always a risky proposition but, looking ahead, two possible scenarios present themselves. One reflects the hopes of millions of people inside and outside the country. The other reflects their fears.

Under the first scenario, Burma's election laws would be revised and the electoral rolls updated, in anticipation of a national poll in 2015.[3] If it is free and fair, there is little doubt the NLD would win a large majority. Not only is there strong support for political change, but also Aung San Suu Kyi remains enormously popular. The NLD's campaign slogan in the 2012 by-elections—that 'a vote for the NLD is a vote for Aung San Suu Kyi'—saw the party win most of the available seats.[4]

More importantly, the 2008 constitution would have to be amended. Other parts of the charter are relevant, but the main obstacle to an Aung San Suu Kyi presidency is Clause 59(f). Under this provision, the president cannot have any children who are citizens of a foreign country, nor can their children's spouses be foreigners. Aung San Suu Kyi's two sons are British subjects and both are married to non-Burmese citizens. Until this clause is amended, she cannot become president—as was doubtless its intention.

Consideration is being given to amending the constitution. Aung San Suu Kyi has declined to discuss the possibility of specific changes to Clause 59(f),[5] but it is apparently a subject of debate within official circles. The government has stated that it does not have a problem with Aung San Suu Kyi becoming president,[6] but the majority USDP has

---

3   The Associated Press, 'Myanmar: A Warning on Voter Lists', *The New York Times*, 8 March 2012, www.nytimes.com/2012/03/09/world/asia/myanmar-a-warning-on-voter-lists.html?_r=0.

4   Kyaw Kyaw, 'Analysis of Myanmar's NLD Landslide', *New Mandala*, 1 May 2012, asiapacific. anu.edu.au/newmandala/2012/05/01/analysis-of-myanmars-nld-landslide/.

5   Daniel Pye and Tha Lun Zaung Htet, 'Aung San Suu Kyi Says Burma to Amend "World's Most Difficult Constitution"', *The Irrawaddy*, May 2013, www.irrawaddy.org/archives/34296 [page discontinued] [now at www.irrawaddy.com/election/news/suu-kyi-says-burma-to-amend-worlds-most-difficult-constitution].

6   'Burma to Allow Suu Kyi's Presidential Bid, Aung Min Tells US Audience', *The Irrawaddy*, 26 April 2013, www.irrawaddy.org/archives/33149 [page discontinued] [now at www.irrawaddy.com/election/news/burma-to-allow-suu-kyis-presidential-bid-aung-min-tells-us-audience].

expressed opposition to the idea.[7] Under the first scenario, however, more than 75 per cent of the parliament would vote in favour of the relevant amendment, clearing the way for Aung San Suu Kyi to be a candidate.

The final step in this process would be for the president to be chosen by an electoral college consisting of members of both houses of the national parliament. Assuming an NLD landslide in the 2015 elections, and the successful amendment of the constitution, this should not present any problems. Even if opposed by the 25 per cent of parliament reserved for serving military officers, the NLD should have the numbers to vote Aung San Suu Kyi into the country's highest office, probably in early 2016.

The second—and possibly more likely—scenario delivers a completely different result.

The *Tatmadaw* has loosened its grip on national politics, but it remains the most powerful political institution in the country.[8] The constitution guarantees it a leading role in Burma's national affairs—something that Commander-in-Chief Min Aung Hlaing reaffirmed at the annual Armed Forces Day parade in March.[9] Should the military leadership and its supporters in government and parliament oppose Aung San Suu Kyi's elevation, it is difficult to see her becoming president.

The easiest way for them to prevent her candidacy would be to oppose any changes to Clause 59(f) in the constitution. The legal requirement for 'more than' 75 per cent of all MPs to vote in favour of an amendment gives the military bloc an effective veto over constitutional change.

The *Tatmadaw*'s views about Aung San Suu Kyi are mixed. Past voting patterns suggest that many in the ranks support her and the NLD's campaign for a genuine democracy. But others seem to worry that she plans to reduce defence spending, dismantle the apparatus that has sustained the armed forces for decades, remove the protections granted by the constitution and deny them their guardianship role. Some officers are

7   'Suu Kyi Won't Be President, Ruling Party Says', *United Press International*, [Washington, DC], 26 April 2013, www.upi.com/Top_News/Special/2013/04/26/Suu-Kyi-wont-be-president-ruling-party-says/67701366992651/.

8   Adam P. MacDonald, 'The Tatmadaw's New Position in Myanmar Politics', *East Asia Forum*, 1 May 2013, www.eastasiaforum.org/2013/05/01/the-tatmadaws-new-position-in-myanmar-politics/.

9   James Hookway, 'Military Asserts its Role in Myanmar Democracy', *The Wall Street Journal*, 27 March 2013, online.wsj.com/article/SB10001424127887323361804578386083999202130.html.

reportedly also concerned about her closeness to foreign powers and her past readiness to use them to support her domestic political agenda—for example, by imposing economic sanctions.

Other presidential candidates are likely also to play a role. Despite poor health, Thein Sein may choose to seek a second term.[10] Another contender could be Shwe Mann, Chairman of the USDP and Speaker of the lower house. *Tatmadaw* chief Senior General Min Aung Hlaing may also throw his hat into the ring. As former and serving generals, all three would probably be considered safer bets by the armed forces hierarchy than a civilian democrat leading a fractious and inexperienced party that has been highly critical of the former military government and its carefully crafted constitution.

All this is known to Aung San Suu Kyi. It has probably been with such issues in mind that she has publicly acknowledged the *Tatmadaw's* important political role and its autonomy in military affairs.[11] While calling for constitutional amendments to strengthen democracy in Burma, she has tried to reassure the armed forces leadership that she does not pose a threat to their interests.[12] This has alienated some of her supporters but, if she manages to win the *Tatmadaw's* trust, it would maintain the momentum of the current reform program and possibly help open the path to the presidency.[13]

Rumours are swirling around Burma about various deals that would permit the relevant part of the constitution to be amended prior to the national elections. However, 2015 is still a long way off and such an outcome is far from certain. Aung San Suu Kyi becoming president, and leading a government and parliament dominated by the NLD, is not a prospect that everyone in Burma looks upon favourably. Over the next two years, the only guarantee is that there will be more than a few people working hard to prevent that from happening.

---

10   Lawi Weng, 'Thein Sein Still a USDP Leader, May Be Party's 2015 Presidential Pick: Lawmaker', *The Irrawaddy*, 3 May 2013, www.irrawaddy.org/archives/33709 [page discontinued] [now at www.irrawaddy.com/election/news/thein-sein-still-a-usdp-leader-may-be-partys-2015-presidential-pick-lawmaker].

11   Soe Than Lynn, 'Identify Causes of Kachin Fighting, Urges Suu Kyi', *Myanmar Times*, [Yangon], 14 January 2013, www.mmtimes.com/index.php/national-news/3775-identify-causes-of-kachin-fighting-urges-nld-leader.html.

12   'Aung San Suu Kyi Reaches Out to Burmese Military', *Voice of America*, 5 March 2012, www.voa news.com/content/aung-san-suu-kyi-reaches-out-to-burmese-military-141581403/179955.html [page discontinued] [now at www.voanews.com/archive/aung-san-suu-kyi-reaches-out-burmese-military].

13   Daniel Ten Kate and Kyaw Thu, 'Suu Kyi Courts Military With Eye on Presidency: Southeast Asia', *Bloomberg*, 12 February 2013, www.bloomberg.com/news/2013-02-11/suu-kyi-courts-military-with-eye-on-presidency-southeast-asia.html.

53

Burma: Conspiracies and other theories

(15:28 AEDT, 5 June 2013)

Myanmar has always attracted its fair share of conspiracy theories, but after the anti-Muslim violence in 2012, they seemed to increase in number and intensity. Some were more credible than others.

There is something about Burma that seems to encourage conspiracy theories. Not only does it create them in abundance, but they tend to be picked up by the international news media and given wide circulation. This in turn gives them a prominence that most do not deserve—at least, not without appropriate caveats and qualifications. To give a few recent examples:

1. When a misguided American tourist invaded Aung San Suu Kyi's home in 2009, there were suggestions he had been put up to it by Burma's Military Intelligence Service to help publicly justify an extension of her house arrest.[1]

2. When President Thein Sein acknowledged Burma's myriad problems and announced an unprecedented reform program in 2011, activists claimed it was merely a ploy to neutralise Aung San Suu Kyi and seduce foreign governments.[2]

---

1   Andrew Selth, 'Conspiracies and Cock-Ups in Burma', *The Interpreter*, 26 May 2009, www.lowy interpreter.org/post/2009/05/26/Conspiracies.aspx [page discontinued] [now at archive.lowyinstitute. org/the-interpreter/conspiracies-and-cock-ups-burma].
2   Bertil Lintner, 'The Limits of Reform in Myanmar', *Asia Times Online*, [Hong Kong], 18 January 2012, www.atimes.com/atimes/Southeast_Asia/NA18Ae03.html [page discontinued].

3. The widespread sectarian violence in Rakhine State in 2012 was described by some commentators as a clever plot by the Thein Sein Government to embarrass Aung San Suu Kyi, who at the time was receiving a rapturous welcome in Europe.[3]

All these theories have been dismissed by serious Burma-watchers.

The latest stories in this vein focus on accusations that the anti-Muslim violence seen in several parts of Burma over the past year constitutes a coordinated campaign by conservative forces either to reassert their national role and stymie Thein Sein's reform program or to achieve some other grand design, such as the expulsion of all non-Buddhists.

There are a number of possible reasons conspiracy theories find such fertile soil in Burma.

First, there is a long tradition of storytelling, social gossip and rumour-mongering. This may have its roots in the country's deeply entrenched 'tea culture',[4] but others point to the restrictions on free speech imposed by successive military governments after 1962, which made the open discussion of many issues dangerous.

Second, news about developments in Burma is now more freely available than it has been for the past 50 years, but there is still a lack of hard, verifiable information about contemporary events. And, as tantalising as some rumours may be, resident diplomats, analysts and journalists cannot investigate every rumour they hear in Rangoon's hothouse environment.[5]

Third, given the volatility of Burma's political scene, the divisions within most major institutions, the fractiousness of the main parties and the emotive nature of international Burma studies, it is little wonder that sensational stories arise and find their way into the public arena. The sources and motives behind these tales are rarely easy to determine.

---

3   Edward Loxton, 'Is Burma Regime Inciting Rakhine Conflict to Discredit Aung San Suu Kyi?', *The Week*, [London], 12 June 2012, www.theweek.co.uk/asia-pacific/burma/47364/burma-regime-inciting-rakhine-conflict-discredit-aung-san-suu-kyi.
4   Bamarlay, 'Teashops in Myanmar', *Today in Myanmar*, 14 December 2008, www.myanmar2day.com/myanmar-life/2008/12/teashops-in-myanmar/.
5   'US Embassy Cables: North Korea Alleged to be Building Secret Underground Missile Site in Burma', *The Guardian*, [London], 10 December 2012, www.guardian.co.uk/world/us-embassy-cables-documents/20129.

Fourth, the news media is now better informed about Burma than in the past, when some myths and misconceptions were the basis of serious reports;[6] a few unlikely claims became the received wisdom.[7] Even so, in today's highly competitive news environment, some outlets and websites still publish stories that warrant more careful handling.

As regards the violence seen since mid 2012, it is evident that there are religious zealots, including some Buddhist monks, who are stirring up trouble and leading attacks against minority communities. There is also a strong racist element directed at those perceived to be foreigners. Rohingyas and other Muslims have been the latest targets, but in the past local Christians and Chinese have been victims.[8]

According to unconfirmed news reports, at least two groups are behind the latest anti-Muslim unrest.[9] One is the 'Swan Arshin', a loose collection of thugs used by the former military regime to attack Aung San Suu Kyi in 2003 and prodemocracy demonstrators in 2007. The other is reportedly a 'Buddhist militia' called the Taung Tha Army, linked to a former general turned politician.

Little is known about either group, but both appear to share the views of the extremist 969 Buddhist Movement headed by radical monk U Wirathu, whose anti-Muslim diatribes have been circulated widely.[10]

Part of the conspiracy narrative are claims that the outbreaks of violence in central and northern Burma this year were well planned and executed, with armed men being brought in from elsewhere to support attacks by locals on Muslim communities. Each outbreak seems to have been sparked by a specific incident, but there have also been suggestions that these were staged with a view to inciting wider violence.

6   Derek Tonkin, 'Political Myths', *Network Myanmar*, www.networkmyanmar.org/index.php/political-myths [page discontinued].
7   Andrew Selth, *Chinese Military Bases in Burma: The Explosion of a Myth*, Griffith Asia Institute Regional Outlook Paper No.10 (Brisbane: Griffith University, 2007), www.griffith.edu.au/__data/assets/pdf_file/0018/18225/regional-outlook-andrew-selth.pdf [page discontinued].
8   Bureau of Democracy, Human Rights and Labor, 'Burma', in *International Religious Freedom Report for 2012* (Washington, DC: US Department of State, 2012), www.state.gov/j/drl/rls/irf/religiousfreedom/#wrapper [page discontinued] [now at 2009-2017.state.gov/j/drl/rls/irf/2012religiousfreedom//index.htm#wrapper].
9   Maung Zarni, 'Myanmar: Old Military Monsters Stirring Up Trouble', *Dr Ko Ko Gyi's Blog*, 2 June 2013, at drkokogyi.wordpress.com/2013/06/02/myanmar-old-military-monsters-stirring-up-trouble/.
10   Matthew J. Walton, 'Myanmar Needs A New Nationalism', *Asia Times Online*, [Hong Kong], 20 May 2013, www.atimes.com/atimes/Southeast_Asia/SEA-02-200513.html [page discontinued].

The apparent reluctance of the army and police to intervene in anti-Muslim riots has been cited as evidence that the security forces, and possibly even the government itself, are complicit in the violence.[11] Little allowance is made for the enormous practical difficulties of responding to such attacks or for Naypyidaw's obvious reluctance to endorse tough measures that might prompt further international censure.

Some reports claim that hardliners in the security forces and USDP are encouraging anti-Muslim unrest to put pressure on Thein Sein.[12] If so, their motives are unclear, but a common explanation is that they want to reassert their dominance in Burma and remind everyone that strong security forces—and strong measures—are necessary to preserve internal stability and national unity.[13]

A few sources have also suggested that powerful vested interests in Burma—notably, corrupt former generals and wealthy businessmen—wish to establish an extraparliamentary power base that can be used to weaken any reforms that threaten their position. Others have claimed that such groups plan to use private militias to eliminate rivals and to protect themselves should Burma's 'disciplined democracy' become less disciplined.

It is difficult to confirm or deny such stories. There is insufficient evidence to draw any firm conclusions. Parts of some reports appear accurate, or draw on known precedents, which give them a degree of plausibility. There is also a troubling pattern to some anti-Muslim riots, which, as Thein Sein has acknowledged, have involved extremists and reactionaries.[14] Other reports, however, simply do not ring true.

---

11   'Burma: Government Forces Targeting Rohingya Muslims', *News* (New York: Human Rights Watch, 31 July 2012), www.hrw.org/fr/node/109214.
12   'Deep-Seated Prejudice, Radical Buddhist Monks Fuel Violence Against Myanmar's Muslims', *The Washington Post*, 1 June 2013, www.washingtonpost.com/world/asia_pacific/deep-seated-prejudice-radical-buddhist-monks-fuel-violence-against-myanmars-muslims/2013/05/31/ab1149e4-ca61-11e2-9cd9-3b9a22a4000a_story_1.html [page discontinued].
13   'Buddhist Top Brass Conspiracy of Muslims Massacre in Myanmar', *Jafria News*, 16 April 2013, jafrianews.com/2013/04/16/buddhist-top-brass-conspiracy-of-muslims-massacare-in-myanmar/.
14   President's Office, 'President U Thein Sein Delivered a Remark on the Report of the Rakhine Investigation Commission', The Republic of the Union of Myanmar, Naypyitaw, 6 May 2013, www.president-office.gov.mm/en/briefing-room/speeches-and-remarks/2013/05/07/id-1989 [page discontinued].

It is undeniable that there are dark undercurrents in Burmese politics. There are elements within the country that hold strong beliefs and seem prepared to go to considerable lengths to pursue them. Not everyone welcomed the creation of a hybrid civilian–military parliament in 2011, Thein Sein's rapprochement with Aung San Suu Kyi and the relaxation of the former regime's control measures. Also, notwithstanding the popular view of Burma as a tolerant Buddhist country, sectarian strife has never been far from the surface. Over the years, social tensions have been exacerbated by a complex mix of political, economic, legal and cultural issues.

The question that now arises, however, is whether these feelings are being exploited by particular individuals and groups for political or economic gain.

The civil unrest of the past year has exposed deep fissures in Burmese society and serious weaknesses in the government. Both have had international consequences. Even if there are no cabals, conspiracies or coverups, as often claimed, these problems can only work to the benefit of those opposed to a more progressive approach to public policy in Burma.

54

Burma and North Korea: Again? Still

(12:58 AEDT, 10 July 2013)

US concerns over Myanmar's shadowy relations with North Korea seemed to fade away after president Thein Sein gave Barack Obama his assurances that Naypyidaw would cut its military ties with Pyongyang. However, a scan of official US documents issued over the past year revealed that the issue remained a factor in the bilateral relationship, albeit not to the extent of prompting the reimposition of broad economic sanctions.

The US Treasury's 'designation' of Lieutenant General Thein Htay, Chief of Burma's Directorate of Defence Industries (DDI), for purchasing military goods from North Korea, surprised many.[1] After Barack Obama's visit to Burma in November 2012, when he was assured by President Thein Sein that such activities would cease, concerns about Naypyidaw's shadowy relationship with Pyongyang seemed to fade.

---

1   US Department of the Treasury, 'Treasury Designates Burmese LT General Thein Htay, Chief of Directorate of Defence Industries', Press Center, Washington, DC, 2 July 2013, www.treasury.gov/press-center/press-releases/Pages/jl1998.aspx.

In March, some suspect dual-use materials from North Korea were seized by Japan, but nothing seemed to come of it.[2] And North Korea did not rate a mention in the official statements and learned commentary related to President Thein Sein's return visit to Washington in May.[3] The State Department fact sheet issued after his visit was all good news.[4]

Yet US concerns about Burma's military links with North Korea have never gone away.

Before Obama's visit to Burma, Naypyidaw's relationship with Pyongyang was the subject of considerable concern. Washington tended to discount a clandestine nuclear weapons program but remained worried about the possible sale to Burma of ballistic missiles and/or missile production facilities.[5] In April 2012, a senior State Department official told Congress that this was 'a top national security priority'.[6]

During the Obama visit, the Burmese Government announced that it would cut its military ties with North Korea. It stated that it had not and would not violate UNSC resolutions 1874 of 2009[7] and 1718 of 2006,[8] both of which banned arms sales from North Korea. Burma also reiterated its commitment to abide by the Nuclear Non-Proliferation Treaty—a claim that has since been accepted by Washington.[9]

---

2   Daniel Schearf, 'Burma's Military Relations with North Korea Under Scrutiny', *Voice of America*, 22 March 2013, www.voanews.com/content/burma-military-relations-with-north-korea-under-scrutiny/1626532.html [page discontinued] [now at www.voanews.com/east-asia/burmas-military-relations-north-korea-under-scrutiny].
3   Murray Heibert and Kathleen Rustici, 'After Half a Century, a Myanmar President Visits Washington', *Critical Questions* (Washington, DC: Center for Strategic and International Studies, 22 May 2013), csis.org/publication/after-half-century-myanmar-president-visits-washington.
4   'Visit of President U Thein Sein of the Republic of the Union of Myanmar/US Assistance', *Fact Sheet* (Washington, DC: US Department of State, 20 May 2013), www.state.gov/r/pa/prs/ps/2013/05/209707.htm [page discontinued].
5   Senior State Department Official, 'Background Briefing on Secretary Clinton's Travel to Burma', Special Briefing, En Route Busan, South Korea, 29 November 2011, www.state.gov/p/eap/rls/rm/2011/11/177896.htm [page discontinued] [now at 2009-2017.state.gov/p/eap/rls/rm/2011/11/177896.htm].
6   'Oversight of US Policy Toward Burma', Hearing before the Subcommittee on Asia and the Pacific, Committee on Foreign Affairs, US House of Representatives, 112th Congress, Washington, DC, 25 April 2012, archives.republicans.foreignaffairs.house.gov/112/74001.pdf [page discontinued].
7   *United Nations Security Council, Resolution 1874 (2009)*, 12 June 2009, www.un.org/ga/search/view_doc.asp?symbol=S/RES/1874(2009).
8   *United Nations Security Council, Resolution 1718 (2006)*, 14 October 2006, www.un.org/ga/search/view_doc.asp?symbol=S/RES/1718(2006).
9   Bureau of Verification, Compliance and Implementation, *Adherence to and Compliance with Arms Control, Nonproliferation and Disarmament Agreements and Commitments* (Washington, DC: US Department of State, August 2012), www.state.gov/documents/organization/197295.pdf [page discontinued].

Following the Obama visit and assurances from several Burmese officials that links with North Korea had indeed been severed, the issue dropped from sight. There were warnings from a few critics of the US rapprochement with Burma, but it was almost as if the issue had been resolved. A survey of official US statements over the past year, however, suggests that Burma's relationship with North Korea has continued to weigh on Washington's mind.

- On 11 July 2012, President Obama issued an executive order stating that Burma's arms trade with North Korea constituted 'an unusual and extraordinary threat to the national security and foreign policy of the United States'.[10] It authorised sanctions against Burmese individuals and institutions engaged in this practice.

- On the basis of this order, the US formally 'designated' Burma's DDI, which, according to the State Department, 'carries out missile research and development at its facilities in Burma, where North Korean experts are active'.[11]

- In February 2013, the Special Representative and Policy Coordinator for Burma, W. Patrick Murphy, told the Tom Lantos Human Rights Commission that the US continued to target those who 'perpetuate military trade with North Korea'.[12]

- Speaking to the Senate Committee on Foreign Affairs' Subcommittee on East Asian and Pacific Affairs on 25 April 2013, a State Department official revealed that the US continued to ask the Burmese Government to demonstrate 'an end of military ties to North Korea'.[13]

---

10   Presidential Documents, 'Executive Order 13619 of 11 July 2012', *Federal Register*, Vol.77, No.135 (Washington, DC: The White House, 2012), www.gpo.gov/fdsys/pkg/FR-2012-07-13/pdf/2012-17264.pdf.

11   Press Center, *Joint Fact Sheet from US Treasury and State Departments: Administration Eases Financial and Investment Sanctions on Burma* (Washington, DC: US Department of the Treasury, 11 July 2012), www.state.gov/r/pa/prs/ps/2012/07/194868.htm [page discontinued] [now at www.treasury.gov/press-center/press-releases/Pages/tg1633.aspx].

12   W. Patrick Murphy, Special Representative and Policy Coordinator for Burma, 'Human Rights in Burma: Testimony', Remarks prepared for delivery to Tom Lantos Human Rights Commission, US Department of State, Washington, DC, 28 February 2013, www.state.gov/p/eap/rls/rm/2013/02/205487.htm [page discontinued] [now at 2009-2017.state.gov/p/eap/rls/rm/2013/02/205487.htm].

13   Joseph Yun, Acting Assistant Secretary, Bureau of East Asian and Pacific Affairs, 'Rebalance to Asia II: Security and Defense—Cooperation and Challenges: Testimony', Statement before the Subcommittee on East Asian and Pacific Affairs, Senate Committee on Foreign Affairs, US Senate, Washington, DC, 25 April 2013, www.state.gov/p/eap/rls/rm/2013/04/207981.htm [page discontinued] [now at 2009-2017.state.gov/p/eap/rls/rm/2013/04/207981.htm].

- On 2 May 2013, in a briefing about the relaxation of economic sanctions against Burma, State Department officials stated that 'specific bad actors' in Burma engaging in trade with North Korea would not be eligible to enter the US.[14]

Looking back over these statements, it would appear that the US has tried to keep up public pressure on Naypyidaw—as it has doubtless been doing in private—but it has not allowed its concerns over continuing Burmese links with North Korea to interrupt the development of bilateral relations. This represents a softening in the US position since Hillary Clinton's December 2011 visit to Burma.[15]

This policy shift may account for the fact that sanctions have been imposed on a single department of Burma's armed forces and an individual army officer. The recent Treasury document specifically states that it is not targeting the Burmese Government, which 'has continued to take positive steps in severing its military ties with North Korea'. It also refers to Naypyidaw's undertaking in 2012 to abide by the relevant UNSC resolutions.

That formulation may satisfy diplomatic etiquette, but it is difficult to see how Lieutenant General Thein Htay or the DDI could maintain links with a foreign power without the knowledge of the armed forces leadership, and probably the President. It is also likely that DDI's acquisitions from North Korea were in formal breach of UNSC resolutions 1874 and 1718. If the transactions were benign, why the strong US response?

As *Network Myanmar*'s Derek Tonkin has pointed out, the Treasury statement did not say when the offences took place or what arms were involved.[16] However, a US spokesman has revealed that the Treasury Department has had concerns about Thein Htay since last November, when he led a Burmese delegation to Beijing. There he met North Korean officials and signed an agreement to expand bilateral military ties.[17]

---

14   Senior State Department Officials, 'Background Briefing on the Administration's Policies Toward Burma Sanctions', Special Briefing, Via Teleconference, US Department of State, Washington, DC, 2 May 2013, www.state.gov/r/pa/prs/ps/2013/05/208897.htm [page discontinued] [now at 2009-2017.state.gov/r/pa/prs/ps/2013/05/208897.htm].
15   Lindsay Murdoch, 'Clinton Seeks a Nuclear Surety from Burma', *Sydney Morning Herald*, 2 December 2011, www.smh.com.au/world/clinton-seeks-a-nuclear-surety-from-burma-20111201-1o98b.html.
16   Derek Tonkin [Comment], 'US Treasury Department Sanctions Myanmar General', *Network Myanmar*, www.networkmyanmar.org/.
17   Nan Tin Htwe, 'Uncertainty Over Thein Htay Sanction', *Myanmar Times*, [Yangon], 8 July 2013, www.mmtimes.com/index.php/national-news/7405-uncertainty-over-thein-htay-sanction.html.

Senator Richard Lugar is no longer around to voice his perennial concerns about secret deals between Pyongyang and Naypyidaw, but Congress has already sounded some warning bells. North Korea was not specifically mentioned, but in June both houses called for greater transparency from the Burmese about military budgets and operations, before the US seeks closer military engagement with their armed forces.[18]

The Burmese Government has expressed surprise at Treasury's recent announcement, and President Thein Sein's office has claimed not to know the evidence on which the latest US sanctions are based.[19] Only last month, the Speaker of Burma's lower house of parliament reportedly told officials in Washington that Burma's arms trade with North Korea had ceased and that Naypyidaw was observing the relevant UNSC resolutions.

The latest developments in this saga raise a number of difficult questions. Is Lieutenant General Thein Htay a maverick, acting alone? Are Burma's armed forces beyond the President's control? Is Naypyidaw trying to squeeze in a few more arms sales and wrap up a secret missile program before cutting its ties with Pyongyang? Is Thein Sein hoping that the US's wish to preserve its good relations with Burma will persuade it to turn a blind eye?

Once again, observers are left bemoaning the lack of hard information, not only about Burma's shadowy relationship with North Korea, but also about what drives the decisions of policymakers in Naypyidaw and Pyongyang—and Washington.

---

18   Walter Lohman, 'Hill Concern Over US–Burma Military Engagement Grows', *The Daily Signal*, 27 June 2013, blog.heritage.org/2013/06/27/hill-concern-over-u-s-burma-military-engagement-grows/.
19   Hannah Hindstrom, 'Burma Denies Military Ties with North Korea', *Democratic Voice of Burma*, 4 July 2013, www.dvb.no/news/burma-denies-military-ties-with-north-korea/29199 [page discontinued].

55

West reaches out to Burma's security sector

(10:13 AEDT, 26 July 2013)

The advent of Thein Sein's reformist government reduced the sensitivity of bilateral security relations with Myanmar and made it possible for Western countries like the US and the UK to contemplate—within limits—the provision of assistance to the country's armed forces and police force.

One of the most striking aspects of Burma's reemergence as an international actor has been the readiness of the Western democracies to renew or strengthen ties with the country's armed forces and police. Before the advent of President Thein Sein's reformist government in 2011, any relationship with Burma's reviled security forces was politically very difficult.

The policy change has been enthusiastically welcomed by Naypyidaw and, albeit more cautiously, by opposition leader Aung San Suu Kyi. It has been condemned as premature and ill-advised by activists and human rights organisations, but it is hoped that foreign assistance can ameliorate the very problems about which Burma's critics are most concerned.

Most of the new initiatives have been expressed in principled terms, including by Thein Sein,[1] but essentially they can be divided into two separate, if related, sets of proposals. One is aimed at increasing the

---

1   Thein Sein, 'Myanmar's Complex Transformation: Prospects and Challenges', Transcript, Chatham House, London, 15 July 2013, at www.networkmyanmar.org/images/stories/PDF15/Chatham-House-Thein-Sein.pdf [page discontinued] [now at www.files.ethz.ch/isn/167435/150713Sein.pdf].

professionalism of the armed forces (*Tatmadaw*) and reducing its political role. The other relates to the modernisation and civilianisation of the Myanmar Police Force (MPF).

After Barack Obama's visit to Burma in November 2012, Naypyidaw was invited to send observers to Exercise Cobra Gold in Thailand.[2] In April 2013, the State Department announced that the US was looking at ways to support 'nascent military engagement' with Burma as a way of encouraging further political reforms.[3]

Pentagon officials have since referred to a 'carefully calibrated' plan[4] that includes Burmese cooperation in the search for the remains of US personnel missing since World War II. *Tatmadaw* officers have participated in events sponsored by the Asia-Pacific Center for Security Studies in Hawai`i, and a military dialogue or 'partnership' has not been ruled out.[5]

During Thein Sein's March 2013 visit to Australia, Canberra announced it was restoring the resident defence attaché's position in Rangoon. Prime Minister Julia Gillard said that this was to permit engagement with the *Tatmadaw* in areas such as peacekeeping, humanitarian assistance and disaster relief and to enhance other dialogues.[6]

The UK has also been active in this area. During Thein Sein's recent visit to the UK, London announced that it, too, was posting a defence attaché (DA) to Rangoon. An arms embargo (sort of)[7] remains in place but the *Tatmadaw* has been offered training courses in human rights, the laws of armed conflict and the accountability of armed forces in democracies. Thirty senior Burmese officers will attend a staff course in the UK next year.

---

2   Daniel Schearf, 'Burma Observers Participate in US-Led Military Exercises in Thailand', *Voice of America*, 11 February 2013, www.voanews.com/content/burma-observers-participate-in-us-led-military-exercies-in-thailand/1601193.html [page discontinued] [now at www.voanews.com/east-asia/burma-observers-participate-us-led-military-exercises-thailand].

3   Erika Kinetz, 'US to Boost Military, Trade Ties to Burma', *The Irrawaddy*, April 2013, www.irrawaddy.org/archives/33140.

4   'US Begins "Calibrated" Defence Engagement with Myanmar', *Zee News*, [Noida, India], 26 April 2013, zeenews.india.com/news/world/us-begins-calibrated-defence-engagement-with-myanmar_844777.html.

5   Barrister Harun ur Rashid, 'US–Myanmar Military Engagement: A Step to Counter China?', *Daily Star*, [Dhaka], 1 December 2012, archive.thedailystar.net/newDesign/news-details.php?nid=259409.

6   Naomi Woodley, 'Australia Further Strengthens Ties with Myanmar', *The World Today*, [ABC Radio], 18 March 2013, www.abc.net.au/worldtoday/content/2013/s3717728.htm.

7   Hanna Hindstrom, 'UK Approves US$5 Million in Arms Export Deals to Burma', *Burma Link*, 18 July 2013, www.burmalink.org/uk-approves-us5-million-in-arms-export-deals-to-burma/.

There has also been considerable international interest in the reform of Burma's police force.[8] While most proposals refer to the need to strengthen the 'rule of law' in Burma, they also seem to envisage direct aid to the MPF. Earlier this year, the UN Office on Drugs and Crime was asked to conduct a survey of the force's strengths and weaknesses, to help focus the provision of foreign assistance.

This process has already begun. The EU has just posted two officers to Burma in response to a request from Naypyidaw for advice on crowd control and community policing. Foreign training in the management of public protests was recommended by Aung San Suu Kyi's commission in its report on the Letpadaung incident last year, when the MPF used excessive force.[9]

The UK sent a police expert on an exploratory mission to Burma in June and appears to be contemplating a relationship with the MPF. While Burmese officials routinely denigrate the colonial administration, including its police forces, both countries acknowledge that the MPF owes much to its British heritage and see this as the basis for fruitful cooperation.

For its part, the US has lifted its embargo on Burmese attendance at the Bangkok-based International Law Enforcement Academy and seems to be considering assistance to the MPF. A US interagency 'rule of law' mission visited Burma earlier this year. Independent organisations like the US Institute of Peace are also looking at ways to help the MPF improve its performance.[10]

The Australian Federal Police (AFP) has maintained an office in Rangoon since 2000. Joint activities and training courses have focused on transnational crime such as narcotics trafficking and people smuggling.[11]

---

8   Andrew Selth, 'Burma Police: The Long Road to Reform', *The Interpreter*, 13 December 2012, www.lowyinterpreter.org/post/2012/12/13/Burmas-police-The-long-road-to-reform.aspx [page discontinued] [now at archive.lowyinstitute.org/the-interpreter/burma-police-long-road-reform].

9   Ei Ei Toe Lwin, 'Fury Over Letpadaung Copper Mine Report', *Myanmar Times*, [Yangon], 18 March 2013, www.mmtimes.com/index.php/national-news/5175-fury-at-copper-mine-report.html.

10   United States Institute of Peace, *USIP Burma/Myanmar Rule of Law Trip Report* (Washington, DC: USIP Rule of Law Center, June 2013), newcrossroadsasia.com/main/images/monthly/usip.pdf [page discontinued] [now at themimu.info/sites/themimu.info/files/documents/Report_Burma-Myanmar_Rule_of_Law_Trip_US_Institute_of_Peace_June2013.pdf].

11   Department of Foreign Affairs and Trade, *Myanmar Country Brief* (Canberra: Australian Government, 2016), www.dfat.gov.au/geo/myanmar/myanmar_brief.html [page discontinued] [now at www.dfat.gov.au/geo/myanmar/Pages/myanmar-country-brief].

It is not known whether there are any plans to increase this level of cooperation, given the MPF's current receptivity to closer foreign ties, but the AFP is well placed to do so.

The risks associated with closer ties to the *Tatmadaw* and MPF will be explored in a follow-up post.

56

Risk and reward with Burma's security sector

(13:26 AEDT, 26 July 2013)

While Western assistance to the Tatmadaw *and MPF became less sensitive after the reformist president Thein Sein took office in 2011, such contacts still attracted strong criticism from activist and exile groups. As these groups were quick to point out, there were no guarantees that any assistance provided to Myanmar would result in significant changes in either the ethos or the behaviour of the security forces.*

The initiatives for closer ties between the West and Burma's police and armed forces, summarised in the previous post,[1] have aroused the ire of the activist community, which has been quick to remind everyone that the armed forces still dominate politics in Burma. The *Tatmadaw* is also engaged in counterinsurgency campaigns against armed ethnic groups and has been guilty of crimes against Muslim Rohingyas. The MPF, too, has been accused of corruption and human rights abuses.

Another criticism has been that assistance to Burma's security forces helps them maintain their grip on Burmese society by increasing their coercive capabilities. Also, formal recognition is seen as giving them a legitimacy

---

1   Andrew Selth, 'West Reaches Out to Burma's Security Sector', *The Interpreter*, 26 July 2013, www.lowyinstitute.org/the-interpreter/west-reaches-out-burmas-security-sector.

they do not deserve.[2] Even the US Senate has warned that there is the potential for 'well-intended engagement [to be] misdirected towards a negative result'.[3]

Some observers sceptical of Thein Sein's reform agenda, and international engagement more generally, believe the real aim of closer relations with Burma's security forces is to outflank China.[4]

Such links can have strategic implications, but these should not be overstated. The aid programs proposed to date are quite modest and seem to be prompted largely by concerns about Burma's domestic situation. In any case, it would take considerable time and effort for the US and its allies to match China's current relationships with the *Tatmadaw* and MPF.[5] And Burma will always try to balance its foreign relations to protect its independence. With the chairmanship of ASEAN next year in mind, Naypyidaw has already asked Beijing for advice on a range of public security issues.

The risks associated with closer ties to the *Tatmadaw* and MPF have clearly been taken into account by the Western democracies. Yet the prevailing view remains that 'positive reinforcement for meaningful reforms' is the best policy, and that such an approach is more likely to change the mindset and behaviour of the Burmese authorities than a return to sanctions and other punitive measures.[6]

This is a persuasive argument, but it must be kept in perspective. The scope for foreign governments and international organisations to change the nature of Burma's security forces is limited.

Outsiders can provide specialist advice, technical assistance and modern equipment. They can help lift the professionalism of the *Tatmadaw* and MPF and encourage the adoption of internationally accepted standards. Such measures can facilitate changes in the character and effectiveness of the country's security forces. But they cannot determine them.

---

2   Saw Yan Naing and Andrew D. Kaspar, 'UK to Resume Military Ties with Burma', *The Irrawaddy*, 16 July 2013, www.irrawaddy.org/archives/40175.
3   Walter Lohman, 'Hill Concern Over US–Burma Military Engagement Grows', *The Daily Signal*, 27 June 2013, blog.heritage.org/2013/06/27/hill-concern-over-u-s-burma-military-engagement-grows/.
4   Bertil Lintner, 'Myanmar Morphs to US–China Battlefield', *Asia Times Online*, [Hong Kong], 2 May 2013, www.atimes.com/atimes/Southeast_Asia/SEA-01-020513.html [page discontinued].
5   Xinhua, 'Chinese Senior Military Official Begins Visit to Myanmar', *Global Times*, [Beijing], 20 July 2013, www.globaltimes.cn/content/798139.shtml.
6   Lohman, 'Hill Concern Over US–Burma Military Engagement Grows'.

Fundamental reforms will depend on a completely new political dynamic in Burma, a shift in the professional culture of the armed forces and police and the development of a genuine relationship of trust with the community. These changes will be difficult and will take a long time. More to the point, they will ultimately depend on the Burmese themselves.

57

Burma: What chance another coup?

(13:47 AEDT, 9 September 2013)

Almost as soon as president Thein Sein took office in 2011, rumours began to circulate that certain elements in the armed forces were unhappy with the new political arrangements and were planning to mount another coup. These reports, however, tended to come from observers who were unfamiliar with the Tatmadaw's careful calculations, designed to retain ultimate power in Myanmar, and its long-term aims.

Whenever Burma-watchers get together these days, one topic that usually gets an airing is the prospect of another military coup.[1] Some analysts have put the likelihood of this happening over the next five years as high as 20 per cent, while others believe the odds are much lower.[2] A few observers have argued that the country is still effectively under military control, so the question of a coup simply does not arise.

Contrary to expectations, President Thein Sein's ambitious reform program has developed a momentum of its own and there is now palpable hope for real change. Opinion is divided[3] on whether or not the process

1   ANU College of Asia and the Pacific, 'Myanmar and Coups', *News & Events*, 16 August 2013, asiapacific.anu.edu.au/news-events/all-stories/myanmar-and-coups.
2   Joshua Kurlantzick and Devin T. Stewart, *Burma's Reforms and Regional Cooperation in East Asia*, Paper (New York: Carnegie Council for Ethics in International Affairs, 24 July 2013), www.carnegie council.org/publications/articles_papers_reports/0164.html/:pf_printable.
3   'Burmese Parliament Speaker Says "Reform Process Irreversible"', *BBC News*, 27 September 2012, www.bbc.co.uk/news/world-asia-19740502.

is 'irreversible'.[4] It is difficult to see Burma going back to the dark days before 2011 but, in certain circumstances, the armed forces (*Tatmadaw*) could be prompted to step in and exert greater direct control.

This issue can be examined at the national, institutional and personal levels.

At the national level, the armed forces are deeply committed to Burma's sovereignty, unity and internal stability, as they judge such matters. These goals were encapsulated in the former government's three 'national causes' and have been enshrined in the 2008 constitution. Any developments that threaten the country in these ways would greatly concern the military leadership and raise the possibility of intervention of some kind.

The perceived external threat to Burma has receded since the international community embraced Thein Sein and his reform program.[5] However, there are still up to 100,000 armed men in the country who do not (or only begrudgingly) recognise Naypyidaw's authority. Some are waging guerilla wars against the central government. Others have been designated Border Guard Forces and technically put under the *Tatmadaw*'s control, but their reliability is suspect.

Also, as seen over the past few years, civil unrest can suddenly erupt over a range of political, economic and social issues. Further religious violence is a real possibility. A failure by Thein Sein to meet rising popular expectations is another potential trigger for protests. Should Aung San Suu Kyi's presidential ambitions be blocked, there is likely to be a domestic and international outcry, arousing the *Tatmadaw*'s deepest fears.[6]

At the institutional level, the armed forces would be concerned at any attempts to deny them their special place in national affairs. This is not only spelt out in the constitution, but was recently reaffirmed by both

---

4   Scott Stearns, 'Aung San Suu Kyi Says Burma Reforms Not Yet Irreversible', *Voice of America*, 18 September 2012, www.voanews.com/content/aung-san-suu-kyi-begins-us-visit/1510124.html [page discontinued] [now at www.voanews.com/east-asia-pacific/aung-san-suu-kyi-says-burma-reforms-not-yet-irreversible].

5   Andrew Selth, *Burma and the Threat of Invasion: Regime Fantasy or Strategic Reality?*, Griffith Asia Institute Regional Outlook Paper No.17 (Brisbane: Griffith University, 2008), www.griffith.edu.au/business-government/griffith-asia-institute/pdf/Andrew-Selth-Regional-Outlook-17v2.pdf [page discontinued].

6   Andrew Selth, 'Will Aung San Suu Kyi Be President of Burma?', *The Interpreter*, 16 May 2013, www.lowyinterpreter.org/post/2013/05/16/Will-Aung-San-Suu-Kyi-be-President-of-Burma.aspx [page discontinued] [now at www.lowyinstitute.org/the-interpreter/will-aung-san-suu-kyi-be-president-burma].

the President[7] and the commander-in-chief.[8] Most military officers are intensely nationalistic and take seriously their role as guardians of the country, with their responsibility to step in and 'save' Burma if it is believed necessary.

The military leadership is also likely to act if the *Tatmadaw* itself was under threat. For example, should the government or parliament drastically reduce the defence budget, or try to seriously restrict the armed forces' sources of off-budget revenue, there is likely to be trouble.[9] The *Tatmadaw* would be particularly concerned if it felt it was being denied the men and materiel necessary to fulfil its duty to 'safeguard the constitution'.

At the personal level, many servicemen would be unhappy about an attempt to remove the clause in the constitution that seems to grant them immunity from prosecution for human rights violations committed under the former government. If opposition politicians, or the international community, revived efforts to put Burmese military personnel on trial for war crimes, that, too, would prompt a strong reaction.[10]

Another scenario that deserves at least passing mention is an attempt by a faction within the armed forces either to slow the reform process or to preserve perks and privileges that seem to be slipping away.[11] It has been suggested, for example, that many younger officers resent the fact that current and proposed changes to Burmese society may deny them the opportunities for personal enrichment enjoyed by their predecessors.

---

7   Anne Gearan, 'Burma's Thein Sein Says Military "Will Always Have a Special Place" in Government', *The Washington Post*, 19 May 2013, articles.washingtonpost.com/2013-05-19/world/39376769_1_president-obama-than-shwe-sanctions [page discontinued] [now at www.washington post.com/world/national-security/burmas-thein-sein-says-military-will-always-have-a-special-place-in-government/2013/05/19/253c300e-c0d4-11e2-8bd8-2788030e6b44_story.html].
8   Lawi Weng, 'In Naypyidaw, Suu Kyi Attends Armed Forces Day', *The Irrawaddy*, 27 March 2013, www.irrawaddy.org/archives/30671.
9   Brian McCartan, 'Myanmar Military in the Money', *Asia Times Online*, [Hong Kong], 28 February 2012, www.atimes.com/atimes/Southeast_Asia/NB28Ae02.html [page discontinued] [now at brianpmccartan.com/wp-content/uploads/2019/04/20120228-Myanmar-military-in-the-money-1.pdf].
10   Marwaan Macan Markar, 'US Joins Calls for Myanmar War Crimes Trial', *Asia Times Online*, [Hong Kong], 20 August 2010, www.atimes.com/atimes/Southeast_Asia/LH20Ae01.html [page discontinued].
11   Euro–Burma Office, *The Tatmadaw: Does the Government Control the Tatmadaw?*, EBO Briefing Paper No.3/2013 (Brussels: Associates to Develop Democratic Burma, 6 May 2013), euro-burma.eu/doc/EBO_Brief_No_3_2013_Tatmadaw.pdf [page discontinued] [now at euroburmaoffice.s3.amazonaws.com/filer_public/bb/2b/bb2ba05e-f7cd-4960-bf19-526dd9d1b73f/ebo_brief_no_3_2013_tatmadaw.pdf].

All that said, the *Tatmadaw* is not the institution it once was, and there are significant constraints on military intervention. There would inevitably be a strong reaction to a coup, both within the country and outside it. Also, Thein Sein's reforms enjoy some support in the ranks and the generals would need to weigh the benefits of a military takeover against the possibility that it could cause a serious breakdown in discipline.

In any case, the armed forces need not resort to anything as crude as a coup. There is some debate over the respective powers of the President and the commander-in-chief but, under the 2008 constitution, the latter can legally take over the running of the country.[12] Short of that, the *Tatmadaw* can exercise considerable influence without actually assuming power.

The government is already dominated by military and ex-military personnel. As Burma scholar Maung Aung Myoe has noted, of 46 ministers at the national level, 37 are from the *Tatmadaw*, including five still on active service.[13] Of the 14 chief ministers of Burma's states and regions, all but one are retired military officers. In all national, state and regional assemblies, 25 per cent of the seats are reserved for serving military personnel. The pro-government USDP consists largely of veterans and 80 per cent of senior civil service positions are occupied by former servicemen.

Some activists have gone further and claimed that Thein Sein's administration is a sham and that the 2008 charter, like Burma's 1974 constitution, is simply a political device that permits the *Tatmadaw* to continue running the country behind the facade of a quasi-civilian government.[14] If that is true, there would be no need for a coup, as the military leadership could simply manipulate the current system to get whatever it wanted.

---

12 Janet Benshoof, 'It's Time for the Int'l Community to Address Burma's Constitution', *Democratic Voice of Burma*, 20 February 2013, www.dvb.no/analysis/its-time-for-the-int%E2%80%99l-community-to-address-burma%E2%80%99s-constitution/26505 [page discontinued].
13 ANU College of Asia and the Pacific, 'Myanmar/Burma Update, 15–16 March 2013', The Australian National University, Canberra, asiapacific.anu.edu.au/sites/default/files/myanmar/MBU-flyer.pdf.
14 Bertil Lintner, 'The Military's Still in Charge', *Foreign Policy*, 9 July 2013, www.foreignpolicy.com/articles/2013/07/09/the_militarys_still_in_charge.

Needless to say, the situation is much more complicated than that.[15] Whatever may have been intended by the authors of the 2008 constitution, politics in Burma is no longer the exclusive domain of the armed forces. However, the *Tatmadaw* remains the ultimate arbiter of power and, as Aung San Suu Kyi has acknowledged, a genuinely democratic system of government cannot be introduced without its agreement and cooperation.

15   Aung Zaw, 'Putting a New Face on Myanmar's Military', *The Irrawaddy*, 12 July 2013, www.irra waddy.org/archives/39914.

58

Burma: Two WMD developments

(16:41 AEDT, 8 October 2013)

Given the dearth of reliable information about developments in Myanmar, authoritative statements about controversial issues by governments and international organisations were always welcome. Not only did they define particular problems but also, as in the case of Myanmar's reputed WMD ambitions, they helped dispel any associated myths and misconceptions. Rarely, however, did such statements prevent continuing discussion and speculation about the regime's possible aims and activities.

There have recently been two noteworthy developments in the long-running saga of Burma's reported interest in acquiring weapons of mass destruction. In different ways, both were welcome but, inevitably, concerns remain.

First, in mid September, the US State Department released the third of its annual reports on foreign military and intelligence assistance to Burma, as required by the *JADE Act* of 2008.[1] As the Act specifically referred to the military regime that was replaced with the Thein Sein Government in March 2011, another report was not expected, but it seems that a short note was required to tie off loose ends.

---

1   *Report to Congress per P.L. 110-286 on Military and Intelligence Aid to Burma for 2011* (Washington, DC: US Department of State, 16 September 2013), www.state.gov/s/inr/rls/burmareport/214291.htm [page discontinued] [now at 2009-2017.state.gov/s/inr/rls/burmareport/214291.htm].

And it certainly is short, even more so than the first two reports, which briefly covered developments in 2009 and 2010.[2] The latest report simply states that, during 2011, Burma's main suppliers of weapons and military-related technology were China, North Korea, Russia and Belarus. Also, firms based in Singapore, Taiwan and Thailand apparently assisted Burma's defence industries in acquiring unspecified production technology.

On North Korea, the report states that, during 2011, Pyongyang 'supported Burma's efforts to build and operate military-related production facilities' and that North Korean arms traders purchased production-related equipment for work in Burma from companies based in Taiwan and China. Despite specific references to it in other official US documents, there was no mention of a possible ballistic missile program in Burma being conducted with North Korean assistance.[3]

Nor was there any treatment in the State Department's report of foreign intelligence cooperation. This was despite some bold claims in 2011 that China, in particular, had established a close relationship with Burma in this field, to the extent of operating intelligence collection stations in Burma.[4] If there were any such bilateral links that year, they were covered in the more comprehensive classified annex of the report, which was presented to Congress.

Second, on 17 September, Burma signed the additional protocol to the IAEA's Comprehensive Safeguards Agreement.[5] This fulfilled a promise made by Thein Sein during Barack Obama's visit to Burma in December 2012.[6] It is a major step forward, not only in terms of Naypyidaw's international respectability, but also because it holds out the promise of a better understanding of Burma's nuclear status—for example, through mutually agreed inspections.

2   Andrew Selth, 'Burma and WMD: Nothing to Report?', *The Interpreter*, 29 March 2012, www.lowyinterpreter.org/post/2012/03/29/Burma-and-WMD-Nothing-to-report.aspx [page discontinued] [now at archive.lowyinstitute.org/the-interpreter/burma-and-wmd-nothing-report].

3   Andrew Selth, 'Burma and North Korea: Again? Still?', *The Interpreter*, 10 July 2013, www.lowyinterpreter.org/post/2013/07/10/Burma-and-North-Korea-Again-Still.aspx [page discontinued] [now at www.lowyinstitute.org/the-interpreter/burma-and-north-korea-again-still].

4   Andrew Selth, *Chinese Military Bases in Burma: The Explosion of a Myth*, Griffith Asia Institute Regional Outlook Paper No.10 (Brisbane: Griffith University, 2007), www.scribd.com/document/155246947/Chinese-Military-Bases-in-Burma-Griffith-Asia-Institute.

5   'Burma Signs New Nuclear Deal with IAEA', *Voice of America*, 17 September 2013, www.voanews.com/content/burma-signs-new-nuclear-deal-with-iaea/1751469.html [page discontinued] [now at www.voanews.com/east-asia/burma-signs-new-nuclear-deal-iaea].

6   Andrew Selth, 'Burma: The Man Has Met The Lady', *The Interpreter*, 23 November 2012, www.lowyinterpreter.org/post/2012/11/23/Burma-The-Man-has-met-The-Lady.aspx [page discontinued] [now at archive.lowyinstitute.org/the-interpreter/burma-man-has-met-lady].

Burma clearly hopes that, by signing the additional protocol, it will remove any lingering fears that the former military regime flirted with the idea of making nuclear weapons. At no time did Burma appear to be in breach of its IAEA or Non-Proliferation Treaty obligations,[7] but there were enough suspicious signs, including the acquisition of some dual-use technology,[8] for the international community to question Burma's intentions. Naypyidaw now wants help with a civilian nuclear program.

As former IAEA inspector Robert Kelley has warned, the signing of the additional protocol is only the beginning of a potentially lengthy process of ratification, administration and declaration.[9] Despite the fact that several suspected nuclear facilities have been identified, it is possible that the Burmese will simply declare they have no sites warranting inspection. That would effectively deny the IAEA access and raise doubts about Naypyidaw's bona fides.

The State Department's latest *JADE Act* report is not likely to remove concerns about North Korea's continuing defence links with Burma or quell suspicions of a secret missile program. However, it contains no surprises and is important for what it does not say. Acceptance of the additional protocol does not immediately clarify Burma's nuclear status, but it is very encouraging.

Burma being Burma, there is still a great deal that we do not know, but the more reliable information the US Government and the IAEA can put on the public record, the more they can help balance the policy debate and dispel the myths and misconceptions that surround Burma's possible WMD ambitions.

---

7   Bureau of Arms Control, Verification and Compliance, *2011 Adherence to and Compliance with Arms Control, Non-Proliferation and Disarmament Agreements and Commitments* (Washington, DC: US Department of State, August 2011), www.state.gov/t/avc/rls/rpt/170447.htm#4e_burma [page discontinued] [now at fas.org/nuke/control/compliance2011.pdf].

8   David Albright, Paul Brannan, Robert Kelley and Andrea Scheel Stricker, *Burma: A Nuclear Wannabe; Suspicious Links to North Korea; High-Tech Procurements and Enigmatic Facilities* (Washington, DC: Institute for Science and International Security, 28 January 2010), www.isis-online.org/isis-reports/detail/burma-a-nuclear-wanabee-suspicious-links-to-north-korea-high-tech-procureme.

9   Robert Kelley, 'Nuclear Burma: A Chance to Cut the Red Tape', *Democratic Voice of Burma*, 22 September 2013, www.dvb.no/analysis/nuclear-burma-a-chance-to-cut-the-red-tape-myanmar-iaea-atomic-energ/32677 [page discontinued] [now at english.dvb.no/analysis/nuclear-burma-a-chance-to-cut-the-red-tape-myanmar-iaea-atomic-energ/32677].

59

Aung San Suu Kyi's risky strategy

(15:07 AEDT, 30 October 2013)

Despite the transition to a hybrid civilian–military government in Myanmar, and a dialogue between Aung San Suu Kyi and president Thein Sein, the opposition leader continued to call upon foreign governments to apply pressure against Naypyidaw, including sanctions, which harmed the general population more than those in power. This strategy ran the risk of being not only ineffective, but also counterproductive.

Aung San Suu Kyi is in Europe, where she recently collected the Sakharov Prize for Freedom of Thought, awarded to her by the European Parliament in 1990 shortly after she was placed under house arrest by Burma's military government.[1] While on tour, she is speaking to senior officials and making public speeches.

As she has done on similar trips in the past, she is urging world leaders to put pressure on Burma's government to increase the scope and pace of reform. On one issue she has been quite specific, stating that

---

1   'Aung San Suu Kyi Finally Collects Her 1990 Sakharov Prize', *RTÉ*, [Donnybrook, Ireland], 22 October 2013, www.rte.ie/news/2013/1022/481997-aung-san-suu-kyi-strasbourg/.

'the European Union must come out unambiguously on the need to change the constitution'.[2] She has also identified the armed forces' 'special position' in Burmese politics as a key problem.[3]

This strategy of publicly calling upon foreign governments and international organisations to help her achieve domestic political goals is not new and, in the circumstances, is perhaps to be expected. However, it carries certain risks.

Between 1990 and 2010, Aung San Suu Kyi spent about 14 years under house arrest at the order of a ruthless military regime. While incarcerated, she had little scope to exercise her enormous popularity to political advantage inside Burma. However, she came to be highly respected outside the country and was able to use her considerable influence to gain the backing of powerful political figures, institutions and governments.[4]

During this period, Aung San Suu Kyi encouraged her foreign supporters to apply pressure against Burma's military government. Accompanied in many cases by tough political and economic sanctions, they repeatedly called for her release and the release of other political prisoners, as well as recognition by the regime of internationally accepted human rights and the creation of a genuinely democratic government.

Since 2011, a new administration has been installed in Naypyidaw and Aung San Suu Kyi has been elected to parliament in free and fair by-elections. The armed forces have stepped back from day-to-day government and the international community is rushing in—some say with indecent haste—with advice and practical assistance.[5] Some issues identified in the past as obstacles to international engagement no longer seem to be problems.[6]

---

2   'Suu Kyi Urges World to Pressure Myanmar Leaders on Reform', *Burma News International*, 22 October 2013, bnionline.net/index.php/news/mizzima/16371-suu-kyi-urges-world-to-pressure-myanmar-leaders-on-reform.html [page discontinued].

3   Jonathan Stearns and Ian Wishart, 'Suu Kyi Says Myanmar Must End Military's "Special Position"', *Bloomberg*, 22 October, www.bloomberg.com/news/2013-10-21/suu-kyi-says-myanmar-must-end-military-s-special-position-.html.

4   David I. Steinberg, 'Aung San Suu Kyi and US Policy Toward Burma/Myanmar', *Journal of Current Southeast Asian Affairs*, Vol.29, No.3, 2010, pp.35–59, doi.org/10.1177/186810341002900302.

5   Rowan Callick, 'Companies Rush to Myanmar "New Frontier" for Opportunities', *The Australian*, 24 May 2013, www.theaustralian.com.au/business/economics/companies-rush-to-myanmar-new-frontier-for-opportunities/story-e6frg926-1226649539387# [page discontinued].

6   Andrew Selth, 'Burma and North Korea: Again? Still?', *The Interpreter*, 10 July 2013, www.lowyinterpreter.org/post/2013/07/10/Burma-and-North-Korea-Again-Still.aspx [page discontinued] [now at www.lowyinstitute.org/the-interpreter/burma-and-north-korea-again-still].

Yet despite these welcome developments, and periodic discussions between her and President Thein Sein, Aung San Suu Kyi still seems determined to use her international standing to apply external pressure on Naypyidaw. This raises the question of whether such a strategy can deliver Aung San Suu Kyi the outcomes she seeks.

Diehard advocates of sanctions still claim that international pressure prompted the paradigm shift in policy that saw the advent of a hybrid civilian–military government in Burma and the launch of an ambitious reform program.[7] Yet there is no evidence to support such a view. Indeed, as US and other officials have admitted, sanctions were no more than a 'modest inconvenience' to the military regime, while making life more difficult for the civilian population.[8]

More to the point, the pressures applied by foreign governments and organisations, and their strong rhetoric, were in some ways counterproductive. By antagonising Burma's military leadership, they encouraged their bunker mentality and the development of a garrison state. Aung San Suu Kyi's public endorsement of sanctions against her own country and calls for regime change were seen by the generals as unpatriotic, if not treasonable.

Nor were incentives to reform any more successful. As Burma's foreign minister put it in 2002: '[G]iving a banana to the monkey and then asking it to dance is not the way. We are not monkeys.'[9] Such behaviour on the part of the international community made the intensely nationalistic military leadership even more determined to resist external pressures and set their own agenda for a managed transition to a new system of government.

This is now the widely accepted explanation for the adoption of the regime's roadmap to a 'disciplined democracy'. It would be naive to claim that external factors did not play some part in the regime's thinking, but it is clear that the policy changes seen since the 2010 elections stem largely from internal factors and the government's interest in modernising Burma, not as a result of economic sanctions or foreign threats.

---

7   Mary Kissel, 'Bush's Burma Policy, Obama's Victory Lap', *The Wall Street Journal*, 18 November 2012, online.wsj.com/news/articles/SB20001424127887324439804578115312833763472 [page discontinued].

8   Derek Tonkin, 'Suu Kyi is Fighting, But How Long For?', *Democratic Voice of Burma*, 11 February 2011, www.dvb.no/analysis/suu-kyi-is-fighting-but-how-long-for/14223 [page discontinued].

9   'Aiding Burma', *The Irrawaddy*, November 2002, www2.irrawaddy.org/article.php?art_id=2768.

Given this conclusion, it is curious that Aung San Suu Kyi seems to be counting on Thein Sein's government being more responsive to external pressure than the former military regime. Even if the President and those around him were susceptible to such measures, the armed forces leadership is unlikely to be so, and its support is crucial not only for the continuation of the reform process, but also for any amendment of the constitution.

Bear in mind, too, that since 2011, foreign governments and international organisations have embraced Thein Sein and publicly praised his reform program. Naturally, they have reserved the right to discuss contentious issues like the 2008 constitution. However, the same governments have been anxious to not do or say anything that might interrupt the momentum of the reform process or reduce their newly acquired influence in Naypyidaw.

In any case, Aung San Suu Kyi has less influence on world affairs than in the past. The Burmese Government is not the only one that has changed. New administrations elsewhere are less in thrall to her iconic status and more sensitive to accusations of interfering in Burma's internal affairs. Aung San Suu Kyi herself has been criticised for failing to speak out in support of oppressed communities in Burma, such as the Muslim Rohingya[10] and the Kachin.[11]

It is also surprising that Aung San Suu Kyi would adopt a strategy that seems so much at odds with her current efforts to gain the trust of Burma's generals.[12] As she has acknowledged, the country cannot make the transition to a genuine democracy without the agreement and support of the armed forces. Nor can she become president without a constitutional amendment that is endorsed by the military bloc in parliament.

With all this in mind, some observers are asking whether Aung San Suu Kyi's continued requests to the international community to apply pressure on Naypyidaw are doing more harm than good. Whether or not foreign governments respond, such a strategy threatens to harm her already shaky relationship with Thein Sein. It is also likely to alienate the generals on whom she depends, not only for the realisation of her own leadership ambitions, but also for the further democratisation of Burma.

10   Azeem Ibrahim, 'The Rohingya of Burma: Betrayed by Aung San Suu Kyi', *The Huffington Post*, 17 May 2013, www.huffingtonpost.com/azeem-ibrahim/aung-san-suu-kyi-rohingya_b_3287191.html.
11   Nang Seng, 'I Feel Betrayed by Aung San Suu Kyi', *The Huffington Post*, 2 October 2012, www.huffingtonpost.co.uk/nang-seng/i-feel-betrayed-by-aung-s_b_1924918.html.
12   'Aung San Suu Kyi Attends Burma's Armed Forces Day', *BBC News*, 27 March 2013, www.bbc.co.uk/news/world-asia-21950145.

60

Bombings in Burma: The long view

(12:33 AEDT, 11 November 2013)

There was no simple explanation for the rash of terrorist bombings that occurred in Myanmar in late 2013. By considering them in the light of the country's long history of such incidents, it was possible to view them in a broader context and appreciate the changing nature of the threat. However, that still did not explain who was responsible for the latest attacks, nor the motives that prompted them. They remained a mystery.

The recent spate of terrorist bombings in Burma[1] has not injured many people or caused much property damage, but it is a reminder of the country's continuing, multifaceted internal security problems. No one seems sure who conducted the attacks, or why, but several explanations have been offered.[2] Some have been more convincing than others, but all need to be considered in the widest context.

Terrorist bombings in central Burma are not new. For decades, small devices have periodically exploded in public meeting places like markets, cinemas and railway stations. Larger bombs have been employed against

---

1   '"Cool Heads" Needed as Bombings Tear Through Burma', *Burma Partnership*, 21 October 2013, www.burmapartnership.org/2013/10/cool-heads-needed-as-bombings-tear-through-burma/.

2   Saw Yan Naing, 'Who's Behind the Bombings in Burma?', *The Irrawaddy*, 18 October 2013, www.irrawaddy.org/burma/news-analysis/whos-behind-bombings-burma.html.

infrastructure targets such as bridges, communications facilities and power plants. Official buildings have also been attacked. The casualties were often light, but the bombings contributed to a persistent low-level threat.

Over the past 20 years, the nature of these attacks has broadened. In 1997, for example, a parcel bomb was sent to a senior military officer from Japan. In 2002, letter bombs were sent to Burma's embassies in Tokyo, Singapore, Kuala Lumpur and Manila. In 2005, two powerful bombs exploded in Rangoon, killing 25 people. At the time, Burma was averaging about one bombing a month, though attacks of this size and sophistication were unusual.[3]

It has never been clearly established who was behind all these incidents. The culprits have probably varied over time. Before 1988, they were most likely members of underground communist cells and armed ethnic groups. After the abortive prodemocracy uprising that year, the Thailand-based All Burma Students' Democratic Front planned a series of bombings inside Burma, and a few other activist groups may also have adopted terrorist tactics.[4]

The attacks against Burma's national infrastructure and official sites doubtless reflected the fact that, for many years, up to 25 armed groups were waging guerilla wars against the military government. The bombings in urban centres were harder to explain, as they achieved no appreciable results—apart from alienating the civilian population and prompting tougher countermeasures by the security forces.

Rarely did any group claim responsibility for terrorist bombings. Indeed, those groups accused by the government—most often ethnic insurgents— invariably denied any involvement. Supported by conspiracy theorists inside and outside the country, such groups claimed that Burma's Military Intelligence Service was staging such attacks to discredit opposition groups and justify the state's powerful coercive apparatus.

---

3   'Bomb Blasts in Burma: A Chronology', *The Irrawaddy*, 18 May 2006, www2.irrawaddy.org/article.php?art_id=5762&page=3.
4   Aung Naing Oo, 'Burma Bombings Raise Questions: Who and Why?', *The Irrawaddy*, 18 January 2007, www2.irrawaddy.org/opinion_story.php?art_id=6619.

From time to time, the authorities announced the arrest of an individual or group that they claimed was responsible for particular incidents. Some may have been guilty, but given the regime's paranoia, its constant search for scapegoats and its penchant for calling all its opponents terrorists, it was difficult to know when to take such claims seriously.[5]

The latest attacks are notable for three reasons.[6] First, they mark the first string of bombings since the inauguration of Thein Sein's reformist government in 2011. Second, they appear to have been part of a coordinated countrywide campaign. And third, a bomb left in a luxury hotel in Rangoon seems to have been specifically aimed at foreign visitors.[7]

If all nine reported incidents are connected—and that is not yet clear—their timing may be related to Burma's recent accession to the ASEAN chair. A nationwide ceasefire agreement with ethnic armed groups is close to being finalised[8] and Burma is due to host the Southeast Asian Games in December.[9] The bombing campaign raises the level of uncertainty about all these developments.

Burma's police have announced that the bombings were carried out by ethnic Karen businessmen to scare off foreign investors.[10] Others have pointed the finger at ethnic insurgents, hardliners in the armed forces, rogue intelligence agents, disgruntled democracy activists, Buddhist fanatics and Muslim extremists.[11] It is the last category that has attracted most attention from foreign observers.

---

5   'Burma: 14 Accused Over Bombing in Fabricated Case', Urgent Appeals Programme (Hong Kong: Asian Human Rights Commission, 19 August 2011), www.humanrights.asia/news/urgent-appeals/AHRC-UAC-145-2011/.
6   'Two More Bombings Kill 1, Wound 6 in Burma', *Voice of America*, 17 October 2013, www.voanews.com/content/burma-bomb-blast-kills-1-in-shan-state/1771348.html [page discontinued] [now at www.voanews.com/east-asia/two-more-bombings-kill-1-wound-6-burma].
7   Andrew Buncombe, 'Myanmar Bombing: Three Held After Blast Hits Luxury Hotel in Burma', *The Independent*, [London], 15 October 2013, www.independent.co.uk/news/world/asia/myanmar-bombing-three-held-after-blast-hits-luxury-hotel-in-burma-8880765.html.
8   Saw Yan Naing, 'All But One Ethnic Group Sign Agreement Supporting Nationwide Ceasefire', *The Irrawaddy*, 3 November 2013, www.irrawaddy.org/burma/ethnic-reach-sign-agreement-sign.html.
9   'Concern for SEA Games Safety in Myanmar', *ABC News*, 19 October 2013, www.abc.net.au/news/2013-10-19/an-phils-myanmar-sea-games-safety/5033150.
10   Lawi Weng, 'Burma Police Say Karen Businessmen Plotted Bombings', *The Irrawaddy*, 18 October 2013, www.irrawaddy.org/burma/burma-police-say-karen-businessmen-plotted-bombings.html.
11   Jonah Blank, 'Who's Bombing Myanmar?', *CNN*, 30 October 2013, globalpublicsquare.blogs.cnn.com/2013/10/30/whos-bombing-myanmar/.

After the sectarian violence in Rakhine State in 2012, and similar outbreaks in central Burma this year, there were warnings that the persecution of Burma's Muslims could prompt action by foreign extremists, both inside Burma and further afield. It was also feared that it could radicalise local Muslims, leading to a campaign of terrorist violence in Burma and the recruitment of Burmese Muslims to conduct terrorist operations elsewhere.

These scenarios are worth briefly considering.

Foreign extremists have been calling for a jihad against Burma's government and 'infidel' population since the 1970s, but with little apparent result. After the 2012 violence, however, spokesmen for Al Qaeda, the Taliban and Jemaah Islamiyah all warned of retaliation for attacks against Muslim Rohingyas.[12] In May 2013, Indonesian authorities foiled an attempt to bomb the Burmese Embassy[13] and in August a Buddhist centre in Jakarta was attacked 'in response to the screams of the Rohingya'.[14]

Whether foreign extremists will increase their efforts to operate inside Burma is difficult to judge. Osama bin Laden stated in 2001 that there were already jihadist cells there—a claim repeated by a few journalists and academics. A small number of Rohingyas has been linked to Al Qaeda–affiliated groups in Bangladesh,[15] but unconfirmed reports of militant groups in Burma with ties to organisations like Jemaah Islamiyah need to be treated carefully.[16]

---

12 *Friends Burma's Rohingya Could Do Without*, Burma Briefing No.20 (London: Burma Campaign UK, March 2013), www.burmacampaign.org.uk/images/uploads/Friends_Burmas_Rohingya_could_do_without.pdf.

13 Ben Otto and I Made Sentana, 'Myanmar's Rifts Make Waves in Indonesia', *The Wall Street Journal*, 3 May 2013, online.wsj.com/news/articles/SB10001424127887324266904578459770982983566.

14 Yenni Kwok, 'Jakarta Bomb a Warning That Burma's Muslim–Buddhist Conflict May Spread', *TIME*, 7 August 2013, world.time.com/2013/08/07/jakarta-bomb-a-warning-that-burmas-muslim-buddhist-conflict-may-spread/.

15 Bureau of Counterterrorism and Countering Violent Extremism, *Country Reports on Terrorism 2008* (Washington, DC: US Department of State, April 2009), www.state.gov/documents/organization/122599.pdf [page discontinued] [now at 2009-2017.state.gov/j/ct/rls/crt/2008//index.htm].

16 Daniel Schearf, 'Indonesia Foils Terror Attack on Burmese Embassy', *Voice of America*, 3 May 2013, newsle.com/article/0/75676637/ [page discontinued] [now at www.voanews.com/east-asia-pacific/indonesia-foils-terror-attack-burmese-embassy].

In the vast literature on international terrorism that has appeared since 9/11, it is easy to find lists of factors that reputedly radicalise religious communities.[17] Considered against these criteria, it is easy to see why some counterterrorism experts fear the possibility of Burma's Muslims turning to terrorism. Experienced Burma-watchers, however, are much more cautious in speaking about homegrown or imported jihadism taking root there.

In the freer atmosphere now prevailing in Burma, a terrorist campaign might be easier to mount, from either inside or outside the country, but it would still be difficult to sustain. Burma possesses an extensive state security system[18] and an alert citizenry that would detect outsiders very quickly. More to the point, an organised campaign of violence would be strongly opposed by the overwhelming majority of Burmese Muslims.

Local Muslims want to be accepted as full citizens of Burma, not risk further marginalisation, or worse. They know that a terrorist campaign would be completely counterproductive. A bomb at a sacred site like the Shwedagon Pagoda, for example, could provoke a massive backlash. Also, such attacks would be exploited by Buddhist extremists ready to seize upon any 'evidence' of Muslim attempts to destroy the dominant culture.[19]

These are complex and sensitive issues, all demanding close attention. However, it is worth keeping in mind that, whoever is behind the latest bombings, they will fail to achieve their objectives, whatever these may be. The government will not fall, nor will major policies be amended, because of terrorism. Unless the scope and nature of the attacks dramatically change, tourists will still visit Burma in unprecedented numbers and foreign companies will continue to pursue opportunities in a country hungry for foreign capital and expertise.

---

17 'What Causes Radicalisation?', *Radicalisation Research*, www.radicalisationresearch.org/features/Francis-2012-causes/ [page discontinued].
18 Andrew Selth, *Burma's Security Forces: Performing, Reforming or Transforming?*, Griffith Asia Institute Regional Outlook Paper No.45 (Brisbane: Griffith University, 2013), www.griffith.edu.au/__data/assets/pdf_file/0011/559127/Regional-Outlook-Paper-45-Selth.pdf [page discontinued].
19 Andrew Selth, 'Burma: Conspiracies and Other Theories', *The Interpreter*, 5 June 2013, www.lowyinterpreter.org/post/2013/06/05/Burma-Conspiracies-and-other-theories.aspx [page discontinued] [now at www.lowyinstitute.org/the-interpreter/burma-conspiracies-and-other-theories].

61

Australia and the Burma/ Myanmar name debate

(10:08 AEDT, 27 November 2013)

When Thein Sein's reformist government came to power in Myanmar in 2011, the Australian Government formally acknowledged the change in the country's official name, which was made by the former military regime in 1989. There were strong rumours in late 2013, however, that the incoming Abbott Government would reverse this decision and go back to calling the country 'Burma'.

Aung San Suu Kyi's visit to Australia this week will throw into sharp relief several aspects of Australia's relationship with Burma. One will be the name by which her country is known.

Ever since 1989, when Burma's military government changed the English name of the country to Myanmar, there have been heated arguments over the decision.[1] The Australian Government shuffled from one to the other to suit the competing demands of policy, popular preference and diplomatic etiquette. It finally accepted the country's new official name last year, but some observers suspect the Abbott Government plans to revisit this issue.

---

1   Swe Win, 'A Burmese Tug of Words', *The New York Times*, 6 July 2012, latitude.blogs.nytimes.com/2012/07/06/neither-myanmar-nor-burma-is-a-good-name-for-my-country/?_r=0.

The name 'Burma' derives from the ethnic Burman (or Bamar) majority and, following local custom, was adopted by the British colonialists in the nineteenth century. Yet the more formal indigenous name, 'Myanmar', has been used for titles, in literature and on official documents for centuries. The English-language version of the 1947 constitution, prepared the year before the country regained its independence, referred to the 'Union of Burma', while the Burmese-language version used the name 'Myanmar'.[2]

The adoption of the more formal name by the military government was part of a wider move to rid the country of the vestiges of the colonial era. At the same time, a range of other names was introduced, which conformed more closely to their original pronunciation in the Burmese language. Thus, Rangoon became Yangon, the Irrawaddy River became the Ayeyarwady River, and so on. In this, the regime was following the practice of many other governments in many other countries.

Internal names are a purely national concern. The international community, however, is required to take a formal position on the name of a country in English.

The name Myanmar was accepted by the UN and most other countries. However, some governments—notably, the US and the UK—chose not to do so. The EU adopted the rather clumsy compromise 'Burma/Myanmar'.[3] These countries wanted to show support for Burma's opposition movement, which clung to the old name as a protest against the military regime. The opposition felt that the country's name could only be decided by the people.[4]

The new name was also controversial at another level. 'Myanmar' can be traced back to the precolonial period when successive kings ruled the central lowlands of Burma and periodically clashed with the states and societies around them. It implies the continuing political dominance of the major ethnic group living within the geographical boundaries inherited from the British in 1948. This is anathema to many among the country's ethnic minorities.

---

2   Derek Tonkin, '"Burma" versus "Myanmar": A Touch of Desperation', *Mizzima News* [Yangon], 23 November 2013, reprinted by the Arakan Rohingya National Organisation, 20 October 2013, www.rohingya.org/burma-versus-myanmar-a-touch-of-desperation/.

3   'Should it be Burma or Myanmar?', *BBC News*, 26 September 2007, news.bbc.co.uk/2/hi/uk_news/magazine/7013943.stm.

4   Min Zin, 'Burma or Myanmar: The Name Game', *Foreign Policy*, 5 July 2012, transitions.foreignpolicy.com/posts/2012/07/05/burma_or_myanmar_the_name_game.

To some, the use of either 'Burma' or 'Myanmar' represented a political position. To call the country Myanmar was deemed by activists to denote sympathy for the military regime. To the government, continued use of the old name was considered insulting.

Yet, many who preferred to use 'Burma' after 1989 did so without wider connotations. Many commentators, myself included, still feel that 'Burma' is more easily recognised than 'Myanmar'. Besides, it lends itself to 'Burmese'; 'Myanmar' does not have an equivalent adjective in English.

Like all other countries, Australia used the name Myanmar in formal diplomatic exchanges, but in public it continued to refer to Burma. Indeed, Kevin Rudd made a point of doing so—for example, when he issued a press release in 2011 announcing 'Foreign Minister to Visit Burma'.[5] In June 2012, however, Bob Carr made an important symbolic gesture to the new civilian–military government in Naypyidaw by publicly calling the country Myanmar.[6]

Since then, official Australian statements and press releases have referred to Myanmar, not Burma. The Department of Foreign Affairs and Trade has a *Myanmar Country Brief* on its website.[7] During President Thein Sein's visit to Australia in March this year, it was evident that Prime Minister Julia Gillard's numerous public references to Myanmar were in keeping with a high-level decision to refer to the country by its formal name.[8]

There are now concerns that the Abbott Government might change this policy. In a recent press release, both names were used,[9] suggesting that Burma may once again become the preferred term. If so, this would probably be in deference to the views of Aung San Suu Kyi, who insists on

5   Minister for Foreign Affairs, 'Foreign Minister to Visit Burma', Media release, Parliament House, Canberra, 24 June 2011, foreignminister.gov.au/releases/2011/kr_mr_110624a.html [page discontinued].

6   Dan Flitton, 'Burma Name Change Signals Symbolic Shift by Australia', *Sydney Morning Herald*, 5 June 2012, www.smh.com.au/federal-politics/political-news/burma-name-change-signals-symbolic-shift-by-australia-20120605-1zsq8.html.

7   Department of Foreign Affairs and Trade, *Myanmar Country Brief* (Canberra: Australian Government, 2016), www.dfat.gov.au/geo/myanmar/myanmar-country-brief.

8   Tom Allard, 'Australia to Forge Closer Ties with Myanmar', *Sydney Morning Herald*, 18 March 2013, www.smh.com.au/federal-politics/political-news/australia-to-forge-closer-ties-with-myanmar-20130318-2ga3x.html.

9   The Hon. Julie Bishop MP, Minister for Foreign Affairs, 'Aung San Suu Kyi to Visit Australia', Media release, Parliament House, Canberra, 5 November 2013, foreignminister.gov.au/releases/2013/jb_mr_131105a.html [page discontinued] [now at www.foreignminister.gov.au/minister/julie-bishop/media-release/aung-san-suu-kyi-visit-australia].

calling her country 'Burma'. Foreign Minister Julie Bishop has admitted to being 'in awe' of the Nobel laureate, who she says inspired her to become involved in national politics.[10]

The former British diplomat Derek Tonkin has argued[11] that the debate over whether to call the country Burma or Myanmar is at root a clash between international protocol and political correctness. Since the advent of Thein Sein's reformist government in 2011, the former has been in the ascendant. 'Burma' is heard less frequently in official UK circles and the EU looks set to abandon its hybrid nomenclature.[12] Even the US is now using the name 'Myanmar' in public, albeit with the explanation that it is a 'diplomatic courtesy'.[13]

If the Abbott Government should revert to the old name—at least outside diplomatic exchanges—it would be in the face of this clear trend. It would also risk isolating Australia on an issue that, however trivial it might first appear, has the potential to complicate not only recent efforts to get closer to Naypyidaw, but also the wider bilateral relationship. The outcome of any policy review should be evident when Aung San Suu Kyi meets senior Australian officials later this week.

Confucius wrote in *The Analects*: 'If names be not correct, language is not in accordance with the truth of things. If language be not in accordance with the truth of things, affairs cannot be carried on to success.'[14] This is as relevant today as it was 2,000 years ago.

10 'Women in Politics: Julie Bishop, Deputy Leader of the Federal Liberal Party', *Australian Women Online*, 13 August 2013, www.australianwomenonline.com/women-in-politics-julie-bishop-deputy-leader-of-the-federal-liberal-party/.

11 'Commentaries by Derek Tonkin', *Network Myanmar*, www.networkmyanmar.org/index.php/commentary [page discontinued] [now at www.networkmyanmar.org/Blogs.html].

12 Banyan, 'Bye-Bye, Burma, Bye-Bye', *The Economist*, 21 May 2013, www.economist.com/blogs/banyan/2013/05/what-s-name-myanmar.

13 Max Fisher, 'Why It's Such a Big Deal that Obama Said "Myanmar" Rather than Burma', *The Washington Post*, 19 November 2012, www.washingtonpost.com/blogs/worldviews/wp/2012/11/19/why-its-such-a-big-deal-that-obama-said-myanmar-rather-than-burma/.

14 Arthur Waley, *The Analects of Confucius* (London: George Allen & Unwin, 1949), Ch.13, p.171.

62

When Aung San Suu Kyi comes to call

(10:24 AEDT, 3 December 2013)

Aung San Suu Kyi's first visit to Australia, from 27 November to 2 December 2013, was in most respects a predictable exercise in hero-worship and cautious diplomacy, but it also highlighted several aspects of Australian policy towards Myanmar that demanded closer attention.

At one level, Aung San Suu Kyi's visit to Australia last week was all high praise, inspiring speeches and standing ovations. At another level, it was hardheaded politics, diplomatic signals and muted criticisms. At times, history was simplified or rewritten to suit the occasion. In other words, there were no surprises and on all sides the visit was considered a resounding success.

Wherever she went, Aung San Suu Kyi was given a rapturous reception. She is clearly held in high regard by the Australian Government, the public and most members of the Burmese community (the Kachins boycotted the visit to protest her failure to speak out against recent military operations in Kachin State).[1] The Nobel laureate's many qualities and accomplishments were acknowledged with awards, honorary degrees and other accolades.

---

1   Deborah Snow, 'Aung San Suu Kyi: Kachin Ethnic Group Boycotts Visit to Opera House', *Sydney Morning Herald*, 28 November 2013, www.smh.com.au/national/aung-san-suu-kyi-kachin-ethnic-group-boycotts-visit-to-opera-house-20131127-2yadu.html [page discontinued].

As packed auditoriums in three capital cities found, Aung San Suu Kyi is a capable and polished performer—quite comfortable in the public eye. In private meetings, too, she can be a persuasive advocate of her party's political causes and its wider aspirations for her country.

In her public speeches and media interviews, Aung San Suu Kyi stressed the themes of 'national reconciliation' and 'the rule of law'. She also embraced 'honest politics' and 'principled compromise'. She rejected the label 'democratic icon', emphasising that she had in fact been a practising politician ever since the formation of her party in 1988.[2] She said little specifically about her ambition to become President of Burma in 2016.[3]

In public and private, Aung San Suu Kyi emphasised that Burma was only at the beginning of the road to a true democracy and that, without major constitutional reforms, real progress towards that goal could not be achieved. On a number of occasions, she warned Australia against accepting the status quo and trying to strengthen relations with the current government in Naypyidaw. Instead, she sought support for her own party and its long-term goals.[4]

How Australia might do this, however, was not made clear. The country's aid, expertise and moral support were welcomed, but how Canberra could or should intervene in sensitive areas of Burma's domestic politics was not spelt out, at least not in public. Nor was there any discussion of whether attempts to influence internal developments in Burma may prove counterproductive—for example, by provoking a backlash from nationalists and other hardliners.[5]

There was some questioning of Aung San Suu Kyi's positions on contentious issues like the repression of Muslims in Burma, the military campaigns against certain armed ethnic groups and her relations with the

2   'Daw Aung San Suu Kyi AC: In Conversation with Dr Michael Fullilove', Lowy Institute, Sydney, 29 November 2013, lowyinstitute.org/news-and-media/videos/a-conversation-with-aung-san-suu-kyi [page discontinued] [now at www.lowyinstitute.org/news-and-media/multimedia/video/daw-aung-san-suu-kyi-ac-conversation-dr-michael-fullilove].

3   'Aung San Suu Kyi Seduces Australia with Presidential Ambitions', *Xinhua*, [Beijing], 29 November 2013, news.xinhuanet.com/english/world/2013-11/29/c_132927795.htm [page discontinued].

4   Australian Associated Press, 'Suu Kyi to Australia: Smart Money's On Us', *News.com*, 28 November 2013, www.news.com.au/national/breaking-news/suu-kyi-to-australia-smart-moneys-on-us/story-e6fr fku9-1226770386242.

5   Andrew Selth, 'Aung San Suu Kyi's Risky Strategy', *The Interpreter*, 30 October 2013, www.lowy interpreter.org/post/2013/10/30/Aung-San-Suu-Kyis-risky-strategy.aspx [page discontinued] [now at www.lowyinstitute.org/the-interpreter/aung-san-suu-kyis-risky-strategy].

country's armed forces. However, it was always respectful, even gentle by Australian standards.[6] She was clearly expecting such issues to be raised and had little difficulty in avoiding direct answers, usually by referring to broad principles and historical examples.

Aung San Suu Kyi's enormous popularity is both a boon and a burden. It will help her achieve some goals, but it will also pose real problems. There is no way she can meet everyone's high expectations, either at home or abroad. As she noted several times during her Australian tour, she has already had to make some difficult choices regarding her own and her party's future. There will be many more such challenges in the years ahead.

Back home, Aung San Suu Kyi faces a much more demanding audience. Her leadership style, policies and performance have been subject to criticism, not only by members of the government and armed forces, but also by people within her own party. Some ethnic communities and other sectors of Burmese society are unhappy with what The Australian National University's Nicholas Farrelly has described as her personal transformation 'from symbol to strategist'.[7]

Also, her popularity worries many conservative Burmese.[8] Not only does it pose a threat to the armed forces' continuing control over the political process, but also they fear the outcome of elections in 2015, which, if free and fair, would likely give the NLD a large majority in the national parliament. The prospect of a relatively liberal, populist civilian president, supported by a fractious and inexperienced party, troubles them deeply.

She may be widely admired, but Aung San Suu Kyi's future, and that of her country, is far from certain.

---

6   'Aung San Suu Kyi Calls for "Genuine Democracy"', *7.30 Report*, [ABC TV], 28 November 2013, www.abc.net.au/7.30/content/2013/s3901329.htm.
7   Nicholas Farrelly, 'Suu Kyi Carries Great Expectations', *The Canberra Times*, 29 November 2013, www.canberratimes.com.au/comment/suu-kyi-carries-great-expectations-20131128-2ycry.html [page discontinued].
8   Sanay Lin and Simon Roughneen, 'A Suu Kyi Presidency Would Bring "Chaos", Says Firebrand Monk', *The Irrawaddy*, 28 November 2013, www.irrawaddy.org/burma/suu-kyi-presidency-bring-chaos-says-firebrand-monk.html [page discontinued] [now at www.irrawaddy.com/election/news/a-suu-kyi-presidency-would-bring-chaos-says-firebrand-monk].

As a footnote to my previous post,[9] it is worth recording that, throughout Aung San Suu Kyi's Australian visit, most of the officials, journalists and academics she met referred to her country as 'Myanmar', or used neutral formulations such as 'your country'. The Australian National University acknowledged the controversy over the country's name but rejected what Chancellor Gareth Evans described as 'linguistic authoritarianism'.[10]

Foreign Minister Julie Bishop has said that she 'adopted the Government's protocol in relation to the use of Burma or Myanmar', but this now seems much more flexible than under the former Labor Government. During a joint press conference with Aung San Suu Kyi at Parliament House on 28 November, the Prime Minister referred to 'Burma' and 'the Government of Burma'.[11] Whether this was a courtesy to his guest, who still uses the country's old name, or is hard evidence of a policy change is difficult to judge.

It may have simply been a gaffe. After all, this was the same occasion when, in an apparent attempt at empathy, the Prime Minister told the world's most famous political prisoner: 'I was an opposition leader myself for four years.'[12]

---

9   Andrew Selth, 'Australia and the Burma/Myanmar Name Debate', *The Interpreter*, 27 November 2013, www.lowyinterpreter.org/post/2013/11/27/Australia-and-the-BurmaMyanmar-name.aspx [page discontinued] [now at www.lowyinstitute.org/the-interpreter/australia-and-burmamyanmar-name-debate].
10   'Aung San Suu Kyi at ANU', November 2013, new.livestream.com/canberradcc/AungSanSuuKyi [page discontinued].
11   Tony Abbott, Prime Minister of Australia, 'Joint Press Conference with Daw Aung San Suu Kyi', [Transcript], Canberra, 28 November 2013, www.pm.gov.au/media/2013-11-28/joint-press-conference-daw-aung-san-suu-kyi [page discontinued] [now at pmtranscripts.pmc.gov.au/release/transcript-23121].
12   'Myanmar Opposition Leader Aung San Suu Kyi Says Mercy Important in Asylum Seeker Debate', *ABC News*, 29 November 2013, www.abc.net.au/news/2013-11-28/aung-san-suu-kyi-weighs-in-on-asylum-debate/5123282.

2014

63

Burma puts its stamp on the world: Philately and foreign policy

(09:02 AEDT, 7 January 2014)

Postage stamps are easily dismissed as colourful curiosities or ephemera unrelated to affairs of state. However, they can provide a window into the domestic and international politics of individual countries. In this regard, Myanmar's philatelic record can offer a number of insights into the thinking of successive governments.

When subjects like soft power and public diplomacy are discussed in forums like this, few people have postage stamps in mind, but there has long been a close connection between philately and foreign policy. In themselves, stamps express sovereignty, but they are also examples of political iconography and visual indicators of official attitudes and policies, aimed at both domestic and international audiences.

The use of stamps as projections of national identity can be traced back to their origin in 1840, when stamps carrying portraits of Queen Victoria began to be used throughout the British Empire. Even before the Universal Postal Union was formed in 1874 to permit the free flow of international mail, stamps were used to mark a country's independence, stake territorial claims, record military victories, honour statesmen and women and support multilateral institutions.

There are now about 600 stamp-issuing entities, or 'authorities', around the world. Over the past century and a half, they have produced an estimated 250,000 different designs. Through the use of unique and often striking visual statements in a small two-dimensional space, they have covered themes as far-ranging as nationalism, history, politics, economics, art, cultural identity and foreign relations.

Authoritarian governments in particular have been quick to recognise the propaganda value of stamps and to utilise them in international campaigns. During the Cold War, for example, the Soviet Union utilised stamps to trumpet the glories of communism. North Korea is still one of the most prolific issuers of stamps portraying icons of its own and other revolutionary movements. Cuba's stamps display a stubborn attachment to such themes.

These days, China has become particularly adept at promoting its relations with other countries through the issue of commemorative stamps, usually celebrating the establishment of diplomatic ties and other major events.[1] Some joint issues have been paid for entirely by Beijing. Not only do such stamps promote China as a friendly global power, they also help strengthen its ties with strategically important states.

It is also possible, through the study of a country's postage stamps, to see the historical development of its foreign relations. Afghanistan's stamp issues between 1948 and 1992, for example, mark the 1973 coup that toppled the monarchy, the 1978 Marxist revolution that overthrew the republic, the Soviet invasion in 1979, the withdrawal of Soviet troops in 1989 and the short-lived government that collapsed in 1992.[2]

In Burma's case, successive governments have been quite conservative in their use of postage stamps as diplomatic tools.[3] Issues have been used almost exclusively to promote official programs and to mark major events within and outside the country. From independence in 1948 to the 1988

---

1   'What Stamps Tell Us (II): Philatelic Imperialism or Social Networking?', *Commonwealth Stamps Opinion*, 3 September 2013, commonwealthstampsopinion.blogspot.com.au/2013/09/301-philatelic-imperialism-or-social.html.

2   Lawrence E. Cohen, 'Afghanistan's Foreign Relations through Philately', *American Philatelist*, September 2012, stamps.org/userfiles/file/AP/feature/Feature_09_12.pdf [page discontinued] [now at digital.ipcprintservices.com/publication/?i=121983&article_id=1143485&view=articleBrowser].

3   Bertil Lintner, 'Stamping Out History', *The Irrawaddy*, January 2008, www2.irrawaddy.org/print_article.php?art_id=9796 [page discontinued] [now at www2.irrawaddy.com/article.php?art_id=9796&page=2].

prodemocracy uprising, about 37 per cent of stamp issues emphasised broad nationalist themes, while 18 per cent were on revolutionary and military subjects.[4]

During this period, the U Nu and Ne Win governments pursued strictly neutral foreign policies. A few countries commemorated state visits to and from Burma on their postage stamps[5] but no bilateral relationships were recognised on Burmese issues. Rather, emphasis was given to multilateral institutions and international events. Between 1948 and 1988, some 40 per cent of Burma's stamps were dedicated to UN-related themes.

After a new military government took over in 1988, however, there were a number of significant changes in this approach.

Over the past 25 years, UN-related themes have almost disappeared from Burmese stamps, probably reflecting the deterioration of relations since the UN began to criticise Burma for its human rights abuses. Emphasis has been given instead to the achievements of the military regime and political milestones, such as the inauguration of a new government in 2011.[6] At the same time, attention has been paid to Burma's evolving foreign relations.

Burma issued a stamp to mark the thirtieth anniversary of ASEAN in 1997—the year it joined the association. In 2007, Burma collaborated with other member states to produce a mini-sheet commemorating ASEAN's fortieth anniversary, and in 2012 it issued a set of stamps to mark the eleventh ASEAN Telecommunications Senior Officials Meeting in Naypyidaw.[7] It is expected that Burma will issue a new stamp this year when it assumes the ASEAN chair.

In a notable break with past practice, Burma and China jointly issued a stamp in 2000 to mark the fiftieth anniversary of the establishment of diplomatic ties. This was followed in 2010 by a stamp to celebrate

---

4   'Stamps of Burma', *Burma Philatelic Blog*, 21 March 2012, burmaphilatelic.blogspot.com.au/.
5   'The State Visit of His Excellency U San Yu, President of the Socialist Republic of the Union of Burma', www.pennfamily.org/KSS-USA/870608-1496.htm [page discontinued].
6   'Myanmar Issues Postage Stamps to Mark Establishment of New Gov't', *Xinhua*, [Beijing], 16 June 2011, news.xinhuanet.com/english2010/world/2011-06/16/c_13933177.htm [page discontinued].
7   'President U Thein Sein Delivered an Address at 11th ASEAN Telecommunications and IT Ministers Meeting (11th TELEMIN) at Myanmar International Convention Centre', President's Office, Republic of the Union of Myanmar, Nay Pyi Taw, 8 December 2011, www.president-office. gov.mm/en/?q=briefing-room/speeches-and-remarks/2011/12/08/id-726 [page discontinued].

the sixtieth anniversary.[8] In 2013, there was another joint issue, this time with Russia, to mark the sixty-fifth anniversary of diplomatic relations between Burma and that country. No other states have been recognised by Naypyidaw in this fashion.

Unlike most other countries, Burma has eschewed portraits of prominent individuals. Independence hero Aung San was an occasional exception before 1988, but even his face disappeared from stamps (and the national currency)[9] after his daughter began to challenge the military regime. It has been suggested that this was in part because Aung San Suu Kyi bore a striking resemblance to her father.

Indeed, when Aung San Suu Kyi's portrait was included in a set of eight stamps issued by Norway in 2001,[10] to mark the centenary of the Nobel Peace Prize, the stamps were banned in Burma.[11] The country's opposition leader has appeared on the stamps of several other countries and on unofficial issues produced to mark special events, such as her receipt of the Sakharov Prize last year.

Another Burmese figure who has been portrayed on foreign postage stamps is former UN secretary-general U Thant. He has been honoured in this way by more than a dozen countries, but not Burma, largely because Ne Win resented the global standing of U Nu's former secretary. In 2009, the UN Postal Administration issued three stamps to commemorate the 100th anniversary of U Thant's birth.[12]

The only time a senior Burmese military figure has been portrayed on a postage stamp was in 2000, when a picture of Senior General Than Shwe (then chairman of the SPDC) was included in the world's largest mini-sheet, which was issued by Liberia. It depicted the heads of state of all 190 UN members.

---

8   'Myanmar Issues New Stamp to Mark Sino-Myanmar Relations Anniversary', *People's Daily*, [Beijing], 8 June 2010, english.peopledaily.com.cn/90001/90776/90883/7017150.html [page discontinued].

9   Htet Naing Zaw, 'Gen Aung San to Once Again Feature on Burma's Banknotes', *The Irrawaddy*, 15 November 2013, www.irrawaddy.org/politics/gen-aung-san-feature-burmas-bank-notes.html.

10   Burma Lawyers' Council, 'Burmese Junta Violates UPU Constitution', *Legal Issues on Burma Journal*, No.10, December 2001, www.burmalibrary.org/docs/LIOB10-BKSen.2.htm [page discontinued].

11   Win Htein, '2,500-Postcards for Aung San Suu Kyi', *The Irrawaddy*, 19 December 2001, www2. irrawaddy.org/article.php?art_id=3650.

12   United Nations Postal Administration, '1st Day of Issue, 6 February 2009: 100th Anniversary U Thant', *Information Circular* (New York: UN Secretariat, 15 January 2009), unstamps.un.org/unpa/en/ products/100th_Anniversary_U_Thant/index.html [page discontinued] [now at digitallibrary.un.org/ record/646761?ln=en].

Some attention is now being paid to postage stamps by academic researchers, but they remain a neglected source. They are easily dismissed as colourful curiosities or ephemera unrelated to affairs of state. However, they can provide a window on to the domestic and international politics of countries. Stamps are emblematic devices that illustrate how the issuing states wish to be seen, not only by their own citizens, but also by those beyond their borders.

It is possible that in this era of email, Skype and social media, the heyday of the postage stamp is over, but they are still important. This is particularly so in countries like Burma, where electronic communications are underdeveloped. In any case, given the dearth of reliable information about Burma's domestic politics and foreign relations, no source should be seen as unworthy of serious consideration.

64

Myanmar becomes Burma, again

(08:32 AEDT, 14 January 2014)

The Abbott Government's unannounced and unexplained decision to revert to use of the name 'Burma', after the previous government finally accepted widespread international practice and started calling the country 'Myanmar', needlessly complicated Australia's relations with Naypyidaw and possibly other regional governments.

There has been no official announcement but, as foreshadowed on *The Interpreter* last year, the Abbott Government seems to have decided to revert to using Burma's old name.[1]

In 2012, former foreign minister Bob Carr declared that Australia would join the overwhelming majority of countries, international organisations and regional institutions that publicly called Burma by its official name, the Union of Myanmar, which was adopted by the country's military regime in 1989.

---

1   Andrew Selth, 'Australia and the Burma/Myanmar Name Debate', *The Interpreter*, 27 November 2013, www.lowyinterpreter.org/post/2013/11/27/Australia-and-the-BurmaMyanmar-name.aspx [page discontinued] [now at www.lowyinstitute.org/the-interpreter/australia-and-burmamyanmar-name-debate].

This step was part of a comprehensive new policy approach by Australia, which included the suspension of political and economic sanctions. It was time, Bob Carr said during a visit to Burma in June 2012, that Australia 'moved beyond coercion'. Such measures had been found 'no longer to contribute to the reform process'.[2]

The decision to call the country Myanmar was timely, given the creation of a new Burmese government in 2011, Naypyidaw's announcement of a sweeping reform program and Canberra's plans to develop closer bilateral relations. As Dan Flitton observed, it was a significant symbolic shift in Australia's position.[3] It was also in keeping with clear global trends.

Following last September's federal election, it was rumoured that the Coalition Government planned to change this approach and, outside official exchanges, once again call the country 'Burma'.

During the visit to Australia of opposition leader Aung San Suu Kyi last November,[4] the Prime Minister referred publicly to 'Burma' and 'the Government of Burma'.[5] Inquiries about these comments made to the Prime Minister's office, the foreign minister's office and the Department of Foreign Affairs and Trade (DFAT) failed to elicit any clear response.

In December 2013, however, DFAT's public website was revised. The 'Myanmar Country Page' is now called the 'Burma Country Page'.[6] The name 'Myanmar' still appears in a few places—for example, on the page referring to the Australian Embassy in Rangoon (Yangon)—but the relevant DFAT 'fact sheet' is clearly headed 'Burma'.[7]

---

2   Hamish McDonald, 'Carr Lifts Sanctions Against Burma', *Sydney Morning Herald*, 8 June 2012, www.smh.com.au/federal-politics/political-news/carr-lifts-sanctions-against-burma-20120607-1zz2j.html.

3   Daniel Flitton, 'Burma Name Change Signals Symbolic Shift by Australia', *Sydney Morning Herald*, 5 June 2012, www.smh.com.au/federal-politics/political-news/burma-name-change-signals-symbolic-shift-by-australia-20120605-1zsq8.html.

4   Andrew Selth, 'When Aung San Suu Kyi Comes to Call', *The Interpreter*, 3 December 2013, www.lowyinterpreter.org/post/2013/12/03/When-Aung-San-Suu-Kyi-comes-to-call.aspx [page discontinued] [now at www.lowyinstitute.org/the-interpreter/when-aung-san-suu-kyi-comes-call].

5   Tony Abbott, Prime Minister of Australia, 'Joint Press Conference with Daw Aung San Suu Kyi', Media release, Parliament House, Canberra, 28 November 2013, www.pm.gov.au/media/2013-11-28/joint-press-conference-daw-aung-san-suu-kyi [page discontinued] [now at pmtranscripts.pmc.gov.au/release/transcript-23121].

6   Department of Foreign Affairs and Trade, *Burma Country Page*, (Canberra: Australian Government), www.dfat.gov.au/geo/burma/ [page discontinued].

7   Department of Foreign Affairs and Trade, *Burma: Country Fact Sheet*, (Canberra: Australian Government), www.dfat.gov.au/geo/fs/burm.pdf [page discontinued].

Just to confuse matters, on 7 January this year, the foreign minister issued a media statement welcoming the release of political prisoners—in 'Myanmar'.[8]

While the Prime Minister's public comments last year remain unexplained, the mixed messages coming from Canberra seem to reflect a wish by the Abbott Government to differentiate between perceived 'internal' and 'external' usages of the country's name. In international diplomacy, however, such distinctions are always difficult to sustain.

Only the US and some EU countries still use the old name. This is largely a gesture to Aung San Suu Kyi, who feels the former military regime had no right to change the country's name without a popular mandate. However, these countries seem increasingly uncomfortable with this legacy of the past, when they were far more critical of Burma's government.[9]

Lest it be thought that this is a minor matter of diplomatic etiquette, the US Government was recently obliged to defend its use of the name 'Myanmar' in a public statement by John Kerry.[10] In what former British ambassador Derek Tonkin has described as an 'utterly unconvincing' explanation,[11] a State Department spokesperson dismissed such usage (including at times by President Obama) as a 'diplomatic courtesy'.[12]

This formula may satisfy the Burma lobby in the US and elsewhere, but Naypyidaw considers the continued use of 'Burma' by Western governments to be gratuitously offensive. Also, given the use of 'Myanmar' in all diplomatic correspondence and a wide range of other official exchanges, from visa applications to UN resolutions, the practice strikes many Burmese officials as faintly ridiculous.

---

8   The Hon. Julie Bishop MP, Minister for Foreign Affairs, 'Australian Government Welcomes Release of Political Prisoners in Myanmar', Media release, Parliament House, Canberra, 7 January 2014, foreignminister.gov.au/releases/Pages/2014/jb_mr_140107.aspx?ministerid=4 [page discontinued] [now at www.foreignminister.gov.au/minister/julie-bishop/media-release/australian-government-welcomes-release-political-prisoners-myanmar].

9   Derek Tonkin, '"Burma" Versus "Myanmar": A Touch of Desperation', *Mizzima News*, [Yangon], 18 October 2013, www.mizzima.com/opinion/commentary/item/10365-burma-versus-myanmar-a-touch-of-desperation [page discontinued].

10   'US Uses "Myanmar" Name as "Diplomatic Courtesy"', *Channel News Asia*, [Singapore], 7 January 2014, www.channelnewsasia.com/news/world/us-uses-myanmar-name-as/945424.html [page discontinued].

11   'Myanmar's Independence Day: Press Statement', *Network Myanmar*, www.networkmyanmar.org/ [page discontinued].

12   Marie Harf, 'Daily Press Briefing', US Department of State, Washington, DC, January 2014, www.state.gov/r/pa/prs/dpb/2014/01/219353.htm#BURMA [page discontinued].

It is difficult to know what has prompted the Australian Government's unexpected policy shift. It could simply be a reflection of the foreign minister's longstanding support for Aung San Suu Kyi.[13] Or it may herald a more critical approach to issues such as Burma's military-biased constitution and the harsh treatment of Muslim Rohingyas.

Whatever the reason, having formally opted for 'Myanmar' less than two years ago, it is curious that Canberra would knowingly—and, some would say, needlessly—complicate its relationship with Naypyidaw and adopt a position that is out of step with all other states in the Asia-Pacific region, including Burma's fellow ASEAN members.

---

13   Julie Bishop, 'Broken Promise on Burma', *Sydney Morning Herald*, 18 February 2010, www.smh. com.au/federal-politics/blogs/the-bishops-gambit/broken-promise-on-burma-20100217-ocll.html [page discontinued].

65

Is Burma really buying submarines?

(11:50 AEDT, 29 January 2014)

For years, there were rumours that Myanmar's armed forces wanted to acquire at least one submarine. None of these stories could ever be confirmed. Some officials may have nursed such ambitions but, as far as any foreign observers could tell from the information publicly available, Myanmar had not purchased any boats, nor did it have the capacity to develop a subsurface warfare capability.

For the past six months, there have been intermittent reports in the news media and on specialist websites stating that Burma (Myanmar) is developing a submarine capability. If this is true, it has important implications not only for Burma and the region, but also for the wider international community.

However, equally dramatic stories about Burma have emerged in the past only to prove misleading or false.

This is not the first time Burma has been linked to a submarine sale. In 2003, it was claimed the military government had held discussions with North Korea on the purchase of one or two small submarines.

The 110-tonne Yugo and 370-tonne Sang-O classes were mentioned. Despite the limitations of both designs, Burma's interest in these boats was said to reflect a wish to police its territorial waters and deter an invasion.[1]

According to *Jane's Defence Weekly* (*JDW*), Burma eventually opted to purchase one Sang-O-class submarine but was forced to abandon the deal in late 2002. It was suggested that the project had been scuppered by the cost of the boat and perhaps belated recognition by the country's military leadership of the technical difficulties of keeping it fully operational.

These reports were never confirmed, but other developments gave them some credibility. For example, after the 1988 uprising, Burma's new military government launched an ambitious plan to modernise and expand the armed forces. This included a naval rearmament program. In 1999, it was reported that Burmese naval officers had undergone unspecified 'submarine training' in Pakistan.

Also relevant was the fact that in the 1990s Burma started to expand its defence ties with North Korea.[2] If the generals were interested in acquiring other weapons from Pyongyang, possibly including ballistic missiles, so the logic went, why not a few submarines? If Korea was prepared to sell Yugo-class boats to Vietnam (which it did in 1997), why not to Burma?

Over the next decade, Burma's navy acquired several new ships, some armed with antisubmarine weapon systems,[3] but the emphasis was clearly on surface warfare. Claims by an activist group in 2010 that India had provided training for Burma on a Foxtrot-class submarine, and that Naypyidaw was considering the purchase of two Foxtrot boats from Russia, could not be verified.[4]

---

1   Andrew Selth, *Burma and the Threat of Invasion: Regime Fantasy or Strategic Reality?*, Griffith Asia Institute Regional Outlook Paper No.17 (Brisbane: Griffith University, 2008), www.griffith. edu.au/business-government/griffith-asia-institute/pdf/Andrew-Selth-Regional-Outlook-17v2. pdf [page discontinued].

2   Clifford McCoy, 'Rogues of the World Unite', *Asia Times Online*, [Hong Kong], 28 April 2007, www.atimes.com/atimes/Southeast_Asia/ID28Ae01.html [page discontinued].

3   Ankit Panda, 'Myanmar to Import India-Developed Submarine Sonar Systems', *The Diplomat*, [Washington, DC], 25 October 2013, thediplomat.com/2013/10/myanmar-to-import-india-developed-submarine-sonar-systems/.

4   'Russian Submarines for Burma Navy: Kilos or Foxtrots?', *Hla Oo's Blog*, 18 July 2013, hlaoo 1980.blogspot.com.au/2013/07/russian-submarines-for-burma-navy-kilos.html.

During a visit to Russia in June 2013, however, Burmese Commander-in-Chief Senior General Min Aung Hlaing reportedly opened discussions for the purchase of two 3,000-tonne Kilo-class diesel submarines. It was also claimed that he secretly visited St Petersburg's naval dockyard. A number of commentators have stated that Burma hopes to create a submarine force by 2015.[5]

Burma was said to have chosen the Russian Kilos over Pakistan's ageing Agosta-70 boats.[6] Also, in April 2013, about 20 Burmese naval officers and ratings reportedly began basic submarine familiarisation and training in Pakistan, probably at the Submarine Training Centre, PNS Bahadur. This prompted *JDW* to suggest that 'Myanmar is finally taking concrete steps towards developing a subsurface capability'.[7]

These reports raise a number of issues that need to be considered.

First, no official announcement has been made, by either Russia or Burma, about a possible Kilo sale. This is not unusual, but it leaves the field to unconfirmed reports in the news media and on activist websites. Most of these outlets have simply recycled earlier claims without giving sources or providing any firm evidence. Indeed, it is difficult to determine where the story originated.

Second, there does not appear to have been any response to these reports from other countries, which again raises questions about their accuracy. In normal circumstances, it might be expected that Burma's possible acquisition of submarines would prompt comments from its neighbours at least, let alone interested powers such as the UK and the US.

Third, Burma's armed forces are much larger, more balanced, better equipped and more capable than they were in 1988. They have also developed a better grasp of conventional warfare doctrines. Yet they still have serious problems, and it is difficult to see Burma being able to develop a viable submarine force in the foreseeable future, let alone by 2015.

---

5   'The Submarine Race in Asia', [Editorial], *The New York Times*, 7 January 2014, www.nytimes.com/2014/01/08/opinion/the-submarine-race-in-asia.html?_r=0.
6   'Myanmar Navy Modernization Plan', *Pakistan Defence*, 18 July 2013, defence.pk/threads/myanmar-navy-modernization-plan.265249/.
7   Anthony Davis, 'Myanmar Navy Starts Submarine Training in Pakistan', *Jane's Defence Weekly*, 20 June 2013, www.janes.com/article/23451/myanmar-navy-starts-submarine-training-in-pakistan [page discontinued].

Two major obstacles will be a lack of resources and a lack of expertise.

Defence gets about 14 per cent of official expenditure, but this allocation is likely to be reduced.[8] Even if it were not, a submarine force would put an enormous strain on Burma's military budget. Also, subsurface warfare is highly specialised, requiring advanced technology, customised support facilities and trained personnel. There have been no signs that this infrastructure has been developed.

Other countries can help in some of these areas, but even modern navies in developed states have found such challenges difficult to overcome.

This issue also raises questions about the government's priorities and the relationship between the President and his Commander-in-Chief, Min Aung Hlaing, who has emphasised Burma's need for 'strong, powerful, modernized and patriotic' armed forces.[9] President Thein Sein agrees, but the defence sector still has to compete for scarce resources against the demands of the government's wideranging reform program and the pressing needs of other portfolios.

The purchase of a submarine or two would also have implications for Burma's external relations.

Several Southeast Asian navies have acquired or are acquiring conventional submarines.[10] After a recent maritime dispute with Burma, Bangladesh intends to buy two Chinese boats.[11] Talk of an 'underwater arms race'[12] may be premature, but these developments have doubtless attracted Naypyidaw's attention. Burma's strategic environment is changing.

---

8   Aung Thura Htun, 'Government Plans to Reduce Military Spending', *Mizzima News*, [Yangon], 15 January 2014, www.mizzima.com/mizzima-news/politics/item/10821-government-plans-to-reduce-military-spending [page discontinued].

9   Zin Linn, 'Burma Army's Boss Calls for Stronger Armed Forces', *Asiancorrespondent.com*, [Bristol, UK], 28 March 2013, asiancorrespondent.com/103472/burma-armys-boss-calls-for-stronger-and-modernized-armed-forces/ [page discontinued].

10   Carl Thayer, 'Southeast Asian States Deploy Conventional Submarines', *The Diplomat*, [Washington, DC], 3 January 2014, thediplomat.com/2014/01/southeast-asian-states-deploy-conventional-submarines/.

11   'PM Says Bangladesh to Buy 1st Submarines', *Defense News*, 24 January 2014, www.defensenews.com/article/20130124/DEFREG03/301240016/ [page discontinued].

12   'Underwater Arms Race Looms between ASEAN and China', *The Nation Thailand*, 11 January 2014, www.nationthailand.com/opinion/30224043.

The US and the UK are tentatively developing military ties with Burma. Australia has just posted a defence attaché to Rangoon, and the Royal Australian Navy has made its first port visit since 1959.[13] Despite Burma's recent naval diplomacy,[14] these and other countries are unlikely to welcome reports that Naypyidaw is acquiring an expensive and possibly destabilising power projection capability.

Strategic analysts often find Burma difficult to read. For example, it was once an accepted fact that China had a large military base in Burma. This later proved to be incorrect. Similarly, it was widely reported that Burma was on track to have a nuclear weapon by 2014. That was never a realistic prospect. Rumours that Naypyidaw was seeking to acquire ballistic missiles aroused scepticism at first, but now appear to be confirmed.

With all these factors in mind, reports of a secret submarine sale need to be treated carefully. Burma has always had the ability to surprise observers, but until there is conclusive evidence of an active subsurface warfare program, or corroboration of a submarine purchase from a reputable official source, a degree of caution seems warranted.

13   Senator the Hon. David Johnston, 'Acting Minister for Defence and Minister for Foreign Affairs, Joint Media Release, Australian Government Strengthening Ties with the Myanmar Government', Department of Defence, Canberra, 20 January 2014, www.minister.defence.gov.au/2014/01/20/acting-minister-for-defence-and-minister-for-foreign-affairs-joint-media-release-australian-government-strengthening-ties-with-the-myanmar-government/ [page discontinued] [now at www.minister.defence.gov.au/minister/david-johnston/media-releases/acting-minister-defence-and-minister-foreign-affairs-joint].
14   John Drennan, 'Myanmar's Navy Gets a Second Wind', *IISS Voices* (London: International Institute for Strategic Studies, 30 September 2013), www.iiss.org/en/iiss%20voices/blogsections/iiss-voices-2013-1e35/september-2013-38d4/myanmars-navy-gets-a-second-wind-880c [page discontinued].

66

Burma: A critical look at those chemical weapons claims

(14:36 AEDT, 25 February 2014)

For decades, insurgents, refugees and others in Myanmar claimed that the armed forces had used chemical weapons (CW) against them. Despite credible reports of a pilot CW program back in the 1970s, and subsequent efforts by various activist groups, none of these claims could be proven. This issue arose again in early 2014, when two Myanmar journalists claimed they had discovered a secret CW plant.

Since the 1988 prodemocracy uprising, strategic analysts monitoring developments in Burma (Myanmar) have been on quite a rollercoaster ride, particularly with regard to WMD.

Over the past 25 years, both the former military regime and President Thein Sein's reformist government have been accused of developing a nuclear device, manufacturing ballistic missiles, deploying biological agents and using CW.[1] These capabilities were reportedly acquired mainly with the help of North Korea and China.

---

1   Andrew Selth, *Burma and Weapons of Mass Destruction: Claims, Controversies and Consequences*, Associate Paper (Perth: Future Directions International, 9 August 2012), www.futuredirections. org.au/files/Associate%20Papers/FDI_Associate_Paper_-_09_August_2012.pdf [page discontinued] [now at www.futuredirections.org.au/publication/burma-and-weapons-of-mass-destruction-claims-controversies-and-consequences/].

Such is the dearth of reliable information about Burma's armed forces and national security that it has been difficult to prove or disprove many of these claims. However, enough of them have been shown to be exaggerated or false to warrant a fair degree of caution when considering any fresh accusations of WMD production or use.

With that in mind, it is worth looking closely at reports in the news media over the past few weeks that a secret CW plant has been discovered in Burma.

The Rangoon-based *Unity Journal* has claimed that, in 2009, a CW factory was built on 12 square kilometres of land confiscated from farmers in Pauk township, near Pakokku in central Burma. Citing local informants, the journal said the complex (possibly known as DI-24) included more than 300 metres of tunnels and was receiving technical help from China.[2]

Following publication of this story, four journalists and one *Unity Journal* executive were charged under the 1923 *State Secrets Act*, which prohibits trespassing on and photographing defence facilities in Burma and divulging classified information.[3] All unsold copies of the weekly journal were seized. Naypyidaw also flatly denied the existence of any CW plant.

Local news outlets have highlighted the perceived attack on freedom of the press in Burma, which has been vigorously exploited since Thein Sein relaxed controls on the media in 2012.[4] International observers seem more concerned about the apparent revelation of a CW plant[5] and Burma's failure to ratify the 1997 Chemical Weapons Convention (CWC).[6]

Some background to the latest claims and Burma's current CWC status might help put these issues into perspective.

---

2   Zarni Mann and Samantha Michaels, 'Burma Govt Rejects Report of Secret Chemical Weapons Factory', *The Irrawaddy*, 4 February 2014, www.irrawaddy.org/burma/burma-govt-rejects-report-secret-chemical-weapons-factory.html.

3   Yen Saning, 'Sixth Unity Journal Staffer Detained for Questioning', *The Irrawaddy*, 5 February 2014, www.irrawaddy.org/burma/sixth-unity-journal-staffer-detained-questioning.html.

4   'Burma (Myanmar)', in *Freedom of the Press 2013* (Washington, DC: Freedom House, 2013), www.freedomhouse.org/report/freedom-press/2013/burma [page discontinued] [now at freedom house.org/sites/default/files/FOTP%202013%20Full%20Report.pdf].

5   Luke Hunt, 'Pardon, Was That a Chemical Weapons Factory in Myanmar?', *The Diplomat*, [Washington, DC], 7 February 2014, thediplomat.com/2014/02/pardon-was-that-a-chemical-weapons-factory-in-myanmar/.

6   Joshua Kurlantzik, 'Chemical Weapons in Myanmar?', *Asia Unbound* (New York: Council on Foreign Relations, 10 February 2014), blogs.cfr.org/asia/2014/02/10/chemical-weapons-in-myanmar/.

Since the mid 1980s, several ethnic armed groups have claimed to be the victims of chemical warfare. They have described attacks by the Burmese armed forces with mortars, artillery, rockets and air-delivered bombs that left insurgents and displaced communities with symptoms including dizziness, nausea, rashes and, in some cases, partial paralysis. There do not seem to have been any fatalities.

Such claims continued to be made after Thein Sein's inauguration in March 2011. In June, for example, Shan insurgents reported that they had been bombarded with artillery shells containing noxious chemicals.[7] Also in 2011, Kachin groups said they had been subjected to 'yellow rain' and 'toxic gas'.[8] Similar claims were made in 2012.[9]

Without independent expert testimony and rigorous scientific analysis, which have so far been lacking, such reports are almost impossible to verify. It has even been difficult to determine what kinds of chemical agents, if any, may have been employed. Some descriptions have been consistent with the use of white phosphorus, tear gas or even toxic defoliants.

That said, claims of CW use have had some support. In 1984, Western newspapers cited what was reportedly a leaked US Special National Security Intelligence Estimate stating that the Ne Win regime had been trying to produce mustard gas since 1981. A West German firm was said to be assisting with the construction of a pilot plant in Burma, with additional equipment imported from Italy.

It was later reported that the US had forced this project to close—in part, by putting pressure on Bonn. No evidence was ever provided to suggest that any chemical agents had been produced, weaponised or tested. However, as late as 1993, Burma was being listed by some US agencies as possibly having an offensive CW capability.[10]

---

7   'Fears Mount Over Chemical Weapons Use', *Democratic Voice of Burma*, 8 June 2011, www.dvb. no/news/fears-mount-over-chemical-weapons-use/16018 [page discontinued].

8   Naw Noreen, '"Yellow Rain" Fuels Chemical Weapons Fears', *Democratic Voice of Burma*, 25 November 2011, www.dvb.no/news/%E2%80%98yellow-rain%E2%80%99-fuels-chemical-weapon-fears/18917 [page discontinued].

9   'Burma Denies Using Chemical Weapons in Kachin', *Democratic Voice of Burma*, 10 January 2013, www.dvb.no/news/burma-denies-using-chemical-weapons-in-kachin/25671 [page discontinued].

10   Walter Friedenberg, 'Chemical Warfare Gaining Acceptance in Some Nations', *Deseret News*, [Salt Lake City], 10 September 1988, www.deseretnews.com/article/18676/CHEMICAL-WARFARE-GAINING-ACCEPTANCE-IN-SOME-NATIONS.html?pg=all.

More recently, a few US politicians have referred to Burmese CW use, but this has been in the context of unconfirmed press reports.[11] Also, the issue has usually been raised in an attempt to discredit Naypyidaw's reform program and the Obama administration's engagement policy. Once again, no evidence was provided to support such claims.

For their part, successive Burmese governments have consistently denied having a CW capability and using CW against domestic opponents. Officials have pointed out that Burma has been a strong supporter of the CWC, which it signed in 1993. Some have been of the view that, as Burma was then directly ruled by a military council, this automatically included ratification.

Despite all the claims made over the years, some of which included descriptions of purported CW facilities,[12] the fact remains that no one really knows whether Burma has ever developed a CW capability or has used CW against armed ethnic groups. There is simply not enough reliable information available from public sources either to dismiss these claims or to confirm them.

As regards the latest reports, it is possible that the site investigated by the *Unity Journal* journalists was another kind of defence industrial plant, as claimed by a government spokesman. Many such facilities have been built since 1988, often for unknown purposes. A number have 'tunnels'; and Burmese authorities have always been very sensitive to breaches of security.

It has been argued that Thein Sein's reforms make chemical weapons 'near redundant'.[13] Burma's circumstances have certainly changed, but CW have enduring strategic applications. If Naypyidaw is developing ballistic missiles, as many suspect, possession of a chemical warhead would constitute a strong deterrent and a powerful bargaining chip in international negotiations.

---

11   Ileana Ros-Lehtinen, Chairwoman, 'Ros-Lehtinen Expresses Concern about Atrocities in Burma, Possible Connections to North Korea, and Secretary Clinton Trip', House Committee on Foreign Affairs, US House of Representatives, Washington, DC, 29 November 2011, archives.republicans. foreignaffairs.house.gov/news/story/?2103 [page discontinued].

12   'Burma Military's Hidden Chemical Weapons Factories', *Blogspot*, 18 December 2011, burma chemicalweapons.blogspot.com.au/.

13   Elliot Brennan, 'Why Myanmar Needs to Ratify the Weapons Conventions', *The Interpreter*, 7 February 2014, www.lowyinterpreter.org/post/2014/02/07/Why-Myanmar-needs-to-ratify-the-Weapons-Conventions.aspx [page discontinued] [now at www.lowyinstitute.org/the-interpreter/why-myanmar-needs-ratify-weapons-conventions].

It is in this context that Burma's ratification of the CWC has become more pressing. Last year, the Organisation for the Prohibition of Chemical Weapons conducted a 'national awareness workshop' in Naypyidaw. The Burmese Government later announced that it would ratify the convention—a decision that has recently been reconfirmed.[14]

This step would doubtless be presented as evidence of Burma's readiness to be a good international citizen and, as such, would be applauded by many. However, it is unlikely to have any appreciable impact on domestic political developments. Indeed, as long as Naypyidaw continues to deny any past CW attacks, ratification will be seen by most ethnic groups as little more than a public relations exercise.

Another reason ratification of the CWC is unlikely to attract unqualified approval is that, despite repeated protestations to the contrary, Burma maintains military ties with North Korea.[15] Thein Sein's government could accede to all the international instruments relating to WMD but, as long as that issue remains unresolved, suspicions about Naypyidaw's bona fides are bound to remain.

14   'Burma Preparing to Ratify Chemical Weapons Ban: Ye Htut', *Democratic Voice of Burma*, 14 February 2014, www.dvb.no/news/burma-preparing-to-ratify-chemical-weapons-ban-ye-htut-burma-myanmar/37250 [page discontinued].
15   Andrew Selth, 'Burma and North Korea: Again? Still?', *The Interpreter*, 10 July 2013, www.lowyinterpreter.org/post/2013/07/10/Burma-and-North-Korea-Again-Still.aspx [page discontinued] [now at www.lowyinstitute.org/the-interpreter/burma-and-north-korea-again-still].

67

Should Burma participate in UN peacekeeping?

(10:19 AEDT, 13 May 2014)

In March 2014, it was widely reported that Myanmar had been invited to participate in UN peacekeeping operations. These reports were inaccurate but provoked an outcry from activist groups. This was a little surprising, as there were good arguments for permitting Myanmar's police and armed forces to get the international exposure and experience that UN peacekeeping operations usually provide.

A few months ago, several activist organisations expressed outrage at reports that the UN had invited Burma (Myanmar) to participate in peacekeeping operations (PKO). The furore has since died down, but Naypyidaw's critics are reasserting themselves in a number of ways and the question will doubtless arise again.

With that in mind, it is helpful to look more closely at Burma's fluctuating relationship with the UN, the reported PKO invitation and recent moves to curb engagement with Burma.

After it regained its independence in 1948, Burma was a strong supporter of the UN. Between 1961 and 1971, a Burmese statesman, U Thant, was twice elected secretary-general. In 1958, Burma participated in the UN Observation Group in the Lebanon (UNOGIL) and, in 1961, it provided a small contingent for the UN Operation in the Congo (ONUC).

After Ne Win's coup in 1962, Burma steered clear of PKO, but it continued to enjoy a good relationship with the UN. Indeed, as it retreated into economic and political isolation, Burma came to rely on the UN for development aid and the ultimate guarantee of its sovereignty.

The 1988 prodemocracy uprising marked a turning point in the relationship. Burma's new military government increasingly saw the UN as a threat, aligned with its Western critics.

Over the past 25 years, four special envoys and five rapporteurs have been appointed by the UN to carry out fact-finding missions in Burma or to facilitate dialogue between the government and opposition movement. Between them, these officials visited Burma about 60 times. The current UN Secretary-General has himself visited Burma three times.[1]

The UN can claim a few modest successes in Burma, but it is difficult to identify any significant policy changes made by the military regime between 1988 and 2011 that were the result of approaches made by UN representatives.[2]

Since the advent of Thein Sein's mixed civilian–military government, there has been an effort on both sides to improve the relationship. The UN is still critical of Burma's human rights record,[3] but it is assisting with development programs and important initiatives such as the reform of the Myanmar Police Force.

Then in March this year, there were news media reports that UN Special Envoy Vijay Nambiar had 'invited' Burma to contribute to PKO.

A UN spokesman later explained that Nambiar had told Burmese Commander-in-Chief Min Aung Hlaing that, like any member state, Burma was 'invited to discuss its interest in specific terms with the Department of Peacekeeping Operations which would consider such a request in accordance with its regular parameters'.[4]

---

1   *Chronology of Visits and Reports* (Bangkok: ALTSEAN-Burma, 2013), www.altsean.org/Research/UN%20Dossier/EnvoysandRapporteurs.htm [page discontinued].
2   Anna Magnusson and Morten B. Pedersen, *A Good Office? Twenty Years of UN Mediation in Myanmar* (New York: International Peace Institute, 2012), www.ipinst.org/images/pdfs/ipi_ebook_good_offices.pdf.
3   'Myanmar Homepage', Office of the UN High Commissioner for Human Rights, www.ohchr.org/en/countries/asiaregion/pages/mmindex.aspx.
4   Matthew Russell Lee, 'Myanmar Invited for UN Peacekeeping by Vijay Nambiar, Ban Ki-moon No Comment on Anti-Muslim Marriage Law', *Inner City Press*, [New York], 27 February 2014, innercitypress.blogspot.com.au/2014/02/myanmar-invited-for-un-peacekeeping-by.html.

This suggests that it was in fact the Burmese side that raised the issue. Nambiar did not 'invite' Burma to participate in PKO, as claimed, nor did he respond positively to any Burmese request. However, he left the door open for the UN to consider Burmese participation in a UN peacekeeping force, should Naypyidaw make a formal approach.

The UN's clarification of Nambiar's remarks did not prevent a strong reaction. Human Rights Watch and other activist organisations were quick to point out that Burma's armed forces (*Tatmadaw*) have a poor human rights record and that efforts to demobilise Burma's child soldiers were incomplete.[5]

Other critics reminded the UN that Burma had an undemocratic constitution, a peace settlement with the country's ethnic armed groups was still a long way off and Rohingya Muslims suffer from official discrimination.[6] Also, Burma maintains military ties with North Korea, in violation of UNSC resolutions.

Despite several countries with dubious human rights records already providing soldiers for PKO, these activist groups felt that any Burmese participation would be incompatible with the high standards the UN was expected to uphold.

There is no question that there are serious problems in Burma. Unsurprisingly, the reform process is proving difficult and there are deep-seated communal tensions that were always going to prove problematic. Indeed, given the scope and nature of the challenges Naypyidaw faces, it is remarkable what has already been achieved.

While it is true that the *Tatmadaw* remains the most powerful institution in Burma, this should not be seen just in negative terms. As a recent International Crisis Group report stated, the *Tatmadaw*'s guaranteed position at the centre of Burma's government has given it the confidence to allow, and in many cases support, a major liberalisation of politics and

5   'UN: Request for Burmese Peacekeepers Misguided', *News* (New York: Human Rights Watch, 13 March 2014), www.hrw.org/news/2014/03/13/un-request-burmese-peacekeepers-misguided.
6   'Mixed Messages from the UN in Burma', *US Campaign for Burma*, 20 March 2014, uscampaign forburma.wordpress.com/2014/03/20/mixed-messages-from-the-un-in-burma/.

the economy.[7] Yet in public commentary, such factors are not always taken into account. Immediate concerns usually overshadow longer-term strategic considerations.

Another problem is that the atmosphere surrounding cooperation with Burma's security forces is changing. In the euphoria that followed the launch of Thein Sein's reform program and the international community's rush to restore relations with Burma, Naypyidaw's critics found it hard to get a hearing. They have now seized on Burma's latest problems and continuing crises to try to wind back the level of foreign contact.

In the US, for example, the Obama administration is in danger of losing control of its Burma policy.[8] There is a Bill before Congress that makes such unrealistic demands that, if passed, it would undercut US goals and reduce US influence in Burma.[9] Indeed, it would strengthen the hand of those elements still opposed to reform.

In such an atmosphere, the likelihood of Burma being invited to participate in UN PKO must be considered slight. Yet it can be argued that now more than ever such a step would be beneficial.

If Burma's security forces are to learn about international norms of behaviour, devise better ways of doing things and be exposed to issues beyond their narrow experience, participation in UN operations offers a way ahead. The alternative is to deny them such opportunities and perpetuate the blinkered thinking that has contributed to Burma's current problems.

There could be other benefits, too. A major reform program has been launched in the MPF, which is rapidly expanding and assuming greater responsibility for internal security. The *Tatmadaw*, too, is rewriting its doctrine to meet changing domestic and strategic circumstances. International training and experience could assist such processes.

---

7   *Myanmar's Military: Back to the Barracks?*, Asia Briefing No.143 (Brussels: International Crisis Group, 22 April 2014), www.crisisgroup.org/-/media/Files/asia/south-east-asia/burma-myanmar/b143-myanmar-s-military-back-to-the-barracks.pdf [page discontinued] [now at www.crisisgroup.org/asia/south-east-asia/myanmar/myanmar-s-military-back-barracks].

8   Steve Hirsch, 'Cracks Appear in US Myanmar Rapprochement', *The Diplomat*, [Washington, DC], 30 April 2014, thediplomat.com/2014/04/cracks-appear-in-us-myanmar-rapprochement/.

9   David I. Steinberg, 'The Problem with H.R. 4377, the Burma Human Rights and Democracy Act of 2014', *cogitASIA* (Washington, DC: Center for Strategic and International Studies, 7 May 2014), cogitasia.com/the-problem-with-h-r-4377-the-burma-human-rights-and-democracy-act-of-2014/.

Although activists remain sceptical, there are many within Burma's police and armed forces who wish to see democratic reform. Members of both institutions want to be better trained, better equipped, more professional and more respected. Participation in PKO would assist in this process and give them a greater investment in positive change.

Burma will continue to experience serious problems for years to come. It would be naive to expect otherwise. The international community thus continues to face the same question it has struggled with since 1988: is progress more likely by isolating and punishing Naypyidaw or by trying to encourage reform through constructive dialogue and positive action?[10]

If the answer is the latter, inviting Burmese soldiers and police to participate in UN PKO would seem an option worth taking seriously.

---

10   Andrew Selth, 'Defence Relations with Burma: Our Future Past', *The Interpreter*, 4 March 2013, www.lowyinterpreter.com.au/post/2013/03/04/Australian-defence-relations-with-Burma-our-future-past.aspx [page discontinued] [now at www.lowyinstitute.org/the-interpreter/defence-relations-burma-our-future-past].

68

Will Aung San Suu Kyi be president? Odds are lengthening

(09:05 AEDT, 30 June 2014)

After an initial effort to cultivate positive relations with the Thein Sein Government and armed forces leadership, Aung San Suu Kyi seemed to draw the conclusion that neither was prepared to change the constitution and permit her to stand for the presidency. She returned to a strategy of seeking to have both domestic and foreign actors apply public pressure on Naypyidaw in an attempt to achieve her ambitions and those of her party.

A year ago, a Lowy Institute panel was asked whether Aung San Suu Kyi would become President of Burma (Myanmar).[1] The question was also raised on *The Interpreter*.[2] The answer on both occasions was that such an outcome was far from certain. Powerful forces in Burma were working hard to prevent it. Few informed observers were optimistic about her future.

1   'Lowy Lecture Series: Burma's Transition—Progress and Prospects', Lowy Institute, Sydney, 9 May 2013, www.lowyinstitute.org/news-and-media/videos/conversation-michael-fullilove-sean-turnell-and-andrew-selth-discuss-reform-process-burma [page discontinued] [now at soundcloud.com/lowyinstitute/lowy-lecture-series-burmas-transition].

2   Andrew Selth, 'Will Aung San Suu Kyi Be President of Burma?', *The Interpreter*, 16 May 2013, www.lowyinterpreter.org/post/2013/05/16/Will-Aung-San-Suu-Kyi-be-President-of-Burma.aspx?COLLCC=3636179620& [page discontinued] [now at www.lowyinstitute.org/the-interpreter/will-aung-san-suu-kyi-be-president-burma].

Since then, the odds on the charismatic opposition leader becoming president have lengthened considerably.

When writing about Burma, it is always prudent to begin by saying that its internal affairs are difficult to read and the country has always had the capacity to surprise. That said, there have been increasing signs that a decision has been made to extend the period of 'disciplined democracy' beyond President Thein Sein's term and that steps are being taken to ensure that Aung San Suu Kyi cannot contest the presidency after the 2015 general elections.

After a mixed civilian–military government was formed in 2011, Aung San Suu Kyi seemed to feel that her best interests, and those of her party, lay in a compromise with Thein Sein, whose ambitious reform program she publicly endorsed. She also tried to get closer to the armed forces (*Tatmadaw*) in an apparent attempt to reassure its leaders that she did not pose a threat to their institutional or personal interests.[3]

Since then, however, Aung San Suu Kyi has clearly become disillusioned with Thein Sein and the slow pace of political reform. She has also failed to weaken the armed forces' commitment to a gradual, controlled, top-down transition to a more democratic system. This seems to have prompted her discussions with powerbrokers like Shwe Mann, the Speaker of the parliament's lower house, in what was probably an attempt to outflank her opponents.

At the same time, she increased her efforts to persuade other countries to put pressure on Naypyidaw.[4] She warned world leaders (including Australia's Prime Minister) not to get too comfortable in dealing with Burma's current government.[5] She also sought their help in getting the 2008 constitution amended to remove those provisions enshrining the *Tatmadaw*'s special place in national politics and preventing her from becoming president.

---

3   'Aung San Suu Kyi Attends Burma's Armed Forces Day', *BBC News*, 27 March 2013, www.bbc.com/news/world-asia-21950145.

4   Andrew Selth, 'Aung San Suu Kyi's Risky Strategy', *The Interpreter*, 30 October 2013, www.lowyinterpreter.org/post/2013/10/30/Aung-San-Suu-Kyis-risky-strategy.aspx [page discontinued] [now at www.lowyinstitute.org/the-interpreter/aung-san-suu-kyis-risky-strategy].

5   Andrew Selth, 'When Aung San Suu Kyi Comes to Call', *The Interpreter*, 3 December 2013, www.lowyinterpreter.org/post/2013/12/03/When-Aung-San-Suu-Kyi-comes-to-call.aspx [page discontinued] [now at www.lowyinstitute.org/the-interpreter/when-aung-san-suu-kyi-comes-call].

Yet, over the past six months, the President[6] and the *Tatmadaw's* Commander-in-Chief[7] have reiterated their commitment to the 2008 constitution and to a 'disciplined democracy'. Both have hinted that they favour another five-year term under a former general. And, on 13 June, a parliamentary committee dominated by pro-government members voted against amending the clause of the constitution that bars from the presidency anyone (like Aung San Suu Kyi) whose family has foreign ties.[8]

As Larry Jagan has observed, Aung San Suu Kyi now seems convinced that an accommodation with the government and armed forces is no longer possible.[9] With the system stacked so heavily against her, she has few options, but she is already pursuing two lines of attack. Both carry considerable risks and neither guarantees success. Indeed, they could prove counterproductive and bring about the opposite results to those she desires.

Aung San Suu Kyi is trying to use her prestige and popularity to increase pressure on the government in Naypyidaw. Constitutional reform is not as high a priority for most Burmese as the provision of basic services,[10] but she has launched a nationwide campaign aimed at winning support for constitutional amendments. She is organising public meetings and widening her message to challenge the *Tatmadaw's* guaranteed allocation of 25 per cent of all parliamentary seats.

Second, she is once again seeking help from the international community.[11] She is downplaying her presidential ambitions and expressing her concerns in terms of genuine democratic elections and the removal of sectoral interests, as enshrined in the constitution. This seems to reflect

---

6   'Speech Delivered by President U Thein Sein on the Occasion of the 3rd Anniversary of the Assumption of Duty at the Pyidaungsu Hluttaw, Naypyitaw, 26 March 2014', *Network Myanmar*, www.networkmyanmar.org/images/stories/PDF16/Thein-Sein-26-03-2014.pdf [page discontinued].

7   'Commander-in-Chief Says Armed Forces Responsible for "Safeguarding Constitution" as 69th Armed Forces Day is Marked with Parade', *New Light of Myanmar*, [Yangon], 28 March 2014, www.networkmyanmar.org/images/stories/PDF16/C-in-C-27032014.pdf [page discontinued].

8   'Suu Kyi's Presidential Hopes Suffer Setback', *Deutsche Welle*, [Bonn], 17 June 2014, www.dw.de/suu-kyis-presidential-hopes-suffer-setback/a-17710999.

9   Larry Jagan, 'Suu Kyi Shifts Pre-Election Tack in Myanmar', *Asia Times Online*, [Hong Kong], 12 June 2014, www.atimes.com/atimes/Southeast_Asia/SEA-01-120614.html [page discontinued].

10   *Survey of Burma Public Opinion, December 24, 2013 – February 1, 2014* (Washington, DC: International Republican Institute, 2014), www.iri.org/sites/default/files/flip_docs/2014%20April%203%20Survey%20of%20Burma%20Public%20Opinion,%20December%2024,%202013-February%201,%202014.pdf.

11   'Myanmar's Suu Kyi Seeks Global Support for Charter Change', *West Australian*, [Perth], 14 June 2014, au.news.yahoo.com/thewest/world/a/24239496/ [page discontinued].

recognition that support for such broad principles is easier for foreign governments than interventions in Burma's domestic politics on behalf of an individual.

A possible third approach is for Aung San Suu Kyi to reach out again to figures like Shwe Mann, or other parties and groups, including the ethnic communities. There have long been rumours of deals that could help Aung San Suu Kyi achieve her personal and party goals. However, Burmese politics is notoriously volatile and such arrangements rarely last long. Also, Shwe Mann is himself a presidential hopeful.

In any case, the armed forces remain the ultimate arbiters of power in Burma. They have stepped back from day-to-day government and allowed other institutions to develop. However, thanks to the 2008 constitution and the appointment of military officers to key positions, the *Tatmadaw* still effectively controls the government and parliament. It also commands the state's coercive apparatus, including the police and intelligence agencies.

Aung San Suu Kyi's confrontational approach already worries the armed forces.[12] Appeals to the *Tatmadaw*'s rank and file for support and calls for foreign governments to put greater pressure on Naypyidaw are likely to confirm the doubts already held by the generals about her readiness to preserve the country's stability, unity and sovereignty—the three 'national causes' to which the armed forces remain deeply committed.

Having chosen to permit a more open political and economic system to develop, the *Tatmadaw* seems determined to retain control over the process. It is not backing away from the goal of a more modern, prosperous and respected country. However, it does not yet seem ready to put its trust in an inexperienced civilian politician, backed by a fractious party, to manage developments in a way that safeguards Burma's national interests, as it sees them.

This impasse poses real dangers for Burma. Civil unrest in support of an Aung San Suu Kyi presidential bid would threaten Burma's already precarious internal stability and make the implementation of reforms even more difficult. Naypyidaw is more sensitive to domestic and international

---

12   Shwe Aung, 'Election Commission Curbs Suu Kyi's Campaign Trail', *Democratic Voice of Burma*, 11 April 2014, www.dvb.no/news/election-commission-curbs-suu-kyis-campaign-trail-burma-myanmar/39558 [page discontinued].

opinion than it was before 2011, but it would not hesitate to send in the police and the army if protests became too disruptive. It could even declare an emergency.

Continued refusal to lift restrictions on Aung San Suu Kyi's presidential candidacy, or tough action against protesters seeking a genuine democracy in Burma, would strengthen the hand of those activists and sceptics who were never convinced of Naypyidaw's commitment to change. They are already trying to wind back the level of engagement by countries like the US and the UK,[13] citing continued human rights abuses and the failure of many promised reforms to materialise.[14]

Yet, an overreaction by Western countries, such as the imposition of unrealistic benchmarks or even a return to sanctions, would help hardliners within the *Tatmadaw* to claim that such fair-weather friends cannot be trusted. It could result in not just a slower pace of reform, but also a greater reliance by Naypyidaw on countries like China, whose interests in Burma are less aligned with the democratic opposition movement and many in the international community.

---

13   Andrew Selth, 'Should Burma Participate in UN Peacekeeping?', *The Interpreter*, 13 May 2014, www.lowyinterpreter.org/post/2014/05/13/Should-Burma-Myanmar-participate-in-UN-peace keeping.aspx?COLLCC=2310905121& [page discontinued] [now at www.lowyinstitute.org/the-interpreter/should-burma-participate-un-peacekeeping].
14   Daniel P. Sullivan, 'Burma's Promise: President Thein Sein's 11 Commitments to Obama', *Foreign Policy in Focus*, 19 November 2013, fpif.org/burmas-promise-president-thein-seins-11-commitments-obama/.

69

Burma and the Biological Weapons Convention

(08:40 AEDT, 15 October 2014)

President Thein Sein's announcement in September 2014 that Myanmar would ratify the Biological Weapons Convention was widely welcomed. It also prompted a look at the historical record and claims by some members of the activist community that the former military government had developed and possibly even used biological weapons against its own citizens.

It was announced last month[1] that Burma's parliament had approved President Thein Sein's request for the country to become a state party to the 1972 Biological Weapons Convention.[2] While in some respects a symbolic gesture, this was an important step that promises to close the book on a security issue that for decades has been mired in controversy.

Burma's position regarding various biological weapons (BW) conventions has long been unclear. According to some sources,[3] upon regaining its independence from the UK in 1948, Burma automatically became a state

---

1   'Myanmar Set to Ratify Biological Weapons Convention', *Eleven*, 30 September 2014, cbrn.dfns. net/2014/09/30/myanmar-set-to-ratify-biological-weapons-convention/ [page discontinued] [now at www.cbrneportal.com/myanmar-set-to-ratify-biological-weapons-convention/].

2   Khin Maung Soe, 'Myanmar Prepares to Ratify Chemical, Biological Weapons Treaties', *Radio Free Asia*, [Washington, DC], 11 December 2013, www.rfa.org/english/news/myanmar/weapons-12112013 192030.html/.

3   'Myanmar Special Weapons', *GlobalSecurity.org*, www.globalsecurity.org/wmd/world/myanmar/.

party to the 1925 Protocol for the Prohibition of the Use in War of Asphyxiating, Poisonous or Other Gases, and of Bacteriological Methods of Warfare.[4]

This view is based on the fact that the UK signed the protocol in 1925 and deposited the necessary legal instruments in 1930, while Burma was still a province of British India. Thus, in 1948, Burma was deemed to have inherited the same obligations. No authorities support this view, however, and Burma has never been listed by the UN as a signatory or a state party to the Geneva Protocol (as it became known).[5]

In 1972, Burma signed the Bacteriological (Biological) and Toxin Weapons Convention.[6] This went further than the 1925 protocol and banned the development, production, stockpiling and acquisition of such weapons. It entered into force in 1975. The Burmese Government did not ratify the convention, but it acknowledged its legal responsibilities and even attended meetings in Geneva to discuss ways to strengthen measures against BW.

After the dissolution of Burma's bicameral parliament in 1988 and the creation of the State Law and Order Restoration Council (SLORC), some military officers claimed Burma had automatically become a state party to the 1972 convention. They felt that, as Burma then had only a single ruling body, it did not need to both sign and ratify such international legal agreements. One formal act of endorsement was considered sufficient.

This position, however, was not accepted by the international community, which pressed the new Burmese Government to ratify the 1972 convention. This pressure mounted as suspicions grew that the regime was secretly developing other WMD, and calls were made for Burma to accede to, or abide by, other multilateral agreements.

Complicating consideration of this issue were accusations that the SLORC had developed and employed BW against its domestic opponents. In 1993, there were reports of unidentified aircraft dropping mysterious

---

4   *Protocol for the Prohibition of the Use in War of Asphyxiating, Poisonous or Other Gases, and of Bacteriological Methods of Warfare* (New York: United Nations Office for Disarmament Affairs, 1925), disarmament.un.org/treaties/t/1925/text.

5   ibid.

6   *Convention on the Prohibition of the Development, Production and Stockpiling of Bacteriological (Biological) and Toxin Weapons and on Their Destruction* (New York: United Nations Office for Disarmament Affairs, 1972), disarmament.un.org/treaties/t/bwc/text.

devices, resembling white boxes, on Karen villages along the Thailand–Burma border.[7] A few weeks later, more than 300 people in the area died after displaying symptoms resembling those of cholera.

In 1994, these claims were investigated by a team from the British human rights group Christian Solidarity International (CSI).[8] It concluded that there was very strong circumstantial evidence that the SLORC had used biological agents against Karen villagers. CSI linked the 'attacks' to BW training reportedly given to the Burmese armed forces by Germany.

The CSI's findings were challenged by the Burmese Government, but the international news media seemed to accept them at face value. In 1998, the defence publisher Jane's went as far as to state, with regard to Burma, that 'a biological warfare capability appears to exist, a fact supported by various well-documented reports, including photographs of air-dropped weapons'.[9]

This assessment has been cited in several publications, including a few academic studies. Also, in 2004, one British MP (apparently misquoting a US think tank) stated that Burma 'probably' had BW.[10] Most analysts were more cautious. However, such was the reputation of Burma's military regime that its possession of BW became widely accepted.

A few activists also claimed that the regime was allowing HIV/AIDS to spread through Burma's frontier areas as a form of 'germ warfare'. In reports reminiscent of stories that used to circulate around Africa, it was said that the virus was being used not only to weaken resistance to military rule, but also as a way of eliminating minority ethnic groups.

Some of these stories are easily dismissed. Without more information, the truth or otherwise of other claims is difficult to determine. However, the case for Burmese possession and use of BW has never been very persuasive.

No hard evidence has ever been produced of a Burmese BW program. Even the Bush administration, which was highly critical of the military government and which had sophisticated intelligence gathering capabilities,

7   'Is the SLORC Using Bacteriological Warfare?', *Karen Human Rights Group*, 15 March 1994, www.khrg.org/2014/07/940315/slorc-using-bacteriological-warfare-preliminary-report-based-information.
8   'British Experts Investigating Possible Germ Warfare in Burma', *Associated Press*, 14 November 1994, www.apnewsarchive.com/1994/British-Experts-Investigating-Possible-Germ-Warfare-in-Burma/id-f7f2030f726aeaa7922ecef6eadcd8b7.
9   'NBC Inventories: Burma (Myanmar)', *Jane's NBC Protection Equipment, 1997–98* (London: Jane's Information Group, 1998).
10   'Mr John Bercow (Buckingham) (Con.)', Parliamentary Business, *Hansard*, 24 November 2004 (London: House of Commons), www.publications.parliament.uk/pa/cm200405/cmhansrd/vo041124/debtext/41124-19.htm.

never accused the regime of engaging in such activities. There was no strategic logic to the claimed attacks in 1993. In any case, it was unlikely that BW would ever be employed so close to an international border.

More to the point, independent investigators, including the UK's Porton Down defence establishment, have been unable to confirm any claims of BW use.[11] The 'white boxes' were found to be harmless radiosondes—routinely used in meteorological surveys. Also, in 1992, a virulent, previously unknown strain of cholera was spreading east from India. This was considered the most likely cause of the deaths reported along the Burma–Thailand border.

Granted, some questions surrounding these issues remain unanswered. However, the rash of reports in the 1990s about a clandestine Burmese BW program appears to be another example of activists and journalists seizing on unconfirmed claims and drawing dire conclusions, knowing that Burma's military regime was capable of terrible human rights abuses and assuming it was prepared to do anything to remain in power.

In a message to parliament prior to the vote last month, President Thein Sein emphasised that Burma was the last member of ASEAN to ratify the BW Convention. He felt it was important that the country not be isolated on such an important matter. He also expressed the hope that ratification would 'head off any suggestions that [Burma] has or is developing biological weapons'.[12]

Whether the recent decision in Naypyidaw puts all suspicions to rest remains to be seen. Burma does not have an unblemished record of abiding by its international obligations, and doubtless there will be some who will remain sceptical of the government's bona fides. Foreign governments and international organisations, however, will welcome this step as another sign of Burma's wish to be accepted as a respectable international citizen.[13]

11 'Burma: Attacks on the Karen People', Written Answers, *Lords Hansard*, Vol.561, No.43 (London: House of Lords, 20 February 1995), www.parliament.the-stationery-office.co.uk/pa/ld199495/ldhansrd/vo950220/text/50220w01.htm [page discontinued] [now at publications.parliament.uk/pa/ld199495/ldhansrd/vo950220/index/50220-x.htm].

12 Pyae Thet Phyo, 'MPs Agree to Join Arms Convention', *Myanmar Times*, [Yangon], 10 October 2014, www.mmtimes.com/index.php/national-news/11904-hluttaw-makes-moves-to-join-bioweapons-accord.html.

13 Elliot Brennan, 'Why Myanmar Needs to Ratify the Weapons Conventions', *The Interpreter*, 7 February 2014, www.lowyinterpreter.org/post/2014/02/07/Why-Myanmar-needs-to-ratify-the-Weapons-Conventions.aspx?COLLCC=4216145380& [page discontinued] [now at www.lowyinstitute.org/the-interpreter/why-myanmar-needs-ratify-weapons-conventions].

70

Aung San Suu Kyi and Kipling's Burma

(10:00 AEDT, 31 October 2014)

Aung San Suu Kyi had long demonstrated her affection for the works of the 'bard of empire', British author Rudyard Kipling, and for classical music. Her tastes were seized upon by both her detractors and her supporters to promote their respective political agendas.

One of the inevitable side effects of Burma's long struggle for democracy has been the demonisation, or canonisation, of its main political actors. This phenomenon has been reflected in countless articles in the news media and on the web about figures like Ne Win (who effectively ruled Burma from 1962 to 1988), Than Shwe (who led the country's military council from 1992 to 2011) and of course opposition leader Aung San Suu Kyi.

There are very few books published (in English) about the country's military leaders. The first full-length biography of Than Shwe appeared in 2010 and a scholarly account of Ne Win's career is currently in preparation. Aung San Suu Kyi, by contrast, has been the subject of more than a dozen biographies, ranging from books for children to major studies. She has also published three semi-autobiographical works.

This is not counting Luc Besson's rather imaginative account of her place in modern Burmese history, as seen in the feature film *The Lady*, starring Michelle Yeoh and released in 2011.[1]

Given the close attention that has been paid to Aung San Suu Kyi's background and career since she first rose to prominence during Burma's 1988 prodemocracy uprising, it would be surprising to discover anything new about her. However, there remain a few areas of her private life that have not been thoroughly explored.

These can sometimes be revealed in unlikely ways.

For example, a Griffith Asia Institute research project about the influence of Rudyard Kipling[2] and popular Western music on perceptions of colonial Burma has unexpectedly thrown a new light on Aung San Suu Kyi's affection for both the 'bard of empire' and classical music.[3]

When Aung San Suu Kyi began to challenge Burma's new military government after 1988—a campaign that saw her awarded the Nobel Peace Prize—Kipling's 1890 poem *Mandalay*[4] was used in state propaganda against her. The generals likened her to the 'unpatriotic' Burma girl who had turned her back on her own race and, by implication, her own country. As David Steinberg has explained:

> They cite the marriage of Aung San Suu Kyi to a British academic, Michael Aris, as disqualifying her from leading the country. This colonial issue, as exemplified in Rudyard Kipling's poem 'The Road to Mandalay' (and its paean to Burmese women who had relations with British soldiers) ... thus continues today.[5]

---

1   Luc Besson, dir., *The Lady* (2011), *IMDb*, www.imdb.com/title/tt1802197/.

2   'Rudyard Kipling', *Wikipedia*, en.wikipedia.org/wiki/Rudyard_Kipling.

3   Griffith Asia Institute, 'On the Road to Mandalay', *Newsletter*, Vol.15, No.2, Winter 2014, pp.1–3, www.griffith.edu.au/__data/assets/pdf_file/0011/637760/Newsletter-Two-2014-web-version-2.1.pdf [page discontinued] [now at issuu.com/griffithasiainstitute/docs/newsletter_two_2014_web_version].

4   Rudyard Kipling, 'Mandalay', *Poetry Lovers' Page*, www.poetryloverspage.com/poets/kipling/mandalay.html.

5   David I. Steinberg, *Burma/Myanmar: What Everyone Needs to Know* (Oxford: Oxford University Press, 2013), pp.39–40, books.google.com.au/books?id=bWBE6Z9U6JsC&pg=PT50&lpg=PT50&dq=david-steinberg-suu-kyi-road-to-mandalay&source=bl&ots=UEPTwmtwQL&sig=ZnmMp_eIOPM8QysHIFQ9FUlJQ5A&hl=en&sa=X&ei=RIhRVKqcJ9fX8gWyzIKwDw&ved=0CB0Q6AEwAA#v=onepage&q=david%20steinberg%20suu%20kyi%20road%20to%20mandalay&f=false.

There is no denying that Aung San Suu Kyi is an admirer of Kipling. In 1972, extracts from *Mandalay*, referring to 'a neater, sweeter maiden in a cleaner, greener land', were read out at her wedding. She and her husband named their second son Kim, after the lead character in Kipling's famous novel of the same name, published in 1901. Also, she ended her first Reith Lecture for the BBC by quoting her favourite lines from Kipling.[6] They were taken from his poem *The Fairies Siege*:

> I'd not give way for an Emperor
> I'd hold my road for a King—
> To the Triple Crown I would not bow down—
> But this is a different thing.
> I'll not fight with the Powers of Air,
> Sentry, pass him through!
> Drawbridge let fall, 'tis the Lord of us all,
> The Dreamer whose dreams come true![7]

Despite the views of some postcolonial scholars, Aung San Suu Kyi seems always to have associated Kipling with the idea of freedom. Referring to his poem *If*, published in 1910, she said 'the poem that in England is often dismissed as the epitome of imperialist bombast is a great poem for dissidents'. The verse most often associated with the opposition leader and her struggle for democracy in Burma was the second:

> If you can dream—and not make dreams your master;
> If you can think—and not make thoughts your aim;
> If you can meet with Triumph and Disaster
> And treat those two imposters just the same;
> If you can bear to hear the truth you've spoken
> Twisted by knaves to make a trap for fools,
> Or watch the things you gave your life to, broken,
> And stoop and build 'em up with worn-out tools:[8]

Aung San Suu Kyi even distributed a Burmese-language version of the poem to inspire her supporters. The report in a recent biography that she translated the poem herself, however, is incorrect.

---

6   'Aung San Suu Kyi: Liberty', *The Reith Lectures*, [BBC Radio 4], 2011, www.bbc.co.uk/programmes/b012402s.
7   Rudyard Kipling, 'The Fairies' Siege', *Poetry Lovers' Page*, www.poetryloverspage.com/poets/kipling/fairies_siege.html.
8   Rudyard Kipling, *If* (Chicago: Poetry Foundation, June 2015), www.poetryfoundation.org/poems/46473/if---.

There is no easy segue from Kipling to classical music, other than to say that, thanks to modern technology, the musical settings of his poetry were often better known than the original texts. Aung San Suu Kyi was familiar with both, but it would appear she preferred the printed versions. Also, if her carefully chosen selection of recordings for the BBC radio program *Desert Island Discs* in 2013 is any guide, her musical tastes, while mixed, are inclined more to the classical than the popular end of the spectrum.[9]

Because of her public standing, and the challenge she posed to Burma's military regime, Aung San Suu Kyi was kept under house arrest for almost 15 years. During that time, part of her daily regimen was to practise on the piano. Until the instrument was completely out of tune, she played pieces by a range of classical composers, including Pachelbel, Telemann, Scarlatti, Bach, Mozart, Clementi and Bartok. At one stage, she was forced to sell much of her furniture to generate money for food. One of the few items she refused to let go was her piano.[10]

As Jonathan Webster wrote in 2013, Aung San Suu Kyi's piano playing 'in rebellious isolation' became a powerful symbol of her continuing resistance to military rule:

> Concerned supporters reportedly snuck within earshot for assurance that she was still alive. Famous Europeans who publicized her struggle sympathised with her as musicians. U2 called her 'a singing bird in an open cage'. Annie Lennox tried to send her a new piano. The top prize in the Leeds International Piano Competition was recently renamed the Daw Aung San Suu Kyi Gold Medal for its fiftieth anniversary.[11]

Aung San Suu Kyi's supporters around the world turned the image of her sitting at the piano in her closely guarded Rangoon home into a symbol of her country's struggle for democracy. Some also equated the military regime's efforts to curb the appreciation of Western music in Burma with

9   'Aung San Suu Kyi', *Desert Island Discs*, [BBC Radio 4], 1 February 2013, www.bbc.co.uk/programmes/b01q7gvl.
10   'Aung San Suu Kyi Under House Arrest', *Facts and Details*, factsanddetails.com/southeast-asia/Myanmar/sub5_5b/entry-3017.html.
11   Jonathan Webster, 'Solitude and *Sandaya*: The Strange History of Pianos in Burma', *The Appendix*, Vol.1, No.3, 7 August 2013, theappendix.net/issues/2013/7/solitude-and-sandaya-the-strange-history-of-pianos-in-burma.

their attempts to silence the respected opposition leader. In 2012, the *Los Angeles Times* even called the piano itself 'a symbol of Myanmar's struggle for democracy'.[12]

In these as in other aspects of Burma's struggles over the past few decades, there is a fair degree of exaggeration and mythmaking—on both sides of the political divide. That said, Aung San Suu Kyi's devotion to Western music and her determination to make Burma a more respectable international citizen have some interesting historical parallels. Also, rather than denoting Aung San Suu Kyi's abandonment of her country, as suggested by her domestic opponents, her affection for Kipling suggests quite the opposite.

Indeed, one could say that, in several ways, the wheel has come full circle. As Burma gradually emerges from its long period of military dictatorship, economic hardship and international isolation, there are millions of people both inside and outside the country who hope that it keeps turning.

12   Mark Magnier, 'Suu Kyi's Piano Tuners Play Small but Key Part in Myanmar History', *Los Angeles Times*, 15 November 2012, www.latimes.com/world/la-xpm-2012-nov-15-la-fg-myanmar-piano-tuner-20121116-story.html.

71

Aung San Suu Kyi's aura is fading

(15:10 AEDT, 18 November 2014)

Two regional summits held in Naypyidaw in November 2014 attracted the world's attention, but the press coverage of those events suggested that international opinion regarding Aung San Suu Kyi was shifting. Increasingly, she was the subject of articles critical of her refusal to speak out on behalf of those in Myanmar—notably, the Kachin and Rohingya minorities—who were suffering from human rights abuses.

The East Asia and ASEAN summit meetings in Naypyidaw last week[1] drew attention to a wide range of issues concerning the Asia-Pacific. They also prompted journalists and commentators around the world to take a closer look at Burma (Myanmar) itself.

There were three kinds of articles about Burma published in the news media earlier this month. Two were expected and aired arguments that have become familiar since the advent of President Thein Sein's mixed civilian–military government in 2011. The third set of articles, however, was unexpected and seems to reflect a major shift in international attitudes towards opposition leader Aung San Suu Kyi.

---

1   Brendan Thomas-Noone, 'Myanmar's Big Week: A Backgrounder', *The Interpreter*, 12 November 2014, www.lowyinterpreter.org/post/2014/11/12/9th-East-Asia-Summit-The-best-on-Myanmar.aspx?COLLCC=2527660672& [page discontinued] [now at www.lowyinstitute.org/the-interpreter/myanmars-big-week-backgrounder].

The first category of articles highlighted the slowing pace of reform in Burma, the government's failure to achieve a ceasefire with ethnic armed groups, continuing discrimination against the Rohingya minority[2] and parliament's refusal to amend the 2008 constitution so that Aung San Suu Kyi can run for the presidency in 2016.[3] World leaders were urged to put more pressure on Thein Sein, even to reimpose sanctions.

The second category of articles included a number of thoughtful commentaries by analysts who took a more strategic view.[4] They recognised Burma's shortcomings but made greater allowances for the enormous challenges faced by Thein Sein and the reformers. After considering the alternatives, they argued strongly for the international community to be patient and to continue supporting the transition process.[5]

As these articles revealed, human rights campaigners and other activists remain focused on Burma's immediate problems. Governments and international organisations, however, are increasingly looking forward to wider reforms. They believe the democratisation process is real but accept that it will be difficult and take a long time.[6] They are clearly unwilling to do anything that might harm the prospects for further change.

While the broad positions outlined in these articles were not new, it was striking how Aung San Suu Kyi no longer seemed to be viewed as central to the resolution of Burma's problems. The focus was clearly on the national government. Indeed, in a third category of articles, published

---

2   Charlie Campbell, 'If Obama Only Talks About One Thing in Burma it Must Be the Rohingya', *TIME*, 13 November 2014, time.com/3582611/obama-rohingya-burma-myanmar/.

3   Matthew Pennington, 'US Lawmakers: Myanmar Vote Unfair without Suu Kyi', *Yahoo News*, 5 November 2014, news.yahoo.com/us-lawmakers-myanmar-vote-unfair-without-suu-kyi-191159697. html [page discontinued].

4   Nirmal Ghosh, 'Little Choice but to Support Reformists in Myanmar', *The Straits Times*, [Singapore], 10 November 2014, www.stasiareport.com/the-big-story/asia-report/blogs/story/little-choice-support-reformists-myanmar-20141110 [page discontinued] [now at www.straitstimes.com/asia/little-choice-but-to-support-reformists-in-myanmar].

5   Priscilla Clapp, *Myanmar: Taking the Long View*, Asia Pacific Bulletin No.286 (Washington, DC: East–West Center, 10 November 2014), www.eastwestcenter.org/sites/default/files/private/apb286.pdf [page discontinued] [now at www.eastwestcenter.org/system/tdf/private/apb286.pdf?file=1&type=node &id=34833].

6   Erin Murphy and James Clad, 'Previewing President Obama's Trip to Myanmar for the East Asia Summit', *Commentary* (Seattle: The National Bureau of Asian Research, 4 November 2014), www.nbr. org/downloads/pdfs/eta/MurphyClad_commentary_110414.pdf [page discontinued] [now at www. nbr.org/publication/previewing-president-obamas-trip-to-myanmar-for-the-east-asia-summit/].

in a number of leading magazines and newspapers, Aung San Suu Kyi was openly and strongly criticised for failing to exert a leadership role on a number of key issues.

As noted on *The Interpreter* last year,[7] there was a time not that long ago when Aung San Suu Kyi was considered to be without peer and beyond reproach. According to one story in *The Times*, she was 'the bravest and most moral person in the world'.[8] Her aura began to fade after she was released from house arrest in 2010 and was elected to parliament in 2012.[9] Few observers, however, anticipated the harsh criticism that she is now receiving.

The first shot in the latest salvo against her was fired by *TIME* on 6 November, in an article headlined 'Aung San Suu Kyi's Silence on Burma's Human-Rights Abuses is Appalling'.[10] This was followed on 12 November by a piece in *The Diplomat* by Tim Robertson under the title 'Aung San Suu Kyi: Colluding with Tyranny'.[11]

On the same day, two other articles appeared. They were a little more measured but were still quite critical of her actions—or lack of them. Jane Perlez published a piece in *The New York Times* under the heading 'For Some, Daw Aung San Suu Kyi Falls Short of Expectations in Myanmar'.[12] On a lesser-known website, Alan Lerner posted a piece entitled 'Obama's Tarnished Saint'.[13]

7   Andrew Selth, 'Aung San Suu Kyi: A Pilgrim's Progress', *The Interpreter*, 7 May 2013, www. lowyinterpreter.org/post/2013/05/07/Aung-San-Suu-Kyi-A-pilgrims-progress.aspx [page discontinued] [now at www.lowyinstitute.org/the-interpreter/aung-san-suu-kyi-pilgrims-progress].

8   R.L. Parry, 'Enjoy Suu Kyi Now: Her Saintliness Won't Last', *The Times*, [London], 18 June 2012, www.networkmyanmar.org/images/stories/PDF12/enjoy-suu-kyi-now.pdf [page discontinued].

9   'Aung San Suu Kyi: The Halo Slips', *The Economist*, 15 June 2013, www.economist.com/news/ asia/21579512-running-president-comes-risks-halo-slips.

10   Charlie Campbell, 'Aung San Suu Kyi's Silence on Burma's Human-Rights Abuses is Appalling', *TIME*, 6 November 2014, time.com/3560353/myanmar-burma-nobel-peace-prize-aung-san-suu-kyi-burma-human-rights-abuses-silence/.

11   Tim Robertson, 'Aung San Suu Kyi: Colluding with Tyranny', *The Diplomat*, [Washington, DC], 12 November 2014, thediplomat.com/2014/11/aung-san-suu-kyi-colluding-with-tyranny/.

12   Jane Perlez, 'For Some, Daw Aung San Suu Kyi Falls Short of Expectations in Myanmar', *The New York Times*, 12 November 2014, www.nytimes.com/2014/11/13/world/asia/for-some-daw-aung-san-suu-kyi-falls-short-of-expectations-in-myanmar.html?emc=edit_tnt_20141112&nlid=21134157& tntemail0=y&_r=2.

13   Adam B. Lerner, 'Obama's Tarnished Saint', *Politico Magazine*, 12 November 2014, www.politico. com/magazine/story/2014/11/obama-myanmar-aung-san-suu-kyi-112844.html#.VGZR4mccRUb.

As the titles of these and other articles suggest, there has been widespread disappointment over the Nobel Peace laureate's refusal to condemn the continuing persecution of the Muslim Rohingyas and military operations against the Kachin and Shan. She has also drawn fire for appearing to support big business and for trying to develop a relationship with the country's armed forces, which still dominate Burma.

There was always going to be an adjustment in popular perceptions once Aung San Suu Kyi ceased being an icon under house arrest and began participating in the rough and tumble of Burmese power politics. She had been invested with such unrealistic hopes and expectations that she was bound to disappoint many. Also, many of her supporters seem to find it difficult to accept that politics requires difficult decisions and that compromises are often necessary.

It is often forgotten, too, that Aung San Suu Kyi, for all her charisma and popular support both at home and abroad, has few means of actually affecting political change in Burma. The constitution gives the government and armed forces control of almost all the levers of power. In that sense, she is the leader of a small, and to all practical purposes, ineffectual group in the national parliament, which to the surprise of many has adopted a low profile.

Aung San Suu Kyi is caught between two fires. She seems anxious to avoid taking any position that will alienate her predominantly ethnic Burman and Buddhist constituency. However, by failing to speak out on major human rights issues, she risks losing the support of her international backers, on whom she has relied to put pressure on the government, the better to achieve her domestic political objectives.[14]

Aung San Suu Kyi has declined to explain her behaviour, falling back as she often does on broad statements of principle.[15] Whatever the reasons for her refusal to speak out on some important issues, her reputation is no

---

14   Christi Parsons, 'Obama–Suu Kyi Visit in Myanmar Reflects Warmth and Differences', *Los Angeles Times*, 14 November 2014, www.latimes.com/world/asia/la-fg-obama-suu-kyi-meeting-20141114-story.html.

15   Anjana Pasricha, 'Aung San Suu Kyi Explains Silence on Rohingyas', *Voice of America*, 15 November 2012, www.voanews.com/content/aung-san-suu-kyi-explains-silence-on-rohingyas/1546809.html [page discontinued] [now at www.voanews.com/east-asia/aung-san-suu-kyi-explains-silence-rohingyas].

longer what it used to be.[16] No one is yet saying that she has feet of clay, but her image as a principled champion of universal human rights and determined fighter for democracy is certainly taking a beating.

In his article, Tim Robertson cites George Orwell's line: 'Saints should always be judged guilty until they are proved innocent.' The sentence, taken from Orwell's 1949 essay *Reflections on Gandhi*, continues, 'but the tests that have to be applied to them are not, of course, the same in all cases'.[17] We need to know more about Aung San Suu Kyi's thinking to get the full picture, but some tests have already been applied and she has not come out of the examination well.

16 Tim Hume, 'Aung San Suu Kyi's "Silence" on the Rohingya: Has "The Lady" Lost Her Voice?', *CNN*, 1 June 2014, edition.cnn.com/2014/04/15/world/asia/myanmar-aung-san-suu-kyi-rohingya-disappointment/.
17 George Orwell, 'Reflections on Gandhi', *Partisan Review*, January 1949, [London: The Orwell Foundation], www.orwellfoundation.com/the-orwell-foundation/orwell/essays-and-other-works/reflections-on-gandhi/.

72

Myanmar Police Force needs more foreign help to reform

(15:07 AEDT, 3 December 2014)

The hopes of both the Myanmar people and the international community were pinned on the reform of the Myanmar Police Force (MPF), both to exercise a greater civilian role in internal security and to strengthen the rule of law. However, to achieve these aims, the MPF needed more support, in terms of recognition, resources and training, including from overseas.

Two years ago,[1] I wrote that the MPF was gradually being recognised as a large, increasingly powerful and influential organisation that, in a more civilianised form, was likely to become a key instrument of state control under the hybrid civilian–military government that was inaugurated in Naypyidaw in 2011.

Since then, there have been a growing number of reports in the news media suggesting that President Thein Sein's comprehensive reform program has slowed or even stalled.[2] With that in mind, it is worth looking at the MPF again, to see how the transition described in my 2012 post is going.

---

1   Andrew Selth, 'Burma Police: The Long Road to Reform', *The Interpreter*, 13 December 2012, www.lowyinterpreter.org/post/2012/12/13/Burmas-police-The-long-road-to-reform.aspx?COLLCC= 2825173060& [page discontinued] [now at archive.lowyinstitute.org/the-interpreter/burma-police-long-road-reform].
2   Jean-Marie Guehenno and Richard Horsey, 'Despite the Headlines, Progress in Myanmar Isn't Slipping Away', *Reuters*, 19 November 2014, blogs.reuters.com/great-debate/2014/11/19/staying-on-course-in-myanmar/.

There have been some positive developments. The MPF has been restructured and includes several new departments, such as the aviation, maritime, border and tourist police. Some modern equipment has been acquired. A major recruitment program is under way and training institutions provide courses on modern policing and human rights. Greater emphasis is being given to tackling transnational crime.

More importantly, perhaps, the MPF is emphasising a 'service-oriented approach' and giving a high priority to issues like accountability, transparency and respect for human rights.[3] There is a new MPF code of conduct. Such rhetoric has been heard before, but recent statements by senior police officers seem to reflect a genuine wish to change the force's image, ethos and behaviour.

In other ways, however, little has changed.[4] The MPF still suffers from a lack of resources, abuses still occur, corruption remains a problem and 'community policing' doctrines have yet to take a firm hold. The transfer of large numbers of men from the armed forces to the police is seen by some as a ruse by Burma's military leaders to maintain their coercive power through less obvious means.

After decades of authoritarian rule, in which the armed forces dominated all aspects of internal security, including law and order, it is unrealistic to expect the MPF to become a modern, capable and internationally respected police force overnight. Mindsets are hard to change. Also, given the pressures on official resources, the force cannot implement many reforms without external help. Yet, such support has been slow in coming.

Since 2011, the MPF has received assistance from the UN, mainly through the UN Office on Drugs and Crime (UNODC), the UN High Commissioner for Refugees (UNHCR) and the UN Children's Fund (UNICEF). The International Committee of the Red Cross has also advised on modern policing standards. MPF officers have attended courses at the Jakarta Centre for Law Enforcement Cooperation and the

---

3   The Republic of the Union of Myanmar, Ministry of Home Affairs, Myanmar Police Force, 'Speech Delivered by the Chief of Police at the 49th Anniversary of the Myanmar Police Force', Ministry of Home Affairs, 1 October 2013, www.unodc.org/documents/southeastasiaandpacific/speech/2013/Speech_-_Chief_of_Police_at_49th_Anniversary_of_MPF.pdf.

4   Andrew Selth, *Police Reform in Burma (Myanmar): Aims, Obstacles and Outcomes*, Griffith Asia Institute Regional Outlook Paper No.44 (Brisbane: Griffith University, 2013), www.griffith.edu.au/__data/assets/pdf_file/0025/118906/Regional-Outlook-Paper-44-Selth-web.pdf.

Bangkok-based International Law Enforcement Academy. The EU has run useful pilot courses in community policing, crowd management and media relations.[5]

There have been a few bilateral initiatives, mainly related to transnational crime.[6] But, despite continuing low-level contacts,[7] most Western democracies seem chary of closer engagement. The MPF's poor reputation makes them cautious and, despite Aung San Suu Kyi's support for police training,[8] activists oppose aid to any components of Burma's 'coercive apparatus'.

With the active support of the MPF, the UNODC conducted a comprehensive survey of the force earlier this year. The study was aimed at gaining a greater understanding of the MPF, including its strengths and weaknesses. It was envisaged that the final report would help guide further reforms and identify specific areas where foreign governments and international organisations could assist.

Given its past close relations with the MPF, the UNODC was in an ideal position to make an honest appraisal of the force. Provided that its observations and recommendations are culturally sensitive and made in a way that encourages their acceptance, the final report could become a blueprint for wideranging changes to the MPF's policies and practices.

The reform of the MPF remains a key part of Thein Sein's attempts to civilianise internal security functions in Burma, strengthen the rule of law and improve judicial processes. As with most of his proposed changes, this process will not be quick or easy. There will be plenty of opportunities for critics—both within and outside Burma—to point out the MPF's shortcomings. Yet it is vital that the momentum built up since 2011 is maintained.

---

5   KG/Xinhua, 'Myanmar EU to Promote Police–Public Relations', *New Europe*, [Brussels], 26 May 2014, www.neweurope.eu/article/myanmar-eu-promote-police-public-relations.
6   'US to Help Combat Narcotics Trade, Police Say', *Eleven*, 7 October 2014, www.elevenmyanmar. com/index.php?option=com_content&view=article&id=7766:us-to-help-combat-narcotics-trade-police-say&catid=44:national&Itemid=384 [page discontinued].
7   Tim McLaughlin, 'Police Train with Bangladeshi Counterparts in United States', *Myanmar Times*, [Yangon], 25 July 2014, www.mmtimes.com/index.php/national-news/11124-myanmar-police-train-with-bangladeshi-counterparts-in-us.html.
8   'EU Begins "Crowd Control" Training for Burmese Police', *Democratic Voice of Burma*, 6 November 2013, www.dvb.no/news/eu-begins-crowd-control-training-for-burmese-police/34210 [page discontinued] [now at english.dvb.no/news/eu-begins-crowd-control-training-for-burmese-police/34210].

The need for continuing police reform can be considered at both practical and political levels.

As regards the first, Burma is facing serious problems caused by population growth, urbanisation and rapid economic change. Crime rates are growing. Arguably, the dramatic influx of foreign influences since 2011 has weakened traditional cultural norms, which helped curb antisocial behaviour.[9] Also, while difficult to quantify, the relaxation of controls over civil society has probably contributed to an increase in civil unrest.

These issues pose major challenges for the police. For example, a recent report by the Center for Strategic and International Studies (CSIS) recommended that the US explore the training of the MPF in cooperation with other democratic countries, on the grounds that 'communal violence has spiralled out of control over the past two years because the police have little or no training and experience in modern crowd control'.[10]

The MPF also needs to be bigger, more efficient and more effective. With 75,000 men and women on its books, the force has a ratio of only 120 officers per 100,000 people. If it achieves its goal of 155,000 personnel by 2020, there will be 256 officers per 100,000, which is comparable to international standards. Even if the force had not been neglected for decades, however, such an expansion will demand a massive infusion of resources.

There are also broader political issues. As a Canadian parliamentary committee noted last year: '[S]ecuring the rule of law in Burma will require the wholesale reform of the entire security apparatus.'[11] The committee drew particular attention to 'the urgent need to begin reforming the Burmese police forces' on the grounds that 'a principled, effective, and accountable police force is a cornerstone of democracy'.

---

9   Belle Hammond, 'Burma's Terrible Beauty', *Griffith News*, 14 March 2013, app.griffith.edu.au/news/2013/03/14/burmas-terrible-beauty/.
10   J. Stephen Morrison, Murray Hiebert, Thomas Cullison, Todd Summers and Sahil Angelo, *Myanmar: Regressed, Stalled, or Moving Forward?*, A Report of the CSIS Global Health Policy Center and the CSIS Sumitro Chair for Southeast Asia Studies (Washington, DC: Centre for Strategic and International Studies, October 2014), csis.org/files/publication/141019_Morrison_Myanmar_Web.pdf.
11   *Conflicting Realities: Reform, Repression and Human Rights in Burma*, Report of the Standing Committee on Foreign Affairs and International Development, Subcommittee on International Human Rights, 41st Parliament, 1st Session (Ottawa: House of Commons, Canada, June 2013), pp.34–36, www.parl.gc.ca/HousePublications/Publication.aspx?DocId=6157999&Language=E.

Traditionally, Burma's security forces have shunned outside influences. Indeed, they have been intensely proud of their ability to manage their own affairs, albeit with limited resources and mixed success rates. Before 2011, for example, few MPF officers were sent overseas for training. Now the security forces are reaching out to the international community and the MPF is taking the lead in seeking advice, training and equipment.

The American sociologist Morris Janowitz once wrote: 'It is a basic assumption of the democratic model of civilian–military relations that civilian supremacy depends upon a sharp organizational separation between internal and external violence forces.'[12] When Indonesia's police force broke away from the army in 1999, it received strong support from the international community.[13] Burma's police force deserves no less.

---

12 Morris Janowitz, *The Military in the Development of New Nations: An Essay in Comparative Analysis* (Chicago: University of Chicago Press, 1964), p.38.

13 David Connery, Natalie Sambhi and Michael McKenzie, *A Return on Investment: The Future of Police Cooperation between Australia and Indonesia*, Special Report (Canberra: Australian Strategic Policy Institute, 25 March 2014), www.aspi.org.au/publications/a-return-on-investment-the-future-of-police-cooperation-between-australia-and-indonesia/SR67_Australia_Indon_police_coop.pdf [page discontinued] [now at www.aspi.org.au/report/return-investment-future-police-cooperation-between-australia-and-indonesia].

73

Surveying public opinion in Burma

(08:01 AEDT, 18 December 2014)

The freedom under president Thein Sein to conduct large-scale public opinion surveys in Myanmar should have resulted in more accurate analyses of the popular mood and more informed decision-making. Unsurprisingly, early polls revealed that democratic systems of government were poorly understood and major political issues like constitutional reform were less important to people than the problems encountered in daily life.

For years—decades even—professional Burma-watchers, activists and other commentators have been making assessments about developments in Burma (Myanmar) on the basis of very little hard information. Government statistics could not be trusted, official spokespeople rarely gave away anything of value and the state-run press largely peddled propaganda. Reports generated outside Burma were often highly politicised and had to be treated carefully.

There were some notable exceptions to this rule, but even well-informed analysts tended to refer to Burma as an intelligence black hole.

In such circumstances, gauging the popular mood in Burma was always fraught with risk. Structured surveys of public opinion were forbidden. There were occasional attempts by embassies and international organisations to informally sound out certain target groups, but access to different parts of the country was difficult and the regime's coercive apparatus was so pervasive that the likelihood of gaining an accurate picture was low.

As a result, Burma-watchers of all kinds were heavily reliant on fragmentary information derived from relatively small numbers of personal contacts, anecdotal sources and gossip. Whenever there was a major incident of any kind, the Rangoon rumour mill went into overdrive. This did not prevent educated speculation about what people in Burma felt about certain issues, but such judgements usually lacked hard evidence.

Since the advent of President Thein Sein's hybrid civilian–military government in 2011, however, the atmosphere within Burma has changed dramatically. There is now much greater freedom of speech, of association and of movement. As a result, it has been possible to conduct comprehensive surveys that give reliable snapshots of public opinion. Two such exercises, both conducted by US institutions with the support of foreign governments, stand out.

The first was published in April this year by the International Republican Institute (IRI) and enjoyed the backing of the US Agency for International Development (USAID). Entitled *Survey of Burma Public Opinion, December 24, 2013 – February 1, 2014*, it canvassed the views of 3,000 adult men and women from 208 rural and 92 urban locations in all 14 states and regions of Burma.[1]

Not surprisingly, the survey showed there was overwhelming support for democracy as the most desirable form of government, although understanding of what 'democracy' actually meant seems to have differed widely. Those surveyed were also generally supportive of the government's reform programs, although their views seem to have been influenced by the optimism then prevailing about Burma's future economic development.

Interestingly, when asked to identify the three biggest problems facing Burma as a whole, respondents identified unemployment, ethnic or sectarian violence and high prices.[2] Almost all other issues raised related

---

1   *Survey of Burma Public Opinion, December 24, 2013 – February 1, 2014* (Washington, DC: International Republican Institute, 3 April 2014), www.iri.org/sites/default/files/flip_docs/2014%20 April%203%20Survey%20of%20Burma%20Public%20Opinion,%20December%2024,%20 2013-February%201,%202014.pdf.

2   'IRI Survey: Burmese Strongly Support Democracy, Express Satisfaction Over Country's Current Trajectory' (Washington, DC: International Republican Institute, 3 April 2014), www.iri.org/news-events-press-center/news/iri-survey-burmese-strongly-support-democracy-express-satisfaction-ove [page discontinued] [now at iri.org/resource/iri-survey-burmese-strongly-support-democracy-express-satisfaction-over-country's-current].

to daily life, such as poor health care, the lack of electricity and inadequate transportation. Politics only featured at the far end of the scale, with the need to amend the constitution scoring lower even than natural disasters.

The second survey has just been released. It was conducted by the Asia Foundation with help from the Australian Department of Foreign Affairs. Entitled *Myanmar 2014: Civic Knowledge and Values in a Changing Society*, it was conducted in May and June this year.[3] It, too, sought the views of 3,000 respondents across all 14 states and regions—once again, through personal interviews.

The Asia Foundation survey was more comprehensive than the IRI exercise and has yielded more nuanced results. It found, for example, that there is very limited knowledge in Burma about the structure and functions of the country's multilevel system of government, particularly at the subnational level. Respondents still hoped for real democracy, but there was little understanding about the principles and practices that underpin a democratic society.[4]

Also, the survey suggests that Burmese are generally positive about the situation in the country and welcome the results of the reform programs introduced since 2011, as far as they go. However, there is a pervasive underlying uncertainty about the future, particularly in the peripheral areas where most of the ethnic minorities live. Governments are still viewed with suspicion, political disagreements are deeply polarising and social trust is low.

Once again, the country's economic fortunes figured prominently in the thinking of those surveyed. As the IRI project also found, economic performance not only serves as a key indicator of how the country is seen, but also strongly affects popular attitudes towards the central government. There is a high expectation that the government will play a strong role in ensuring economic growth and an equitable and inclusive society.

None of these conclusions will be surprising to those who have followed Burma closely. Also, there is still a dearth of reliable information about many critical issues, such as the political views of the armed forces

3   *Myanmar 2014: Civic Knowledge and Values in a Changing Society* (San Francisco: The Asia Foundation, 2014), asiafoundation.org/resources/pdfs/MyanmarSurvey20141.pdf.
4   'The Asia Foundation Releases Results of Nationwide Myanmar Public Opinion Survey', Press release (San Francisco: The Asia Foundation, 12 December 2014), asiafoundation.org/news/2014/12/the-asia-foundation-releases-results-of-nationwide-public-opinion-survey-in-myanmar/.

leadership. However, these and other surveys can provide the basis for more reliable judgements about the public mood in Burma and the wishes of the Burmese people. They should also result in better-informed policy decisions.

If there is an underlying message in both surveys, it is that, since 2011, Burma's reforms have had a positive impact. The country is still facing serious problems, resulting in attendant caution, but there are now palpable hopes for a more democratic system of government and (in particular) a higher standard of living. These trends are to be welcomed and encouraged. That will require not just moral support, but also technical advice, practical assistance and patience.

2015

74

Second thoughts on the civil unrest in Burma

(16:28 AEDT, 14 April 2015)

The brutal suppression of demonstrations in Myanmar in March 2015 was a cause for widespread concern and resulted in demands for foreign assistance to the MPF to be suspended. However, the picture was not as black and white as portrayed in the news media and on activist websites. In any case, a strong argument could be made that these events argued for more help to the police force, not less.

Now that the dust has settled on last month's civil unrest in Burma, it is worth pausing to reflect on the protests and official responses to see whether any important factors have escaped public attention. I am also prompted to do so because the conventional narrative does not completely match what I heard in Rangoon at the time.

To briefly summarise recent events, in January, protesters began marching from major provincial cities to Rangoon, demanding changes to the National Education Law, which was passed by parliament last September. Protests were also held in other parts of the country.[1] Among the protesters' demands were a greater devolution of power to universities, the freedom to form student unions and mother-tongue language instruction in ethnic minority areas.

---

1   'Updates: National Education Law—Student Protests', *Burma Partnership*, www.burma partnership.org/updates-national-education-law-student-protest/.

On 5 March, up to 150 protesters outside Rangoon City Hall were forcibly dispersed by the MPF.[2] The police were assisted by civilian 'auxiliaries' wearing armbands proclaiming them to be 'on duty'.[3] Several protesters were reported injured and eight were arrested. The following day, about 200 protesters at Letpadan, 140 kilometres north of Rangoon, attempted to overcome a police blockade and resume their march on the city. Five people were arrested.

On 10 March, after negotiations with the authorities, the protesters at Letpadan were given permission to continue their journey to Rangoon under certain conditions. Some protesters refused to accept the agreed terms, however, and began dismantling police barricades. This sparked violent action by MPF security battalions, which were assisted by local Bago region members of the MPF.[4] Officials later said 127 people had been detained.

These events have been portrayed by most journalists and activists in stark, dualistic terms as clashes between peaceful, idealistic students and brutal, hardline police—reminiscent of the bloody confrontations under the former military regime. On this basis, calls have been made for the EU to suspend its MPF training program and for all other international contacts with Naypyidaw to be reviewed.

Clearly, the authorities at both the regional and the national levels could have handled the protests much better, and the MPF's brutal behaviour at Letpadan was inexcusable. The strong responses from foreign governments and human rights groups[5] to the two incidents were understandable and justified.[6]

2   'Police Crack Down on Student Protesters in Rangoon', *The Irrawaddy*, 5 March 2015, www.irra waddy.org/burma/police-crack-down-on-student-protestors-in-rangoon.html.
3   'Plainclothes Vigilantes Make a Comeback in Rangoon', *The Irrawaddy*, 5 March 2015, www.irrawaddy.org/burma/plainclothes-vigilantes-make-a-comeback-in-rangoon.html.
4   'Myanmar Riot Police Beat Student Protesters with Batons', *BBC News*, 10 March 2015, www.bbc.com/news/world-asia-31812028.
5   Colin Hinshelwood, 'International Voices Decry Police Crackdown on Students', *Democratic Voice of Burma*, 9 March 2015, www.dvb.no/news/international-voices-decry-police-crackdown-on-students-burma-myanmar/49066 [page discontinued] [now at images.dvb.no/news/international-voices-decry-police-crackdown-on-students-burma-myanmar/49066].
6   David Stout, 'Washington Condemns Burma's Violent Student Crackdown', *TIME*, 11 March 2015, time.com/3740141/burma-crackdown-student-protests-letpadan/.

Speaking to well-informed observers in Rangoon at the time, however, I was given a more nuanced account of events. Among the points made to me were the following:

- The protesters have invariably been labelled 'students'. This implies not only a direct and justifiable interest in educational reform, but also a status and respectability deriving from student participation in Burma's past pro-independence and prodemocracy struggles. Not all the protesters, however, were in fact students. Also, as the government has claimed, some probably had wider political goals in mind, such as regime change.[7]

- Most people to whom I spoke last month believed that, prior to the incidents in Rangoon and Letpadan, Naypyidaw had made a number of unexpected concessions to the protesters. Some of their demands had already been incorporated into the education law. Others (such as the allocation of 20 per cent of the annual budget to education) were seen as unrealistic by a parliamentary committee that included members of the opposition parties.

- The MPF units at Letpadan initially adopted a cautious and conciliatory approach. For example, at one stage, female police officers were deployed in an apparent attempt to present a friendly official face and to reduce the likelihood of violence.[8] It was only after five days of negotiations, when some protesters tired of what they saw as police obstructionism and openly began to challenge the police blockade, that the security battalions were sent in.

None of my interlocutors in Burma last month tried to excuse the MPF's violent tactics. Clearly, excessive force was used at Letpadan in what was described by one onlooker as 'a complete breakdown of police discipline'.[9]

---

7   Min Zin, 'Burma Takes a Big Step Backwards', *Foreign Policy*, 12 March 2015, foreignpolicy. com/2015/03/12/burma-takes-a-big-step-backwards/.

8   Yen Snaing, 'Authorities in Letpadan Block Student Protest March', *The Irrawaddy*, 2 March 2015, www.irrawaddy.org/multimedia-burma/authorities-letpadan-block-student-protest-march.html/ nggallery/page/8 [page discontinued].

9   'Scenes of Indiscriminate Violence in Letpadan as Police Attack Ambulance Workers, Students, Reporter', *The Irrawaddy*, 10 March 2015, www.irrawaddy.org/photo/scenes-of-indiscriminate-violence-in-letpadan-as-police-attack-ambulance-workers-students-reporter.html [page discontinued] [now at www.irrawaddy.com/news/burma/scenes-of-indiscriminate-violence-in-letpadan-as-police-attack-ambulance-workers-students-reporter.html].

Yet, as was also pointed out to me, on 10 March, some officers—probably from the Bago region MPF—attempted to curb the behaviour of the security battalions and even tried to protect protesters and bystanders.

Those actions highlight an aspect of the disturbances that has not been addressed in the news media—namely, that the uncompromising attitude of the security battalions was not representative of the entire MPF. Indeed, one senior police officer told me that many in the force were shocked and disappointed by events. They regretted what had occurred and recognised the damage the Letpadan incident in particular could do to the MPF's reform program and its attempts to regain public confidence.

Another issue that seems to have divided the MPF last month was the recruitment of civilian 'auxiliaries' to 'assist' the police in Rangoon. These untrained, poorly led and ill-disciplined 'vigilantes'—usually local unemployed youths—publicly undercut the authority of the MPF. Who actually directs such groups during an incident is unclear, but for the police, they make the management of civil unrest more problematic.

Another point of discussion last month was the extent to which the harsh response to the protests was instigated by the authorities in Rangoon, Bago or Naypyidaw. The security battalions are a national asset, but it does not necessarily follow that the notoriously hardline home affairs minister ordered violent tactics to be used. The recruitment of the civilian 'auxiliaries', for example, was by Rangoon ward officials, on orders from the region's chief minister.

It is also noteworthy that the security battalions deployed in Rangoon and Letpadan do not appear to have received any training in crowd management from the EU. The violent tactics employed by them are therefore hardly an indictment of the international training program. In any case, the EU has to date only undertaken to train 4,000 police—a small proportion of the estimated 12,500 in Police Security Command. Also, as it has no operational control over these forces, the EU cannot be held responsible for any of their actions.[10]

---

10   Andrew D. Kasper and Lawi Weng, 'EU Says Police Training "Still Needed" After Crackdowns Draw Criticism', *The Irrawaddy*, 11 March 2015, www.irrawaddy.org/burma/eu-says-police-training-still-needed-after-crackdowns-draw-criticism.html.

Despite this, the security battalions' behaviour has prompted calls from activist groups and others for a cancellation of the EU training program. It has also cast a shadow over the efforts of others—notably, the UNODC—to help reform Burma's police force.[11] How the MPF can be encouraged to raise its standards when the very elements dedicated to helping it reach those goals are withdrawn is not clear. If anything, recent developments argue for even closer engagement by the international community.

When incidents of this sort occur in Burma, it is often difficult to work out precisely what happened, and why. Even harder to discern is the thinking behind some of the decisions taken—on both sides. As is so often the case, the picture is more complicated than it first appears and any responses need to be considered with this in mind.

---

11   'Burma Crackdown on Students: EU, UK & USA Have Questions to Answer', *Burma Campaign UK*, 11 March 2015, burmacampaign.org.uk/burma-crackdown-on-students-eu-uk-usa-have-questions-to-answer/.

75

Burma: The return of the 'vigilantes'

(08:01 AEDT, 22 April 2015)

The use of civilian 'vigilante' groups to help the national police quell two cases of civil unrest in Myanmar raised a number of questions about these shadowy organisations, the motives behind their employment by the authorities and even the reform process itself.

In 2011, Burma's hybrid civilian–military government launched an ambitious reform program that, among other things, envisaged the transfer of primary responsibility for Burma's internal security from the armed forces to the national police force. Given Naypyidaw's firm and public commitment to this policy, it was surprising last month to see 'vigilante' groups being used by the authorities to help quell civil unrest.

In Burma, the use of such groups to 'assist' in the resolution of political disputes has a long history. In the 1950s, for example, political bosses employed gangs of enforcers. During the Ne Win era (1962–88), the Burma Socialist Programme Party was used to help monitor the mood of the civilian population, generate support for the government and in various ways encourage compliance with the regime's laws and regulations.

After the armed forces took back direct political control of the country in 1988, 'unofficial' civilian groups played a more direct role, including in the security arena.

In 1993, Burma's ruling military council created the Union Solidarity Development Association (USDA). Its main purpose was to mobilise the population in support of the regime's policies. Not long after its formation, there were reports of the creation of a USDA-sponsored 'militia', designed to provide paramilitary, intelligence and law enforcement services to the regime.[1] The militia's structure was believed to broadly mirror that of the civil administration, but it had no legal status.[2]

One part of this militia was later identified as the Swan Ah Shin (SAS; literally, 'Masters of Force'). This was essentially a loose collection of civilians attached to local councils that included members of the fire brigades, first aid organisations, women's organisations and the USDA, as well as criminals released from jail, members of local gangs, the unemployed and the very poor.[3] At different times, reports have put SAS groups under the command of the civil authorities, intelligence agencies, the army and police.

These organisations first prompted international scrutiny in 1996, when Aung San Suu Kyi's car was attacked in Rangoon by about 200 USDA supporters. In 2003, her motorcade was set upon by a much larger mob at Depayin in Upper Burma. These 'government-affiliated forces' (as they were described by the US State Department)[4] appear to have been organised in an effort to intimidate (or, in the latter incident, possibly even assassinate) the popular opposition leader.[5] At Depayin, dozens of her followers were killed and many more were injured.

The SAS also played a part in the suppression of the so-called Saffron Revolution in 2007. Up to 600 criminals were said to have been released from jail and given basic training in crowd control. They were initially used

1   *The White Shirts: How the USDA Will Become the New Face of Burma's Dictatorship* (Mae Sot, Thailand: Network for Democracy and Development, 2006), burmacampaign.org.uk/media/USDA-2.pdf.

2   *Crackdown: Repression of the 2007 Popular Protests in Burma*, Report, Vol.19, No.18(C) (New York: Human Rights Watch, December 2007), www.hrw.org/sites/default/files/reports/burma1207web.pdf.

3   United Nations General Assembly, *Human Rights Situations That Require the Council's Attention: Report of the Special Rapporteur on the Situation of Human Rights in Myanmar*, A/HRC/6/14 (New York: UN Human Rights Council, 7 December 2007), burmalibrary.org/docs4/HRC2007-12--SRM-A-HRC-6-14-en.pdf.

4   Richard Boucher, Spokesman, 'Burma: Second Anniversary of Attack on Aung San Suu Kyi', Press statement, US Department of State, Washington, DC, 26 May 2005, 2001-2009.state.gov/r/pa/prs/ps/2005/46836.htm.

5   'Premeditated Depayin Massacre', www.ibiblio.org/obl/docs/Yearbook2002-3/yearbooks/Depayin%20report.htm [page discontinued].

to intimidate protesters[6] but, after the anti-government demonstrations grew in size and scope, SAS members acted in concert with the police and army. The state-run *New Light of Myanmar* described them as 'peace-loving people' preventing 'instigators from trying to cause instability and unrest'.[7] Aung San Suu Kyi has called them Burma's Brown Shirts.

Since 2007, there have been claims that shadowy groups like the SAS have been involved in other outbreaks of civil unrest. For example, several commentators and activist groups have suggested that the Buddhist extremists active in 2012 and 2013 had official sanction—accounting for the apparent reluctance of the police and army to prevent the anti-Muslim violence that occurred in those years.[8] No firm evidence of such sponsorship, however, has yet been produced.

Indeed, it was hoped that, with the advent of a new and reformist government in 2011, the use of groups like the SAS would cease. Naypyidaw emphasised the management of internal security through an expanded and modernised civil police force, which publicly embraced modern doctrines such as community policing.[9] The role of the armed forces was reduced and greater emphasis was given to 'the rule of law'.

Such hopes, however, have been dashed.

Last month, 100 or so civilian 'auxiliaries' were used to break up the remnants of a garment workers' strike at the Shwepyithar Industrial Zone.[10] Auxiliaries were also deployed outside Rangoon City Hall during a protest against the National Education Law. Wearing red armbands stating that they were 'on duty', they assaulted the protesters and helped police to detain eight of them.

---

6   Michael Van Es, 'Burmese People-Power Powder Keg', *Himal Southasian*, [Kathmandu], 10 December 2008, old.himalmag.com/component/content/article/1315-burmese-people-power-powder-keg.html [page discontinued] [now at www.himalmag.com/burmese-people-power-powder-keg/].
7   'Burmese Vigilante Group Arrests Citizens', *Fifty Viss*, 20 May 2007, viss.wordpress.com/2007/05/20/burmese-vigilante-group-arrests-citizens/.
8   Francis Wade, 'Burma Recruits Vigilante "Duty" Mobs to Quell Student Protests', *Asian Correspondent*, 6 March 2015, asiancorrespondent.com/author/insideburma/ [page discontinued].
9   Andrew Selth, *Police Reform in Burma (Myanmar): Aims, Obstacles and Outcomes*, Griffith Asia Institute Regional Outlook Paper No.44 (Brisbane: Griffith University, 2013), www.griffith.edu.au/__data/assets/pdf_file/0009/512379/Regional-Outlook-Paper-44-v.2-Selth.pdf [page discontinued].
10   Fiona MacGregor, 'Garment Workers Deserve Support Too', *Myanmar Times*, [Yangon], 16 March 2015, www.mmtimes.com/index.php/opinion/13530-garment-workers-deserve-support-too.html#.VQjyCfgAjWQ.facebook.

These 'vigilantes' were recruited by ward officials at the order of the Chief Minister of Rangoon Region. Most seem to have been unemployed men who were offered meals and modest daily payments to 'assist' the authorities maintain law and order. Some were only teenagers.[11] They were untrained, ill-disciplined and, as far as can be determined, poorly led. During the Rangoon protest, they appear to have ignored or exceeded police orders.

Strictly speaking, the popular label 'vigilante' is a misnomer. These auxiliaries were not self-appointed. Nor were they acting without legal authority. As both regional and national officials have pointed out, according to Article 128 of the Burmese Code of Criminal Procedure (which dates from 1898), magistrates and police station chiefs have the right to recruit civilians to assist in the breaking up of protests and to help make arrests.[12]

On 10 March, President Thein Sein ordered an investigation into whether or not the security forces acted properly in Rangoon, and whether the authorities acted in accordance with the law. The commission's report was due on 30 March but has not been released.[13] It is unlikely to find the authorities at fault, but it may help answer some of the questions surrounding the use of deputised civilians.

Whether or not the recruitment of such groups is found to be legal, the thinking behind their use is hard to fathom. The Shwepyithar and Rangoon protests were quite small and could easily have been handled by police security battalions. Even if the auxiliaries did not behave badly, they had no legitimacy in the eyes of the public. Their use thus undercut the authority of the national police. Indeed, to many police officers, they threaten a key goal of the force's reform program, which is to win back the respect of the population through higher standards, adherence to the rule of law and better community relations.

---

11   Nobel Zaw, 'Students, Activists Allege Violence in Rangoon Protest Crackdown', *The Irrawaddy*, 6 March 2015, www.irrawaddy.org/burma/students-activists-allege-violence-in-rangoon-protest-crack down.html.
12   'Plainclothes Vigilantes Make a Comeback in Rangoon', *The Irrawaddy*, 5 March 2015, www.irra waddy.org/burma/plainclothes-vigilantes-make-a-comeback-in-rangoon.html.
13   Ye Mon, 'Govt Keeps Report on Vigilantes Under Wraps', *Myanmar Times*, [Yangon], 6 April 2015, www.mmtimes.com/index.php/national-news/13925-govt-keeps-report-on-vigilantes-under-wraps.html.

There has been an outcry in Burma and abroad against what many see as a return to the 'bad old days' of 'officially sponsored thugs' being used to crush popular dissent.[14] The use of such tactics has added to growing scepticism about the November elections and the government's willingness to permit criticism of its policies in the leadup to the poll. Some commentators have even cited the recent use of 'vigilantes' to raise doubts over the entire reform process.[15]

This is drawing rather a long bow, but after last month's events Naypyidaw certainly has some serious questions to answer.

---

14   'Behind the Mask', *Mizzima News*, [Yangon], 7 April 2015, www.mizzima.com/news-features/behind-mask.
15   'Sliding Backwards to 1962?', *Mizzima Weekly*, [Yangon], 26 March 2015, www.mizzima.com/news-opinion/sliding-backwards-1962.

76

Burma: Police reforms expand women's roles

(08:49 AEDT, 1 May 2015)

Historically, women have not played a significant role in Myanmar's security forces. However, a master plan developed under president Thein Sein included a proposal to recruit more women into the MPF and expand the roles they perform. This has already made an impact inside and outside the country.

There was a time when there were very few women in Burma's national police force and they were practically invisible. Under an ambitious plan to enlarge, modernise and reform the MPF, however, that situation is rapidly changing. Not only are there now many more female police officers in Burma, but also their roles are expanding, both locally and internationally.

Burma had always prided itself on the fact that, compared with other Asian countries, its women enjoyed high social status.[1] They were not considered the equal of men (after all, one had to be born a man to become a Buddha), but under both custom and the law, they were accorded many rights denied to their sisters elsewhere. This picture changed after the 1962 military coup,[2] but women have played an important role in modern Burmese history, rising to senior positions in politics, the civil service and business.

---

1   Daw Mya Sein, 'The Women of Burma', *The Atlantic*, 1 February 1958, www.theatlantic.com/magazine/archive/1958/02/the-women-of-burma/306822/.
2   *The Gender Gap and Women's Political Power in Myanmar/Burma*, Report (New York: Global Justice Centre, 22 May 2013), www.globaljusticecenter.net/index.php?option=com_mtree&task=att_download&link_id=103&cf_id=34 [page discontinued] [now at www.globaljusticecenter.net/publications/advocacy-resources/267-the-gender-gap-and-women-s-political-power-in-myanmar-burma].

There were some occupations, however, for which women were seen as unsuitable, such as the armed forces and the police. In the latter case, this posed problems, as it was considered unacceptable for men to physically restrain women at demonstrations, at crime scenes or in custody. Women detained by the police could only be searched by other women— sometimes requiring the force to enlist the help of members of the public.

During the British colonial period, this problem became acute when women protested against the denial of female representation and voting rights (granted in 1929) and, during the 1930s, became more active in the nationalist movement. Occasionally, the wives of local police officers were recruited for temporary duty, but Burma remained well behind metropolitan Britain, where policewomen were on the beat from 1914.[3]

After Burma regained its independence in 1948, the new government faced similar problems. Yet it was not until 1959 that the then Burma Police established a women's division. In 1960, it accepted five female recruits.[4] In 1964, the renamed People's Police Force recruited 25 women. Over the next 25 years, intakes of women were still infrequent, but class sizes began to number in the hundreds. In those days, female officers tended to be restricted to routine administrative and traffic duties.

At present, only about 4 per cent of the MPF are women. This compares with 3.5 per cent in Indonesia, 6 per cent in Thailand, 12 per cent in Malaysia and 16 per cent in Singapore. However, according to its latest master plan—under which the force will be expanded from 72,000 to 155,000 total personnel—the MPF hopes to increase its female component to 25 per cent. This is roughly comparable with countries such as Australia.[5]

If successful, this move would not only see the MPF reflect Burmese society more accurately (about 52 per cent of Burma's population is female),[6] but also help it embrace a modern 'community policing' model.

3   'Some 95 Years of Women Police Officers', *Mirror*, [London], 20 September 2009, www.mirror. co.uk/news/uk-news/some-95-years-of-women-police-officers-419827.

4   'Burma Policewomen Will Go Home with Fresh Ideas', *Singapore Free Press*, 22 September 1961, eresources.nlb.gov.sg/newspapers/Digitised/Article/freepress19610922-1.2.11.aspx.

5   Rachelle Irving, *Career Trajectories of Women in Policing in Australia*, Trends & Issues in Crime and Criminal Justice No.370 (Canberra: Australian Institute of Criminology, February 2009), www.aic.gov. au/publications/current%20series/tandi/361-380/tandi370.html [page discontinued].

6   *Republic of the Union of Myanmar, The Population and Housing Census of Myanmar, 2014: Summary of the Provisional Results* (Naypyidaw: Department of Population, Ministry of Immigration and Population, August 2014), unstats.un.org/unsd/demographic/sources/census/2010_phc/Myanmar/ MMR-2014-08-28-provres.pdf [page discontinued] [now at myanmar.unfpa.org/en/publications/ summary-provisional-results-0].

The MPF has already launched a vigorous recruitment program, the results of which are obvious to any visitor to Burma.[7] Female police officers in smart new uniforms are now a common sight at airports and tourist venues. During the 2014 ASEAN summit meeting in Naypyidaw, policewomen played a prominent role directing traffic and providing security for the delegates.

Most female officers are based at MPF headquarters in Naypyidaw and in the forces of the 14 states and regions. However, they have also been posted to specialist units such as the Highway Police, the Tourist Police, the Aviation Police, the Anti-Trafficking in Persons Division and the Division Against Transnational Crime. They can also be found in the Criminal Investigation Department and Special Branch.

The highest-ranking female officer in the MPF is a police lieutenant colonel—a position she reached after 30 years in the force.[8] Most other commissioned women are around the police captain level.

Women joining the MPF are required to undergo routine physical examinations, but they are not subject to the degrading virginity and beauty tests applied to female recruits in Indonesia.[9] Other ranks are expected to remain unmarried for their first three years in the force but, after that, they can marry and have children. Female officers are entitled to 12 weeks' maternity leave. At present, about two-thirds of the women in the MPF are married.

As shown in a recent promotional video, Myanmar's 'police ladies' undergo the same training as male recruits, although some training sequences are performed separately.[10] With a few exceptions, they are eligible to perform

---

7   Si Thu Lwin, 'Women Look to Join the Police Force', *Myanmar Times*, [Yangon], 8 July 2013, www.mmtimes.com/index.php/national-news/7406-women-respond-to-police-force-training-call. html.

8   'Myanmar's Gender Status Analysis Gets the Go-Ahead', *News* (Yangon: United Nations Population Fund, 18 January 2015), countryoffice.unfpa.org/myanmar/2015/01/18/11267/myanmar _rsquo_s_gender_status_analysis_gets_the_go_ahead/ [page discontinued] [now at myanmar.unfpa. org/en/news/myanmar%E2%80%99s-gender-status-analysis-gets-go-ahead].

9   Sharyn Graham Davies, 'Beautiful Virgins: The Hard Road to Becoming an Indonesian Policewoman', *Asian Currents*, 21 April 2015, asaablog.tumblr.com/post/116987426401/beautiful-virgins-the-hard-road-to-becoming-an [page discontinued] [now at asaa.asn.au/beautiful-virgins-the-hard-road-to-becoming-an/].

10   Myo Chit Ko Ko, 'Myanmar Special Police Woman', *YouTube*, www.youtube.com/watch?v=KJj QldUMTUY [page discontinued].

the same duties as men, drive motor vehicles and carry weapons. As a rule, however, they do not work night shifts, out of concern for their safety and due to Burma's conservative social mores.

There are no female officers in the MPF's Security Command, which is responsible for area security, crowd control and the protection of diplomatic missions. However, during the confrontation between police and protesters at Letpadan in March, policewomen from Bago region were deployed in an apparent attempt to present a friendlier official face.[11] They employed basic crowd management techniques but were withdrawn before the security battalions were sent in to break up the protest.[12]

Policewomen are still necessary for the management of female protesters.[13] They are also called upon in cases involving women and children and sexual violence. The latter crimes tend to be underreported in official statistics, as most are handled informally through social networks and community-based organisations.[14] With a larger number of female police officers, however, the MPF should be able to improve its management of gender-based offences.

There are important international dimensions to this issue. In recent years, the MPF has participated in regional meetings—for example, at the Jakarta Centre for Law Enforcement Cooperation[15]—that relate to female policing in Asia and the impact on women of transnational crimes such as people and narcotics trafficking. Female police officers have also attended workshops or training courses in several European countries, most ASEAN member states, the US and Australia. Participation in future UN peacekeeping operations remains an option.

---

11   'Myanmar Students Defy Deadline to Disperse', *BBC News*, 3 March 2015, www.bbc.com/news/world-asia-31716169.

12   'First Training of Mass-Handling to Over 60 Policewomen', *Burmese Classic*, 1 November 2014, www.burmeseclassic.org/news_detail.php?id=2866&type=3.

13   Nobel Zaw, 'Students, Activists Allege Violence in Rangoon Protest Crackdown', *The Irrawaddy*, 6 March 2015, www.irrawaddy.org/burma/students-activists-allege-violence-in-rangoon-protest-crackdown.html.

14   David Baulk, 'Burma's "Transition" Leaves Women's Rights Behind', *New Internationalist Blog*, 3 December 2014, newint.org/blog/2014/12/03/burma-womens-rights/.

15   'The 2nd Asia Region Women Police Conference', Jakarta Centre for Law Enforcement Cooperation, 5 June 2014, 222.124.21.46/index.php?option=com_content&task=view&id=341&Itemid=2 [page discontinued].

Inside Burma, international organisations like the UN Office on Drugs and Crime are active in this area, albeit as part of broader initiatives. To date, little has been done through bilateral schemes. However, as in other areas of security sector reform in Burma, there is scope for foreign countries to develop assistance programs specifically tailored for female officers.[16] On present indications, this would be warmly welcomed by the MPF's senior leadership.

16 ActionAid, '5 Ways We Are Tackling Violence against Women in Burma', *ReliefWeb*, 15 January 2015, reliefweb.int/report/myanmar/5-ways-were-tackling-violence-against-women-myanmar.

77

Burma: Beware of unrealistic expectations

(10:03 AEDT, 18 June 2015)

Speakers at The Australian National University's 2015 Myanmar Update conference were almost unanimous in warning against being too optimistic about Myanmar's democratisation process and reform programs. With national elections in Myanmar due in November 2015 and the election of a new president early the following year, this seemed a timely warning.

The spirit of Kevin Rudd seemed to be stalking the lecture theatres of The Australian National University earlier this month, when it staged the latest Myanmar/Burma Update conference. This was not because the former Australian Prime Minister had showed any particular interest in, or understanding of, Burma when in office, but because of his 2013 injunction to overexcited journalists that 'everyone should take a long, cold shower'.[1]

The Australian National University is one of only two academic institutions around the world that regularly stages international meetings to discuss developments in Burma (officially known since 1989 as Myanmar).[2] Over the past 25 years, 13 conferences in Canberra have canvassed a wide range

---

1   Gemma Jones, Simon Benson and Wires, 'Take a Cold Shower, Says Former PM Rudd as He Denies Leadership Challenge Claims', *News.com.au*, 5 February 2013, www.news.com.au/national/take-a-cold-shower-say-former-pm-kevin-rudd-as-he-denies-claims-leadership-challenge-claims/story-fncynjr2-1226570317321.
2   '2015 Myanmar/Burma Update: Making Sense of Conflict ', The Australian National University, Canberra, 5–6 June 2015, asiapacific.anu.edu.au/asiapacific-region/2015-myanmarburma-update.

of subjects of current interest, producing nine major research publications that captured the knowledge and judgements of dozens of foreign and Burmese scholars.[3]

The conference on 5–6 June was of particular interest, staged as it was before Burma's national elections this November and the election of a new president early in 2016.[4] The peace negotiations between Naypyidaw and ethnic armed groups have reached a critical stage,[5] while some economic and social reforms appear to be stalling. Other issues have attracted international attention—notably, the plight of the Muslim Rohingyas[6] and the resurgence of Burma's narcotics production.[7]

It was in relation to all these matters that Kevin Rudd's remark came to mind. For, despite high hopes for the future and optimistic forecasts by journalists and commentators, most speakers at the ANU conference presented sobering accounts of the obstacles facing democratisation in Burma and the likely pace of reform over the next few years. Not counting the keynote address by the Speaker of Burma's upper house of parliament, which was predictably upbeat,[8] the consistent message was to beware of unrealistic expectations.

This message was directed primarily at foreign observers and activists, but it could equally have been aimed at the Burmese population. Despite, or perhaps even because of, decades of crushed hopes and disappointed dreams, many people in Burma still seem to think that genuine democracy

---

3   '2015 Myanmar/Burma Update', *Update Publications* (Canberra: The Australian National University, 2015), asiapacific.anu.edu.au/asiapacific-region/2015-myanmarburma-update#acton-tabs-link--qt-2015_myanmar_burma_update_quickt-ui-tabs4.

4   Larry Jagan, 'Parties Brace for a Bitter Election Battle', *Bangkok Post*, 7 June 2015, www.bangkok post.com/news/special-reports/584481/parties-brace-for-a-bitter-election-battle.

5   Min Zin, 'Why There's Less to Burma's Peace Process Than Meets the Eye', *Foreign Policy*, 26 May 2015, foreignpolicy.com/2015/05/26/why-theres-less-to-burmas-peace-process-than-meets-the-eye-burma-myanmar/.

6   'Southeast Asia: Accounts from Rohingya Boat People', *News* (New York: Human Rights Watch, 27 May 2015), www.hrw.org/news/2015/05/27/southeast-asia-accounts-rohingya-boat-people.

7   Tom Kramer, *The Current State of Counternarcotics Policy and Drug Reform Debates in Myanmar*, TNI Burma Project Report (Amsterdam: Transnational Institute, 1 May 2015), www.tni.org/briefing/current-state-counternarcotics-policy-and-drug-reform-debates-myanmar?context=70443.

8   U Khin Aung Myint, 'Future Lies in Reconciling Present with the Past', *New Mandala*, 5 June 2015, asiapacific.anu.edu.au/newmandala/2015/06/05/myanmars-future-lays-in-reconciling-the-present-with-the-past/#respond [page discontinued] [now at www.newmandala.org/myanmars-future-lays-in-reconciling-the-present-with-the-past/].

is just around the corner. There is also a widespread belief that, once Aung San Suu Kyi becomes president (as large numbers of Burmese confidently expect), all the country's problems will somehow be solved.

As most speakers at the ANU conference warned, none of these things is going to happen, at least not soon and not without considerable difficulty.

There are still a few naysayers who deny any progress has been made since 2011, when a hybrid military–civilian government took over the country and President Thein Sein launched an ambitious program of reforms. These may not have gone as far or as fast as most would have liked, but it is undeniable that the country has changed dramatically over the past four years, and for the better. Burma is still not free, but it is hard to see it returning to the bad old days of direct military rule and widespread repression.

That said, it is important to put these developments into perspective and to keep in mind the enormous problems that Burma still needs to overcome to achieve real and lasting change. Quite apart from the constraints imposed by the armed forces, transforming the country from an internally fractured, economically challenged and diplomatically isolated military dictatorship to a stable, modern, prosperous and respected member of the international community was always going to be difficult. Above all, it was going to take time.

On present indications, even if they are free and fair, this year's elections are unlikely to result in the landslide for the NLD that many have predicted. Aung San Suu Kyi's chances of becoming Burma's next president are slight. While they have stepped back from day-to-day government, the country's armed forces have no intention of surrendering their national political role.[9] The ethnic and religious divisions plaguing the country are far from resolved, and abuses of power will still occur.

The economic and social reforms that have been pursued under President Thein Sein will continue after 2016, but not at the pace, or with the scope, that everyone would like to see. The process will be held back by a continuing lack of infrastructure, insufficient technical and managerial expertise, a weak bureaucracy and the absence of a respected legal

---

9   Larry Jagan, 'Army Set for Top Brass Shift Before Polls', *Bangkok Post*, 16 May 2015, www.bangkok post.com/opinion/opinion/563043/army-set-for-top-brass-shift-before-polls.

system.[10] Also, as Sean Turnell has pointed out, corruption and financial irregularities underpin almost all major transactions in Burma and this situation is unlikely to change soon.[11]

These harsh realities need to be understood and accepted. Inflated expectations already pose major challenges for Thein Sein's government, but widespread disappointment over the election results, the choice of a new president and setbacks in the peace negotiations would seriously undermine confidence in the reform program. Failure to deliver anticipated economic and social benefits could also lead to popular protests. Widespread communal unrest, particularly if accompanied by violence, may invite a military response.

Most foreign governments understand the enormous challenges faced by Naypyidaw and the difficulty of implementing such a wide range of major reforms over a relatively short period. As a result, countries like the US and the UK have cut Naypyidaw considerable slack and (in private, at least) supported the government's calls for patience. However, if events in Burma do not go as many in the West hope, the democracies will come under greater pressure to publicly criticise Naypyidaw, further complicating the reform process.

It does not help that, over the past 25 years, Burma has been held to a higher standard of behaviour than any other regional country, including North Korea.[12] Despite the scarcity of ASEAN examples, a liberal Western-style democracy and a socially responsible capitalist economy were adopted long ago as goals by many inside and outside Burma. Inspired by these ideals—personified by charismatic opposition leader Aung San Suu Kyi— popular expectations were raised to levels that were always difficult to justify when measured against objective criteria.

---

10   Larry Jagan, 'Myanmar in Transition', *Bangkok Post*, 8 June 2015, www.bangkokpost.com/business/news/585797/myanmar-in-transition.

11   Thomas Fuller, 'Profits of Drug Trade Drive Economic Boom in Myanmar', *The New York Times*, 5 June 2015, www.nytimes.com/2015/06/06/world/asia/profits-from-illicit-drug-trade-at-root-of-myanmars-boom.html.

12   David I. Steinberg, 'Disparate Sanctions: US Sanctions, North Korea and Burma', *East Asia Forum*, 23 June 2011, www.eastasiaforum.org/2011/06/23/disparate-sanctions-us-sanctions-north-korea-and-burma/.

There are no magical solutions to Burma's myriad problems, which, as Timothy Garton Ash once wrote, are 'fiendishly complex'.[13] Some predate the colonial era and most have bedevilled Burma since it regained its independence in 1948. Others have been caused, or at least exacerbated, by 50 years of inept and repressive military rule. No single group, let alone individual, has it within their power to solve them. Foreign assistance can help, but ultimately Burma's problems will require agreed Burmese solutions, and that will take time.

---

13   Timothy Garton Ash, 'Beauty and the Beast in Burma', *The New York Review of Books*, 25 May 2000, www.ibiblio.org/obl/docs/Beauty_and_the_Beast_in_Burma.htm [page discontinued] [now at www.nybooks.com/articles/2000/05/25/beauty-and-the-beast-in-burma/].

78

Is Naypyidaw setting the agenda in US–China–Burma relations?

(10:15 AEDT, 18 September 2015)

Analysts looking at Myanmar's relations with China tended to fall into three groups. These were broadly defined as the domination school, the partnership school and the rejectionist school. In considering the range of views offered, it was important to bear in mind that Myanmar was not simply a pawn in a game between the major powers, but an actor in its own right, possibly even setting the agenda and pace of developments.

Since 1988, when Burma appeared to abandon its strictly neutral foreign policy and drew closer to China, contacts between the two countries have been watched closely. Bilateral ties have developed and matured, as has analysis of them, which has begun to include consideration of the US's interests and possible role.

Questions as to how Burma's relations with China have changed over the past 25 years, and what factors may have played a role in this process, were highlighted at a conference staged last week by The Australian National University's Strategic and Defence Studies Centre.[1]

---

1   'Southeast Asian Strategies Towards the Great Powers', Conference Launching the Graduate Research and Development Network on Asian Security (GRADNAS), Strategic and Defence Studies Centre, The Australian National University, Canberra, 7 September 2015, www.gradnas.com/gradnas-launch.

Before the advent of President Thein Sein's reformist government in 2011, Western studies of Burma–China relations fell into three broad schools of thought. There were many areas of agreement, but they were distinguished by some key differences of view. For the sake of argument, they can be called the domination school, the partnership school and the rejectionist school.

The domination school harked back to the great power politics and strategic balances of the Cold War and argued that small, weak and isolated Burma would inevitably succumb to the pressures of its larger neighbour, becoming a pawn in China's bid to achieve world-power status. In the mid 1990s, this school was confidently predicting that, by the turn of the century, Burma would be a 'satellite' or 'client state' of an expansionist China.

To support this view, it cited China's 'stranglehold' over Burma, as exercised through loans, arms sales, trade and political influence, including along their shared border. In these circumstances, it was felt, Burma would have little choice but to conform to China's wishes. As evidence of this trend, the school claimed that Burma was the site of several Chinese military bases.[2]

The second, or partnership, school broadly accepted the main arguments of the domination school but was much more cautious in its predictions of how and when China would draw Burma into its sphere of influence. This school rejected the idea that China would simply impose its wishes on a weak and reluctant Burma, suggesting instead that the process would be more gradual and develop along the lines of a more even-handed strategic alliance.

The partnership school argued that the bilateral relationship was part of a pattern of expanding Chinese activity around the Indian Ocean, which included Sri Lanka and Pakistan—the 'string of pearls' theory.[3] While its members doubted that there were any Chinese bases in Burma, they believed that Beijing wished eventually to establish a permanent military presence there.

---

2   Andrew Selth, *Chinese Military Bases in Burma: The Explosion of a Myth*, Griffith Asia Institute Regional Outlook Paper No.10 (Brisbane: Griffith University, 2007), www.griffith.edu.au/__data/assets/pdf_file/0018/18225/regional-outlook-andrew-selth.pdf [page discontinued].

3   Billy Tea, 'Unstringing China's Strategic Pearls', *Asia Times*, [Hong Kong], 11 March 2011, www.atimes.com/atimes/China/MC11Ad02.html [page discontinued].

The third, or rejectionist, school consisted mainly of scholars with a specialised knowledge of Burma and Sinologists sceptical of China's purportedly expansionist designs. Its arguments consisted of three main points.

1. Its members pointed out that Burma had always been very suspicious of China and only turned to Beijing in 1989 out of dire necessity after it was ostracised by the West and placed under a range of sanctions. This change of policy was adopted reluctantly and by no means represented a permanent shift in Burma's focus or allegiance.

2. The rejectionist school pointed out that China was not as successful in winning Burma's confidence and support as was often reported. Despite their new closeness, Beijing did not always get its own way with Burma's notoriously prickly government.[4] This school argued that Burma would never agree to host Chinese military bases.

3. While it suited Burma to develop the bilateral relationship, it always had the option of drawing back from Beijing's embrace. China carried such enormous strategic weight that the thought of Naypyidaw being able to resist its advances or reduce its level of engagement seemed far-fetched. Yet, Burma has made a concerted effort to balance its ties to China with links to other states and international organisations.[5]

Despite their differences, most of these early studies were informative and stimulating. However, their authors encountered a range of obstacles that sometimes made balanced and accurate analyses difficult. Since 2011, anyone examining Burma's foreign relations and their implications for the strategic environment has enjoyed certain advantages, of which four stand out.

First, while Burma before 1988 was sadly neglected by scholars and officials, it has since been the focus of close and sustained attention in many countries and routinely attracts the attention of journalists and

---

4   Fan Hongwei, 'China's "Look South": China–Myanmar Transport Corridor', *Ritsumeikan International Affairs*, Vol.10, 2011, pp.43–66, www.ritsumei.ac.jp/acd/re/k-rsc/ras/04_publications/ria_en/10_04.pdf'China's [page discontinued] [now at www.oilseedcrops.org/wp-content/uploads/2014/02/Chinas-Look-South-to-the-Myanmar-China-Transport-Corridor.pdf].

5   Stephen McCarthy, *The Black Sheep of the Family: How Burma Defines its Foreign Relations with ASEAN*, Griffith Asia Institute Regional Outlook Paper No.7 (Brisbane: Griffith University, 2006), www.griffith.edu.au/__data/assets/pdf_file/0018/18234/regional-outlook-volume-7.pdf [page discontinued].

other commentators.[6] This has generated a more wideranging, rigorous and nuanced public debate about Burma and its security, including its relations with China and the US.[7]

Second, many issues are still poorly understood, but Burma's opening up since 2011 has permitted much greater access to local politicians, analysts and members of the public, most of whom can now speak openly.[8] Also, more statistics[9] and documentary sources—both Burmese and Chinese—are available, leading to better-informed and more detailed analyses.[10]

Third, it is now possible to discuss Burma more freely than was sometimes the case before 2011, when the activist community was very influential and debates over contentious subjects were dominated by political and moral issues.[11] There is still an ideological element to discussions about Burma's relations with China and the US, but strategic analyses tend to be more objective and evidence-based.

Last, this greater awareness and understanding of, and even sympathy for, Burma's fiendishly complex problems has permitted—perhaps even encouraged—Western analysts and commentators to give greater weight to Burma's own concerns and to consider the points of view of all Burmese institutions and actors across the entire political spectrum.

For example, greater weight is being given to Burma's intense nationalism, its historical reluctance to become aligned with other states and Naypyidaw's strong commitment to principles such as national

---

6   Andrew Selth, 'Burma/Myanmar: Bibliographic Trends', *New Mandala*, 16 February 2015, asiapacific.anu.edu.au/newmandala/2015/02/16/burmamyanmar-bibliographic-trends/.

7   Jürgen Haacke, *Myanmar: Now a Site for Sino–US Geopolitical Competition?*, IDEAS Reports: Special Reports, edited by Nicholas Kitchen, LSE IDEAS SR015 (London: London School of Economics and Political Science, 2012), eprints.lse.ac.uk/47504/.

8   Nicholas Farrelly and Stephanie Olinga-Shannon, *Establishing Contemporary Chinese Life in Myanmar*, ISEAS Trends in Southeast Asia No.15 (Singapore: ISEAS–Yusof Ishak Institute, 2015), sealinguist.files.wordpress.com/2015/08/chinese-life-myanmar.pdf.

9   Andrew Selth, 'Surveying Public Opinion in Burma', *The Interpreter*, 18 December 2014, www.lowyinterpreter.org/post/2014/12/18/Surveying-public-opinion-in-Burma.aspx [page discontinued] [now at www.lowyinstitute.org/the-interpreter/surveying-public-opinion-burma].

10   David I. Steinberg and Hongwei Fan, *Modern Myanmar–China Relations: Dilemmas of Mutual Dependence* (Copenhagen: NIAS Press, 2012), www.niaspress.dk/books/modern-china-myanmar-relations.

11   David I. Steinberg, 'Aung San Suu Kyi and US Policy Toward Burma/Myanmar', *Journal of Current Southeast Asian Affairs*, Vol.29, No.3, 2010, doi.org/10.1177/186810341002900302.

independence, sovereignty and territorial integrity.[12] These factors have been underestimated in quite a few analyses of Burma's foreign relations and place in the region.

Increasingly, Burma is accorded independent agency in debates about the regional strategic environment. Instead of being seen simply as a minor player, or the victim of larger powers, it is being recognised as an important actor in its own right, with specific attitudes, policies, capabilities and resources that influence wider developments.

Indeed, it can be argued that, in some respects, in the evolving three-way relationship between Burma, China and the US, it is not Beijing or Washington that is currently setting the agenda and the pace of developments, but Naypyidaw.

---

12   Chenyang Li and James Char, *China–Myanmar Relations Since Naypyidaw's Political Transition: How Beijing Can Balance Short-Term Interests and Long-Term Values*, RSIS Working Paper No.288 (Singapore: S. Rajaratnam School of International Studies, 16 March 2015), www.rsis.edu.sg/wp-content/uploads/2015/03/WP288_150316_China-Myanmar-Relations.pdf.

79

Burma's *Tatmadaw*: A force to be reckoned with

(11:32 AEDT, 22 October 2015)

Despite Myanmar's transition from a military dictatorship to a 'disciplined democracy' under a hybrid civilian–military government, the country's armed forces remained the most powerful political institution in the country. The Tatmadaw *was also becoming a stronger and more professional military force, supported by continuing high budgets, major arms acquisitions and new operational doctrines.*

Shashank Joshi's recent post on 'India's Incredible Shrinking Air Force'[1] prompts a closer look at Burma's armed forces (the *Tatmadaw*). Since the accession of President Thein Sein in 2011, the *Tatmadaw*'s continuing political role has been examined closely.[2] Less attention has been given to strictly military issues, yet the *Tatmadaw*'s combat capabilities not only underpin its domestic position, but also help determine Burma's strategic influence.

---

1   Shashank Joshi, 'India's Incredible Shrinking Air Force', *The Interpreter*, 21 September 2015, www.lowyinterpreter.org/post/2015/09/21/Indias-incredible-shrinking-air-force.aspx [page discontinued] [now at www.lowyinstitute.org/the-interpreter/indias-incredible-shrinking-air-force].
2   Robert H. Taylor, *The Armed Forces in Myanmar Politics: A Terminating Role?*, Trends in Southeast Asia No.2 (Singapore: Institute of Southeast Asian Studies, 2015), www.iseas.edu.sg/images/pdf/Trends_2015_2.pdf.

Despite its dominance of Burma's national affairs for decades, the *Tatmadaw* remains in many respects a closed book.[3] Even the most basic data are beyond the reach of analysts and other observers. For example, the *Tatmadaw*'s current size is a mystery, although most estimates range between 300,000 and 350,000 personnel. Official statistics put Burma's defence expenditure this year at 3.7 per cent of gross domestic product (GDP), but the actual level is unknown.[4]

Given this uncertainty, all reports about the *Tatmadaw* need careful handling. It is clear, however, that since 2011, Commander-in Chief Min Aung Hlaing has implemented wideranging plans to make the *Tatmadaw* more professional and to improve its order of battle. The latter includes an ambitious arms acquisition program that some have compared with the dramatic expansion and modernisation of Burma's armed forces during the 1990s.

In recent years, the army has upgraded its inventory of armoured vehicles with Ukrainian, Russian and Chinese armoured personnel carriers, as well as Ukrainian T-72 and Chinese MBT-2000 tanks. As seen at recent Armed Forces Day parades,[5] it has new surface-to-air missile systems such as the Chinese HQ-12/KS-1A[6] and the Russian Pechora-2M. It has also shown an interest in obtaining more heavy artillery and unmanned ground vehicles.

Under a 2009 agreement with Russia, the air force is acquiring 50 Mi-35 Hind E attack helicopters. In 2010, Burma reportedly bought 50 more K-8 Karakorum jet trainers. The following year, a contract was signed for

3   Andrew Selth, *Burma's Armed Forces: Looking Down the Barrel*, Griffith Asia Institute Regional Outlook Paper No.21 (Brisbane: Griffith University, 2009), www.griffith.edu.au/__data/assets/pdf_file/0003/148350/Selth-Regional-Outlook-Paper-21.pdf [page discontinued].

4   Jon Grevatt, 'Myanmar Announces 2015 Budget of USD 2.5 Billion', *IHS Jane's 360*, 27 January 2015, www.janes.com/article/48370/myanmar-announces-2015-budget-of-usd2-5-billion [page discontinued].

5   Dylan Malyasov, 'Photo: Myanmar Military Parade to Mark Armed Forces Day 2015', *Defence Blog*, 29 March 2015, defence-blog.com/army/photo-myanmar-military-parade-to-mark-armed-forces-day-2015.html.

6   Dylan Malyasov, 'Myanmar Receive First Batch SAM missiles HQ-12/KS-1A', *Defence Blog*, 16 June 2015, defence-blog.com/news/myanmar-receive-first-batch-sam-missiles-hq-12-ks-1a.html.

an additional 20 MiG-29 Fulcrum fighters and, in 2014, an unspecified number of CAC/PAC JF-17 Thunder multirole combat aircraft was ordered.[7] It has also received new transport aircraft and air-to-air missiles.[8]

A particular effort has been made to improve Burma's naval capabilities.[9] In 2012, China delivered two decommissioned Jianghu II–class frigates. In 2011, a locally built Aung Zeya frigate was launched and another two in the same class followed in 2014. Five more are planned. A third Anawrahta-class corvette was launched in 2014 and construction has begun on a fleet of fast attack craft. Rumours that Burma will purchase two submarines, however, remain unconfirmed.[10]

At the same time, Burma's naval diplomacy has increased and Naypyidaw has signed defence agreements with several foreign countries. Some arrangements—like those with China, Russia, Ukraine and Belarus—seem to relate mainly to local defence production, but others are more broadly based, such as that with India.[11] Burma claims it has severed military ties with North Korea, but some, including the US, dispute this.[12]

There have been repeated claims that Burma has tried to develop, or has even acquired, WMD. The former government's interest in nuclear technology fell well short of a weapons program, however, and no hard evidence has been produced to support reports the *Tatmadaw* has chemical and biological weapons. Accusations that Burma is producing ballistic missiles are harder to dismiss, but reliable data are scarce.

Together, all these developments invite a number of observations.

---

7   Zachary Keck, 'Burma to Purchase Chinese–Pakistani JF-17 Fighter Jets', *The Diplomat*, [Washington, DC], 25 June 2014, thediplomat.com/2014/06/burma-to-purchase-chinese-pakistani-jf-17-fighter-jets/.

8   Mrityunjoy Mazumdar, 'Myanmar Commissions Helos, Transport Aircraft', *IHS Jane's 360*, 16 July 2015, www.janes.com/article/53049/myanmar-commissions-helos-transport-aircraft [page discontinued].

9   Shahryar Pasandideh, 'Modernization of the Myanmar Navy', *NATO Association of Canada*, 17 August 2015, natocouncil.ca/modernization-of-the-myanmar-navy/ [page discontinued] [now at natoassociation.ca/modernization-of-the-myanmar-navy/].

10   Andrew Selth, 'Is Burma Really Buying Submarines?', *The Interpreter*, 29 January 2014, www.lowyinterpreter.org/post/2014/01/29/Burmas-submarine-dream.aspx [page discontinued] [now at www.lowyinstitute.org/the-interpreter/burma-really-buying-submarines].

11   Prashanth Parameswaran, 'India, Myanmar Eye Future Defense Cooperation', *The Diplomat*, [Washington, DC], 28 July 2015, thediplomat.com/2015/07/india-myanmar-eye-future-defense-cooperation/.

12   Andrew Selth, 'Burma and North Korea: Again? Still?', *The Interpreter*, 10 July 2013, www.lowyinterpreter.org/post/2013/07/10/Burma-and-North-Korea-Again-Still.aspx [page discontinued] [now at www.lowyinstitute.org/the-interpreter/burma-and-north-korea-again-still].

First, several of these acquisition and construction programs were initiated before the handover of power to the hybrid civilian–military government in 2011. This suggests the then ruling military council wanted to ensure that the *Tatmadaw* had the revenue and hardware necessary to handle any challenges that arose after that time. The programs launched after 2011 illustrate the *Tatmadaw*'s continuing political clout.

Second, the military leadership still sees a need to guard against both internal and external threats. Before the recent ceasefires, the *Tatmadaw* faced more than 72,000 armed insurgents.[13] Also, the security environment has changed. A US invasion is no longer considered likely, but Burma's neighbours are improving their own armed forces and the Bay of Bengal is fast becoming an arena for economic and strategic competition.[14]

Third, in the 1990s, Burma largely bought cheap, obsolete weapons. More modern systems are now both available and affordable. The helicopter gunships seem aimed primarily at countering insurgencies, while the fighters, tanks and surface-to-air missile (SAMs) are a hedge against conventional threats. The new naval vessels are to help police Burma's resource-rich territorial waters and protect it against developing maritime threats.[15]

Fourth, the proportion of Burma's budget allocated to defence is likely to remain high, not only to pay for these new weapon systems, but also to keep them operational. Of the US$1.15 billion (A$1.82 billion) allocated to defence in 2013, for example, more than US$600 million (A$947 million) was earmarked for the procurement of military hardware. About $200 million (A$315 million) was reserved for aircraft, $93 million (A$147 million) for ships and $30 million (A$47.3 million) for military vehicles.[16]

---

13   Ye Mon and Lun Min Mang, 'Ceasefire Pact is "Historic Gift": President', *Myanmar Times*, [Yangon], 16 October 2015, www.mmtimes.com/index.php/national-news/17051-ceasefire-pact-is-historic-gift-president.html.

14   David Brewster, 'The Bay of Bengal: The Indo-Pacific's New Zone of Competition', *The Strategist*, 2 December 2014, www.aspistrategist.org.au/the-bay-of-bengal-the-indo-pacifics-new-zone-of-competition/.

15   Pushan Dash, 'A "Three-Dimensional" Bangladesh Navy in the Bay of Bengal', *The Diplomat*, [Washington, DC], 12 February 2015, thediplomat.com/2015/02/a-three-dimensional-bangladesh-navy-in-the-bay-of-bengal/.

16   Tha Lun Zaung Htet, 'Burma Parliament Approves Controversial Defence Budget', *The Irrawaddy*, 1 March 2013, www.irrawaddy.org/military/burma-parliament-approves-controversial-defense-budget.html.

Some observers have seen the latest arms contracts in more political terms. The reforms announced since 2011 have developed a life of their own, and probably exceed what was envisaged by the former military regime, but arguably they have occurred only because the armed forces have allowed them to. The continuing flow of funds and hardware to the *Tatmadaw* is seen by many as a payoff for stepping back from day-to-day politics.

If this is so, it remains to be seen whether such an arrangement can survive a new administration. Should the opposition win a majority of seats in the national parliament next month—as many predict—the *Tatmadaw*'s relationship with the central government will change. The NLD has long been critical of the fact that the defence sector receives more in the annual budget than education and health combined.[17]

However, major cutbacks to defence spending would be difficult to implement. The *Tatmadaw* remains Burma's most powerful political institution. Also, the military leadership will try to persuade the new government that its latest modernisation program is justified. It knows that, regardless of who is in power in Naypyidaw, Burma's internal stability, sovereignty and independence will remain important factors in any consideration of the country's military capabilities and its annual defence expenditure.

---

17 'Statement: Suu Kyi's NLD Slams Burma Junta's Budget', *Democracy for Burma*, 6 March 2011, democracyforburma.wordpress.com/2011/03/06/statementsuu-kyi%E2%80%99s-nld-slams-burma-junta%E2%80%99s-budget/.

80

All change: Election result may see another round of the Burma/Myanmar name game

(08:35 AEDT, 18 November 2015)

The Australian Government's incomprehensible flip-flopping over the question of what name to call Myanmar looked like taking another turn when Aung San Suu Kyi and the NLD won the November 2015 elections.

Shortly after the Abbott Government took office in September 2013, it overturned the decision by Labor foreign minister Bob Carr in 2012 to recognise Burma's new official name, Myanmar. This had long been the country's traditional name, but it was only adopted as the official name in English by the military government in 1989.[1]

The new name had been accepted by most countries, the UN and other major international organisations. However, a few governments, some political groups and certain high-profile individuals (notably,

---

1   Andrew Selth, 'Australia and the Burma/Myanmar Name Debate', *The Interpreter*, 27 November 2013, www.lowyinterpreter.org/post/2013/11/27/Australia-and-the-BurmaMyanmar-name.aspx [page discontinued] [now at www.lowyinstitute.org/the-interpreter/australia-and-burmamyanmar-name-debate].

then opposition leader Aung San Suu Kyi) clung to the old name as a protest against the military regime's failure to consult the people about the change.[2]

The Abbott Government decreed that, in all official communications with Naypyidaw, Australia was to refer to 'Myanmar' and 'the Government of Myanmar', as required by diplomatic protocol. In all internal correspondence, however, and on the DFAT website, the name 'Burma' was to be used.[3]

The word around Canberra at the time was that this was another 'captain's call' by Tony Abbott, who insisted the old name be used despite concerns expressed by the Australian Embassy in Rangoon (Yangon), DFAT and possibly even the foreign minister's office.

The new policy led to some strange results. In some media releases, both Myanmar and Burma were used, depending on the context.[4] The DFAT website also used both terms, but, because it was often difficult to differentiate between so-called internal and external communications, it was often not clear why one name was used in preference to the other.

The situation was made more confusing by the policy's inconsistent application. For example, during the visit to Australia in November 2013 of Aung San Suu Kyi, Prime Minister Abbott publicly referred to 'Burma' and 'the Government of Burma'. Repeated requests for clarification of the policy were ignored.

The decision to revert to the old name took observers in Australia and elsewhere by surprise, as it seemed to lack any rationale, let alone any benefit to Australia. As I told Dan Flitton of the *Sydney Morning Herald* earlier this year, it was 'an inexplicable retrograde step that can only have harmed Australia's interests, both in Burma and the region'.[5]

---

2   Gwen Robinson, 'Suu Kyi Refuses to Use "Myanmar" Name', *Financial Times*, [London], 3 July 2012, www.ft.com/intl/cms/s/0/2db68340-c51e-11e1-b6fd-00144feabdc0.html#axzz3r1iMqulW.

3   Andrew Selth, 'Myanmar Becomes Burma, Again', *The Interpreter*, 14 January 2014, www.lowy interpreter.org/post/2014/01/14/Myanmar-becomes-Burma-again.aspx [page discontinued] [now at www.lowyinstitute.org/the-interpreter/myanmar-becomes-burma-again].

4   The Hon. Julie Bishop MP, Minister for Foreign Affairs, 'Aung San Suu Kyi to Visit Australia', Media release, Parliament House, Canberra, 5 November 2013, foreignminister.gov.au/releases/Pages/2013/jb_mr_131105a.aspx?ministerid=4 [page discontinued] [now at www.foreignminister. gov.au/minister/julie-bishop/media-release/aung-san-suu-kyi-visit-australia].

5   Daniel Flitton, 'Australia Urged to Change Official Names for Macedonia, Burma', *Sydney Morning Herald*, 5 April 2015, www.smh.com.au/federal-politics/political-news/australia-urged-to-change-official-names-for-macedonia-burma-20150331-1mcg3q.html.

There are now rumours circulating that, under Australia's new and less idiosyncratic Prime Minister, it has been decided once again to use the name Myanmar in all official publications, statements and correspondence. Such a decision would be welcomed by all those trying to work, and develop better relations, with the government in Naypyidaw.

However, the picture is still unclear.

Media releases issued by the foreign minister[6] refer only to Myanmar and the Myanmar Government,[7] but the DFAT website still has a country profile for Burma.[8] Other links on the site refer to both Burma and Myanmar. For example, there is an 'Overview of Australia's Aid Program to Burma'[9] linked to a publication titled *Aid Investment Plan Myanmar: 2015–2020*.[10]

Ironically, a question may now arise over the preferred terminology of the new government elected on 8 November. Already there has been speculation that the victory of Aung San Suu Kyi and the NLD may see a more relaxed attitude towards the use of Burma, or possibly even another formal name change. The issue could even be put to the people for a final decision.

If a decision has already been made for Australia to use the name Myanmar again, then, like the 2013 decision to revert to Burma, it seems to have been made without any public announcement, let alone explanation. This leaves observers both in Australia and abroad to speculate about the possible reasons for the change.

One can only imagine what the people of Burma/Myanmar make of all this.

---

6   The Hon. Julie Bishop MP, Minister for Foreign Affairs, 'Signing of Nationwide Ceasefire Agreement in Myanmar', Media release, Parliament House, Canberra, 16 October 2015, foreign minister.gov.au/releases/Pages/2015/jb_mr_151016.aspx?w=tb1CaGpkPX%2FlS0K%2Bg9ZKEg%3D%3D [page discontinued] [now at www.foreignminister.gov.au/minister/julie-bishop/media-release/signing-nationwide-ceasefire-agreement-myanmar].

7   The Hon. Julie Bishop MP, Minister for Foreign Affairs, 'Myanmar Elections Observation', Media release, Parliament House, Canberra, 5 November 2015, foreignminister.gov.au/releases/Pages/2015/jb_mr_151105.aspx [page discontinued] [now at www.foreignminister.gov.au/minister/julie-bishop/media-release/myanmar-elections-observation].

8   Department of Foreign Affairs and Trade, *Burma* (Canberra: Australian Government), dfat.gov.au/geo/burma/Pages/burma.aspx [page discontinued].

9   Department of Foreign Affairs and Trade, *Overview of Australia's Aid Program to Burma* (Canberra: Australian Government), dfat.gov.au/geo/burma/development-assistance/Pages/development-assistance-in-burma.aspx [page discontinued].

10   Department of Foreign Affairs and Trade, *Aid Investment Plan Myanmar: 2015–2020* (Canberra: Australian Government), dfat.gov.au/about-us/publications/Pages/aid-investment-plan-aip-myanmar-2015-20.aspx.

2016

81

The potential for army–police rivalry in Myanmar

(10:40 AEDT, 2 February 2016)

Rumours that the commander-in-chief of Myanmar's armed forces was investigating several police and intelligence officers for corruption raised the question of the broader relationship between the Tatmadaw *and the MPF. Given past tensions between these two organisations, the possibility of a new rift in the security forces would be of concern to both sides of domestic politics.*

Since December 2015, a rumour has been circulating in Yangon that the commander-in-chief of Myanmar's armed forces is investigating several police and intelligence officers for corruption. If that is true, it is a timely reminder of the often-tense relationship between components of the country's coercive apparatus, just as Aung San Suu Kyi and the NLD are forming a new government in Naypyidaw.

Over the past five years, the armed forces (known as the *Tatmadaw*) and the MPF have consistently received strong support from President Thein Sein. In large part, this has been to help them modernise and introduce wideranging reform programs. Both have modified their organisational structures, acquired new arms and equipment and made an effort to win back public respect through innovative public relations campaigns.

Also, the *Tatmadaw* has stepped back from day-to-day politics and given a higher priority to territorial defence. It aims to become smaller, but more capable, more professional and better connected internationally. In an effort to civilianise Myanmar's internal security operations, the

MPF plans to expand from 80,000 to 155,000 personnel by 2020. With foreign help, it is receiving training in human rights, community policing and modern methods of crowd control.[1]

The army and police have always worked closely together, patrolling Myanmar's borders, conducting counterinsurgency campaigns and putting down internal unrest. In intelligence operations, the military agencies have shared a range of interests with the Special Branch and the Bureau of Special Investigations (BSI). There has always been rivalry between the armed forces and police, however, and this has sometimes caused problems.

After Myanmar regained its independence in 1948, U Nu's fledgling government created two police forces. One was a civil organisation that dealt with everyday policing. The other was a paramilitary force called the Union Military Police (UMP). It helped deal with problems that demanded the application of lethal force, such as operations against army mutineers, ideological and ethnic insurgents and armed bandits known as *dacoits*.

The UMP cooperated with the *Tatmadaw*, but the two always competed for status and scarce resources. Their relations were complicated by the fact that they answered to different ministers, who were themselves rivals for political power. In 1958, the Minister for Home Affairs ordered UMP units to march on Rangoon. He claimed it was to forestall a coup, but it was probably to settle a personal disagreement with the defence minister.

General Ne Win always resented the fact that the *Tatmadaw* did not enjoy a monopoly of the means to exercise state force. In 1958, when his 'caretaker' administration took over Myanmar's government for two years, he renamed the UMP the Union Constabulary, drafted army officers into its ranks, ordered policemen to attend military-style training camps and reduced police resources.

After Ne Win's coup d'état in 1962, all paramilitary police units were absorbed into the army. In 1964, the civil arm was reformed as the People's Police Force (PPF), with a military-style rank structure. Army

---

1   Andrew Selth, *Burma's Security Forces: Performing, Reforming or Transforming?*, Griffith Asia Institute Regional Outlook Paper No.45 (Brisbane: Griffith University, 2013), www.griffith.edu.au/__data/assets/pdf_file/0011/559127/Regional-Outlook-Paper-45-Selth.pdf [page discontinued].

officers were posted into senior police positions. For the next 20 years, the PPF was considered the 'younger brother' of the *Tatmadaw* but continued to be given a low priority for funds, arms and equipment.[2]

The PPF developed a reputation for corruption and incompetence. After it was created in 1974, the PPF's paramilitary 'riot squad', or *Lon Htein*, became known for its arrogance and brutality. During the abortive 1988 prodemocracy uprising, it was considered even more ruthless than the armed forces. Myanmar's ruling military council later allocated the PPF more resources and tried to lift its standards, but with little apparent success.

When Thein Sein took office in 2011, the government recognised that it needed to do something about the (renamed) MPF. Not only did it require radical reform, but it was also seen as a means of permitting the armed forces to relinquish some of its internal security duties and become a more conventional military organisation. Before long, blue uniforms began to replace green uniforms on the streets of Myanmar's population centres.

A clearer differentiation between police and army roles seemed an obvious step, but it carried certain risks. For example, when the Indonesian police force split from the army in 1999, disputes arose over their respective roles and responsibilities and the allocation of resources. Both personal and institutional jealousies arose. There were a number of armed clashes as members of the two forces competed for control of off-budget finances.

Such problems are much less likely in Myanmar. The *Tatmadaw* is still the country's most powerful institution, it commands the lion's share of the budget and, under the 2008 constitution, the Minister of Home Affairs is always a serving army officer. Also, the expansion of the MPF is being achieved in part through transfers from the armed forces. The Chief of Police and about 10 per cent of MPF officers are former military personnel.[3]

---

2   Andrew Selth, *Burma's Police Forces: Continuities and Contradictions*, Griffith Asia Institute Regional Outlook Paper No.32 (Brisbane: Griffith University, 2011), www.griffith.edu.au/__data/assets/pdf_file/0008/372761/Selth-Regional-Outlook-Paper-32.pdf [page discontinued].
3   Andrew Selth, *Police Reform in Burma (Myanmar): Aims, Obstacles and Outcomes*, Griffith Asia Institute Regional Outlook Paper No.44 (Brisbane: Griffith University, 2013), www.griffith.edu.au/__data/assets/pdf_file/0009/512379/Regional-Outlook-Paper-44-v.2-Selth.pdf [page discontinued].

That said, the MPF is trying to develop its own ethos and esprit de corps. Police officers are being encouraged to see themselves as separate from the armed forces, with different responsibilities requiring different methods. If the force is able to develop independently, and receives reasonable budget allocations, then serious tensions between the *Tatmadaw* and the MPF can be avoided. However, any obvious intrusion into police affairs by members of the armed forces could cause tensions.

In Myanmar, all unconfirmed rumours should be treated with caution, but it is in this context that the recent story regarding the commander-in-chief becomes interesting.

Senior General Min Aung Hlaing has reportedly ordered an investigation into claims that several officers from the MPF's Special Branch and the BSI have been involved in drug trafficking. In one sense, this comes as no surprise. Myanmar is ranked as one of the most corrupt countries in the world.[4] However, the accused officers are from the two agencies in the Ministry of Home Affairs with specific responsibilities for rooting out such practices. This might be why the *Tatmadaw*, and someone as senior as the commander-in-chief, is said to be involved.

Both civilian and military leaders in Myanmar would have an interest in this case. Aung San Suu Kyi has long emphasised the rule of law and opposed corruption. She would want to be seen as supporting a strong response to any official misconduct. Also, division within the security forces is a recurring nightmare for Myanmar's generals. Past attempts to weaken the cohesion and loyalty of the state's coercive apparatus have prompted firm action.

The significance of this rumour should not be overstated. However, if it is true, we may be seeing an early and welcome example of the country's most senior leaders acting together to tackle a problem of shared concern.

---

4   Transparency International, *Corruption Perceptions Index 2015* (Berlin: Transparency International, 2015), www.transparency.org/cpi2015.

82

Democracy in Myanmar: Who can claim victory?

(08:45 AEDT, 29 March 2016)

Despite all the claims made by foreign governments, activist organisations and others, credit for the creation of an NLD government in 2016 goes to the Myanmar people. This must include the armed forces, which consciously permitted the carefully controlled, top-down transition to a 'disciplined democracy' to occur. It did so not as a sign of weakness, however, but as a sign of strength.

Paraphrasing the Roman historian Tacitus, US president John F. Kennedy said in 1961 that 'victory has a thousand fathers but defeat is an orphan'.[1] This aphorism springs to mind as Aung San Suu Kyi and the NLD prepare to assume power as the first popularly elected government in Myanmar for more than 50 years.

There is no shortage of foreign governments, activist organisations and individuals claiming credit for the extraordinary events of the past five years:[2] the paradigm shift that saw Myanmar's armed forces (or *Tatmadaw*)

---

1   While this version is the one most often quoted, Kennedy actually said: 'Victory has a hundred fathers and defeat is an orphan.' See 'President Kennedy's News Conference, No.10', Washington, DC, 21 April 1961, US Information Agency, *YouTube*, www.youtube.com/watch?v=AYx6MG6NkjU.
2   Andrew Selth, 'Burma Reforms: Foreigners Can't Take Much Credit', *The Interpreter*, 30 January 2012, www.lowyinterpreter.org/post/2012/01/30/Burma-reforms-foreigners-cant-take-credit.aspx [page discontinued] [now at archive.lowyinstitute.org/the-interpreter/burma-reforms-foreigners-cant-take-much-credit].

step back and permit the creation of a hybrid civilian–military government; the launch of an unprecedented reform program; and the elections in 2015 that resulted in a landslide victory for the NLD.[3]

Despite some early scepticism about the *Tatmadaw*'s motives and the validity of President Thein Sein's reforms,[4] it is now accepted that Myanmar has undergone a remarkable transformation. There are still many difficult issues to be resolved, not least the continuing political role of the armed forces, economic problems, religious tensions and ethnic insurgencies, but the Myanmar of 2016 is a far cry from the Myanmar of 2011.

Following the 1988 prodemocracy uprising, governments, international organisations, activist groups and others worked long and hard to achieve such an outcome. They threw much needed light on a country that had long been in darkness and a population that had suffered for decades. Looking back, however, it is difficult to see any evidence that external factors contributed significantly to the evolution of a new era in Myanmar.

The Myanmar people themselves deserve most of the credit for the transition and, like it or not, that includes the armed forces. It may seem a harsh judgement, but examined objectively, it is hard to escape the conclusion that Aung San Suu Kyi and the NLD are forming a new government this week largely because the generals have allowed them to do so, as part of a long-term plan formulated by the former military regime.

Despite 25 years of international action, economic sanctions and other measures designed to isolate and punish Myanmar's military government, it just kept growing stronger. In strategic, political, military and economic terms, it was more powerful in 2011 than at any time since 1988, possibly even since the 1962 military coup. Granted, it was very unpopular and faced serious domestic problems, but when it eventually handed over the reins to Thein Sein, the regime was firmly entrenched in power.[5]

---

3   Stephen Collinson, 'Hillary Clinton Celebrates Myanmar Vote and Her Role In It', *CNN Politics*, 12 November 2015, edition.cnn.com/2015/11/12/politics/hillary-clinton-myanmar-election-role/.

4   Bertil Lintner, 'Burmese Change Aplenty but It's Only Skin Deep', *The Australian*, 17 October 2011, www.theaustralian.com.au/news/world/burmese-change-aplenty-but-its-only-skin-deep/story-e6frg6ux-1226167961805?nk=44baf9d25c180cf6a9855726ee7cfd27-1458696390 [page discontinued].

5   Andrew Selth, *Civil–Military Relations in Burma: Portents, Predictions and Possibilities*, Griffith Asia Institute Regional Outlook Paper No.25 (Brisbane: Griffith University, 2010), www.griffith.edu.au/__data/assets/pdf_file/0016/215341/Selth-Regional-Outlook-25.pdf [page discontinued].

There are still diehard proponents of sanctions, but most governments now acknowledge that, in Myanmar's case, they had only a marginal effect.[6] They did not change the regime's thinking or policies on a single key issue. Indeed, they made it more resentful of external interference, strengthened its bunker mentality, inhibited the development of civil institutions in Myanmar and made daily life even harder for its people.[7]

Also, while the regime saw internal threats everywhere, its hand was not forced by civil strife or military defeat. Its readiness to allow a more liberal form of government was not a sign of weakness but a sign of strength. As part of a 'seven-point roadmap' announced in 2003,[8] it promulgated a constitution in 2008 that guaranteed the *Tatmadaw*'s central place in national affairs and heralded a controlled transition to a 'disciplined democracy'.

This transition may have gone further and faster than anticipated, but the 2015 elections were held, were relatively free and fair and produced an accurate result, because the armed forces leadership permitted them to occur and did not interfere. As history attests, it could have intervened at any stage of the process and ensured that the elections were cancelled, postponed or manipulated to give a different outcome.

Also, given their intelligence sources and control of Myanmar's internal affairs, the generals must have known that an honest election would result in a decisive victory for the NLD. The final statistics may have come as a surprise (before the poll, some analysts were doubtful the party could achieve a landslide)[9] but the outcome could not have been in doubt.

---

6   Thihan Myo Nyun, 'Feeling Good or Doing Good: Inefficacy of the US Unilateral Sanctions Against the Military Government of Burma/Myanmar', *Washington University Global Studies Law Review*, Vol.7, No.3, 2008, openscholarship.wustl.edu/cgi/viewcontent.cgi?article=1117&context=law_globalstudies.

7   US Government, 'Myanmar: Prepared Testimony by Dr Thant Myint U Before the East Asia Sub-Committee of the Senate Foreign Relations Committee', *ReliefWeb*, 30 September 2009, reliefweb.int/report/myanmar/myanmar-prepared-testimony-dr-thant-myint-u-east-asia-sub-committee-senate-foreign.

8   David Arnott, *Burma/Myanmar: How to Read the Generals' 'Roadmap'—A Brief Guide with Links to the Literature*, Geneva, 2004, www.ibiblio.org/obl/docs/how10.htm [page discontinued] [now at www.burmalibrary.org/sites/burmalibrary.org/files/obl/docs/how10.htm].

9   Andrew Selth, 'Burma: Beware of Unrealistic Expectations', *The Interpreter*, 18 June 2015, www.lowyinterpreter.org/post/2015/06/18/Burma-Beware-of-unrealistic-expectations.aspx [page discontinued] [now at www.lowyinstitute.org/the-interpreter/burma-beware-unrealistic-expectations].

This being the case, it can be assumed that, before the election, the *Tatmadaw*'s senior leadership, in consultation with Thein Sein, collectively decided to accept the final result. There is no tradition in Myanmar of sharing political power, but the leadership must also have faced the prospect of negotiating the future governance of the country with the NLD.

Aung San Suu Kyi has apparently agreed a *modus vivendi* with Commander-in-Chief Min Aung Hlaing that permits the NLD to form government and the *Tatmadaw* to retain certain powers and privileges. She did not get everything she wanted—notably, a constitutional amendment that would have let her become president. However, both sides seem to have set aside their differences for the time being.

It remains to be seen whether this arrangement survives the test of time. The NLD is certain to adjust the former government's priorities for attention and funding and to propose more far-reaching reforms. Also, Aung San Suu Kyi's blunt dismissal of the President's constitutional position and determination to make all major policy decisions herself is likely to cause other problems.[10]

The generals will be reluctant to accept the constraints on the *Tatmadaw*'s power that are required for Myanmar to become a genuine democracy. As Robert Taylor has written: '[O]nly the army can end its own role in Myanmar's politics, and that decision is dependent on its perception of the civilian political elite's ability to manage the future.'[11] He might have added, 'and protect the *Tatmadaw* as a national institution'.

This being the case, the question arises: why did the armed forces initiate a reform process that was bound to increase the NLD's power and reduce its own?

The military regime's decision to permit far-reaching changes to Myanmar was not forced upon it. Nor was it a miscalculation or the result of astrological predictions. Rather, it was the outcome of a careful assessment

---

10   Min Zin, 'Burma's Puppeteer-in-Chief Takes Charge', *Foreign Policy*, 12 March 2016, foreignpolicy.com/2016/03/12/burmas-puppeteer-in-chief-takes-charge-aung-san-suu-kyi/.

11   Robert Taylor, 'Myanmar Military Preserves Its Autonomy, For Now', *Nikkei Asian Review*, 16 March 2015, asia.nikkei.com/Viewpoints/Perspectives/Myanmar-s-military-preserves-its-autonomy-for-now.

of the political state of the country, its complex security problems, its needs in terms of economic and social development and, of course, the future role and requirements of the armed forces.

It may not fit the accepted narrative, but over a decade ago the generals seem to have decided that Myanmar's interests would be best served if it became more modern, more liberal, more prosperous, more open to the outside world and more respected internationally. This was most likely to be achieved if the *Tatmadaw* allowed a more democratic government to evolve, which could undertake the necessary reforms.

Albeit with qualifications, it is a decision that Aung San Suu Kyi and the new NLD Government would probably find easy to endorse.

83

Old Burma hands write on the 'odd man out in Asia'

(12:40 AEDT, 6 June 2016)

There are not many memoirs by diplomats who were posted to Myanmar, but of those published, Australians have contributed a large proportion.

The recent release of former ambassador Trevor Wilson's book, *Eyewitness to Early Reform in Myanmar*,[1] prompts a brief look at other diplomatic memoirs by Australians and, in particular, those written by officers posted to Australia's embassy in Rangoon (now Yangon) since it opened in 1956.

Australia has a strong tradition of diplomatic memoirs. Many ambassadors and other officials have recorded their experiences and impressions of international events. Books by Walter Crocker, Alan Watt, Richard Woolcott, Alan Renouf and Peter Henderson spring to mind. The National Library of Australia (NLA) holds the papers of others and has recorded the reminiscences of many more as part of its oral history project.

Also, between 1988 and 1998, Griffith University's Centre for the Study of Australia–Asia Relations (CSAAR) published 22 monographs under the collective title *Australians in Asia*. Edited by Hugh Dunn, they included diplomatic memoirs by Dunn himself, Keith Waller, John Rowland and Harold Marshall, among others. The series was a timely reminder of the contributions made by Australian officials to regional affairs.

---

1   Trevor Wilson, *Eyewitness to Early Reform in Myanmar* (Canberra: ANU Press, 2016), .doi. org/10.22459/EERM.03.2016.

Until 1966, all female members of the Australian Foreign Service were forced to resign on getting married and none appears to have written a memoir. However, the partners of Australian diplomats have also contributed to the literature. In 1968, for example, Jean Spender wrote *Ambassador's Wife*, and in 2013 Rachel Miller (herself a 'diplomatic spouse') edited a collection of interviews entitled *Wife and Baggage to Follow*.[2]

Relatively few Australian diplomats or their partners, however, have published books about their postings to Burma (as the country was known before 1989).

The CSAAR series included memoirs by Francis Stuart, who visited Burma in 1947; Alf Parsons and Pierre Hutton, both of whom served there in the 1950s; and by Richard Gate, who was ambassador from 1980 to 1982. In 1991, Edwin Ride published a memoir that described his experiences as a junior officer in Rangoon in the mid 1960s and Richard Broinowski's autobiography included an account of life in Burma during the early 1970s.

Other former diplomats have given presentations or published papers[3] that throw light on their Burmese days. The memoirs of some—like Roy Fernandez (ambassador in Rangoon from 1968 to 1970), Garry Woodard (ambassador from 1973 to 1975) and Geoff Allen (ambassador from 1989 to 1993)—have been recorded by the NLA. A few old Burma hands, such as Garry Woodard, have also deposited their private papers in the NLA.

Rachel Miller's book includes a chapter by Pat Milne, whose husband, Frank, was twice posted to Burma, for the second term as Head of Mission, from 1983 to 1986.

The relative dearth of Burma memoirs is perhaps not surprising, given that Rangoon was for many years considered a minor diplomatic post. It was on the fringes of Australia's main areas of interest in the region. Also, as Alf Parsons wrote in 1998, Burma was the 'odd man out in

---

2 '"Wife and Baggage to Follow": DFAT Launches a Social History of Women and Wives in Australia's Foreign Service', Public Diplomacy Activities (Canberra: Department of Foreign Affairs and Trade, 6 November 2013), dfat.gov.au/people-to-people/public-diplomacy/programs-activities/pages/wife-and-baggage-to-follow-dfat-launches-a-social-history-of-women-and-wives-in-australias-foreign-service.aspx.

3 Andrew Selth, 'Burma after Forty Years: Still Unlike Any Land You Know', in *Griffith Review 68: Getting On*, edited by Ashley Hay, 26 April 2016, griffithreview.com/articles/burma-after-forty-years/.

Asia'.[4] After General Ne Win's 1962 coup d'état, the country pursued the 'Burmese way to socialism'—a system characterised by economic autarky and a strictly neutral foreign policy.

Until this year, Australian memoirs about Burma were confined to the 'democratic era' (1948–62) or the period under General Ne Win, who ruled for 26 years. None covered the 'new' Myanmar, which began to take shape after the abortive 1988 prodemocracy uprising and the rise of opposition leader Aung San Suu Kyi. This gap has now been filled, at least in part, by Trevor Wilson's memoir, which focuses on the period 2000–03.

All these authors commented on political and social developments in Burma, but few did so in any detail. Not only did the country stagnate under Ne Win, but so, too, did its relations with Australia. One exception is Wilson's more focused account of his three-year posting, by which time the local political scene was starting to change, posing fresh challenges for those responsible for managing the bilateral relationship.

Most of these memoirs are notable for their accounts of daily life in a country that, after 1962, seemed frozen in time. This encouraged descriptions of Burma's natural beauty, its lack of modern amenities, the difficulty of getting things done and colourful local personalities. Given the exotic nature of the posting and the lack of major diplomatic initiatives, amusing anecdotes tended to be given more space than serious analysis.[5]

That said, most of these memoirs do throw some light on Australian policy towards Burma/Myanmar from officials directly involved in its development and implementation—areas where contemporary scholarship is largely absent. For example, as Trevor Wilson points out in his book, under foreign minister Alexander Downer, Australia adopted a different approach than most other Western countries, by supporting human rights training for Burmese officials.

---

4   Alf Parsons, *South East Asian Days*, Australians in Asia Paper No.22 (Brisbane: Centre for the Study of Australia–Asia Relations, Griffith University, April 1988), p.30.
5   See, for example, Andrew Selth, 'The Rats of Rangoon', *New Mandala*, 29 March 2016, asiapacific.anu.edu.au/newmandala/2016/03/29/the-rats-of-rangoon/.

Also, such memoirs help reveal the inner workings of a Western diplomatic mission in Burma and its relationships with the home country, the receiving government and local society. Over the years, Australian officers have provided insights on a wide range of contemporary issues of a kind that are often difficult to find elsewhere. This includes frank observations about key personalities. From his personal contacts with her, for example, Wilson writes that Aung San Suu Kyi is an impressive figure but 'very conscious of her own importance' and 'prickly to deal with'.

Australian memoirs of Burma are all the more interesting for the fact that few other foreign diplomats posted there seem to have recorded their experiences. One exception is Aleksandr Kaznacheev's *Inside a Soviet Embassy*, about his time in Rangoon during the late 1950s, before he defected to the US.[6] Another is Takashi Suzuki's Japanese-language memoir, *A Country Called Burma: Its History and Memoir*, about his posting to Burma as Tokyo's envoy from 1971 to 1974. Also, Preet Malik has just published *My Myanmar Years*, covering his posting as Indian ambassador from 1990 to 1992.

A rare example of a Burma memoir written by a foreign diplomat's wife is *Five Years in a Forgotten Land* by Cristina Pantoja-Hidalgo, whose husband was the resident UNICEF representative from 1984 to 1989. Also, the NLA is not alone in recording the memories of Rangoon veterans. The Association for Diplomatic Studies and Training, for example, has interviewed nearly 40 US officials who served in Burma between 1947 and 1998.[7]

The Canadian academic George Egerton once noted that memoirs 'have but a brief flowering in the attention of the public and popular media, finding resurrection, if ever, only as sources in the hands of curious historians'.[8] Be that as it may, over the past 30 years or so, Australian accounts of diplomatic postings to Burma/Myanmar have provided useful and entertaining snapshots of a country that has long been the subject of myths and misconceptions.

---

6   Matthew N. Caslon, 'Book Review of Inside a Soviet Embassy by Aleksandr Kaznacheev', *Studies Archives Indexes*, Vol.7, No.3 (Langley, VA: Center for the Study of Intelligence, Central Intelligence Agency, 2007), www.cia.gov/library/center-for-the-study-of-intelligence/kent-csi/vol7no3/html/v07i3a12p_0001.htm.

7   *Burma: Country Reader*, Country and Subject Reader Series (Arlington, VA: Association for Diplomatic Studies and Training), adst.org/wp-content/uploads/2012/09/Burma-Myanmar.pdf.

8   George Egerton (ed.), *Political Memoir: Essays on the Politics of Memory* (London: Routledge, 1994).

84

More name games in Burma/Myanmar

(13:34 AEDT, 10 August 2016)

The long saga of what Australian officials should call Myanmar finally seemed to be over when State Counsellor Aung San Suu Kyi told a public gathering that she did not mind whether the country was called Burma or Myanmar. However, she sparked a fresh controversy over names by requesting that civil servants and diplomats in Myanmar not use the term 'Rohingya' for one of the country's Muslim minorities.

Regular readers of *The Interpreter* will know that, over the past few years, this site has closely followed the Australian Government's efforts to grapple with the diplomatic implications of the formal change of Burma's name in 1989 to Myanmar. The indications are that this saga may finally be over.

At first, Australia followed the lead of the US, the UK and other Western democracies opposed to the new military regime and continued to call Burma by its old name. This was also in accordance with the wishes of the country's main opposition leader, Aung San Suu Kyi, who took the view that a country can only change its name if there is a popular mandate to do so.[1]

---

1   Laura McQuillan, 'Suu Kyi: It's Burma, Not Myanmar', *Sydney Morning Herald*, 23 November 2012, www.smh.com.au/world/suu-kyi-its-burma-not-myanmar-20121122-29wlh.html.

Aung San Suu Kyi also felt that 'Myanmar' was not an inclusive term, as it was merely a literary form of 'Burma', which referred only to the majority ethnic Bamar, or Burmans.[2] How her preferred name 'Burma'—a colonial creation based on exactly the same premises as 'Myanmar'—was more representative of the country's 135 or more national races was not explained.

By following this line, Australia was forced to adopt a two-track approach to the country. Canberra's formal correspondence with the military government always referred to 'Myanmar', as required by diplomatic protocol. However, in all official statements and press releases, and on the DFAT website, the Australian Government called the country 'Burma'.[3]

This policy complicated relations both with the authorities in Rangoon (later Naypyidaw) and with other capitals in the region, where 'Myanmar' was readily accepted. However, the mixed approach was deemed symbolically important. Canberra claimed that it helped register concern over human rights abuses by the military government and was a gesture of support for the country's embattled democracy movement.

This clumsy arrangement ended in 2012 when foreign minister Bob Carr accepted that a confrontationist approach to the military regime made it more difficult to promote meaningful reforms. Australia had fallen out of step with the international community, which increasingly favoured the use of 'Myanmar'. Carr decided that Canberra would henceforth call the country by its formal name—a rule that was observed during president Thein Sein's state visit to Australia in March 2013.

This position, however, was unexpectedly reversed in 2014 by Tony Abbott. In what appears to have been one of his 'captain's calls', the new prime minister decreed that, in all 'internal' correspondence (including on the DFAT website), the country would once again be called Burma.[4] Only in cases of 'external' usage, such as formal diplomatic exchanges, would it be referred to as Myanmar.

2   Peter Lloyd and Tony Eastley, 'Burma Bans Officials' Use of "Rohingya" to Describe Minority Ahead of UN Report', *PM*, [ABC Radio National], 22 June 2016, www.abc.net.au/pm/content/2016/s4487158.htm [page discontinued].
3   Andrew Selth, 'Australia and the Burma/Myanmar Name Debate', *The Interpreter*, 27 November 2013, www.lowyinterpreter.org/post/2013/11/27/Australia-and-the-BurmaMyanmar-name.aspx [page discontinued] [now at www.lowyinstitute.org/the-interpreter/australia-and-burmamyanmar-name-debate].
4   Andrew Selth, 'Myanmar Becomes Burma, Again', *The Interpreter*, 14 January 2014, www.lowyinterpreter.org/post/2014/01/14/Myanmar-becomes-Burma-again.aspx [page discontinued] [now at www.lowyinstitute.org/the-interpreter/myanmar-becomes-burma-again].

The reason for this about-face has never been explained. Indeed, the instruction appears to have been issued by the prime minister's office against the advice of the Australian Embassy in Rangoon, DFAT and possibly even the foreign minister's office. To make matters worse, the new policy was applied inconsistently, including by the Prime Minister himself.

It is difficult to see any benefits for Australia in adopting this approach. Indeed, it needlessly offended the Naypyidaw government at a critical time and upset other ASEAN members. Also, it is unlikely to have been appreciated by Aung San Suu Kyi, who by then was herself using the name Myanmar in certain circumstances. The result of the change was confusion and, in the eyes of some knowledgeable observers, a loss of credibility by Australia on Burma-related issues.

After Malcolm Turnbull became Prime Minister last year, there was speculation that common sense would prevail and Canberra would once again accept that, whatever their nature and reputation, all governments have the right to choose the name of their own country. Also, by that time, only a couple of countries (notably, the US) and a number of activist groups still insisted on using 'Burma'.[5]

To add another complication, in March this year, Aung San Suu Kyi and the NLD took government after surprisingly free and fair national elections. This led some commentators to wonder whether the country's de facto leader (Aung San Suu Kyi is denied the presidency by the 2008 constitution) would change the name of the country back to Burma (notwithstanding the practical difficulties and administrative costs of doing so).

It now appears this will not happen. In April, Aung San Suu Kyi told the Rangoon diplomatic corps that it does not matter whether her country is called Burma or Myanmar, as 'there is nothing in the constitution that says you must use any term in particular'.[6] (In fact, the constitution clearly states that the country is called the Republic of the Union of Myanmar.)

5   Andrew Selth, 'All Change: Election Result May See Another Round of the Burma/Myanmar Name Game', *The Interpreter*, 18 November 2015, www.lowyinterpreter.org/post/2015/11/18/All-change-Election-result-may-see-another-round-of-the-BurmaMyanmar-name-game.aspx [page discontinued] [now at www.lowyinstitute.org/the-interpreter/all-change-election-result-may-see-another-round-burmamyanmar-name-game].
6   'Aung San Suu Kyi: You Can Call My Country Myanmar or Burma', *Independent*, [Ireland], 22 April 2016, www.independent.ie/world-news/asia-pacific/aung-san-suu-kyi-you-can-call-my-country-myanmar-or-burma-34651556.html.

She told the assembled foreign officials that she personally preferred 'Burma' but would use 'Myanmar' from time to time, to make everyone 'feel comfortable'.

As in previous cases when Australian policy on this issue has shifted, there has not been any public announcement, but it would appear that Canberra has quietly gone back to the 2012 rules. The 'Burma' country page on the DFAT website has been renamed the 'Myanmar' page.[7] All other references to the country—in public speeches, media releases and data sheets—are now to 'Myanmar'.

For example, when Foreign Minister Julie Bishop addressed Aung San Suu Kyi at the ASEAN meeting in Laos on 25 July 2016, she specifically referred to Myanmar, not Burma.[8] Bishop again referred to Myanmar when announcing Australia's latest tranche of humanitarian assistance earlier this month.[9] This followed discussions between her and the 'State Counsellor', as Aung San Suu Kyi is now called.

Lest anyone think this has all been a storm in a tea cup, important only to those who operate in the rarefied atmosphere of diplomatic protocol, it is worth bearing in mind that in June this year Aung San Suu Kyi instructed all Burmese officials to stop using the term 'Rohingyas' to refer to the hundreds of thousands of disenfranchised local residents whom she prefers to call 'people who believe in Islam in Rakhine State'.[10]

Foreign embassies in Burma and international organisations like the UN have been advised of the State Counsellor's views, in the expectation that they will respect them. The US Ambassador in Rangoon has since announced that he and his government would continue to use the term

---

7   Department of Foreign Affairs and Trade, *Myanmar* (Canberra: Australian Government), dfat. gov.au/geo/myanmar/Pages/myanmar.aspx.
8   The Hon. Julie Bishop MP, Minister for Foreign Affairs, 'ASEAN–Australia Ministerial Meeting: Opening Remarks', Speech, Vientiane, 25 July 2016, foreignminister.gov.au/speeches/Pages/2016/ jb_sp_160725.aspx [page discontinued] [now at www.foreignminister.gov.au/minister/julie-bishop/ speech/asean-australia-ministerial-meeting-opening-remarks].
9   The Hon. Julie Bishop MP, Minister for Foreign Affairs, 'Additional Humanitarian Assistance to Myanmar', Media release, Parliament House, Canberra, 1 August 2016, foreignminister.gov.au/ releases/Pages/2016/jb_mr_160801.aspx [page discontinued] [now at www.dfat.gov.au/news/news/ Pages/additional-humanitarian-assistance-to-myanmar].
10   Peter Lloyd, 'Burma Leader Aung San Suu Kyi Bans Use of Rohingya Name for Oppressed Muslims', *ABC News*, 22 June 2016, www.abc.net.au/news/2016-06-22/aung-san-suu-kyi-bans-use-of-rohingya-name/7534410.

'Rohingya' on the grounds that all such groups have the right to identify themselves.[11] However, the EU has fallen into line, stating that it would avoid use of the controversial term.[12]

Australian officials have referred to 'Rohingyas' many times in the past, in many different contexts. The government's position on Aung San Suu Kyi's latest 'request' is not yet clear, but it is interesting that Bishop's media release on 1 August referred only to aid for 'displaced communities', when the Rohingyas are an obvious target group. Names, it seems, still have the potential to cause diplomatic problems in Burma/Myanmar.

11   'US Defies Myanmar Government Request to Stop Using Term Rohingya', *The Guardian*, 11 May 2016, www.theguardian.com/world/2016/may/11/us-defies-myanmar-government-rohingya-muslims.
12   Antoni Slodkowski, 'Myanmar: Rohingya Will Not be Called Rohingya by the EU', *Sydney Morning Herald*, 23 June 2016, www.smh.com.au/world/myanmar-rohingya-will-not-be-called-rohingya-by-the-eu-20160622-gppsah.html.

85

Aung San Suu Kyi's fall from grace

(08:48 AEDT, 8 December 2016)

When she took office in March 2016, Aung San Suu Kyi inherited enormous problems and compounded them by making promises that she could never keep. Also, she had no control over the activities of the armed forces. She remained popular within Myanmar, but increasingly attracted criticism from abroad. This was not for failing to meet unrealistic popular expectations, however, but for disappointing all those who expected a more vigorous defence of human rights.

The people of Myanmar have always been able to capture complex issues in pithy, often humorous, expressions. One joke currently doing the rounds is that, after decades of trying to get into the driver's seat of the rickety old bus that is modern Myanmar, State Counsellor Aung San Suu Kyi has discovered that the steering wheel is not connected, the accelerator does not work and the passengers all want to go in different directions.

Aung San Suu Kyi was never going to meet the expectations of her supporters, both in Myanmar and abroad. They were quite unrealistic, given all the problems she inherited on taking power in March. Every sector of government begged for drastic reform and increased resources. Added to that, several new challenges have arisen over the past eight months that have stretched her inexperienced administration almost to breaking point.

Aung San Suu Kyi compounded these difficulties by making a number of rash promises. For example, she stated that a nationwide peace agreement with the country's armed ethnic groups was her 'single most important goal'.[1] Yet such an outcome was always going to be very difficult to achieve. Another stated aim was to end corruption—a deepseated problem in Myanmar that few believed could be solved easily or quickly.[2]

Most informed observers have been prepared to cut her some slack, recognising that the new government does not control all the levers of power. The armed forces (or *Tatmadaw*) are arguably still the country's most powerful political institution and they enjoy complete autonomy in military affairs. The economy is dominated by former military officers and their 'capitalist cronies'. Social, ethnic and religious tensions remain high and have the potential to erupt unexpectedly.

Even so, few observers anticipated that Aung San Suu Kyi would fall from grace so quickly. A scan of the headlines in major news outlets and websites reveals an almost uniform chorus of criticism—even, at times, condemnation.

Perhaps the loudest complaint heard against her is that, apart from appointing former UN secretary-general Kofi Annan to lead an advisory commission, she has failed to do anything about the plight of the mostly stateless Rohingya Muslims.[3] International concern has grown since October, when militants attacked three Myanmar security posts, triggering a harsh crackdown against the Rohingyas in northern Rakhine State.

David Mathieson of Human Rights Watch was more polite than most when he said: 'Suu Kyi risks shredding what residual credibility she still has on human rights if she fails to speak out.'[4] She has been accused of abandoning the principles for which she was awarded the 1991 Nobel

---

1   Shibani Mahtani and Myo Myo, 'Aung San Suu Kyi Calls Securing Peace in Myanmar Her Priority', *The Wall Street Journal*, 4 January 2016, www.wsj.com/articles/aung-san-suu-kyi-calls-securing-peace-in-myanmar-her-priority-1451899867.

2   Shibani Mahtani and Myo Myo, 'Myanmar's Suu Kyi Puts Corruption Fight at Centre of Campaign', *The Wall Street Journal*, 12 October 2015, blogs.wsj.com/frontiers/2015/10/12/myanmars-suu-kyi-puts-corruption-fight-at-center-of-campaign/ [page discontinued].

3   Anushay Hossain, 'Aung San Suu Kyi's Tragic Silence Over Rohingya', *CNN*, 1 December 2016, us.cnn.com/2016/12/01/opinions/aung-san-suu-kyi-failing-rohingya-hossain/index.html.

4   Kayleigh Long, 'Myanmar: Rohingya Muslims Displaced, Starving Amid Allegations of Human Rights Abuses by Security Forces', *ABC News*, 25 November 2016, www.abc.net.au/news/2016-11-25/suu-kyi-under-pressure-on-mynmar-human-rights-abuse-claims/8054976.

Peace Prize.[5] Other critics have claimed that her government is 'legitimising genocide',[6] endorsing collective punishment and 'ethnic cleansing'[7] and threatening regional stability.[8]

In the US, Aung San Suu Kyi already risks losing critical support. Some members of Congress have expressed reservations about President Obama's decision, made during Suu Kyi's visit to Washington in September, to lift all economic sanctions against Myanmar. One congressman has said he was 'appalled by her dismissive reaction' to concerns he raised with her about human trafficking in Myanmar.[9]

In addition to military operations in Rakhine State, the *Tatmadaw* is waging a fierce campaign against four armed ethnic groups in northern Myanmar. Since mid November, the Kachin Independence Army (KIA), T'ang National Liberation Army, Myanmar National Democratic Alliance Army and the Arakan Army have launched attacks along the sensitive border with China. There has also been renewed fighting in Shan State.

The KIA attended Aung San Suu Kyi's much vaunted but ultimately unsuccessful 21st Century Panglong Conference in August. The other three insurgent groups were not invited because they refused to lay down their arms before the meeting. In a masterly understatement, a government spokesman said the latest round of fighting would 'complicate the peace process'.[10] This is now effectively in the hands of the armed forces leadership.

5   'Bangladesh Pushes Back Rohingya Refugees Amid Collective Punishment in Myanmar', *News* (London: Amnesty International, 24 November 2016), www.amnesty.org/en/latest/news/2016/11/bangladesh-pushes-back-rohingya-refugees-amid-collective-punishment-in-myanmar/.

6   Nyshka Chandran, 'Myanmar's Suu Kyi Under Fire as Rohingya Crisis Escalates in Rakhine', *CNBC*, 24 November 2016, www.cnbc.com/2016/11/24/myanmars-aung-san-suu-kyis-under-fire-as-rohingya-crisis-escalates-in-rakhine.html.

7   'Myanmar Wants Ethnic Cleansing of Rohingya: UN Official', *BBC News*, 24 November 2016, www.bbc.com/news/world-asia-38091816.

8   Ye Mon and Shoon Naing, 'Duelling Protests as Tensions Rise between Myanmar and Malaysia', *Myanmar Times*, [Yangon], 5 December 2016, www.mmtimes.com/index.php/national-news/24035-duelling-protests-as-tensions-rise.html.

9   Patricia Zengerle, 'US Senator Blasts Suu Kyi's "Dismissive" Reaction on Trafficking', *Reuters*, 15 September 2016, uk.reuters.com/article/uk-usa-myanmar-senator-idUKKCN11K1Z3.

10   'Kachin Independence Army Teams Up with Other Fighters in Myanmar Attack', *Radio Free Asia*, [Washington, DC], 21 November 2016, www.rfa.org/english/news/myanmar/kachin-independence-army-teams-11212016141619.html.

Aung San Suu Kyi is also being criticised for other reasons. She has failed to reduce the *Tatmadaw*'s political power, preventing her from amending the promilitary constitution. Both were major election commitments. Many political prisoners have been released but draconian laws remain on the books, resulting in fresh arrests. Freedoms of speech and the press are still curtailed.[11] The poverty level hovers around 26 per cent.

Without making any excuses for Aung San Suu Kyi, it must be recognised that she is in a very difficult position. Security operations in Myanmar are managed by the armed forces, which, under the 2008 constitution, control all military affairs. Her ability to intervene is limited. Also, if her current delicate relationship with the *Tatmadaw* should break down, her ability to govern the country and introduce a range of much-needed reforms over the longer term is jeopardised.

Since Aung San Suu Kyi came to power, armed forces Commander-in-Chief Min Aung Hlaing has reminded audiences both in Myanmar and overseas of the *Tatmadaw*'s central role in national affairs and its legal right to take back the formal reins of power under certain circumstances.[12] He has also warned of the dangers of an unstable government and restated the need to end all armed conflicts. Most people assume that he was sending messages to the State Counsellor.

Comedians may joke about Aung San Suu Kyi's failure to change Myanmar as quickly as everyone hoped, but the public mood seems to be shifting. The Lady, as she is known, is still seen as preferable to the military leaders of the past, but the euphoria of last year's election landslide has faded. There is now increasing scepticism about the government's willingness to make the necessary reforms and, more to the point, its ability to do so.

The country is not yet at a tipping point. The criticisms heard overseas about the harsh treatment of the Rohingyas are not being made by many people within Myanmar, where anti-Muslim sentiment is strong. The *Tatmadaw*'s operations against minority ethnic groups in the

---

11   San Yamin Aung, 'Analysis: Burma's Military Remains Intolerant of Press Freedom', *The Irrawaddy*, 6 July 2016, www.irrawaddy.com/news/burma/analysis-burmas-military-remains-intolerant-of-press-freedom.html.

12   Lun Min Mang, 'Tatmadaw Chief Defends Military's Political Role at EU Meet', *Myanmar Times*, [Yangon], 11 November 2016, www.mmtimes.com/index.php/national-news/23616-tatmadaw-chief-defends-military-s-political-role-at-eu-meet.html.

north have little impact in the central lowlands, where most of the population lives. Grumblings about the slow rate of democratisation and modernisation are not a threat to stability—at least not yet.

Should the current arrangement between Aung San Suu Kyi and Min Aung Hlaing break down, however, it will not matter who is in the driver's seat. The wheels would come off Myanmar's vehicle of state, with the inevitable result.

2017

86

Myanmar and Aung San: The resurrection of an icon

(09:12 AEDT, 31 March 2017)

After independence hero Aung San was shunted into the background by the former military regime, Aung San Suu Kyi has restored her father to the pantheon of national heroes and to a prominent position in Myanmar's official iconography. It could be argued, however, that at times she has pushed this policy too far.

In a recent post on *The Interpreter*,[1] Andray Abrahamian drew attention to the Myanmar Government's decision to name a bridge in southern Mon State after the country's national hero, Aung San, rather than leave the matter in the hands of the regional authorities. As the post noted, the issue has become a source of tension between the ruling NLD and the local community—one that could easily have been avoided.

This case highlights the central government's continuing dominance of the 14 provincial assemblies in Myanmar, which have long struggled to exercise a substantive role.[2] There is another way of looking at the bridge-naming controversy, however, and that is as an example of the shift

---

1   Andray Abrahamian, 'Myanmar: NLD Scores Own Goal in Mon State', *The Interpreter*, 22 March 2017, www.lowyinstitute.org/the-interpreter/myanmar-nld-scores-own-goal-mon-state.
2   Hamish Nixon, Cindy Joelene, Kyi Pyar Chit Saw, Thet Aung Lynn and Matthew Arnold, *Executive Summary: State and Region Governments in Myanmar* (Yangon: Asia Foundation, September 2013), asiafoundation.org/resources/pdfs/MyanmarStateandRegionGovernmentsExecutiveSummary.pdf.

in the country's political iconography that began under president Thein Sein in 2011 and has picked up pace since Aung San Suu Kyi took power in 2016.

Ever since the country regained its independence from the UK in 1948, successive governments in Myanmar (known until 1989 as Burma) have placed considerable importance on the use of flags, crests and other symbols to foster a sense of shared history, encourage national unity and in various ways promote loyalty to the government of the day.

The most potent of these symbols has been the hero of Myanmar's independence struggle, General Aung San, who was assassinated with his provisional cabinet in 1947. His image was appropriated by the armed forces and, after Ne Win's coup in 1962, was widely used to help legitimise socialist rule. For decades, Aung San's picture hung alongside Ne Win's in all government offices and at many public venues.

After a new military council took over in 1988, Ne Win's portrait was taken down. That was not unexpected, but those of Aung San posed a different kind of problem. For, during the 1988 prodemocracy uprising, and again during the 2007 'Saffron Revolution', pictures of the national hero were used by demonstrators to drum up popular support and call for regime change. They were also potent reminders that Aung San was the father of opposition leader Aung San Suu Kyi.

Before they were regulated by the regime, NLD publicity materials depicted Aung San alongside Aung San Suu Kyi, emphasising not only the familial connection but also the striking physical similarity between them. Aung San Suu Kyi often received visitors at her Yangon home surrounded by photos and paintings of her father, and she routinely referred to him (and their blood relationship) in her speeches.

The military regime countered by reducing Aung San's public profile. Most of his portraits were removed. Also, in a major break from past practice, none of the banknotes issued by the Central Bank of Myanmar after 1990 included a portrait of Aung San. His image was replaced with neutral designs like the mythical *chinthe*, or leogryph. Nor did Aung San's portrait appear on any of the country's new postage stamps.[3]

---

3   Andrew Selth, 'Burma Puts Its Stamp on the World: Philately and Foreign Policy', *The Interpreter*, 7 January 2014, www.lowyinstitute.org/the-interpreter/burma-puts-its-stamp-world-philately-and-foreign-policy.

This policy was not without risks, as the regime exploited the fact that Aung San had helped create modern Myanmar and founded the armed forces. However, it resented efforts by other sectors of society to claim him as their own. When Aung San Suu Kyi returned to Myanmar from the UK in 1988 and began to campaign for democracy, she directly challenged the military government's efforts to monopolise Aung San's legacy.[4]

In response, the regime tried to undermine Aung San Suu Kyi's claim to her father's mantle. It emphasised her marriage to a foreigner and her education abroad (in India and the UK). The state-controlled press accused her of turning her back on her country and 'prostituting herself' to the West. She was labelled a 'traitor puppet'. The regime even refused to cite her full name, referring to her as Mrs Michael Aris (her husband's name) or simply *Ma* (a diminutive form of address) Suu Kyi.

After the inauguration of Thein Sein's reformist government in 2011, however, this policy was abandoned. Aung San was once again permitted to be part of the public consciousness. In 2012, for example, the refurbished Aung San museum in Yangon resumed normal visiting hours (since 1999, it had been open for only three hours each year). Official restrictions were lifted on the portrayal of Aung San in local movies.[5]

This shift in attitude was perhaps best demonstrated by a photo published in 2014 of the new president meeting Aung San Suu Kyi under a portrait of her father.[6] One topic discussed at this meeting was the reintroduction of Aung San's image to public life.[7] In 2016, Aung San Suu Kyi and the armed forces chief attended a ceremony at the Martyrs' Mausoleum, which was dedicated to her father and other fallen independence heroes.

---

4   'The Legacy of General Aung', *SBS News*, 26 August 2013, www.sbs.com.au/news/article/ 2012/03/30/legacy-general-aung.

5   Calum MacLeod, 'Rival Movies Break Taboo on Burma's National Hero', *USA Today*, 31 January 2015, [Updated 1 February 2015], www.usatoday.com/story/news/world/2015/01/31/burma-movie-aung-san/21396503/.

6   Kyaw Phyo Tha, 'Burma's Suu Kyi Holds Talks with President Thein Sein', *The Irrawaddy*, 10 March 2014, www.irrawaddy.com/news/burma/burmas-suu-kyi-holds-talks-president-thein-sein.html.

7   'Myanmar Independence Hero Aung San Back in the Limelight', *Deutsche Welle*, [Bonn], 7 October 2011, www.dw.com/en/myanmar-independence-hero-aung-san-back-in-the-limelight/a-6633306.

Most recently, on 17 March this year, a postage stamp was issued to commemorate the seventieth anniversary of the Ministry of Foreign Affairs. It depicts Aung San, who is described as the 'father of modern-day Myanmar and the country's first foreign minister'.[8] There are still no banknotes in circulation that carry his portrait, but a new currency issue is being considered that may do so.[9]

Several explanations have been offered for Aung San's return to the pantheon of national heroes and reappearance in Myanmar's official iconography.

One obvious reason is the advent of governments that openly acknowledge Aung San's commitment to national unity and democratic rule. Despite his politicisation by both the military regime and the opposition movement, he remains a popular icon that almost everyone in Myanmar can embrace. In that sense, he is like Sun Yat Sen—the only person depicted on the postage stamps of both Taiwan and the People's Republic of China.

Another reason is the election of the NLD Government in 2015 and, in particular, the appointment last year of Aung San Suu Kyi as State Counsellor. She has strong political and personal interests in promoting Aung San, both as a national hero and as the father of the country's de facto leader. It is probably not a coincidence that Aung San Suu Kyi is also Myanmar's foreign minister—the position commemorated on the latest postage stamp.

A third possible reason is to remind everyone of Aung San's key role in the 1947 Panglong Agreement between his provisional government and three major ethnic groups. Conveniently forgotten are the agreement's flaws, its limitations and the later broken promises, but public references to her father help boost Aung San Suu Kyi's own attempts to forge a nationwide peace agreement through the '21st Century Panglong' process.

---

8   Ministry of Information, 'Bogyoke Aung San Stamps and Envelopes to be Sold', News release (Naypyitaw: Republic of the Union of Myanmar, 13 March 2017), www.moi.gov.mm/moi:eng/?q=news/8/11/2018/id-10197.
9   Zon Pann Pwint, 'Aung San Returns to Kyat Notes', *Myanmar Times*, [Yangon], 24 November 2013, www.mmtimes.com/index.php/lifestyle/8868-aung-san-returns-to-kyat-notes.html.

Despite the machinations of the military regime, Aung San was never forgotten by the people of Myanmar.[10] His official rehabilitation is long overdue. To push this policy at the expense of national harmony, however, would be to take the matter too far. Indeed, by overriding the wishes of the Mon State authorities simply to name a bridge, Naypyidaw is threatening the very unity and stability that Aung San tried so hard to establish 70 years ago.

---

10   Naomi Gingold, 'He's Still a Rock Star in Burma, 7 Decades After His Death', *Public Radio International*, [Minneapolis, MN], 6 November 2015, www.pri.org/stories/2015-11-06/man-who-gets-top-billing-next-aung-san-suu-kyi.

87

Suu Kyi's Myanmar, one year on

(09:10 AEDT, 27 April 2017)

Observers conducting a review of Aung San Suu Kyi's government after one year in office usually came away disappointed. There were factors over which the new administration had no control, but it had to be held responsible for many of its failures. In particular, it was felt that Aung San Suu Kyi needed to be held to account for her failure to speak out on human rights abuses against groups like the Rohingyas.

Twelve months ago, Aung San Suu Kyi was appointed State Counsellor of Myanmar, becoming the de facto leader of the NLD Government that swept to power in (relatively) free and fair elections in 2015. Over the past several weeks, both the government and Aung San Suu Kyi herself have been subject to searching reviews by Myanmar-watchers and other commentators.

To varying degrees, most have expressed disappointment with the NLD's performance during its first year in office.[1] Even allowing for the unrealistically high expectations held both within and outside the

---

1   Feliz Solomon, 'One Year On, Aung San Suu Kyi Struggles to Unite a Fractured Myanmar', *TIME*, 30 March 2017, time.com/4714808/myanmar-burma-aung-san-suu-kyi-anniversary/.

country, the new government has failed to deliver on its promises.[2] Foreign observers have been particularly critical of Aung San Suu Kyi's repeated refusal to intervene on behalf of the mostly stateless Muslim Rohingyas.[3]

Since the publication of these reviews, a number of Aung San Suu Kyi's supporters and apologists for her government have leapt to her defence, arguing that it is too early to judge the new administration.[4] They have pointed out the dreadful state of Myanmar when it took power. Some have also sought to deflect criticism of Aung San Suu Kyi towards the armed forces (*Tatmadaw*), which they see as the root cause of all her problems.[5]

The NLD's defenders make some good points. However, before dismissing Aung San Suu Kyi's critics, it is worth considering some of the issues that have been raised.

First, in 2016, Myanmar was suffering from more than 50 years of inept and self-serving military rule, which had left every portfolio of government apart from Defence begging for greater attention and more resources. President Thein Sein's government had taken tentative steps towards reform between 2011 and 2015, but he had only picked the low-hanging fruit and most critical issues had been left unresolved.

Second, the 2008 constitution gave the *Tatmadaw* a powerful role at the centre of government, with 25 per cent of all seats in provincial and national assemblies reserved for serving military officers. Also, the armed forces directly controlled three key ministries: Home Affairs (which included the police force), Defence and Border Affairs. In all security matters, the *Tatmadaw* operated completely independently from the government.

2   Richard C. Paddock, 'After Aung San Suu Kyi's First Year in Power, Dismay Swirls in Myanmar', *The New York Times*, 8 April 2017, www.nytimes.com/2017/04/08/world/asia/myanmar-aung-san-suu-kyi-first-year.html?_r=0.

3   Jon Emont, 'Is This the Real Aung San Suu Kyi?', *The New Republic*, 23 December 2016, newrepublic.com/article/139476/real-aung-san-suu-kyi.

4   Lindsay Murdoch, 'Aung San Suu Kyi "Hung Out to Dry", Say East Timorese, Australian Leaders', *Sydney Morning Herald*, 14 April 2017, www.smh.com.au/world/aung-san-suu-kyi-hung-out-to-dry-say-east-timorese-australian-politicians-20170414-gvkwxf.html.

5   Mark Farmaner, 'It's Time to Talk About Min Aung Hlaing', *The Huffington Post*, 13 April 2017, www.huffingtonpost.co.uk/mark-farmaner/min-aung-hlaing_b_15001514.html.

Third, Aung San Suu Kyi inherited an economy that was responding to new regulations, inflows of foreign capital and increased aid. However, it was still in dire straits. As a percentage of GDP, the budget deficit had increased threefold over the last year of Thein Sein's administration. Poverty levels averaged 26 per cent; in rural areas, they were even higher.[6] Myanmar also lacked infrastructure, a modern fiscal regime and a reliable legal system.

Fourth, as Robert Taylor recently pointed out,[7] the NLD inherited a moribund bureaucracy stacked with former military officers and lacking managerial expertise. After decades of a hierarchical command culture, there was no tradition of public servants taking initiative, challenging decisions or even reporting policy failures. All this made the consideration and implementation of new initiatives very difficult.

As if these problems were not enough, the NLD took over a country that was deeply divided by political, ethnic and religious conflicts, some of which dated back to colonial days. The national peace process had virtually collapsed as a result of mutual distrust, historical grievances, incompatible goals and fresh outbreaks of fighting. The widespread antagonism felt towards Muslims (Rohingyas in particular) was of international concern.[8]

Sixth, the NLD and Aung San Suu Kyi created some of their own problems. The party initially lacked detailed policies on almost all major issues. Few of its members had any experience in government. Aung San Suu Kyi's imperious personal style and tendency to micromanage led to resentment and administrative inefficiencies. Public relations have been handled poorly—at times, even prompting comparisons with the former military regime.

In some ways, Aung San Suu Kyi had set her government up to fail. She had promised to amend the constitution and reduce the power of the armed forces, neither of which was likely in the short term. She also undertook to eliminate corruption—another remote prospect. She said she would give her highest priority to the peace process, before turning to

---

6   United Nations Development Programme, *About Myanmar* (Yangon: UNDP in Myanmar), www.mm.undp.org/content/myanmar/en/home/countryinfo.html.

7   Robert H. Taylor, 'Discord, Not Devotion, Will Help Aung San Suu Kyi Succeed', *Nikkei Asian Review*, 30 March 2017, asia.nikkei.com/Viewpoints/Robert-H.-Taylor/Discord-not-devotion-will-help-Aung-San-Suu-Kyi-succeed.

8   'UN Report Details "Devastating Cruelty" Against Rohingya Population in Myanmar's Rakhine Province', *UN News*, 3 February 2017, www.un.org/apps/news/story.asp?NewsID=56103.

other domestic matters. Yet the peace process was effectively in the hands of the generals and most of the population cared more for issues that affected them directly.

Aung San Suu Kyi has belatedly acknowledged the growing chorus of criticism and asked for more time to tackle outstanding problems.[9] She has said that she and her government would step down if that was the popular wish.[10] This offer was rather disingenuous, given that she has no obvious successor (she has made sure of that) and the only viable alternative to the NLD is another military government, which no one in the country (including the generals) wants.

What is perhaps most perplexing about Aung San Suu Kyi's behaviour since taking office has been her failure to capitalise on her greatest political asset: her own popularity. She has made few personal appearances. Her rare public statements have focused on abstract concepts like national reconciliation and the rule of law.[11] She has left it to others to convey the government's views on specific issues. Over the past 12 months, she has only given three interviews—all to foreign broadcasters.[12]

Outside Myanmar, Aung San Suu Kyi's reputation as a democratic icon and defender of human rights has taken a battering.[13] Her silence on the plight of the Rohingyas and her government's refusal to respond to what the UN has described as 'genocide' and 'crimes against humanity'[14] have undermined her global status and weakened her ability to attract international support. Already, waning confidence in her administration seems to be affecting Myanmar's economic growth and regional influence.[15]

---

9   'NLD Government Asks for "More Time" as Public and Pundits Take Stock', *Myanmar Times*, [Yangon], 19 July 2016, www.mmtimes.com/index.php/in-depth/22181-nld-government-asks-for-more-time-as-public-and-pundits-take-stock.html.
10   Associated Press, 'Myanmar's Aung Suu Kyi Addresses Letdowns, Says She is Prepared to Step Down', *ABC News*, 31 March 2017, www.abc.net.au/news/2017-03-31/suu-kyi-says-she-is-prepared-to-step-down-amid-letdowns/8403304.
11   Mary Callahan, 'Aung San Suu Kyi's Quiet, Puritanical Vision for Myanmar', *Nikkei Asian Review*, 29 March 2017, asia.nikkei.com/Features/The-lady-in-question/Aung-San-Suu-Kyi-s-quiet-puritanical-vision-for-Myanmar2.
12   Fergal Keane, 'Myanmar: Aung San Suu Kyi Exclusive Interview', *BBC News*, 5 April 2017, www.bbc.com/news/world-asia-39510271.
13   Fiona MacGregor, 'Suu Kyi's State of Denial', *New Mandala*, 4 March 2017, www.newmandala.org/suu-kyis-state-denial/.
14   Jonah Fisher, 'Myanmar Muslim Minority Subject to Horrific Torture, UN Says', *BBC News*, 10 March 2017, www.bbc.com/news/world-39218105.
15   'Aung San Suu Kyi's First Year Running Myanmar Has Been a Letdown', *The Economist*, 1 April 2017, www.economist.com/news/asia/21719802-economy-has-slowed-along-pace-reform-aung-san-suu-kyis-first-year-running-myanmar.

Considered in the widest perspective, however, Myanmar's first year of (disciplined) democracy should not be written off. For all its faults, the NLD Government has made modest progress in some areas, and more is promised. Also, the international community needs to measure Myanmar against the same standards as those applied to other countries. There are many examples around the world of democratic transitions that have stalled. Some have even gone backwards.[16] Compared with them, it can be argued that Myanmar is not doing too badly.

Aung San Suu Kyi's supporters are right to point out the complex problems she inherited a year ago and to remind us that she has no control over the *Tatmadaw*, which is responsible for security operations in Myanmar. And yes, she needs to take into account popular sentiment, while maintaining a *modus vivendi* with the armed forces, to implement much-needed and long-awaited reforms. As she has said herself, she is a politician, not an icon, and that means making 'principled compromises'.[17]

However, Aung San Suu Kyi's failure to show greater moral courage and demonstrate political leadership on a critical issue like the Rohingyas cannot be sheeted home to the armed forces, her party or anyone else. For that, she alone must take responsibility.

---

16   Isobel Coleman and Terra Lawson-Remer, 'A User's Guide to Democratic Transitions', *Foreign Policy*, 18 June 2013, foreignpolicy.com/2013/06/18/a-users-guide-to-democratic-transitions/.

17   Deborah Snow and Judith Ireland, 'Suu Kyi: I Am Neither Saint Nor Icon', *Sydney Morning Herald*, 28 November 2013, www.smh.com.au/nsw/suu-kyi-i-am-neither-saint-nor-icon-20131128-2ybpk.html.

88

Incident at Three Pagodas Pass

(13:09 AEDT, 31 May 2017)

An official visit to Three Pagodas Pass by the Director of Australia's Defence Intelligence Organisation (DIO) in 1994 did not go exactly as planned and could have caused a diplomatic incident.

After decades of strained bilateral relations, Australia's defence ties with Myanmar are gradually being restored.[1]

The office of the defence attaché (DA) in the Australian Embassy in Yangon (formerly Rangoon), which closed in 1979, was reopened in 2014. This coincided with a port visit by HMAS *Childers*—the first by a Royal Australian Navy vessel since the frigate HMAS *Quiberon* called in 1959.[2] With the inauguration of Aung San Suu Kyi's semi-civilian government in early 2016, defence engagement has been given a higher priority. The inaugural meeting of the Australia–Myanmar Strategic Dialogue was held in Yangon in March 2017.[3]

---

1   Andrew Selth, 'Defence Relations with Burma: Our Future Past', *The Interpreter*, 4 March 2013, www.lowyinstitute.org/the-interpreter/defence-relations-burma-our-future-past.
2   Senator the Hon. David Johnston, 'Acting Minister for Defence, and Minister for Foreign Affairs: Joint Media Release—Australian Government Strengthening Ties with the Myanmar Government', Media release, Department of Defence, Canberra, 20 January 2014, www.minister.defence.gov.au/minister/david-johnston/media-releases/acting-minister-defence-and-minister-foreign-affairs-joint.
3   Senator the Hon. Concetta Fierravanti-Wells, Minister for International Development and the Pacific, 'Australia–Myanmar Strategic Dialogue', Speech, 13 March 2017, ministers.dfat.gov.au/fierravanti-wells/speeches/Pages/2017/cf_sp_170313.aspx [page discontinued].

These developments are well documented, but over the years there have been others that are not as well known. One in particular springs to mind.

In 1994, an incident occurred at Three Pagodas Pass on the Thailand–Myanmar border, west of Bangkok. While minor in itself, it had the potential to complicate the diplomatic relationship between Australia and Myanmar at a difficult time. Known only to a few people at the time, it deserves at least a footnote when the history of Australia's relations with Myanmar is finally written.

In September that year, Major General John Hartley, Director of Australia's Defence Intelligence Organisation (DIO) from 1992 to 1995, was invited to Thailand as the guest of his Thai counterpart, Royal Thai Army (RTA) Major General Teerawat Patumanonda. General Hartley was accompanied on his visit by two DIO analysts—one an army lieutenant colonel and the other a civilian. While in Thailand, he was escorted by the Australian DA in Bangkok, who was an army colonel.

As part of a familiarisation tour, General Hartley was taken by UH-1H helicopter from the RTA Ninth Infantry Division's Camp Surasri in Kanchanaburi Province to Three Pagodas Pass. Located in the First Army Region, the Ninth Infantry Division was the RTA unit responsible for border affairs in Kanchanaburi. A special task force within the division was charged with coordinating security and refugee affairs at the local level, including around the pass.

Three Pagodas Pass is of considerable historical importance. For centuries, it was one of the main land routes between Burma (as Myanmar was known before 1989) and Siam (as Thailand was known before 1939). During World War II, it was where the infamous 'death railway' from Ban Pong to Thanbyuzayat crossed the border. For years, an old Japanese C56 locomotive was preserved there as a monument to the 13,000 Allied prisoners of war and 80,000 Asian labourers who died working on the railway.

Now a major tourist attraction, the pass receives thousands of visitors every year. However, in 1994, due to its strategic significance and political sensitivity, it was a restricted area.

The pass played an important role in Myanmar's civil wars. During the 1980s, it was the scene of bitter fighting between the Myanmar Army (MA) and insurgents from the separatist New Mon State Party (NMSP), which effectively controlled the area until 1990. After the SLORC took power in Myanmar in 1988, more than 35 ethnic armed groups agreed to ceasefires. The NMSP made such a pact in 1995, but in 1994, tensions around Three Pagodas Pass were still high.

The pass also fell within the operating area of the larger and more powerful Karen National Liberation Army (KNLA), which had been fighting Myanmar's central government since the country regained its independence from the British in 1948. The KNLA was a tough and determined force that sought a separate Karen state. By 1994, a number of breakaway Karen groups had negotiated ceasefires with the SLORC, but the KNLA had refused to do so (this policy would not change until 2012).

These tensions affected Myanmar–Thai relations. Insurgents from the ethnic armed groups routinely crossed the border into Thailand, both to recuperate and to outflank MA positions. Yangon (then Myanmar's capital) believed that Bangkok was secretly aiding the rebels to weaken the MA and destabilise the new military government. Local villagers displaced by the fighting sought sanctuary in Thailand. In July 1994, 6,000 people did so after the MA attacked and destroyed a large Mon refugee camp near Three Pagodas Pass.

Adding to these complications, the demarcation of the border in this area was disputed. The boundary between the two countries was broadly defined in negotiations between the East India Company and the King of Siam in 1826, and through subsequent Anglo-Siamese border commissions, but ambiguities still existed around Three Pagodas Pass. The actual town and border checkpoint that carry this name lie at the end of a thin 1.5-kilometre–long sliver of Thai territory, surrounded by Myanmar on three sides.

It was for all these reasons that General Hartley had asked to visit the area.

The Iroquois helicopter carrying the DIO delegation landed on Thai territory near the eponymous three pagodas, where General Hartley was greeted by the local military commander, an RTA colonel. While they were chatting, a utility truck pulled up and an MA colonel alighted. He was greeted warmly by the RTA colonel, who introduced him to General Hartley as his Myanmar counterpart. Despite occasional political tensions between Bangkok and Yangon, the two enjoyed a friendly working relationship.

The two colonels briefly spoke together. The MA colonel then got back into his utility, gave an instruction to his driver and they drove off. The RTA colonel invited General Hartley and his party to get into a couple of jeeps that were standing nearby. They then followed the MA vehicle. The Australian party soon realised that they had crossed the international border. On being questioned about this, the Thai colonel explained that the Myanmar colonel had invited them to his house 'for tea', and it would have been impolite to refuse.

At this point, it should be noted that General Hartley, the Australian DA, the DIO lieutenant colonel and the Thai colonel were all wearing military uniforms. Only the civilian DIO analyst was in mufti.

The MA colonel's 'house' turned out to be a bunker within a heavily fortified army base, about 3 kilometres inside Myanmar. It was protected by berms and fences crowned with razor wire. Machine-gun posts were visible by the main gate and at various points around the perimeter. The mixed Australian–Thai party crowded into the MA commander's rather cramped living quarters, where they were seated around a table. Introductions were made by the Thai colonel, who acted as a translator.

While this was happening, a woman assumed to be the colonel's wife passed out cups of sweet, milky tea. The civilian DIO analyst, however, had a particular fondness for the local green tea—a taste he had picked up during a diplomatic posting to the Australian Embassy in Yangon in the 1970s. He asked the colonel's wife whether he could have a cup of that instead. As a courtesy, and because he doubted the woman could speak English, he spoke in Burmese.

The colonel's wife was rather startled to hear her own language spoken by a foreigner, but immediately went away and brought him a cup of green tea. This time, however, she was accompanied by an MA major, who squeezed in alongside the analyst and immediately began quizzing him in Burmese. He had obviously been tipped off by the colonel's wife that one of the foreign visitors spoke their language.

The major was keen to know who General Hartley was and what he was doing in Thailand. He was also curious to know how the DIO analyst came to speak Burmese. As far as his limited knowledge of the language allowed, the analyst explained the circumstances of the general's unscheduled visit to the MA base and gave a little of his own background. In doing so, he was acutely aware that Australia's relations with Myanmar at that time were rather strained.

In 1988, Canberra had strongly condemned the way in which Myanmar's armed forces crushed a nationwide prodemocracy uprising. Before Ne Win's moribund socialist regime was replaced with the SLORC, more than 3,000 demonstrators were killed. The Australian foreign minister had also expressed his government's concern in 1990, after opposition leader Aung San Suu Kyi was placed under house arrest and the SLORC ignored the NLD's landslide victory in general elections held that year.

More to the point, bilateral military contacts were politically sensitive. Since 1979, the Australian DA in Bangkok had been dually accredited to Myanmar, to help him monitor developments there. However, after the 1988 uprising, defence cooperation had been suspended. Australia had joined Western efforts to isolate and punish the new regime. In 1991, Canberra imposed an embargo on arms sales, excluded Myanmar officers from attending Australian military colleges and halted defence visits.

It quickly became apparent that the MA major was a member of Myanmar's powerful Military Intelligence Service (MIS). In answering his questions, the DIO analyst was conscious that whatever he said would probably be reported back to MIS headquarters in Yangon, and he framed his replies accordingly. While General Hartley's visit to Myanmar was unplanned—indeed, inadvertent—it was also unauthorised. If made public, it had the potential to prompt some awkward questions in both Yangon and Canberra.

Happily, for the Australians, morning tea was soon over and, after friendly farewells, the party was driven back to Thailand and their waiting RTA helicopter. Despite an unscheduled landing in a paddy field on the flight back, due to bad weather, the party disembarked at Camp Surasri that evening none the worse for their experience.

While perhaps minor in itself, this vignette seems worth recording. It is offered here as a small contribution to the history of the Australia–Myanmar relationship, and of contacts between the armed forces of the two countries at a time of momentous changes in both.

89

A big step back
for Myanmar

(07:17 AEDT, 13 September 2017)

The Tatmadaw's massive overreaction to a series of small-scale attacks by Rohingya insurgents in 2016 and 2017 created a situation in Myanmar in which everyone was worse off. The Rohingyas were of course the greatest losers, but so, too, in different ways were Aung San Suu Kyi's new government, the armed forces and civil society. The democratic transition process in Myanmar, such as it was, was set back years—possibly even decades.

It is always difficult to know exactly what is happening in Myanmar, particularly when eyewitness accounts and reliable reports are dismissed by the Naypyidaw government as 'misinformation' and 'fake news', when false images of atrocities are posted on the web alongside genuine ones, when statistics vary wildly and when passion and propaganda compete with informed and objective analysis for attention in the international news media.

That said, it is clear that, with respect to the current Rohingya crisis, developments in Myanmar over the past year can only be described as a disaster for all concerned that will have far-reaching consequences. There will be no winners. Everyone loses.

Those who stand to lose most are the Rohingyas, as the stateless Muslims concentrated in Myanmar's Rakhine State call themselves. Attacks against three police posts by the Arakan Rohingya Salvation Army (ARSA) in October 2016, and against 30 police posts and an army post this August, have resulted in a massive security crackdown. An unknown number of Rohingya villages have been destroyed by the army, police and Buddhist vigilantes. There have been an estimated 1,000 deaths—almost all Rohingyas—and up to 275,000 people have fled to makeshift refugee camps in Bangladesh.[1]

These developments have been a political and personal disaster for Aung San Suu Kyi, Myanmar's de facto leader.[2] Since the security forces launched their 'area clearance operations' in 2016, she has been condemned for failing to speak out against human rights abuses, which have been described by the UN as 'devastating cruelty' and possibly even 'crimes against humanity',[3] bordering on genocide.[4] More recently, foreign commentators have been scathing in their criticisms of her clumsy attempts to deny the latest atrocities and shift the blame for the unfolding humanitarian nightmare. Calls for her to be stripped of her Nobel Peace Prize are growing louder.[5]

As Aung San Suu Kyi's international reputation has collapsed, so, too, has that of her government. It clearly has no control over the country's armed forces (the *Tatmadaw*), which, under the 2008 constitution, act independently in security matters. It also seems afraid of arousing Myanmar's deep-seated anti-Muslim prejudices.[6] This has left it looking weak and ineffectual, if not complicit in human rights abuses. The report prepared by former UN secretary-general Kofi Annan, on which the government had pinned its hopes for a solution to the broader Rohingya issue, has had to be shelved.[7]

---

1   Max Bearak, 'More Than a Quarter-Million Rohingya Have Fled Burma in the Past Two Weeks, UN Says', *The Washington Post*, 8 September 2017, www.washingtonpost.com/news/worldviews/wp/2017/09/08/more-than-a-quarter-million-rohingya-have-fled-burma-in-the-past-two-weeks-u-n-says/.

2   Andrew Selth, *Aung San Suu Kyi and the Politics of Personality*, Griffith Asia Institute Regional Outlook Paper No.55 (Brisbane: Griffith University, 2017), www.griffith.edu.au/__data/assets/pdf_file/0004/1088590/Regional-Outlook-Paper-55-Selth-web.pdf [page discontinued].

3   'UN Report Details "Devastating Cruelty" Against Rohingya Population in Myanmar's Rakhine Province', *UN News*, 3 February 2017, www.un.org/apps/news/story.asp?NewsID=56103.

4   Liam Cochrane, 'Myanmar Could be On the Brink of Genocide, UN Expert Says', *ABC News*, 6 September 2017, www.abc.net.au/news/2017-09-06/myanmar-on-brink-of-genocide-un-expert-say/8879858.

5   Jacob Judah, 'Strip Aung San Suu Kyi of Her Nobel Prize', *The New York Times*, 7 September 2017, www.nytimes.com/2017/09/07/opinion/strip-aung-san-suu-kyi-of-her-nobel-prize.html?mcubz=0.

6   Fred Strasser, 'No Quick Answers on Burma's Rohingya, Mitchell Says', *Analysis and Commentary* (Washington, DC: US Institute of Peace, 8 September 2017), www.usip.org/blog/2017/09/no-quick-answers-burmas-rohingya-mitchell-says.

7   *Final Report of the Advisory Commission on Rakhine State*, www.rakhinecommission.org/.

The *Tatmadaw* currently seems to have the whip hand. Yet, for it too, developments over the past year can be seen as a setback. Around 2011, the commander-in-chief (C-in-C) embarked on a program to make the armed forces more modern, more professional and better respected. Myanmar's embattled ethnic communities were never persuaded that the high command's mindset had really changed, however, and this view has now been confirmed by the cynical strategy and brutal tactics adopted by the police (which are controlled by the C-in-C) and the army in Rakhine State.[8]

The *Tatmadaw*'s reputation inside Myanmar does not seem to have suffered greatly—most locals view the Rohingyas unsympathetically, as illegal Bengali immigrants—but its standing in international circles has fallen dramatically. There is now little chance that Western countries will relax their restrictions on bilateral defence engagement. This is a significant loss for the *Tatmadaw*, which is keen to learn about foreign military policies and practices. Such contacts would have also helped its officers learn about international norms of behaviour and the role of armed forces in democracies.[9] Any hopes the *Tatmadaw* might have had to acquire Western arms and equipment can be forgotten.

The events of the past year have also been a disaster for Myanmar's civil society. As the International Crisis Group has pointed out, the last anti-Muslim riots were in 2013, but religious tensions have remained high.[10] There have been calls within Myanmar for a peaceful solution to the Rohingya problem but recent developments in Rakhine State have strengthened the hand of Buddhist extremists who have been waiting for an opportunity to reassert themselves. Even if the *Tatmadaw*'s prediction of ARSA attacks in Myanmar's cities proves incorrect, there is the risk of further communal violence.

In other ways, too, the Rohingya crisis is a disaster for Myanmar. With the government's gaze and resources focused on Rakhine State, less attention is being paid to other parts of the country and other pressing issues.

---

8   Andray Abrahamian, 'The Tatmadaw Returns to the "Four Cuts" Doctrine', *The Interpreter*, 4 September 2017, www.lowyinstitute.org/the-interpreter/tadmadaw-ominous-return-four-cuts-doctrine.
9   William C. Dickey and Nay Yan Oo, 'Myanmar's Military Holds Key to Further Reform', *Nikkei Asian Review*, 18 August 2017, asia.nikkei.com/Viewpoints/William-C.-Dickey-and-Nay-Yan-Oo/Myanmar-s-military-holds-key-to-further-reform.
10   *Buddhism and State Power in Myanmar*, Asia Report No.290 (Yangon/Brussels: International Crisis Group, 5 September 2017), www.crisisgroup.org/asia/south-east-asia/myanmar/290-buddhism-and-state-power-myanmar.

A nationwide peace agreement with ethnic armed groups, for example, seems an even more distant prospect. Fewer funds will be available to fill gaping holes in the budget, in critical areas like health and education. The crisis and declining international confidence in Aung San Suu Kyi[11] have already had a negative impact on foreign direct investment and Myanmar's economic growth.[12]

Over the longer term, the Rohingya crisis is a disaster for Myanmar's planned transition from authoritarian rule to a more democratic system of government.

When it announced its intention to launch a violent campaign on behalf of the Rohingyas, ARSA played into the hands of conservative elements in the armed forces. While there is little evidence that it supports a transnational Islamist agenda, ARSA was immediately cast as a member of an international terrorist conspiracy.[13] This made it a clearly identifiable threat to Myanmar's sovereignty, unity and stability—the three 'national causes' enshrined in the 2008 constitution and, for over half a century, the armed forces' highly publicised raison d'être.

As former US ambassador to Myanmar Derek Mitchell has pointed out, the *Tatmadaw*'s roles as Myanmar's 'saviour' and protector of the country's majority-Buddhist values have been confirmed.[14] The Rohingya crisis has pushed the generals to the forefront of government decision-making, where their hard line is likely to remain the default policy position. The armed forces' claim to a central place in national political life has been reaffirmed. By the same token, the standing and influence of Aung San Suu Kyi and her quasi-civilian government have been diminished.

---

11   Peter Janssen, 'Suu Kyi's Fading Allure Repels Foreign Investors', *Asia Times*, [Hong Kong], 6 September 2017, www.atimes.com/article/suu-kyis-fading-allure-repels-foreign-investors/ [page discontinued] [now at asiatimes.com/2017/09/suu-kyis-fading-allure-repels-foreign-investors/].

12   Gwen Robinson and Yuichi Nitta, 'Rakhine Crisis Blights Myanmar Economic Outlook', *Nikkei Asian Review*, 5 September 2017, asia.nikkei.com/Politics-Economy/Economy/Rakhine-crisis-blights-Myanmar-economic-outlook.

13   'Yemeni Al Qaeda Leader Calls for Attacks in Support of Myanmar's Rohingya', *The Irrawaddy*, 3 September 2017, www.irrawaddy.com/news/yemeni-al-qaeda-leader-calls-attacks-support-myanmars-rohingya.html.

14   Matthew Pennington, 'Obama's Myanmar Legacy in Trouble and It's Not Trump's Fault', *The Denver Post*, 2 September 2017, www.denverpost.com/2017/09/02/barack-obama-myanmar-legacy-donald-trump/.

Myanmar has also lost ground in foreign policy terms. Governments of all colours have expressed grave concern over the Rohingya crisis and its international implications.[15] Indonesia even sent its foreign minister to Naypyidaw to speak directly to Aung San Suu Kyi.[16] The UN has been particularly critical of the Myanmar Government's handling of the crisis, including its accusations that NGOs were assisting the ARSA. For the UN Secretary-General, the Rohingyas were 'an undeniable factor in regional destabilisation' that demanded a 'holistic' solution.[17]

Given current attitudes in Myanmar, the Rohingya tragedy could drag on for years. ARSA will not achieve its aims, but Muslim anger both within Myanmar and overseas will remain. Religious divisions in the country will harden. Hundreds of thousands of refugees will be left in squalid camps in Bangladesh, unwanted by anyone and facing a bleak future. The *Tatmadaw* will consolidate its political gains, while Aung San Suu Kyi and her government will find it even harder to implement much-needed reforms. The democratic transition process in Myanmar, such as it was, has been set back years—possibly decades.

In these circumstances, no one wins. Everyone loses.

---

15   'Asian Neighbours Add Pressure on Suu Kyi to Act on Rohingya Crisis', *Nikkei Asian Review*, 5 September 2017, asia.nikkei.com/Politics-Economy/International-Relations/Asian-neighbors-add-pressure-on-Suu-Kyi-to-act-on-Rohingya-crisis.
16   Erwida Maulia, 'Indonesian Minister Meets Suu Kyi as Rohingya Crisis Deepens', *Nikkei Asian Review*, 4 September 2017, asia.nikkei.com/Politics-Economy/Policy-Politics/Indonesian-minister-meets-Suu-Kyi-as-Rohingya-crisis-deepens.
17   Thu Thu Aung, 'UN Secretary-General Calls for "Holistic Solution" in Rakhine', *The Irrawaddy*, September 2017, www.irrawaddy.com/news/burma/un-secretary-general-calls-holistic-solution-rakhine.html.

90

The Rohingya crisis and Myanmar's military responses

(14:00 AEDT, 24 November 2017)

Observers trying to identify the Tatmadaw's *strategy in Rakhine State identified four schools of thought. The official line was that Naypyidaw was responding to international terrorism, while others saw it as a massive overreaction to a minor insurgent threat. A third school believed the armed forces had a long-term plan to expel all Rohingyas from the country, while a fourth school insisted it was all a plot directed by foreign powers. Whatever the formal strategy may have been, the security forces were determined to pursue their own agenda regardless of international opinion.*

Since October 2016, when militants from the ARSA attacked three border police posts in Myanmar's Rakhine State, developments in that part of the world have dominated the headlines. Denied access to western Myanmar, most reporters have focused on the plight of the 600,000 or more Muslim Rohingyas who are now living in squalid refugee camps in Bangladesh.[1]

---

1   'Myanmar Rohingya: What You Need to Know about the Crisis', *BBC News*, 19 October 2017, [Updated 23 January 2020], www.bbc.com/news/world-asia-41566561.

Given the nature of the crisis—described by the UN as 'a humanitarian and human rights nightmare' and 'the largest mass refugee movement in the region for decades'[2]—the flood of reports about the Rohingyas in the news media and online is understandable. However, a few important issues have slipped through the cracks and demand closer attention.

There have been passing references in news stories to the 'area clearance operations' conducted by Myanmar's armed forces (the *Tatmadaw*) and police force and countless reports of specific incidents, but few observers have stepped back and tried to examine the broad strategy being pursued by the security forces in northern Rakhine State. Yet, without an understanding of the long-term military and political goals, it is difficult to look beyond current problems and anticipate future challenges.

It is widely acknowledged that Aung San Suu Kyi's government, while hardly blameless, has little control over the security forces, which seem to be pursuing an agenda of their own. However, what that agenda might be and the thinking behind it are difficult to determine. Broadly speaking, four schools of thought have emerged to explain military operations in Rakhine State. They range from the plausible to the improbable.

First, the official line is that the security forces are responding to a serious threat to Myanmar's unity, stability and sovereignty from Rohingya terrorists, who are supported by international Islamist groups. Naypyidaw has offered few details to back up these statements, preferring to emphasise the attacks against 34 police and army posts over the past year, the 21 soldiers, policemen and civil servants killed in the line of duty and the need to recover the arms captured by ARSA.

As always, hard data are scarce, but the International Crisis Group (ICG) is probably right in stating that ARSA does not have a transnational Islamist or jihadist agenda.[3] That said, questions remain over its possible

---

2   Associated Press, 'UN Chief Urges Myanmar to End Military Operations in Rohingya Crisis', *The Guardian*, 29 September 2017, www.theguardian.com/world/2017/sep/28/un-chief-calls-for-end-to-myanmar-military-operations-in-rohingya-crisis.

3   *Myanmar: A New Muslim Insurgency in Rakhine State*, Asia Report No.283 (Yangon/Brussels: International Crisis Group, 15 December 2016), www.crisisgroup.org/asia/south-east-asia/myanmar/283-myanmar-new-muslim-insurgency-rakhine-state.

connections with other extremist groups.[4] Also, as the ICG has warned, there is the potential for the Rohingya crisis to be exploited by foreign terrorists and for them to launch attacks both in Myanmar and abroad.[5]

Naypyidaw is not alone in taking such threats seriously. Regional governments have expressed concern over the emergence of a new Rohingya militant group and the spread of religious violence.[6] Quite apart from the presence in Thailand, Malaysia, India and elsewhere of thousands of exiled Rohingyas, South and Southeast Asia's Muslim communities have reacted strongly to the harsh treatment accorded their co-religionists in Myanmar.[7]

After what appears to have been a rather confused response to the initial ARSA attacks,[8] Myanmar's security forces have reportedly implemented a comprehensive 'four cuts' counterinsurgency strategy to deprive the militants of food, funds, intelligence and recruits.[9] As seen elsewhere in Myanmar, this is essentially a scorched-earth policy under which villages are burned, crops destroyed, minefields laid and populations displaced.

A second school of foreign observers has seen this strategy as a massive overreaction to a minor threat from a small band of poorly armed and ill-trained Rohingya exiles and their local supporters, driven to act by decades of institutionalised persecution by successive Myanmar governments. Indeed, an ARSA military victory was never a realistic proposition, suggesting that its leaders deliberately provoked an excessive response by the security forces to attract international attention and raise support for the Rohingya cause.

---

4   'ARSA Linked to Foreign Extremist Groups: Bertil Lintner', *The Irrawaddy*, 22 September 2017, www.irrawaddy.com/news/burma/arsa-linked-foreign-extremist-groups-bertil-lintner.html.
5   'The Rakhine State Danger to Myanmar's Transition', Media statement, International Crisis Group, Yangon/Brussels, 8 September 2017, www.crisisgroup.org/asia/south-east-asia/myanmar/rakhine-state-danger-myanmars-transition.
6   Nyshka Chandran, 'Terror Groups May Take Advantage of Myanmar's Rohingya Crisis', *CNBC*, 13 September 2017, www.cnbc.com/2017/09/13/myanmar-rohingya-crisis-islamic-terror-groups-may-take-advantage.html.
7   Basma Elbaz, 'Myanmar … Terrorism Hotbed in the Making', *The Huffington Post*, 17 September 2017, www.huffingtonpost.com/entry/myanmarterrorism-hotbed-in-the-making_us_59bd6fd4e4b02c642e4a1717.
8   Antoni Slodkowski, Wa Lone, Simon Lewis and Krishna Das, 'Rohingya Exodus: How a Two-Week Army Crackdown Reignited Myanmar's Rohingya Crisis', *Reuters Investigates*, 25 April 2017, www.reuters.com/investigates/special-report/myanmar-rohingya-crisis2/.
9   Andray Abrahamian, 'The Tatmadaw Returns to the "Four Cuts" Doctrine', *The Interpreter*, 4 September 2017, www.lowyinstitute.org/the-interpreter/tadmadaw-ominous-return-four-cuts-doctrine.

Also, ARSA's leadership knew that anti-Muslim feelings were rife in Myanmar and the Rohingyas were reviled as illegal Bengali immigrants. Whether or not Naypyidaw gave specific orders to terrorise Rohingya communities, ARSA would have known from other conflicts in Myanmar that poor leadership and lax discipline, combined with racial and religious prejudices, would lead to widespread human rights abuses.[10] It doubtless anticipated that this, too, would generate international sympathy for the Rohingyas.

A third school of analysts believes that the generals seized on the ARSA attacks in 2016 to launch a long-term plan to expel all Rohingyas from northern Rakhine State.[11] A second round of ARSA attacks in August 2017 gave this strategy of 'ethnic cleansing' added impetus. It has been suggested that, under such a plan, the Rohingyas were to be driven into Bangladesh and physical obstacles such as barbed-wire fences and minefields put in place to prevent their return.[12]

According to this theory, any Rohingyas able to survive the stringent citizenship 'verification process'[13] and cleared to return to Myanmar would be resettled further south, where they would be less susceptible to manipulation by Bangladesh-based extremists. The Rohingya lands left vacant in the north could be reallocated to Rakhine Buddhists. This would create a *cordon sanitaire* between Myanmar and Bangladesh populated by Naypyidaw loyalists and organised into local militias to provide additional security.

The fourth school consists of those popular pundits who insist on seeing the Rohingya crisis in terms of a global conspiracy. A few have even described it as a proxy war between the great powers, with the US (helped by its

---

10   'They Tried to Kill Us All': Atrocity Crimes against Rohingya Muslims in Rakhine State, Myanmar, Bearing Witness Report (Washington, DC: Simon-Skjodt Centre for the Prevention of Genocide and Fortify Rights, November 2017), www.fortifyrights.org/downloads/THEY_TRIED_TO_KILL_US_ALL_Atrocity_Crimes_against_Rohingya_Muslims_Nov_2017.pdf?ct=t(Fortify_Rights_USHMM_New_Report11_14_2017)&mc_cid=25c9323497&mc_eid=0bd7a6922f.

11   'Myanmar Violence a Deliberate Strategy to Expel Rohingya, United Nations Says', ABC News, 12 October 2017, www.abc.net.au/news/2017-10-12/myanmar-violence-deliberate-straegy-to-expel-rohingya-un-says/9042884.

12   Krishna N. Das, 'Burma Laying Landmines Near Bangladesh Border "To Prevent Return of Rohingya Muslims"', Independent, [London], 6 September 2017, www.independent.co.uk/news/world/asia/burma-rohingya-muslims-landmines-bangladesh-border-prevent-return-dhaka-persecution-genocide-a7931576.html.

13   Alyssa Ayres, 'Repatriating "Verified" Rohingya: Don't Hold Your Breath', Asia Unbound Blogs (New York: Council on Foreign Relations, 4 October 2017), www.cfr.org/blog/repatriating-verified-rohingya-dont-hold-your-breath.

ally Saudi Arabia) somehow using the Rohingyas to undermine China's influence in Myanmar.[14] Another commentator has suggested that the US and the EU precipitated the crisis to interfere in the internal affairs of Myanmar, which was described as a US 'client state'.[15]

No serious observers entertain such far-fetched notions. However, the other explanations put forward to account for the behaviour of the army and police deserve consideration.

It would be surprising if the *Tatmadaw*'s high command was not exploiting the Rohingya crisis for its own purposes. The generals are already flexing their muscles in Naypyidaw, reminding Aung San Suu Kyi's government of the armed forces' continuing key role in national affairs.[16] They are also capitalising on anti-Muslim sentiments in Myanmar to reinforce their claim to be the defenders of the country's majority Buddhist culture. And a long-term solution to the 'Rohingya problem' has always been a high priority.

Regardless of whether the *Tatmadaw*'s strategy has been dictated by genuine security concerns, crude nativism, political opportunism or a secret plan to permanently change the ethnic balance of northern Rakhine State, one thing is clear: Myanmar's security forces are determined to pursue their own agenda. Aung San Suu Kyi may be responsive to foreign demands for more humane policies, but the generals are unlikely to change their long-term goals because of anything the international community might say or do.

---

14   Moon of Alabama, 'The Rohingya of Myanmar: Pawns in an Anglo-Chinese Proxy War Fought by Saudi Jihadists', *Global Research*, 4 September 2017, www.globalresearch.ca/the-rohingya-of-myanmar-pawns-in-an-anglo-chinese-proxy-war-fought-by-saudi-jihadists/5607605.
15   Tony Cartalucci, 'Shifting Blame as US Agenda Unfolds in Myanmar', *New Eastern Outlook*, 25 October 2017, journal-neo.org/2017/10/25/shifting-blame-as-us-agenda-unfolds-in-myanmar/.
16   Andrew Selth, 'A Big Step Back for Myanmar', *The Interpreter*, 13 September 2017, www.lowy institute.org/the-interpreter/step-back-myanmar.

2018

91

The Rohingya question: Determining whom to hold to account

(09:30 AEDT, 20 April 2018)

The brutal treatment meted out to the Rohingyas by Myanmar's security forces raised a number of questions about the legal culpability of those involved. However, despite clear indications that Myanmar had repeatedly acted contrary to international humanitarian law, the international community had few realistic options and there was little likelihood that anyone would be held to account.

Ever since the 1988 prodemocracy uprising, ethnic minority groups, human rights advocates and others have argued that Myanmar's armed forces (or *Tatmadaw*) should be held legally accountable for a wide range of offences. Their concerns were dramatically highlighted in late 2016 and 2017, after the *Tatmadaw* and police launched 'area clearance operations' against the mainly Muslim Rohingya minority in northern Rakhine State.

More than 650,000 refugees were driven into Bangladesh. These events prompted calls for the Myanmar Government and security forces to be brought before an international tribunal for crimes against humanity, including ethnic cleansing and genocide.[1]

---

1   'UN Myanmar Expert Wants Genocide Investigation', *US News*, 9 March 2018, www.usnews. com/news/world/articles/2018-03-09/un-myanmar-expert-wants-genocide-investigation.

For decades, Myanmar's military leaders have been haunted by the prospect that, one day, they may lose the power to control events and be brought before a court to account for their actions. These fears have been heightened by periodic attempts by the UN Human Rights Council and other bodies to investigate crimes in violation of humanitarian law committed in Myanmar.[2]

To date, international scrutiny, pressure and diplomatic engagement have not resulted in any meaningful changes. Those implicated in human rights violations have effectively enjoyed impunity. Due to the latest Rohingya crisis, however, pressure to hold them in some way criminally accountable is mounting.

Should this matter ever come before an international court, many issues will need to be considered.[3] Most will relate directly to the atrocities perpetrated against the Rohingyas and those who ordered them and carried them out. However, the tribunal would also need to consider a range of issues to do with the *Tatmadaw*'s organisation and structure, its training and ethos and, most importantly, issues relating to command and control.

Given the dearth of reliable information available about the *Tatmadaw*, the consideration of such matters will be difficult. However, they could prove critical to questions of culpability and thus ultimate responsibility for the actions of the security forces in Rakhine State.

The *Tatmadaw* is a 'fully functioning military', as the term is popularly understood.[4] It has a clearly defined organisation, a logical division of specialist responsibilities, a hierarchical rank structure and an identifiable chain of command. It has a tested system of internal communications and a recognisable disciplinary code. It can also be described as effective, in that it is able to convert its diverse resources into combat power.

---

2   'Myanmar' (Geneva: United Nations Human Rights, Office of the UN High Commissioner for Human Rights), www.ohchr.org/EN/Countries/AsiaRegion/Pages/MMIndex.aspx.
3   *Myanmar: Questions and Answers on Human Rights Law in Rakhine State*, ICJ Global Redress and Accountability Initiative Briefing Note (Geneva: International Commission of Jurists, November 2017), www.burmalibrary.org/docs23/ICJ-2017-11-Rakhine-Advocacy-Briefing-Paper-2017-en-.pdf.
4   Andrew Selth, *'Strong, Fully Efficient and Modern': Myanmar's New Look Armed Forces*, Griffith Asia Institute Regional Outlook Paper No.49 (Brisbane: Griffith University, 2015), www.griffith.edu.au/__data/assets/pdf_file/0017/118313/Regional-Outlook-Paper-49-Selth-web.pdf.

However, the question must be asked: who is responsible for the behaviour of troops in the field? The easy answer is the commander-in-chief. In practice, however, the exercise of military power in Myanmar—and, in the recent case of the Rohingyas, its gross misuse—tends to be more complicated.

There are, in effect, two *Tatmadaw*s. One operates according to formal structures and regulations and places a high value on patriotism, professionalism and personal integrity. Its members are enjoined to observe both military and civil laws and to 'preserve the noble dignity of the *Tatmadaw*'.[5]

The other *Tatmadaw* operates from day to day according to a more informal set of rules and practices that allows for considerable flexibility, including in the observance of military directives and humanitarian law. Particularly during operations against ethnic minorities and the Rohingyas there is a high degree of tolerance, at all levels, of egregious human rights abuses.

Abuse victims and activist groups believe that human rights violations in Myanmar are official policy, ordered by the *Tatmadaw*'s high command. They argue that troops on operations are told to commit atrocities as deliberate acts of psychological warfare, to undermine the morale of the opposing forces, to intimidate noncombatants or to force them to leave contested areas.

This has given rise to the oft-repeated claim that atrocities like rape are used as 'weapons of war'.[6] In the case of the Rohingyas in Rakhine State, the systematic nature of the abuses, and the similarity between atrocities perpetrated in different locations, has encouraged the view that they are directed from Naypyidaw.

It is not difficult to find evidence of abuses being committed by soldiers and policemen in Myanmar, but it is difficult to find hard evidence of them specifically being ordered to do so. This is not surprising in the circumstances, but it does argue for caution in claiming that systematic state terror has been and is routinely used by the *Tatmadaw*'s high command to achieve strategic goals.

---

5   'Tatmadaw Has Bounden Duty to Safeguard State's Independence and Sovereignty', *Eleven*, 2 December 2017, www.elevenmyanmar.com/politics/12632 [page discontinued].
6   Shayna Bauchner, 'Rape Puts Myanmar Army on UN "List of Shame"', *Dispatches* (New York: Human Rights Watch, 16 April 2018), www.hrw.org/news/2018/04/16/rape-puts-myanmar-army-un-list-shame.

Certainly, that appears to be the implicit thinking behind the harsh 'four cuts' strategy, as demonstrated in many parts of Myanmar over decades.[7] Also, even if orders are not given, the widespread tolerance of abuses and consistent failure of the military system to punish those guilty of such crimes must encourage them.

In any case, one thing is clear. The latest pogrom against the Rohingyas has been a disaster for everyone.[8] Quite apart from the Rohingyas themselves—more than half a million of whom seem destined to remain in squalid refugee camps in Bangladesh for the foreseeable future—no one has benefited from the events of the past 18 months. Aung San Suu Kyi, her government, the armed forces and the people of Myanmar have all lost, in different ways.

Despite the promise of a more democratic, humane and prosperous society following the 2015 elections, the country has stepped back into its dark past. This poses real challenges for the international community. For decades, successive governments in Myanmar have strongly resisted external pressures to adopt or adapt particular policies. There are no signs that this record will change in the foreseeable future.

Indeed, with regard to the Rohingyas, there is a rare consensus between the government, armed forces and population that will strengthen Naypyidaw's determination to decide its own agenda and timetable for any changes.[9] Unless there are significant shifts in attitude inside Myanmar—which seems unlikely—a fair, durable and long-term solution to the 'Rohingya question', let alone a formal legal accounting for the events of the past 18 months, will remain a distant prospect.

This article draws from a forthcoming report to be published by the US Institute of Peace, Myanmar's Armed Forces and the Rohingya Crisis.

---

7   Andray Abrahamian, 'The Tatmadaw Returns to the "Four Cuts" Doctrine', *The Interpreter*, 4 September 2017, www.lowyinstitute.org/the-interpreter/tadmadaw-ominous-return-four-cuts-doctrine.

8   Andrew Selth, 'A Big Step Back for Myanmar', *The Interpreter*, 13 September 2017, www.lowy institute.org/the-interpreter/step-back-myanmar.

9   *Myanmar's Rohingya Crisis Enters a Dangerous New Phase*, Asia Report No.292 (Brussels: International Crisis Group, 7 December 2017), www.crisisgroup.org/asia/south-east-asia/myanmar/292-myanmars-rohingya-crisis-enters-dangerous-new-phase.

92

The Rohingyas: A new terrorist threat?

(06:00 AEDT, 6 September 2018)

The Rohingya crisis of 2016–17 sparked widespread fears of an increased terrorist threat, both in the region and beyond. There were worries that some of the refugees in Bangladesh would become radicalised, that they would be recruited by extremists based elsewhere and that foreign Islamist groups would conduct fresh attacks in their name.

(This is the final in a series of three articles on the Rohingya crisis, featuring Morten Pedersen[1] on the domestic drivers of conflict and Nicholas Farrelly on the consequences for neighbouring Bangladesh.[2])

There have been a small number of militant Muslim groups in Myanmar, but they were usually weak and disorganised. A few had tenuous international links, mainly to Islamists in South Asia, but these ties had no appreciable impact on their goals or operational capabilities. When international groups recruited Rohingyas, as they did occasionally, they tended to be from exile communities in countries such as Pakistan.

---

1   Morten B. Pedersen, 'No Safe Return for Rohingya Refugees', *The Interpreter*, 4 September 2018, www.lowyinstitute.org/the-interpreter/no-safe-return-rohingrea-refugees.

2   Nicholas Farrelly, 'The Rohingya Are Stuck', *The Interpreter*, 5 September 2018, www.lowy institute.org/the-interpreter/rohingya-are-stuck.

Most Rohingyas in Myanmar kept their heads down and tried to avoid being noticed by the central and Rakhine State governments and the local Buddhist population.[3] Their focus was on staying alive and, if possible, improving their lot, not the overthrow of the regime. Indeed, most Rohingyas saw violence as counterproductive.

In 2012, however, an outbreak of sectarian violence in Rakhine State encouraged the formation of the Arakan Rohingya Salvation Army (ARSA) by a group of Rohingya exiles. Its attacks against Myanmar's security forces in the state's north in 2016 and 2017, and the subsequent exodus of more than 750,000 Rohingyas to Bangladesh, dramatically changed the picture.

These developments have prompted three questions:

1. Are more Rohingyas, either inside Myanmar or outside it, likely to be radicalised by recent events and turn to terrorism?
2. Are Rohingyas and their supporters likely to be recruited by international Islamist groups for terrorist activities?
3. Will Islamist groups, both in the region and further afield, take up the Rohingya cause and launch terrorist campaigns with their plight in mind?

Violent extremism stems from a kaleidoscope of factors, creating infinite individual combinations.[4] However, it is possible to identify several factors that are usually found in processes of political radicalisation. Specific circumstances such as the presence of a charismatic preacher or recruiter can be critical.

---

3   Andrew Selth, *Burma's Muslims: Terrorists or Terrorised?*, Canberra Papers on Strategy and Defence No.150 (Canberra: Strategic and Defence Studies Centre, The Australian National University, 2003), sdsc.bellschool.anu.edu.au/sites/default/files/publications/attachments/2016-03/150_Burma's_Muslims__Terrorists_or_Terrorised_%28Canberra_Papers_on_Strategy_and_Defence%2C_150%29__p_073155437X_0.pdf.
4   Magnus Ranstorp, *The Root Causes of Violent Extremism*, RAN Issues Paper (Amsterdam: Radicalisation Awareness Network Centre of Excellence, 4 January 2016), ec.europa.eu/home-affairs/sites/homeaffairs/files/what-we-do/networks/radicalisation_awareness_network/ran-papers/docs/issue_paper_root-causes_jan2016_en.pdf.

Looking at the refugees in Bangladesh, almost every factor identified by radicalisation experts can be found, to a greater or lesser degree. This is partly due to the harsh treatment of the Rohingyas before 2016, but much more so as a result of their brutal expulsion from Myanmar—described by the UN as ethnic cleansing and probably genocide.[5]

This has made the Rohingya refugee camps in Bangladesh potential breeding grounds for extremism.

Counting the 250,000 Rohingya refugees in Bangladesh before 2016, there are now over one million desperate and effectively stateless people living in squalid camps, entirely dependent on foreign aid. Despite discussions between Naypyidaw and Dhaka, there is no chance they will be repatriated soon, even if it was safe for them to return home.

The refugees—a large proportion of them women and children—currently seem preoccupied with their daily survival. There are no obvious signs that they are about to embark on an international campaign of violence. However, it would only take a very small percentage of them to be radicalised for there to be a major security problem.

As the ICG has stated, ARSA does not appear to have a pan-Islamist narrative.[6] Also, ARSA has been at pains to emphasise that it 'has no link with any terrorist group around the world'.[7] Even so, questions remain over ARSA's external connections.

There have been reports of 'a smattering of foreigners' in ARSA's ranks, hailing from South, Southeast and Central Asia.[8] Also, several observers have pointed out circumstantial links between ARSA and other extremist groups, including global organisations such as Islamic State of Iraq and Syria (ISIS) and Al Qaeda.

---

5   *Independent International Fact-Finding Mission on Myanmar* (Geneva: United Nations Human Rights Council, 2017–19), www.ohchr.org/en/hrbodies/hrc/myanmarffm/pages/index.aspx.
6   *Myanmar: A New Muslim Insurgency in Rakhine State*, Asia Report No.283 (Yangon/Brussels: International Crisis Group, 15 December 2016), www.crisisgroup.org/asia/south-east-asia/myanmar/283-myanmar-new-muslim-insurgency-rakhine-state.
7   Arakan Rohingya Salvation Army, Press release, *Rohingya Blogger*, 29 March 2017, www.rohingyablogger.com/2017/03/statement-of-arakan-rohingya-salvation.html?zx=3dadbfa57ab523a7.
8   Nirmal Ghosh, 'Myanmar's "Bengali Problem" Threatens to Embroil the Region', *The Straits Times*, [Singapore], 6 September 2017, www.straitstimes.com/opinion/myanmars-bengali-problem-threatens-to-embroil-the-region.

Even if Islamist links to the Rohingyas were marginal before 2016, the potential now exists for them to be developed. There is a risk, too, that radicalised Rohingyas will be recruited by international terrorist groups. Also, Muslim communities in South and Southeast Asia have been outraged by the treatment accorded to their co-religionists in Myanmar, making them vulnerable to Islamist recruiters.

The dire situation in Myanmar and Bangladesh has already attracted the attention of various extremist groups, prompting the former Malaysian prime minister to warn of a serious security threat to the entire region.[9] In Singapore last month, Aung San Suu Kyi pointedly warned that the 'terrorism' that sparked the Rohingya crisis could spread beyond Myanmar.[10]

Before 2016, the Rohingyas' plight was not a major concern for Islamist groups, but the dramatic events of the past two years and the publicity given to the refugees are prompting greater attention. There is also the possibility that foreign fighters may be attracted to the region, as occurred in the Philippines, to open new Islamist fronts.[11]

In addition to ISIS and Al Qaeda, most South and Southeast Asian extremist groups have already been linked to the latest Rohingya crisis in some way.[12] For example, there have been media reports of hundreds of jihadists from regional countries training for terrorist operations in Myanmar or being put on standby to go to Bangladesh.

It is not clear whether any of these reports are accurate, but the possibility of increased terrorist activity in the region on behalf of the Rohingyas needs to be taken seriously.

---

9   'ASEAN Summit: IS Could Exploit Rohingya—Malaysian PM', *SBS News*, 17 March 2018, www.sbs.com.au/news/asean-summit-is-could-exploit-rohingya-malaysian-pm.
10   Aaron Low, 'Rohingya Crisis: Terrorism May Spread Beyond Myanmar, Suu Kyi Warns', [This Week in Asia], *South China Morning Post*, [Hong Kong], 21 August 2018, www.scmp.com/week-asia/politics/article/2160716/rohingya-crisis-terrorism-may-spread-beyond-myanmar-suu-kyi-warns.
11   Nyshka Chandran, 'Terror Groups May Take Advantage of Myanmar's Rohingya Crisis', *CNBC*, 13 September 2017, www.cnbc.com/2017/09/13/myanmar-rohingya-crisis-islamic-terror-groups-may-take-advantage.html.
12   Francis Chan, 'ISIS, Al-Qaeda Drawn to Crisis in Rakhine Strait', *The Straits Times*, [Singapore], 20 September 2017, www.straitstimes.com/asia/se-asia/isis-al-qaeda-drawn-to-crisis-in-rakhine-state.

The ICG believes the Rohingya crisis is a 'game changer' for Myanmar. The violence in Rakhine State in 2016 and 2017 was qualitatively different from anything seen before.[13] It also occurred in a more interconnected world, with a greater potential to influence others. It has already changed the region's strategic environment.

An increased terrorist threat is not inevitable—if the Rohingya crisis is handled sensitively, adequate practical assistance is provided and the refugees in Bangladesh are given reason to hope for meaningful change. Such measures would not eliminate the danger of future terrorist attacks, but they could significantly reduce it.

Unfortunately, there are no signs of anything happening along those lines. Hundreds of thousands of Rohingyas are doomed to remain in Bangladesh for the foreseeable future, under terrible conditions, with all the attendant risks of radicalisation and exploitation, in Myanmar and beyond.

---

13   Andrew Selth, *Myanmar's Armed Forces and the Rohingya Crisis*, Peaceworks Report No.140 (Washington, DC: US Institute of Peace, August 2018), www.usip.org/sites/default/files/2018-08/ pw140-myanmars-armed-forces-and-the-rohingya-crisis.pdf.

2019

93

Myanmar's intelligence apparatus under Aung San Suu Kyi

(10:00 AEDT, 12 April 2019)

Under Aung San Suu Kyi, Myanmar's intelligence apparatus seems to have remained much as it was before the transition to a mixed civilian–military government in 2011. There have been changes in the way the intelligence agencies operate, but these appear to have been shifts in manner and style, rather than in substance. All the key agencies remain under the control, directly or indirectly, of the armed forces commander-in-chief.

When Aung San Suu Kyi and the NLD took office in 2016, a wave of euphoria swept over Myanmar—shared by many people in other parts of the world.

At the time, there was a rather naive belief that everything would suddenly be transformed. It was widely assumed, for example, that the key components of the old regime would be dismantled and the repressive military government that had ruled the country for the past half-century would soon become a bad memory.

That has not happened and was never going to happen.

It might have helped the pundits to keep in mind veteran Myanmar-watcher Robert Taylor's observation that military intelligence had always served as a means of social control in Myanmar, to ask whether and how the NLD planned to depart from this pattern and whether the armed forces (known as the *Tatmadaw*) would allow this to occur. As expected, Aung San Suu Kyi has faced many of the same challenges as the military regime but, to the surprise of many, she has relied on similar mechanisms and methods to tackle them.

Indeed, eight years after the armed forces stepped back from direct rule, and despite promises of sweeping reforms, there are few indications that Myanmar's approach to security matters has significantly changed. The vast intelligence apparatus that underpinned military rule is still in place. It is no longer dominated by the military agencies but, either directly or indirectly, it is still controlled by the *Tatmadaw*. There have been changes in the way the intelligence apparatus operates, but these have been more shifts in manner and style than in substance.[1]

For example, there is now a greater reliance on the use of quasilegal, rather than extralegal, means to enforce tight controls over Myanmar's citizens and society.[2] Indeed, a few observers have suggested that in some respects individual freedoms are more restricted under the NLD than they were under former administrations.[3] Also, the extraordinary increase in the use of mobile telephones and the internet in Myanmar has encouraged the intelligence agencies to rely more on electronic monitoring and manipulation of the population, rather than its network of spies and informers.

The intelligence apparatus still displays many of the characteristics that made it a powerful and feared arm of the military regime before Myanmar's adoption of a quasi-civilian government in 2011. In some areas of the country—notably, Rakhine, Kachin and Shan states—the key agencies have demonstrated a continuing commitment to the *Tatmadaw*'s narrow and uncompromising vision of a unitary, compliant and independent Myanmar, dominated by ethnic Burman Buddhists.[4]

1   Karin Dean, 'Myanmar: Surveillance and the Turn from Authoritarianism?', *Surveillance and Society*, Vol.15, No.3–4, 2017, pp.496–505, doi.org/10.24908/ss.v15i3/4.6648.
2   Victoria Milko, 'In Aung San Suu Kyi's Myanmar, Free Press Hopes Wither', *Al Jazeera*, 12 December 2018, www.aljazeera.com/news/2018/12/aung-san-suu-kyi-myanmar-free-press-hopes-wither-181207065931858.html.
3   *Dashed Hopes: The Criminalization of Free Expression in Myanmar* (New York: Human Rights Watch, 31 January 2019), www.hrw.org/report/2019/01/31/dashed-hopes/criminalization-peaceful-expression-myanmar.
4   Andrew Selth, *Myanmar's Armed Forces and the Rohingya Crisis*, Peaceworks Report No.140 (Washington, DC: US Institute of Peace, August 2018), www.usip.org/sites/default/files/2018-08/pw140-myanmars-armed-forces-and-the-rohingya-crisis.pdf.

Aung San Suu Kyi's relationship with the armed forces and the national intelligence apparatus is a complicated one. As State Counsellor, she is the de facto leader of Myanmar and, in her own words, acts 'above the President'. However, she has little actual control over the country's extensive security apparatus, almost all elements of which answer, directly or indirectly, to Senior General Min Aung Hlaing, the *Tatmadaw*'s powerful Commander-in-Chief (C-in-C).

Under the terms of the 2008 constitution, the C-in-C appoints the Minister for Defence, who controls the Office of the Chief of Military Security Affairs (OCMSA). He appoints the Minister for Home Affairs, who has responsibility for the MPF's Special Branch and the ministry's Bureau of Special Investigations. The C-in-C also appoints the Minister for Border Affairs, who manages other intelligence assets. All three ministers are serving military officers.[5]

Aung San Suu Kyi is also the Minister for Foreign Affairs and, as such, is responsible for Myanmar's diplomatic service and overseas missions. This gives her a say in the collection and analysis of open-source intelligence, but the country's defence attachés are controlled by the *Tatmadaw* and the activities of intelligence officers posted abroad (some under diplomatic cover) are usually guided by OCMSA or the Special Branch. She thus cannot be held directly responsible for the behaviour of most elements of Myanmar's intelligence apparatus.

Indeed, Aung San Suu Kyi seems to have adopted a strategy of bypassing the apparatus as much as possible and avoiding any circumstances in which she can be held to account for its behaviour. Even in terms of briefings, it appears that she has tried to put some distance between herself and the intelligence agencies. It is not known what intelligence product she routinely receives as the State Counsellor, but she has made it clear that she wants to tap into independent sources of data and assessments.

The appointment of a career diplomat as her national security advisor in 2017, for example, seems to be in part at least an attempt to reduce her reliance on the military-dominated national intelligence apparatus. His responsibility is 'to advise the President and the Union Government on

---

5   Andrew Selth, 'Myanmar's Intelligence State', *Australian Outlook*, Weblog of the Australian Institute of International Affairs, Sydney, 20 September 2018, www.internationalaffairs.org.au/australianoutlook/myanmars-intelligence-state/.

internal and external threats, by assessing situations from a strategic point of view'.[6] It is not clear, however, how this role differs from those of other ministers or government agencies.

There has been some progress in 'civilianising' internal security in recent years, but the NLD does not seem to have given serious consideration to restructuring the intelligence system to make it more accountable and reflective of the transition to a more democratic form of government.[7] Also, despite her earlier calls for universal human rights and the rule of law, Aung San Suu Kyi has shown little inclination to curb the excesses of the intelligence apparatus or to change the way Myanmar's laws are being misused to silence dissent.

That said, Aung San Suu Kyi's ability to change Myanmar's current security arrangements is very limited. When the 2008 constitution was being drafted, the armed forces were careful to ensure that control of the country's coercive apparatus, including its main intelligence agencies, would remain under the C-in-C. Significant changes to the constitution, while a longstanding goal of the NLD, are very difficult to achieve. This is likely to remain the case, leaving intelligence matters firmly in the hands of the armed forces for the foreseeable future.

---

6   Prashanth Parawesmaran, 'What's Behind Myanmar's New National Security Adviser Post?', *The Diplomat*, [Washington, DC], 11 January 2017, thediplomat.com/2017/01/whats-behind-myanmars-new-national-security-adviser-post/.
7   Andrew Selth, *Be Careful What You Wish For: The National League for Democracy and Government in Myanmar*, Griffith Asia Institute Regional Outlook Paper No.56 (Brisbane: Griffith University, 2017), www.griffith.edu.au/__data/assets/pdf_file/0012/1087977/Regional-Outlook-Paper-56-Selth-web.pdf [page discontinued].

94

Myanmar: Pariah status no bar to defence modernisation

(15:00 AEDT, 7 May 2019)

Despite widespread condemnation of Myanmar's armed forces for their brutal 'area clearance operations' against the Rohingyas and other ethnic groups, the Tatmadaw *continues to acquire modern arms and develop the country's defence industries. Geostrategic and commercial considerations on the part of Myanmar's neighbours and friends clearly trumped any concerns expressed over its violations of international law and universal human rights.*

It has been more than two years since military 'clearance operations' against Myanmar's Rohingyas began in October 2016. Since then, the international community has relied on public criticism, unilateral sanctions and a range of measures in the UN and the International Criminal Court to hold Myanmar's government and armed forces (known as the *Tatmadaw*) accountable for their actions.

Myanmar's political and military leaders have refused to acknowledge the crimes committed in Rakhine State—described by UN officials as ethnic cleansing, if not genocide.[1] As it has done so often in the past, Naypyidaw seems to be relying on the weakness of the international system and the passage of time to escape any serious consequences.

From the lack of effective measures taken against Myanmar to date, this strategy seems to be working.[2]

Indeed, a survey of recent security developments reveals that, despite all the criticisms levelled against it, the sanctions introduced and the embargoes imposed, Myanmar is still strengthening its defence relations with neighbours and friends and the *Tatmadaw* is continuing to acquire modern arms.

Since the advent of a 'disciplined democracy' in Myanmar in 2011, China has sold it two Jianghu II–class frigates, 76 Type-92 armoured vehicles, 12 CASC CH-4 unmanned aerial vehicles and up to 16 CAC/PAC JF-17 fighters, at an estimated cost of almost US$1 billion (A$1.6 billion).[3] Most of these arms have already been delivered. The first four JF-17s were commissioned by the Myanmar Air Force in December 2018.

The JF-17 was jointly developed with Pakistan, which has joined in criticism of Myanmar over its treatment of the Muslim Rohingyas. However, this does not appear to have affected the current contract. Two two-seater JF-17B training variants were delivered to Myanmar in March this year.

Since 2016, the Myanmar Air Force has also received 12 Yakovlev Yak-130 jet trainers from Russia, with a reported four more due for delivery. In October 2017, four of the Myanmar Air Force's Mil Mi-24P helicopter gunships were serviced in Russia. In January 2018, Myanmar and Russia agreed on the sale of six Sukhoi Su-30 multirole fighters. The contract is reportedly worth about US$204 million (A$321 million).

---

1   'Prosecute Myanmar Army Chief for Rohingya "Genocide": UN Envoy', *Al Jazeera*, 25 January 2019, www.aljazeera.com/news/2019/1/25/prosecute-myanmar-army-chief-for-rohingya-genocide-un-envoy.

2   Asia Pacific Centre for the Responsibility to Protect and University of Queensland, 'Regional Atrocity Risk Assessment', *Asia Pacific Regional Outlook*, No.11, April 2019, r2pasiapacific.org/files/3292/AsiaPacificOutlookV11%20FINAL.pdf.

3   'How Dominant is China in the Global Arms Trade?', *China Power* (Washington, DC: Center for Strategic and International Studies, 2018), chinapower.csis.org/china-global-arms-trade/.

In December 2018, it was announced that India would donate six HAL HJT-16 Kiran jet trainers to the Myanmar Air Force and station a team in Myanmar to help train their pilots and ground crew. India has also agreed to help Myanmar's army and navy upgrade their arms and equipment as part of an expanding defence partnership.[4] It is currently considering the sale of offshore patrol boats to the Myanmar Navy.

Last year, the Myanmar Air Force commissioned two French/Italian ATR 72-500 transport aircraft and an Airbus AS365 Eurocopter. They were purchased despite EU arms embargoes, suggesting that the sale involved a third party. While both types are designated as civilian aircraft, the *Tatmadaw* has stated that they will be used to upgrade Myanmar's defence capabilities.[5]

Shortly before the Rohingya crisis began, Israel agreed to provide the Myanmar Navy with four or more Super-Dvora Mk III gunboats. Despite an international outcry against the sale, it went ahead, with the first two boats being delivered in April 2017. According to media reports, the contract is part of a broader defence relationship.[6]

In some cases, with foreign help, Myanmar's defence industries are continuing to produce a wide range of arms and equipment, including armoured vehicles, missiles and naval vessels.[7]

In March this year, it was announced that Ukrspecexport, Ukraine's military import/export agency, had signed a joint-venture agreement with Myanmar to build a plant capable of manufacturing BTR-4U wheeled armoured personnel carriers and 2S1U Gvozdika self-propelled howitzers.[8] The new facility is due to start production in late 2020.

4   Bibhu Prasad Routray, 'India's Defence Diplomacy with Myanmar: State of Play', *Mantraya*, 30 January 2019, mantraya.org/analysis-indias-defence-diplomacy-with-myanmar-state-of-play/.

5   Thomas Kean, 'Despite EU Embargo, Tatmadaw Buys European Aircraft', *Frontier Myanmar*, 9 January 2019, frontiermyanmar.net/en/despite-eu-embargo-tatmadaw-buys-european-aircraft.

6   Ali Abunimah, 'Myanmar Shows Off Its Israeli Weapons', *The Electronic Intifada*, 23 October 2017, electronicintifada.net/blogs/ali-abunimah/myanmar-shows-its-israeli-weapons.

7   'Myanmar Navy Commissions Seven Vessels to Commemorate 71st Anniversary', *The Global New Light of Myanmar*, [Yangon], 25 December 2018, www.globalnewlightofmyanmar.com/myanmar-navy-commissions-seven-vessels-to-commemorate-71st-anniversary/.

8   Bertil Lintner, 'Myanmar, Ukrainian Firm Ink Arms Plant Deal', *Asia Times*, [Hong Kong], 9 March 2019, www.asiatimes.com/2019/03/article/myanmar-ukrainian-firm-ink-arms-plant-deal/.

Myanmar has also been engaged in an active program of defence diplomacy. Senior *Tatmadaw* officers have made visits overseas and several foreign officials have visited Myanmar.[9]

Myanmar has participated in several naval exercises, including one with China in 2017, another with ASEAN (and 10 other invitees) the same year and two more with India, in 2018 and 2019. Warships from China, India and Russia have made port calls. Earlier this year, frigates from Vietnam and Brunei both made their first 'friendship visits' to Myanmar. In March, a Myanmar Navy vessel attended the seventieth anniversary celebrations for China's People's Liberation Army Navy.

All these developments underscore three enduring characteristics of Myanmar's foreign relations and defence policies.

First, geostrategic and commercial considerations on the part of Myanmar's neighbours and friends trump any concerns expressed over its violations of international law and universal human rights. China and India appear untroubled by the widespread condemnation of the *Tatmadaw* for its harsh treatment of the Rohingyas. Russia, the Ukraine and Israel are still prepared to sell arms to Myanmar if there is a profit to be made.

Second, even under Nobel Peace Prize laureate Aung San Suu Kyi, Myanmar is determined to decide its own policies and set its own priorities, regardless of international opinion. In these circumstances, and bearing in mind the support Myanmar receives in the UN and elsewhere from China and Russia, the international community is quite restricted in what it can do to hold Naypyidaw to account for its appalling treatment of the Rohingyas.

Third, regardless of the widespread condemnation of its military operations in Rakhine State, not to mention atrocities perpetrated in other parts of the country, the *Tatmadaw* is still able to secure funds for its ambitious arms acquisition program and the expansion of its military support

---

9   'Renewed EU Sanctions Don't Affect Us: Military Spokesperson', *The Irrawaddy*, 30 April 2019, www.irrawaddy.com/news/world/renewed-eu-sanctions-dont-affect-us-military-spokesperson.html? fbclid=IwAR190_9AEEWz8agjKJKgDQG3EMdLuwI1qwNeQFOxHjLwoulvdxRHGc2bnqM.

facilities. Myanmar's defence budget increased dramatically just before power was transferred to a quasi-civilian government in 2011, and it has remained high ever since.[10]

This is not to argue against concerted efforts by governments and multilateral organisations to hold Myanmar to account for its actions. Even symbolic gestures are important to uphold the laws and principles of conduct that have been endorsed by the international community. Also, there is still much to be done in practical terms to assist the million or more Rohingya refugees in Bangladesh and elsewhere.

However, expectations regarding the outcomes of such measures must be tempered by an understanding of Myanmar's intense nationalism and determination to conduct its own affairs—a position made easier by the readiness of some countries to help pariah states strengthen their coercive capabilities and escape retribution for unacceptable behaviour.

---

10   'Myanmar: Arms Imports in Constant Prices of 1990', *World Data Atlas*, knoema.com/atlas/Myanmar/Arms-imports.

95

With new coastguard, Myanmar looks to improve maritime security

(06:00 AEDT, 9 September 2019)

A proposal by the Myanmar Ministry of Defence to create a coastguard had wide support from within and outside the region. However, a number of challenges would need to be overcome before the new force could make a significant contribution to both national and international maritime security.

In March this year, Myanmar's Defence Ministry submitted a proposal to parliament to establish a national coastguard.[1] Given strong support for the idea from the main political parties, the armed forces and the public, it is expected that the necessary legislation will be passed without undue delay.

Myanmar is one of the few countries in the wider Asian region that does not already have a coastguard or similar force.[2] Responsibility for maritime security is currently shared between the Myanmar Navy and the Maritime Police, which is a part of the MPF. However, they cannot meet all the demands being made upon them, nor can they provide the operational and diplomatic benefits of a paramilitary coastguard.

1   Htoo Thant, 'Defence Submits Coast Guard Plan to Parliament', *Myanmar Times*, [Yangon], 14 March 2019, www.mmtimes.com/news/defence-submits-coast-guard-plan-parliament.html.
2   Prashanth Parameswaran, *Managing the Rise of Southeast Asia's Coast Guards*, Asia Program Report (Washington, DC: Wilson Centre, February 2019), www.wilsoncenter.org/publication/managing-the-rise-southeast-asias-coast-guards.

The new force's remit would be to help safeguard Myanmar's 1,930-kilometre coastline and 23,070 square kilometres of territorial waters, which include about 1,000 islands.

The coastguard would deal primarily with 'non-traditional security threats', such as human trafficking, narcotics smuggling and terrorism. It would enforce maritime law, conduct search-and-rescue operations, combat piracy, safeguard natural resources, protect the environment, prevent illegal immigration, provide security for offshore oil rigs and their associated infrastructure, assist in disaster relief and secure ports, harbours and jetties.

The coastguard would also help the navy protect Myanmar's national sovereignty and share management of Myanmar's sensitive (and in some areas disputed) maritime borders with Bangladesh, India and Thailand. Myanmar's coastal surveillance radar system reportedly cannot detect any vessel smaller than 300 tonnes, making an enhanced inshore patrol capability particularly welcome.

Outside the country's territorial waters (beyond 22 km), operations would be the responsibility of the navy, with its larger, more capable vessels and combat-trained crews. Myanmar has an exclusive economic zone of 532,775 sq km—in some areas, extending more than 370 km from the mainland.

A coastguard would expand the options available to Myanmar in approaching maritime security issues and permit greater flexibility in responding to particular problems. As analyst Sam Bateman has observed, in many roles, 'a coast guard offers a cost-effective alternative to a navy'.[3]

One potential problem is the future management of maritime security, which in Myanmar involves several agencies. It is envisaged, however, that the navy will take the lead in forming an integrated command centre that can coordinate operations and facilitate information exchanges between the armed forces, Maritime Police, Customs, Immigration, the Marine Administration Department, the Myanmar Port Authority and the Fire Services Department.

---

3   Sam Bateman, *Coast Guards: New Forces for Regional Order and Security*, Asia Pacific Issues No.65 (Honolulu: East–West Center, January 2003), www.eastwestcenter.org/system/tdf/private/api065.pdf?file=1&type=node&id=31902.

It is interesting that the proposal for a coastguard was put to parliament by the Defence Ministry. It had been speculated that, as part of its efforts to 'civilianise' security affairs, Aung San Suu Kyi's government would put the new force under the Ministry of Transport and Communications or even the President's Office. Some officials still insist the coastguard will be under civilian control, with the navy merely exercising a coordinating role.

That may eventually occur, but the 2008 constitution clearly states that all armed forces in Myanmar fall under the control of the Chief of Defence Services, and the coastguard will doubtless be lightly armed. Also, it could not operate effectively without the help of the navy. Ideally, the creation of the force will prompt the emergence of a new level of cooperation between civilian and military agencies, but that cannot be guaranteed.

There are other challenges to consider, such as how the coastguard will be funded, equipped and manned.

In recent years, the navy has been investing heavily in modern warships and more sophisticated weapon systems, and it is keen to acquire more, possibly including submarines.[4] The Maritime Police, which was formed in 2012 to maintain law and order on internal waterways and in coastal waters, only has about 20 boats; most are less than 40 metres. A new coastguard would likely take much-needed funds away from both these forces.

There are also questions over personnel. As always in Myanmar, accurate statistics are hard to come by, but there are probably some 20,000 officers and other ranks in the navy and about 600 in the Maritime Police. A coastguard would, initially at least, need to draw on both these forces for support and, even after a rationalisation of duties, it would doubtless compete with them for recruits. Many members of the Maritime Police are former navy personnel.

That said, Myanmar is not starting from scratch. In 2006 and 2007, it acquired four BN-2 'Defender' maritime surveillance aircraft from India.[5] India has also provided some coastguard-related training to

---

4   'Myanmar to Receive its First Kilo Class Submarine from India', *Navy Recognition*, 30 July 2019, www.navyrecognition.com/index.php/news/defence-news/2019/july/7327-myanmar-to-receive-its-first-kilo-class-submarine-from-india.html.

5   Rahul Bedi, 'Myanmar Gets India's Maritime Aircraft', *Hindustan Times*, [New Delhi], 12 May 2007, www.hindustantimes.com/india/myanmar-gets-india-s-maritime-aircraft/story-Ex5EUD2cztE4 egrQNVcXIP.html.

Myanmar in other areas. The chief of the Indian Coast Guard visited Myanmar last year, as did four Indian Coast Guard vessels. There is the potential for Myanmar to extend such links to other countries and international organisations.

Myanmar's armed forces are being shunned by many countries for their brutal operations against the Rohingya in 2016 and 2017, which the UN human rights chief at the time described as ethnic cleansing. Ties with an ostensibly civilian coastguard focusing on nontraditional security threats and maritime policing would not be as sensitive and would offer opportunities for a range of bilateral linkages and joint exercises.

Indeed, most regional countries have developed coastguard forces and are conducting a range of exercises.[6] ASEAN in particular has seen coastguards as a noncontroversial way to tackle cross-border security issues such as piracy and people smuggling. These efforts have been encouraged by countries like the US and Japan, which are keen to tackle transnational threats and keep open sea lanes through the region.

Even if the current proposal goes through parliament smoothly, it will be some time before Myanmar will be able to boast an effective coastguard. Also, there will always be the possibility that the force will be dominated by the navy. Nonetheless, the idea of a new coastguard has widespread support both within and outside the region, and the potential exists for it to make a significant contribution to both national and international maritime security.

6   Ni Komang Erviani, 'Southeast Asian Countries Complete Maritime Law Enforcement Exercise', *The Jakarta Post*, 30 June 2019, www.thejakartapost.com/seasia/2019/06/30/southeast-asian-countries-complete-maritime-law-enforcement-exercise.html.

96

Myanmar: Postage stamps and political signals

(06:00 AEDT, 30 September 2019)

A set of postage stamps issued on 8 August 2019 once again underscored the Myanmar Government's attachment to the formula of eight 'national races' and 135 ethnolinguistic groups in the country. This implicitly but emphatically ruled out recognition of the Rohingyas as an indigenous ethnic minority with all the status and privileges that implied.

Myanmar's former military regime often used new issues of the country's postage stamps to send political signals, not only to its own people but also to the international community.[1] It appears that this practice is also being followed by Aung San Suu Kyi's quasi-democratic government, which took office in 2016.

This was suggested recently by the issue of a new set of stamps by Myanmar Post, an agency of the reorganised Ministry of Transport and Communications. In two mini-sheets of eight stamps each, and on the associated first-day covers, there are depictions of the country's eight recognised 'national races'—namely, the Bamar (Burman), Kachin, Kayah (Karenni), Karen (Kayin), Chin, Mon, Rakhine (Arakanese) and Shan communities.

---

1   Andrew Selth, 'Burma Puts its Stamp on the World: Philately and Foreign Policy', *The Interpreter*, 7 January 2014, www.lowyinstitute.org/the-interpreter/burma-puts-its-stamp-world-philately-and-foreign-policy.

Myanmar is one of the most ethnically diverse countries in the world and the use of such labels to categorise the population has long attracted controversy. The composition and status of the eight races are highly vexed questions.[2] So, too, is their division by Ne Win's socialist regime (1962–88) into 135 ethnolinguistic groups.[3] The 8/135 formula, however, is now a well-established part of the official narrative. For example, it was a key component of the 2014 census.

There are precedents for the division of the population in this way. For example, when Myanmar (then known as Burma) regained its independence from Britain in 1948, the first constitution identified the same eight national races.[4] Seven were represented on the national flag by five stars, with the Bamar, Mon and Arakanese being grouped together as one. (There was no star for Kayah State as, technically speaking, it did not join the new union until 1951.)

Also, it was not long before the country was divided into 14 administrative units. There were seven states representing the main ethnic minorities and seven divisions covering the areas where the Bamar were seen to be in the majority. Under the 2008 constitution, there are still seven provinces based on ethnic groupings, hence Kachin, Kayah, Karen, Chin, Mon, Rakhine and Shan states. The seven divisions dominated by the ethnic Bamar are now called regions.

When a new national flag was introduced in 1974, following the promulgation of a revised constitution, the 14 states and divisions were each represented by a small star, surrounding the gearwheel and rice stalk logo of the Burma Socialist Programme Party. Until a different national flag was introduced in 2010, the old banner figured prominently on the country's postage stamps, publicly reinforcing the division of the population into eight national races.

The latest stamp issue follows a pattern set by the former military regime. A similar set of stamps was released in 1974, depicting the national costumes of the main ethnic groups. The same eight races were identified.

---

2   Sai Wansai and Shan Herald Agency for News, '2014 Population Census: The Problematic of 135 Ethnic Groups Categorisation', *Burma Link*, 5 December 2017, www.burmalink.org/2014-population-census-problematic-135-ethnic-groups-categorization/.

3   Gamanii, '135: Counting Races in Burma', *Shan Herald Agency for News*, 26 September 2012, panglongenglish.blogspot.com/2012/09/135-counting-races-in-burma.html.

4   *Constitution of 1947*, Myanmar Law Library, www.myanmar-law-library.org/law-library/laws-and-regulations/constitutions/1947-constitution.html.

The higher-denomination stamps were reissued in 1989 and again in 1990, when the country's name was changed from the Socialist Republic of the Union of Burma back to the Union of Burma and then to the Union of Myanmar.

That Naypyidaw was using postage stamps for political purposes was also indicated by the issue in 2017 of a stamp depicting Aung San Suu Kyi's father, who was described not as the country's independence hero, but as Myanmar's first foreign minister—a position currently held by his daughter. The stamp was part of a campaign to resurrect Aung San as a political icon and give greater legitimacy to the NLD administration.[5]

The significance of the latest set of postage stamps is not so much that they follow a pattern set by previous governments, but that they signal clearly to both domestic and international audiences the determination of Aung San Suu Kyi's government to stand by the 8/135 formula. This effectively rules out the possibility that any other ethnic communities, such as the Muslim Rohingya, might one day be accorded formal status.

The Rohingya are not recognised as Myanmar citizens, despite the fact that many of them can trace their local roots back for generations. If any can prove that their ancestors were resident in Myanmar prior to the first British colonial incursions in 1824, they may be granted a form of citizenship.[6] However, they would still be denied recognition as members of an indigenous ethnic group, with the rights and privileges that status implies.

Indeed, in Myanmar, even the term 'Rohingya' is avoided. In 2016, for example, Aung San Suu Kyi asked local officials and resident diplomats to refer instead to 'people who believe in Islam in Rakhine State'.[7] In 2017, in a historic speech following the military 'clearance operations' labelled ethnic cleansing by the UN, she did not use the word 'Rohingya' once, referring only to 'Muslims in Rakhine State'.

---

5   Andrew Selth, 'Myanmar and Aung San: The Resurrection of an Icon', *The Interpreter*, 31 March 2017, www.lowyinstitute.org/the-interpreter/myanmar-and-aung-san-resurrection-icon.
6   Mark Farmaner, 'Myanmar 2020—Rohingya Citizenship: Now or Never?', *South Asia@LSE Blogs* (London: London School of Economics South Asia Centre, 2 November 2018), blogs.lse.ac.uk/southasia/2018/11/02/rohingya-citizenship-now-or-never/.
7   Peter Lloyd, 'Burma Leader Aung San Suu Kyi Bans Use of Rohingya Name for Oppressed Muslims', *ABC News*, 22 June 2016, www.abc.net.au/news/2016-06-22/aung-san-suu-kyi-bans-use-of-rohingya-name/7534410.

Others in Myanmar, including senior military figures, routinely dismiss the Rohingya as 'illegal Bengali immigrants', or worse.

Countries have been using postage stamps to make political statements since their introduction by the British in 1840. Since 1948, Myanmar has employed stamps to express its sovereignty, project its national identity, promote official policies and mark important events. In a not very subtle way, Aung San Suu Kyi's government is continuing this practice—in the latest case, implicitly but emphatically denying the Rohingya the recognition, and thus the status, that they crave.

97

Aung San Suu Kyi: Why defend the indefensible?

(14:00 AEDT, 12 December 2019)

On 11 December 2019, State Counsellor Aung San Suu Kyi rose in the International Court of Justice in The Hague and defended her country against charges of genocide against the Muslim Rohingyas. Her blanket denial of crimes against humanity was not unexpected. Given the overwhelming evidence against Myanmar, however, and the risks to her personal reputation of appearing, the question needed to be asked: why did Aung San Suu Kyi decide to attend the hearing and present Myanmar's case herself?

This week, the world was treated to an extraordinary sight. Aung San Suu Kyi, the Nobel Peace Prize winner once hailed as 'the bravest and most moral person in the world … the immaculate heroine who allows us all to feel a little better about human nature',[1] sat in the International Court of Justice (ICJ) in The Hague and defended her country against charges of genocide.

The brutal 'clearance operations' by Myanmar's security forces against the Muslim Rohingya population in Rakhine State between October 2016 and the end of 2017 have been extensively documented by governments and international organisations. In 2018, for example, an independent UN fact-finding mission released a 444-page report that described in

---

1   Cited in Andrew Selth, 'The Fallen Idol: Aung San Suu Kyi and the Politics of Personality', *ABC Religion and Ethics*, 12 September 2017, www.abc.net.au/religion/the-fallen-idol-aung-san-suu-kyi-and-the-politics-of-personality/10095394.

horrific detail case after case of murder, torture, sexual assault and the destruction of property by the armed forces (known as the *Tatmadaw*) and the police.[2]

The UN Human Rights Council stated that these operations demonstrated 'genocidal intent'.[3] A more politically nuanced US State Department investigation conducted at the same time stopped short of calling the atrocities in Myanmar genocide, but recorded broadly similar findings.[4] Both reports noted that there were almost one million Rohingya refugees living in squalid camps in Bangladesh who stood as evidence of the crimes against humanity perpetrated against them.

In her testimony at the ICJ, Aung San Suu Kyi claimed that the allegations against Myanmar represented an 'incomplete and misleading factual picture of the situation'.[5] Implying that no one outside Myanmar could fully understand the situation in Rakhine State, she said it was 'complex and not easy to fathom'. The troubles there went back centuries. The latest problems were caused by the Arakan Rohingya Salvation Army (ARSA), which she said had received support from Afghan and Pakistani militants. Security operations in Rakhine State were taken in response to attacks by ARSA 'terrorists', as part of an 'internal conflict'.

Aung San Suu Kyi said: 'It cannot be ruled out that disproportionate force was used by members of the defence services in some cases, in disregard of international law', or that 'they did not distinguish clearly enough between ARSA fighters and civilians'. She went on: 'There may also have been failures to prevent civilians from looting or destroying property after fighting or in abandoned villages.' In a rare concession, she expressed sympathy for the refugees in Bangladesh (but without calling them 'Rohingyas').

---

2   *Myanmar: UN Fact-Finding Mission Releases its Full Account of Massive Violations by Military in Rakhine, Kachin and Shan States* (Geneva: United Nations Human Rights Council, 18 September 2018), www.ohchr.org/EN/HRBodies/HRC/Pages/NewsDetail.aspx?NewsID=23575&LangID=E.

3   *Report of the Independent International Fact-Finding Mission on Myanmar*, Report A/HRC/39/64 (Geneva: United Nations Human Rights Council, 12 September 2018), www.ohchr.org/Documents/HRBodies/HRCouncil/FFM-Myanmar/A_HRC_39_64.pdf.

4   Jennifer Hannsler, '"I Had to Choose Between My Children and My Mother": US Report Documents Atrocities Against Rohingya', *CNN*, 25 September 2018, edition.cnn.com/2018/09/25/politics/state-department-rohingya-report/index.html.

5   Owen Bowcott, 'Aung San Suu Kyi Tells Court: Myanmar Genocide Claims "Factually Misleading"', *The Guardian*, 11 December 2019, www.theguardian.com/world/2019/dec/11/aung-san-suu-kyi-tells-icj-myanmar-genocide-claims-factually-misleading.

Apparently oblivious to the fact that Myanmar's judicial system (both civil and military) is notorious for its corruption and lack of independence, Aung San Suu Kyi also stated that, if there were any suspicions of improper conduct, they would be fully investigated. As most observers would already know, several internal commissions of inquiry have already investigated various charges against the security forces and cleared them of any wrongdoing.

Considered overall, it was an astonishing performance that left many observers wondering at times whether Aung San Suu Kyi actually believed the nonsense she was peddling. The State Counsellor's carefully crafted testimony was an attempt to defend the indefensible. Strictly legal factors aside, it failed completely. At a personal level, it saw the last tattered remnants of her reputation as a champion of universal human rights shredded in the eyes of the international community.

Given the global attention being given to this case, and the overwhelming evidence against Myanmar, this was bound to happen, raising the question: Why would Aung San Suu Kyi put herself in such a position? Why would she expose herself to the inevitable international criticism—even mockery—in such a way? What could she possibly gain from putting her once immense moral authority and personal prestige on the line, knowing what the outcome (at least in the court of public opinion) would be?

Foreign observers have put forward three reasons to account for her actions.

First, most have suggested that, with the 2020 national elections in mind, Aung San Suu Kyi is keen to be seen defending Myanmar against external criticism. She knows that the clearance operations in Rakhine State in 2016 and 2017 were popular with many of her Burman Buddhist constituents, who have long viewed the Rohingyas as illegal Bengali immigrants who follow an alien and potentially dangerous religion. Not to have stood up against the ICJ could have had electoral consequences for her NLD.

Second, it has also been pointed out that Aung San Suu Kyi is currently governing Myanmar as part of a coalition with the *Tatmadaw*, which arguably remains the strongest political institution in the country. If she is to survive as State Counsellor and implement the wide range of reforms being promoted by her party, she needs to keep the generals onside. She cannot stand by and allow the international community to attack them, for fear of making them even more hostile to her government.

In this regard, it is relevant that Myanmar's armed forces were created by her father, independence hero Aung San. For them to be publicly disgraced not only would bring discredit to the institution itself, but also could reflect on its revered founder and, by implication, Aung San Suu Kyi herself. Interestingly, huge billboards have recently appeared around the country showing Aung San Suu Kyi with three smiling generals, emphasising the close links between them and implying her support for their military operations.[6]

A few pundits have postulated a third motive. For all her criticisms of the former military regime and attempts as a political prisoner to win the support of foreign governments, Aung San Suu Kyi has always been a strong Myanmar nationalist. She shares with the generals a deep commitment to the country's independence and sovereignty and, particularly since taking power herself, has put her country before wider considerations. She also knows that people in Myanmar do not like seeing their country publicly attacked by foreigners.

There is a fourth possible reason. Aung San Suu Kyi has a profound sense of personal destiny. She has always seen herself as the daughter of Myanmar's founding national hero, who was assassinated in 1947. For decades, she worked to become Myanmar's president and to take her place in the pantheon of Myanmar's most revered leaders. With that in mind, she may have felt she could not remain silent while her country and, technically speaking, her government and herself were accused of crimes against humanity.

Even when she was a prisoner of conscience and revered by the international community as a democratic icon, Aung San Suu Kyi always insisted she was a politician. This has been borne out by her actions (or lack of action) since taking power in 2016. Whether her appearance in the ICJ is further evidence of the demands of realpolitik, stems from a sense of duty towards her country or is derived from deeper personal feelings is difficult to say.

However, the result will be the same: her popularity in Myanmar may rise, but outside the country, her reputation will reach a new low.[7]

---

6   Kyaw Ye Lynn, 'Genocide Lawsuits Prompt Mixed Reactions in Myanmar', *Anadolu Agency*, [Ankara], 6 December 2019, www.aa.com.tr/en/asia-pacific/genocide-lawsuits-prompt-mixed-reactions-in-myanmar/1665573.
7   Maung Zarni, 'Aung San Suu Kyi Drives Final Nail in Myanmar's Moral Coffin', *Anadolu Agency*, [Ankara], 10 December 2019, www.aa.com.tr/en/analysis/opinion-aung-san-suu-kyi-drives-final-nail-in-myanmar-s-moral-coffin-/1669596.

Epilogue

Sam Roggeveen, Director,
International Security Program, Lowy Institute,
and founding editor of *The Interpreter*

In hindsight, it seems obvious that the Lowy Institute would have an inhouse publication such as *The Interpreter*. But back in 2007, when *The Interpreter* was first published, things looked a little different. For a young think tank that had already established a reputation for rigorous policy analysis and that had ambitions for a global profile, the idea of a blog might have seemed a little ... frivolous. To many, a glossy print magazine or a quarterly journal of international affairs would have been more in keeping with the Lowy Institute's character.

The institute's founding executive director, Allan Gyngell, made the bold and farsighted decision to set aside those concerns. The institute would have its own blog—a forum for Lowy Institute scholars to publish their assessments on breaking international events. It would be a source of high-quality analysis for foreign policy professionals and all intelligent (but non-expert) readers, and a way to project the institute's voice even if there was no space on the opinion pages of our newspapers or interest from TV and radio producers.

But neither Allan Gyngell nor I, as the founding editor of *The Interpreter*, had any idea of what it was to become. The transformation began early. I expected *The Interpreter* to be overwhelmingly a platform for the Lowy Institute's own scholars but, within months, the site became a popular forum for commentators from around Australia and, increasingly, the world. Andrew Selth was one of the first such experts to appear on *The Interpreter* and, as you will read in these pages, he remains one of our best and most valued contributors.

Andrew and *The Interpreter* were a perfect fit. Here was a writer who specialised in analysing the politics of a nation that was critical for Southeast Asia and important to Australia, but which only occasionally enjoyed mainstream media attention. *The Interpreter* soon became a place where experts such as Andrew could write for a readership they had never reached before—one that hungered for news and analysis that they could not find from a struggling mainstream media.

The internet has changed a lot since 2007, and *The Interpreter* has reflected some of those changes. The site started as a blog, with that familiar reverse-chronological format that spoke to the immediacy and vibrancy of the diary-style medium. Yet political blogging never caught on in Australia as it did in the US. There were not enough Australian foreign policy blogs out there to sustain a true 'blogosphere', with debates and readers moving freely among them.

Instead, over the course of the 2010s, Australian political debate moved to social media, particularly Twitter. It did not mean that longer-form writing was suddenly sidelined; readers remain hungry for smart and informed perspectives on world events, as *The Interpreter*'s steadily growing readership attests. But, after reading a piece they like (or hate), they comment about it on Twitter, and the debate flourishes there.

Social media also changed the way readers discovered articles. Instead of bookmarking a list of their favourite sites and then visiting regularly, they would use social media as a way to have interesting articles recommended to them by people they trusted. It allowed for exposure to a new range of sources, but it also meant that readers stopped returning daily to regular online haunts. Blogs could not rely on brand loyalty anymore.

It made sense, in that environment, for *The Interpreter* to complete its slow evolution from blog to an online magazine. We dispensed with the reverse-chronological format and built a true front page—an online version of a magazine cover—with links to lots of standalone articles that did not assume the reader had kept up with a long debate thread or had even visited the site before. It is a shift that has suited Andrew, who writes deeply considered, richly researched magazine-style pieces that emerge from decades of immersion in his chosen subject.

Over this same period, we have also witnessed a change of mood about the internet and particularly social media. In the early 2000s, techno-optimists argued that the internet would be a tool of political liberation in authoritarian societies. That mood peaked in 2010 and 2011 when it looked like Twitter and Facebook would help overthrow dictatorships around the Middle East.

But the liberal hopes of the Arab Spring gave way to repression, civil wars and new dictatorships. Around the same time, we began to learn more about the colossal scale of China's efforts to censor the internet. More recently, we have read of cyber operations by Russia and China against their Western adversaries.

The mood suddenly changed. For authoritarian countries, the internet had become a tool of repression and surveillance at home and one they could use to manipulate opinion—and even elections—abroad. In its own small way, this shift was reflected in Myanmar, where early promise of liberal reform emerged in 2008 with the announcement of a new constitution. The widespread adoption of mobile phones and social media soon followed. Yet this promise was crushed over the following decade by the clay feet of Aung San Suu Kyi and the cruelty of the military's repression of the Rohingya people.

Yet we should not assume that the pessimists, and the authoritarians, have won. The internet is barely 30 years old; Twitter and Facebook less than 20 years. To argue that this issue is settled would be like saying that the impact of the printing press could have been realistically assessed less than one lifetime after it was invented. This judgement is especially true of weak states such as Myanmar, where governments can easily lose control over public information and suffer a fatal loss of trust with those they claim to lead.

The internet has barely begun, and so has *The Interpreter*. The Lowy Institute is proud to have made a contribution to Australia's online debate about international policy, and particularly to our collective understanding of contemporary Myanmar.

Index

1925 Protocol for the Prohibition
    of the Use in War of Asphyxiating,
    Poisonous or Other Gases, and
    of Bacteriological Methods of
    Warfare, *see* Geneva Protocol
1995 Bangkok Treaty 148
21st Century Panglong Conference
    407
21st Century Panglong process 416
88 Generation Students Group 38,
    212
969 Buddhist Movement 233

Abbott Government 271, 273, 274,
    287, 289, 379–80, 400
Abbott, Tony 400
Abrahamian, Andray 413
'active pacifism' 37, 39
Afghanistan 34, 131, 282, 476
AFP, *see* Australian Federal Police
Africa 317
air force
    India 373
    Myanmar xxiii, 63, 208, 374,
        462, 463
aircraft 316–17, 375, 463
aircraft, military 175, 376
    ATR 72-500 463
    BN-2 'Defender' 469
    CAC/PAC JF-17 375, 462
    CASC CH-4 unmanned aerial
        vehicles 462
    HAL HJT-16 Kiran 463

    K-8 Karakorum 374
    MiG-29 Fulcrum 375
    Sukhoi Su-30 462
    Yakovlev Yak-130 462
Alaungpaya 58
Albright, David 134
Albright, Madeleine 131
All Burma Students' Democratic
    Front 38, 111, 266
Allen, Geoff 396
Al Qaeda 268, 451, 452
America, *see* United States
Amnesty International 95
Amyotha Hluttaw (House of
    Nationalities) xxvi
Anawratha 58
Andropov, Yuri 203
Anglo-Burmese War 217
Annan, Kofi 406, 432
anti-Muslim
    extremists 189, 234
    propaganda 191, 192, 233, 269
anti-Muslim riots 219, 224, 234
    2013 215, 433
    Mandalay (1997) 218
    Meiktila (2013) 218
    Sittwe (2001) 218
    Toungoo (2001) 218
    Yamethin (2013) 218
anti-Muslim sentiment 189, 191,
    408, 432, 440, 441
    as cause of radicalisation 268
    as cause of terrorism 268, 269

anti-Muslim violence 215, 231, 232, 233
  official encouragement of 234, 351
  security forces' failure to intervene in 234, 351
Arafat, Yasser 204
Arakan 217
Arakan Army 407
Arakan Rohingya Salvation Army (ARSA) 433, 435
  agenda 434, 438, 440, 451
  attacks on police 406, 431–2, 437, 440, 450, 476
  capture of arms 438
  responses to 439, 440
Arakan State xxi, 190, 199, 209, 215, 223
  see also Rakhine State
Arakanese 471, 472
'area clearance operations' 3, 4, 432, 438, 445, 461, 473, 475, 477
Aris, Michael 320, 415
armed forces, see *Tatmadaw*
Armed Forces Day 224, 229, 374
armoured vehicles 79, 97, 374, 463
  BTR-4U 463
  Type-92 462
arms
  Buddhist monks seeking 39
  capture by Arakan Rohingya Salvation Army 438
  conventional 45, 63, 101, 108, 140, 185
  embargoes 95–8, 170, 244, 429, 463
  force of 15, 97–8, 120
  from ASEAN members 96
  from Belarus 174
  from Bulgaria 96
  from China 26, 96, 122, 150, 174, 368, 462
  from India 26, 96
  from Israel 96, 464
  from Italy 96

  from North Korea 26, 44, 62–3, 96, 101, 108, 174, 185, 239, 240, 241
  from North Korea, interdiction of 101
  from North Korea, prohibition of 88, 100, 238
  from Pakistan 96
  from Poland 26, 96
  from Russia 26, 96, 174, 464
  from Serbia 96, 174
  from Singapore companies 258
  from Slovakia 96
  from South Korea 96
  from Taiwan companies 258
  from Thailand companies 258
  from Ukraine 26, 96, 174, 464
  independent dealers 97, 463
  lack of access to 62, 433
  Myanmar's manufacture of 27, 97, 98, 105, 463
  North Korean manufacture of 63
  police acquisition of 385, 387
  race 294
  small 62, 97
  Tatmadaw's acquisition of 3, 26, 89, 95, 122, 373, 374, 377, 385, 461, 464
  US policy on 173
  see also artillery; weapons
artillery 62, 139, 186, 299, 374
  2S1U Gvozdika self-propelled howitzer 463
  see also arms
ASEAN, *see* Association of Southeast Asian Nations
Ash, Timothy Garton 365
Ashton, William 109, 111
Asia 132, 395–8, 426, 467
  diplomatic intervention in 143, 171
  human rights in 143
  occult in 75–6
  status of women in 355, 358

US relations with 34, 194
use of pseudonyms in 109
see also Asia-Pacific; Central Asia;
    East Asia summit; South Asia;
    Southeast Asia
Asia Foundation 339
Asia-Pacific 160, 290, 325
Asia-Pacific Center for Security
    Studies 244
Asian Development Bank 122
Asian of the Year 201
Association of Southeast Asian
    Nations (ASEAN) xxvi, 96, 364,
    464, 470
    and philately 283
    Australia's relations with 290, 401,
      402
    Burma's membership of 82, 106,
      130, 143, 150, 171, 318
    charter 146
    'constructive engagement' policy
      48, 82
    Hillary Clinton at 68
    influence on Myanmar 171
    internal tensions 131
    meetings of 325, 357, 402
    member states 4, 93, 358
    Myanmar as chair 145–8, 153,
      248, 267, 283
    Myanmar's relations with member
      states 122, 147–8
    Obama administration's embrace
      of 82, 195
    opposition to armed intervention
      142
    rules out sanctions on Myanmar
      14, 96
    Secretary-General 148
    Singapore as chair of 14
    US Ambassador to 79
ASEAN Telecommunications Senior
    Officials Meeting 283

astrology 73–6, 110, 392
    see also feng shui; magic;
      numerology; occult;
      superstition; *yadaya*
Aung San 110, 181, 284, 413–17,
    473, 478
Aung San Suu Kyi 2, 156–7, 166,
    169, 210, 255
    'active pacifism' 37, 39
    alienating supporters 158, 168,
      230
    and 1990 elections 38, 92
    and ASEAN xxvi, 79, 147
    and Aung San 284, 413, 414,
      415, 416, 473, 478
    and civilianisation of security
      forces 469
    and intelligence apparatus 457–60
    and Min Aung Hlaing 409
    and 'national races' 471, 473
    and Obama administration 79,
      193, 195, 407
    and philately 284, 416, 471, 473,
      474
    and political iconography 413–14,
      415, 416
    and use of Burma/Myanmar name
      xxii, 7, 271, 273–4, 289, 290,
      380, 399–400, 401–2
    as de facto leader xxvi, 2, 392,
      432, 459
    as Minister for Foreign Affairs
      xxvi, 416, 459
    as opposition leader 19, 36, 37,
      38, 48, 142, 147, 165, 397,
      399, 429
    as state counsellor 2, 5, 402, 416,
      419, 459
    at International Court of Justice
      3, 6, 475–8
    at World Economic Forum 172
    attempts to reduce influence of
      54, 55, 120, 231, 232, 415

attempts to win trust of military
230, 264, 309–10, 312
Australian visit (2013) 271, 274,
275–8, 288, 380
calls for international sanctions
230, 261–4, 276, 309, 310,
311–12, 326
challenge to power of military
255, 261–4, 309, 310–11
commitment to peace settlements
3, 406, 407, 416
damage to reputation of 2, 221,
327, 328–9, 405–9, 422, 432,
434, 477, 478
decision to join political process
155–8, 166
declining international support
for 325–9, 422, 434
defence of genocide 3, 475, 476–8
denying status of Rohingya 190,
474, 476
depiction in popular culture 213,
319–20
discussions with Thein Sein 147,
159, 261, 263
downside of international
popularity 195, 223, 277
election to parliament (2012)
178, 186, 202, 262, 327
election victory (2015) 2, 5, 379,
381, 401
exclusion from presidency xxvi,
2, 99, 156, 227–9, 252, 264,
309–11, 213, 326, 363, 392,
401
failure to condemn ethnic
violence 223–4, 264, 275,
276–7, 325, 328
formation of government xxii,
385, 389–90, 392, 405, 425
house arrest xxiii, 2, 14, 222, 261,
262, 322, 429
extension of 55
international lobbying to end
54, 81
military refusal to release from
47–8, 50, 92
release from 123, 147, 327
trial 51, 54
UN pressure for dialogue
on 36
unauthorised visitors during
51, 53–5, 231
in government 1, 4, 431
influence on US policy 143–4,
171
influence on Western policy 171,
210, 222–3, 262
inquiry into Letpadaung incident
197, 223, 245
internal criticism of 221, 223–4,
230, 277, 415, 421, 422
international accolades for 201,
202, 222, 275
international criticism of 39, 190,
221, 223, 224–5, 264, 325–9,
405–8, 419–20, 422, 432
international praise for 22, 157,
195, 201, 222, 232, 275, 327
Jawaharlal Nehru Award for
International Understanding
202
lack of action on Rohingyas 6,
325, 328, 406, 419, 420, 422,
423, 431, 435
lack of control over military 406,
408, 423, 432, 438, 441, 459
lack of experience 225, 277, 405,
421
lack of leadership 39, 327, 423
lack of policy 157, 222, 421
lack of power 328, 459, 460
lack of progress on reform 328,
408, 431, 435, 481
lack of support for human rights
2–3, 6, 190, 325, 328–9,
405–7, 419, 432

loss of international influence
264, 325–9, 407
military's influence on 5
Nobel Peace Prize (1991) 2, 193,
202, 203, 213, 222, 274, 275,
320, 328, 406–7, 432, 464,
475
opposition to within military 229,
263, 264, 277, 312, 477
personal life 228, 319–23
personal qualities 76, 213, 222–3,
225, 276, 398
political ambition 2, 227–8, 252,
264, 276, 309, 311, 312, 477,
478
political failures 419–22, 423,
432, 448
political inflexibility 39, 225, 392,
421
popularity in Myanmar 22, 157,
228, 230, 262, 277, 311, 328,
405, 413, 422, 478
portrayal as icon 195, 213, 221–
5, 276, 327, 413, 475, 478
President Bush's support for 33,
35
prohibition of use of 'Rohingya'
402–3, 473, 476
refusal to condemn military 3, 6,
328
relationship with Thein Sein 165,
195, 235, 309–10
resistance to iconic status 3, 276,
423, 478
responsiveness to international
opinion 441, 464
Sakharov Prize for Freedom
of Thought 202, 261, 284
stand against corruption 385,
388, 406, 421
success in 2011 elections xxv, 2
support for police training 333
support for policy reform 172,
243, 310, 393

support for role of military 230,
262, 478
support for within military 229
supporters 223, 322, 328, 420,
423
Swan Arshin attacks on 233, 350,
351
talks with Shwe Mann 310, 312
transition to politician 168, 221,
223–5, 328
unrealistic expectations of 2, 222,
328, 363, 364, 405, 419
US Congressional Gold Medal
of Honour 35, 202
US support for 19, 22, 33, 35,
131
warnings about terrorism 452
willingness to work with Thein
Sein 166, 167, 168
Australia 18, 29
accolades for Aung San Suu Kyi
275
aid to Myanmar 191, 276, 381,
402
alliance with US 208
and arms embargo 95, 96, 97, 429
and Myanmar's nuclear status 87
and use of Burma/Myanmar name
xxii, 271–4, 278, 287–90,
379–81, 399–403
anti-Muslim sentiment 189, 191
Aung San Suu Kyi's visit to 271,
274–8, 288, 380
contact with *Tatmadaw* 245–6,
429
defence attaché in Myanmar 208,
244, 295, 425
defence links with Myanmar
207–10, 295, 425, 429–30
diplomacy 380, 395–8, 399, 400,
401, 426–9
discussions with Aung San Suu
Kyi 274, 402
elections 288

Embassy in Rangoon (Yangon)
1n.1, 191, 288, 380, 395,
401, 425, 428
expressions of concern about
Myanmar 189, 191, 429
films 124
humanitarian intake 191
intervention in Myanmar 27
media 65–7, 124, 479–81
Myanmar policy 49, 130, 189–92,
271, 275, 276, 288, 290, 361,
397, 402
policing 199, 356, 358
policymakers 1
position on Rohingyas 189–92,
290, 403
punitive measures against
Myanmar 14, 208, 288, 429
relations with ASEAN 290, 401,
402
relations with Myanmar 271,
274, 276, 287, 310, 380, 397,
400–1, 425, 429
response to prodemocracy
uprising 429
response to repression of Muslims
290
Thein Sein's visit to 244, 273, 400
training of *Tatmadaw* 207–8, 210
see also Department of Foreign
Affairs and Trade
Australian Broadcasting Corporation
(ABC) 124
Australian Federal Police (AFP) 245,
246
Australian–Myanmar Strategic
Dialogue 425
Australian National University
(ANU), The 116, 277, 278, 361,
362, 363, 367
Australian Strategic Policy
Institute 18
'auxiliaries' 344, 346, 351, 352
see also militias; vigilantes

Aviation Police 332, 357
Ayeyarwady River xxi, 272
see also Irrawaddy River

Bacteriological (Biological) and Toxin
Weapons Convention 316
see also Biological Weapons
Convention
Bago 344, 346, 358
Bahadur Shah II (Zafar) 57, 58, 59
ballistic missiles 139–40
air-to-air 88, 139, 375
anti-ship 63, 88, 139
anti-tank 139
intercontinental 105, 139
liquid-fuelled 187
medium-range 88, 105, 139, 187
Myanmar's acquisition of 88, 89,
103, 295
Myanmar's capability 187, 188
Myanmar's development of 67,
161, 176, 195
Myanmar's manufacture of 297,
300, 375
North Korean help to develop 89,
101, 105, 148, 175, 185, 187,
238, 258
North Korean sales of 89, 101,
143, 238, 292
short-range (SRBM) 87, 88, 89,
90, 105, 139, 148
surface-to-air (SAM) 139, 374,
376
surface-to-surface 63, 88, 89, 139
tactical 88, 139
see also missiles; rockets
Bamar (Burman) xxi, xxiv
as majority population 3, 272,
400
as 'national race' 471
regional division of 472
see also Burman
Ban Ki-moon 142
Ban Pong 426

Bangkok 208, 245, 426, 429
Bangladesh 58, 451
    disputed borders with Myanmar
        294, 468
    extremist groups in 268, 440,
        449, 451, 452
    illegals in Burma 217
    Rohingya refugee camps in 190,
        191, 218, 432, 435, 437, 440,
        445, 448, 450–1, 453, 465,
        476
    war of independence 217
Barry, Lyndal 124
Barry, Sophie 124
Bateman, Sam 468
Bay of Bengal 153, 376
Bayinnaung 58
BBC (British Broadcasting
    Corporation) 321, 322
Begin, Menachem 204
Beker, Brian 124
Bengali 216, 217, 433, 440, 474, 477
Bermudez, Joseph 89
Besson, Luc 213, 320
bin Laden, Osama 268
biological weapons (BW) 5, 140, 297,
    316, 317, 318, 375
Biological Weapons Convention
    315–18
Bishop, Julie 274, 278, 402, 403
Black, Michael 111
Blair, Eric 110
    see also Orwell—George
Blair, Tony 130
Blaxland, John 207
Bloodworth, Dennis 57
Bombay 58
Boot, William 111
Border Guard Forces 252
border police 332, 386, 437
Brezhnev, Leonid 76
Britain, see United Kingdom
British Empire 281
    see also United Kingdom

Broinowski, Richard 396
Brown, Gordon 95, 222–3
Brunei 464
BSI, see Bureau of Special
    Investigations
Buddha, images of 73
Buddha's tooth 59
Buddhism 3, 58, 73, 355
    969 Movement 233
    and Muslims 192, 218, 269
    and Rohingya lands 440
    as state religion 197–8, 217, 235,
        434, 441, 450, 458
    Burman 458, 477
    clergy 27, 212
    dominance in army 15, 27
    expulsion of non-Buddhists 232
    insult to 192, 218
    social dominance of 3
Buddhist
    Aung San Suu Kyi as 76, 157,
        221, 222, 328, 477
    bomb 106
    extremists 233, 267, 269, 351,
        433
    'militia' 233
    vigilantes 432
    violence against 190, 268
Buddhist monks
    participation in 'Saffron
        Revolution' 13, 27, 39
    violence against 27, 197
Bulgaria 96
Bureau of Special Investigations (BSI)
    386, 388, 459
Burma
    anti-British sentiment in 58
    Bangladeshi illegals in 217
    colonial rule of 110, 217, 245,
        272, 316, 356
    conquest of xxii, 58, 59, 110,
        216, 473
    development of Islam in 217–18
    Indians in 216, 217, 398

membership of ASEAN 82, 106,
130, 143, 150, 171, 318
nuclear proliferation by 106
support for nuclear
nonproliferation 44
UN Special Rapporteur on 142,
304
US special envoy to 133, 173
Burma/Myanmar, name of
Aung San Suu Kyi's views on xxii,
7, 271, 273–4, 289, 290, 380,
399–400, 401–2
Australian use of xxii, 271–4, 278,
287–90, 379–81, 399–403
UK use of 272, 274, 399
UN use of xxii, 272, 289, 379
US use of 272, 274, 289, 399,
401, 402
Western use of 7, 289, 399
Burma Socialist Programme Party xxv,
349, 472
Burman xxi
as 'national race' 471
as majority population 400, 458
as source of 'Burma' 272, 400
Aung San Suu Kyi as 224, 328, 477
dominance of government 167
see also Bamar
Burmese Code of Criminal Procedure
352
Burmese Freedom and Democracy Act
(US) 34
Bush administration
criticism of Myanmar 66
policy failures 35, 47, 48, 79, 81,
82, 83, 159, 171, 172
policy on Myanmar 51, 82, 93,
99, 135, 171, 194
silence on WMD 44, 64, 67, 317
see also United States
Bush, George W. 22, 33, 34, 35, 79
memoir 130
State of the Union speech (2006)
34

visit to Thailand (2008) 33–6
see also United States
Bush, Laura 33, 34, 35, 130, 131,
223

Camp Surasri 426, 429
Campbell, Kurt 81, 101, 106, 160
on US policy 79, 81, 82
testimony to US Congress 177–9
visit to Myanmar 99–101
Canada 334
Canberra 361, 380
CARE 191
Carr, Bob 191, 273, 287, 288, 379,
400
Center for Strategic and International
Studies (CSIS) 334
Central Asia 451
Central Bank of Myanmar 414
Centre for the Study of Australia–Asia
Relations (CSAAR) 395, 396
chemical weapons (CW) 5, 46, 89,
140, 186, 297–301, 375
Chemical Weapons Convention
(CWC) 298, 300, 301
Chiang Kai-shek 203
Chin xxiv, 471, 472
China 21, 48, 59, 109, 110, 131,
142, 143, 168, 294, 407, 481
arms sales to Myanmar 26, 96,
122, 174, 258, 297, 298,
374–5, 462
closer ties with Myanmar 48, 80,
170, 195, 367
diplomatic support for Myanmar
4, 14, 122, 150, 464
ethnic Chinese in Myanmar 216,
217, 233
influence in Myanmar 150, 153,
368, 441
infrastructure 149, 151, 152,
153–4
military presence in Myanmar 5,
150, 174–5, 258, 295, 368

military ties with Myanmar 4,
248, 375, 464
Myanmar as military threat to 90
philately 282, 283, 416
relations with Myanmar 14, 154,
171, 209, 240, 313, 367–71
strained relations with Myanmar
149, 151–2, 153
strategic competition with US
153, 160, 194–5, 248,
367–71
Christian Solidarity International
(CSI) 317
Christianity xxiv, 30, 76, 192, 233
Chun Doo-hwan 181, 183
Churchill, Winston 76
civil war, *see* war—civil
'clearance operations', *see* 'area
clearance operations'
Clinton, Bill 131
Clinton, Hillary 51, 67, 83, 178,
187, 194
Myanmar policy review 47–8
on North Korea links 67–8, 160
on sanctions 48, 49
visit to Myanmar (2011) 159–62,
175, 185, 240
coastguard 467–70
see also Maritime Police; Myanmar
Navy
Cold War 282, 368
constitution, of 1947 217, 272, 472
constitution, of 1974 254, 472
constitution, of 2008 2, 116, 481
aims of 116, 121, 168, 255
amendment to allow Aung San
Suu Kyi to run for presidency
223, 227, 228–30, 264, 309
amendments to strengthen
democracy 230, 311
and ASEAN 146
and composition of parliament
40, 91, 115, 156, 312

and intelligence services 460
and role of commander-in-chief
254, 459
and role of *Tatmadaw* xxiii, xxvi,
121, 229, 252–3, 310, 312,
328, 391, 408, 420, 432, 469
Aung San Suu Kyi calls for
international pressure to
change 262, 264
blocking of Aung San Suu Kyi
from presidency xxvi, 2, 310,
401
criticism of 230, 254, 305
immunity from prosecution for
military 253
international criticism of 35, 82,
172
legal allegiance to 92
military veto over change to 229
name of Burma/Myanmar 401
promilitary bias of 166, 209, 290,
387, 408
promulgation of xxi
provincial divisions in 472
referendum on xxv, 2, 14, 121
refusal to amend 309, 311, 326,
392, 408
Tatmadaw's commitment to 311
Tatmadaw's safeguarding of 253
three 'national causes' enshrined
in 252, 434
undemocratic nature of 305
constitutional reform 264, 276, 311,
337, 339, 421, 460
Convention on the Prohibition of
the Development, Production
and Stockpiling of Bacteriological
(Biological) and Toxin Weapons
and on their Destruction, *see*
Biological Weapons Convention
Corso, Arnold 111
counterterrorism 269
Cowell, Adrian 124

crimes against humanity 203, 422,
432, 445, 446, 475, 476, 478
see also 'ethnic cleansing';
genocide; war—crimes
Crocker, Walter 395
Cuba 282
Cyclone Nargis 17, 19, 20, 21, 22,
23, 25, 27, 28, 32, 35, 48, 114

Dalrymple, William 58
Dantes, Edmond 111
DDI, *see* Directorate of Defence
Industries
Defence Intelligence Organisation
(DIO) 425, 426, 427, 428, 429
Defence White Paper (2013) 207,
208
de Gaulle, Charles 76
De Klerk, F.W. 204
democracies
guided 122
military accountability in 244,
334, 335, 433
Western 224, 243, 248, 333, 334,
364, 399
democracy 337, 338, 339, 448
activists 267, 313
ASEAN support for 146, 364
Aung San Suu Kyi as icon of 3,
54, 195, 221, 222, 223, 276,
321, 322–3, 329, 422, 478
Aung San Suu Kyi's calls to
strengthen 230, 311
Bush administration's
commitment to 33–4
campaign for 229, 415
hopes for return to 36
intervention to restore 20, 21, 32
movement 33, 400
police as cornerstone of 334
principles of 146, 157, 203, 222,
339
struggle for 222, 319, 321, 322–3

transition to 200, 255, 264, 276,
310, 392, 423, 431, 434, 435,
460
US support for 81, 135
Western-style 364
see also democratisation;
'disciplined' democracy;
prodemocracy movement;
prodemocracy uprising
democratic
change 2, 33
'era' 397
see also undemocratic
democratic government
Aung San Suu Kyi's quasi- 471
Aung San's commitment to 416
efforts to create 123, 255, 262, 340
evolution of 118, 393
restoration of 135
democratic principles, *see*
democracy—principles of
democratic reform 100, 159, 209, 210
support within military for 307
US policy on 81, 162
see also democratisation
Democratic Voice of Burma (DVB)
103–6, 107, 108, 124, 134
democratisation 146, 212, 214, 264,
326, 361, 362, 409
Department of Foreign Affairs and
Trade (Australia) (DFAT) 288,
339, 380, 381, 400, 401, 402
Depayin 350
de Tocqueville, Alexis 115
DFAT, *see* Department of Foreign
Affairs and Trade
Dhaka 451
Directorate of Defence Industries
(DDI) 187, 237, 239, 240
'disciplined' democracy 234, 311, 462
elections for 115, 120
extension of 310
foreign acceptance of 147, 201,
423

limits of 168
parliament as centrepiece of 40
recognition of 122
roadmap to 2, 14, 263
transition to 3, 91, 373, 389–93
see also democracy
Dobell, Graeme 129
Downer, Alexander 397
Dulles, John Foster 159
Dunlop, Nic 125
Dunn, Hugh 395

East Asia summit 325
East India Company 427
East Pakistan 217
see also Bangladesh
Egerton, George 132, 398
election law revision 91–4, 96, 99,
  121, 228
elections 124, 146, 311, 481
  Australian 288
  irregularities xxv, 178
  proposed 82
  US presidential 36, 48
  US response to 99, 178
elections, 1990
  and Aung San Suu Kyi 38, 92
  NLD win 92, 121, 156
  result ignored 38, 156, 429
elections, 2010 xxv, 14, 50, 55, 91,
  93, 115–18, 119–22, 123, 263
elections, 2011 xxv, 2
elections, 2012 xxv, 155, 156, 165,
  178, 228, 262
  Aung San Suu Kyi's success in
    178, 186, 202, 262, 327
elections, 2015 xxv, xxvi, 2, 227,
  229, 230, 277, 310, 353, 361–4,
  379–81, 391–2, 401, 408, 416,
  419, 448
  Aung San Suu Kyi's victory in 2,
    5, 379, 381, 401
elections, 2020 477

elections, National League for
  Democracy
  in 1990 38, 92, 121, 156, 429
  in 2011 xxv–xxvi
  in 2012 178, 228
  in 2015 228, 229, 230, 277 363,
    379, 381, 390, 391, 416, 419
embargo, *see* arms—embargoes
England, *see* United Kingdom
'ethnic cleansing' 4, 407, 440, 445,
  451, 462, 470, 473
  see also crimes against humanity;
    genocide; war—crimes
Europe 88, 89, 104, 358
  support for Aung San Suu Kyi
    232, 261, 322
European Union (EU) 262
  and ASEAN 146
  and Rohingyas 403, 441
  and use of Burma/Myanmar name
    272, 274, 289
  as threat to Myanmar 21
  policy on Myanmar 49, 170–1
  sanctions against Myanmar 14,
    80, 96, 463
  training programs 245, 333, 344,
    346, 347
Evans, Gareth 278
Exercise Cobra Gold 210, 244
Extremely Severe Cyclonic Storm
  Nargis, *see* Cyclone Nargis
extremism 3, 450
  see also terrorism
extremists
  969 Buddhist Movement 233
  anti-Muslim 189, 234
  Buddhist 233, 267, 269, 351, 433
  foreign Islamic 268, 438–9, 449,
    451, 452
  Islamic 131, 219, 267, 451
  South Asian 268, 440, 449, 451,
    452
  Southeast Asian 452
  see also jihadists; terrorists

Farrelly, Nicholas xviii, 193, 277, 449
feng shui 76
    see also astrology; magic;
        numerology; occult;
        superstition; *yadaya*
Fernandez, Roy 396
Fire Services Department xxiii, 468
Flitton, Dan 288, 380
force of arms, *see* arms—force of
Foreign Policy (magazine) 109, 201
'four cuts' strategy 439, 448
Fowle, Ali 107
France 22, 48, 115, 463
Fraser, Malcolm 130
frigates
    Aung Zeya 375
    Jianghu II class 375, 462

Gaddafi, Muammar 141, 142
Gandhi, Indira 75
Gandhi, Mahatma 329
Gate, Richard 396
Geneva Protocol 316
genocide 3, 30, 407, 422, 432, 445,
    451, 462, 475, 476
    see also crimes against humanity;
        'ethnic cleansing'; war—
        crimes
Gillard, Julia 192, 244, 273
Global Financial Crisis 131
Griffith Asia Institute 320
Griffith University 395
guerilla war, *see* war—guerilla
Gumnit, Ruth 124
gunboat
    Super-Dvora Mk III 463
    see also helicopter gunships

Hallacy, Jeanne 124
hardware, military 27, 376, 377
Hartley, John 1, 426, 427, 428, 429
Hawai`i 244
Hegner, Isabel 124
helicopter gunships 376

Mil Mi-24P 462
    see also gunboat; helicopters
helicopters 429
    Airbus AS365 Eurocopter 463
    Iroquois 427
    Mi-35 Hind E 374
    UH-1H 426
    see also helicopter gunships
Henderson, Peter 395
Highway Police 357
Hindus 58
Hitler, Adolf 76, 203
HMAS Childers 425
HMAS Quiberon 425
Hong Kong 76
House of Nationalities, see *Amyotha
    Hluttaw*
House of Representatives, see *Pyitthu
    Hluttaw*
Howard, John 130
Human Rights Watch 95, 305, 406
humanitarian law, *see* laws—
    humanitarian
Hurricane Katrina 18
Hutton, Pierre 396

IAEA, *see* International Atomic
    Energy Agency
India 57–9, 110, 318, 373, 415
    arms sales to Myanmar 5n.12,
        26, 96
    as nuclear power 143
    border with Myanmar 468
    defence ties with Myanmar 463,
        464
    military support for Myanmar 5,
        292, 469–70
    relations with Myanmar 14, 375
    relations with US 48–9, 143
    Rohingyas in 439
    strategic competition with China
        153, 171
    support for Myanmar 90, 464
Indian Imperial Police 110

Indian Ocean 368
Indian Ocean tsunami (2004) 20
Indians, in Burma 216, 217, 398
Indonesia 75, 146, 268
    and Rohingyas 435
    separation of army and police
        200, 335, 387
    women police in 356, 357
Institute for Science and International
    Security 134, 138–9
International Atomic Energy Agency
    (IAEA) 104, 107, 134, 138
    guidelines 70, 135
    inspections 71, 72, 161
    Myanmar signing additional
        protocol 161, 179, 195,
        258–9
    on reports of Myanmar weapons
        program 64, 67, 69, 87, 135
    reactor safeguards 44, 70
International Committee of the Red
    Cross 332
    see also Myanmar Red Cross
International Court of Justice (ICJ) 3,
    6, 475, 476, 477, 478
International Criminal Court 141,
    461
International Crisis Group (ICG)
    202, 203, 305, 433, 438, 439,
    451, 453
International Institute for Strategic
    Studies (IISS) 69, 71, 72
International Law Enforcement
    Academy 245, 333
international law, see laws—
    international
International Republican Institute
    (IRI) 338, 339
Inya Lake 55
Iran 34, 43–6, 66, 105
Iraq 22, 34, 45, 46, 66, 131
Irrawaddy (Ayeyarwady) River xxi,
    17, 27, 153, 272

Islam
    development in Burma 217–18
    'people who believe in Islam in
        Rakhine State' 402, 473
    see also anti-Muslim; Muslims;
        Rohingyas
Islamic
    extremism 131, 219, 267, 268,
        438–9, 440, 449, 450, 451,
        452
    pan-Islamist narrative 434, 438,
        451
    see also jihadists
Islamic State of Iraq and Syria (ISIS)
    451, 452
Israel 72, 96, 463, 464
Italy 96, 299, 463

JADE Act, see Tom Lantos Block
    Burmese JADE (Junta's Anti-
    Democratic Efforts) Act
Jagan, Larry 311
Jakarta 268
Jakarta Centre for Law Enforcement
    Cooperation 332–3, 358
Jane's Defence Weekly (JDW) 292, 293,
    317
Janowitz, Morris 335
Japan xxvi, 49, 89, 96, 110, 216, 238,
    266, 398, 426, 470
Jemaah Islamiyah 268
jets, see aircraft
jihadists 268, 269, 438, 452
    see also Islamic extremism;
        terrorists
Joshi, Shashank 373

Kachin xxiv, 152, 264, 299, 472
    as 'national race' 213, 471
    insurgents 166, 186
    lack of support from Aung San
        Suu Kyi 264, 275, 325, 328
    refugees 186

Kachin Independence Army (KIA)
152, 407
Kachin State 458, 472
conflict in 178, 209, 223
infrastructure development 149
military operations in 275, 328
Kamans 216
Kanchanaburi Province 426
Kang Nam 1 62, 63, 88, 100
Karen (Kayin) xxi, xxiv, 29, 267, 317
and *Rambo* 29, 31
as 'national race' 213, 471, 472
insurgents 31, 165, 427
see also Kayin
Karen National Liberation Army
(KNLA) 427
Karen State 29, 31, 427, 472
Karenni, *see* Kayah
Kayah (Karenni) 471, 472
Kayin xxi, 471
see also Karen
Kaznacheev, Aleksandr 398
Kelley, Robert 107, 134, 259
Kennan, George 109
Kennedy, John F. 169, 389
Kerry, John 289
Khomeini, Ayatollah 203
King of Siam 427
Kipling, Rudyard 319–23
Korean Peninsula 6, 183
Kuala Lumpur 266

Larkin, Emma 111, 113, 114
law, rule of 190, 245, 276, 331, 333,
334, 351, 352, 388, 422, 460
law and order 190, 198, 332, 352
laws
Aung San Suu Kyi's lack of
control over 157
civil 447
compliance with 349, 350, 352
for reforms 196
humanitarian 445, 446, 447

international 70, 445, 461, 464,
465, 476
maritime 468, 469
marriage 218
military 447
National Education 343, 345, 351
of armed conflict 244
on women 355
property 218
repressive 178, 408, 460
to create state counsellor position
xxvi
see also election law revision
Lee Kuan Yew 132
Lee Myung-bak 181, 183
Letpadan 344, 345, 346, 358
Letpadaung 223, 245
Liberia 284
Libya 141–4
Lon Htein (riot police) 198, 387
London 69
Lord Palmerston 141, 143
Los Angeles Times 323
Lowy Institute 51, 227, 309, 479, 481
Lugar, Richard (Dick) 136, 160, 241

McConnell, Mitch 93
magic 73, 74, 75, 76
see also astrology; *feng shui*;
numerology; occult;
superstition; *yadaya*
Magny, Helene 124
Malay Muslims, or Pashu 216
Malaysia 190, 266, 356, 439, 452
Malik, Preet 398
Mandalay xxii, 58, 218
Mandalay (poem) 320, 321
Manila 266
Marciel, Scot 79
maritime law, *see* laws—maritime
Maritime Police 332, 467, 468, 469,
470
see also coastguard; Myanmar
Navy

Marshall, Harold 395
Mathieson, David 406
Maung Aung Myoe 254
Maymyo (Pyin Oo Lwin) xxi, 45
Meiktila 218
Merrill, Kay 109, 111
Middle East 142, 481
Mignault, Pierre 124
military, see *Tatmadaw*
military hardware, *see* hardware—
    military
Military Intelligence (MI) xxiii, 457
Military Intelligence Service (MIS)
    xxiii, 231, 266, 429
militias xxiii, 233, 234, 350, 440
    see also 'auxiliaries'; Swan Arshin;
        vigilantes
Miller, Rachel 396
Milne, Pat 396
Min Aung Hlaing 229, 230, 293,
    294, 304, 374, 388, 408, 459
    agreement with Aung San Suu Kyi
        392, 409
Ministry of Defence 467, 469
Ministry of Foreign Affairs 416
Ministry of Home Affairs 388, 459
Ministry of Transport and
    Communications 469, 471
missiles 88, 137, 139–40, 174
    anti-tank 139
    claims of North Korean help to
        manufacture 43, 89, 105, 148,
        175, 185, 187, 238–9, 241,
        258–9
    claims of North Korean shipments
        62, 63, 70, 88, 101, 143, 160,
        238, 292
    component embargo 100
    Hwasong-6 88
    Myanmar's manufacture of 463
    proliferation 131, 171
    Scud-type 88, 139
    see also ballistic missiles; rockets
Mitchell, Derek 135, 434

Mitterrand, Francois 76
Mon 427, 471, 472
Mon State 413, 417, 472
Moscow 96
MPF, *see* Myanmar Police Force
Mughal emperor 57
Munro, Hector 110
Murphy, W. Patrick 239
Muslim
    countries' concern about
        Rohingyas 189, 439, 452, 462
    'threat' 192, 269
    see also anti-Muslim; Islam;
        Islamic; Rohingyas
Muslims in Myanmar 1, 58, 215–19
anger of 435
    Arakan kingdom 217
    'area clearance operations' against
        3, 4, 432, 438, 445, 461, 473,
        475
    as Sunnis 216
    attack on Buddhists 190
    attitudes towards 215, 421, 432
    Aung San Suu Kyi's position on
        repression of 276
    Australian response to repression
        of 290
    bans on government employment
        217
    Burmese suspicions of 192
    Chinese 216, 217
    denied recognition 189, 215, 399,
        473
    desire for acceptance 269
    divisions among 218
    extremists 131, 219, 267, 451
    fear of economic domination by
        218
    harsh treatment of 202
    Indian 216–17
    inflows from Subcontinent
        216–17
    insurgent groups 218, 449
    loss of rights 217

Malay 216
marginalisation of 218
numbers of 189, 215
opposition to violence 269
persecution of 268, 276
radicalisation of 268, 269
rights in 1947 constitution 217
Rohingyas as largest group of 216
violence against 192
see also anti-Muslim; Islam;
  Islamic; Rohingyas
'Myanaung' U Tin 110
Myanmar Air Force xxiii, 63, 208,
  374, 462, 463
see also *Tatmadaw*
Myanmar Army, see *Tatmadaw*
Myanmar, name of, *see* Burma/
  Myanmar—name of
Myanmar National Democratic
  Alliance Army 407
Myanmar Navy
  as part of *Tatmadaw* xxiii
  attends China's celebrations 464
  Australian training of 208
  diplomacy 295, 375
  exercises with ASEAN 464
  exercises with China 464
  exercises with India 464
  foreign naval visits 464
  local vessel manufacture 463
  Pakistan training of 292, 293
  personnel numbers 469
  rearmament 292, 375, 463
  responsibilities of 467, 468, 469,
    470
  ship acquisition 292, 376, 463, 469
  submarine acquisition 5n.12, 469
  see also coastguard; Maritime
    Police; submarines; *Tatmadaw*
Myanmar Police Force (MPF) xxiii,
  267
  abuses by 247, 332, 447, 476
  accountability of 198, 332
  and Swan Arshin 350, 351

Anti-Trafficking in Persons
  Division 357
apology for excessive use of force
  197–8
'area clearance operations' 438,
  445
as instrument of state control 199
attacks against 431, 437, 438
Aung San Suu Kyi's support for
  training of 333
brutality of 245, 343, 345, 433
capability 199, 200, 333, 334
civilian 'auxiliaries' 344, 346,
  349–53
civilianisation of 199, 244, 331,
  333, 385–6
code of conduct 332, 388
colonial 245
command structure 346, 386
community policing 199, 245,
  332, 333, 351, 352, 356, 386
community trust in 346, 352, 385
complicity in anti-Muslim
  violence 234, 351
corruption 198, 199, 247, 332,
  385, 388
Criminal Investigation
  Department 357
criticism of 179, 333
crowd control 245, 333, 334,
  358, 386
discipline 199, 345, 347
Division Against Transnational
  Crime 357
funding 198, 332, 386
increase in power of 198, 199, 331
independence of 388
modernisation of 199, 244, 332,
  351, 355, 385
official neglect of 198–9, 386, 387
operations against Rohingyas 432
paramilitary/UMP xxiii, 199,
  350, 386, 387
peacekeeping 303, 307

personnel transfers from army 332, 387

poor image of 213, 333, 344

professionalisation of 197, 199, 200, 248, 249

rank and file 346, 352

recruitment 199, 332, 355

reform of 197–8, 304, 306, 331–5, 346, 347, 349, 355, 385, 387

relations with China 24

relations with *Tatmadaw* 386, 200

response to protests 245, 313, 343–5

response to 'Saffron Revolution' 27, 199

riot squad 198, 387

rivalry with army 385–8

Security Command/battalions 199, 344, 346, 347, 352, 358

size of 199, 334, 355, 386, 387

strategy 333, 433

subservient to *Tatmadaw* 198, 387

support for democratic reform 307

tactics 433, 441, 447

transfer of responsibilities 306, 349, 387

under control of *Tatmadaw* 312, 420

undermining of authority 346, 352

Western assistance to 243, 245–7, 248, 304, 331–5, 343, 344, 346, 347, 358–9

women in 345, 355–9

see also People's Police Force; police; Special Branch; Swan Arshin; *Tatmadaw*; Union Military Police

Myanmar Port Authority 468

Myanmar Red Cross xxiii

see also International Committee of the Red Cross

Myitsone Dam 149–50, 151–4

Nambiar, Vijay 304, 305

National League for Democracy (NLD) xxvi, 121, 393, 422, 423, 473, 477

and 1990 elections 38, 92, 121, 156, 429

and 2010 election laws 92

and 2011 elections xxv–xxvi

and 2012 elections 178, 228

and 2015 elections 228, 229, 230, 277 363, 379, 381, 390, 391, 416, 419

and constitutional change 460

and peace agreements 5, 421

Aung San Suu Kyi's lack of leadership over 39

claims for legitimacy 121, 156

criticism of 2010 election laws 91

criticism of defence spending 377

disappointment with 419–20

ethnic distrust of 157

failures of 5, 421

formation of government 2, 4, 385, 389, 390, 392, 401, 457

individual freedom under 457–8, 460

internal tensions 38–9, 212

military members' support for 229

negotiations with *Tatmadaw* 392

opposition to 230

political boycott 155

publicity use of Aung San 414

rejoining political process 155, 156, 157–8

tensions with community 413

tensions with other groups 212

US recognition of 34

National Library of Australia (NLA) 395, 396, 398

'national races' 213, 218, 400, 471, 472

navies 294

navy, *see* Myanmar Navy; Royal
    Australian Navy; Royal Thai
    Navy; US Navy
Naypyidaw 99, 160, 301, 435
    Armed Forces Day parade 224
    as seat of government xxii, 80,
        116, 120, 147, 199, 262, 400
    ASEAN meetings in 283, 325,
        357
    creation of xxii, 58, 75
    East Asia summit in 325
    lack of NLD base in 156
    MPF headquarters in 357
    origin of name 59
    Shwedagon Pagoda replica in 59
Ne Win 284, 319, 414
    1962 coup xxv, 111, 198, 207,
        214, 216, 304, 386–7
    and chemical weapons 299
    foreign policy 208, 283, 397
    nom de guerre xxiv, 110
    reliance on astrology/numerology
        74, 75
    rule of xxiv, 208, 349, 386, 397,
        429, 472
New Light of Myanmar 351
New Mon State Party (NMSP) 426,
    427
NLD, *see* National League for
    Democracy
Nobel Peace Prize 203–4, 284
    Aung San Suu Kyi 2, 193, 202,
        203, 213, 222, 274, 275, 320,
        328, 406–7, 432, 464, 475
    Barack Obama 193, 204
    calls to strip Aung San Suu Kyi
        of 432
    laureates 54, 95
    Thein Sein's nomination 201, 202
Nobel Peace Prize Committee 203,
    204
Non-Proliferation Treaty 45, 135,
    238, 259
Nordic countries 96

North Korea 143, 186, 195
    activity in Syria 71
    arms sales to Myanmar 26, 62–3,
        88, 89, 96, 143, 174, 185,
        187, 237, 239, 240, 241, 258
    arms shipments, interdiction of
        101, 238
    as information black hole 61, 62,
        71, 136, 241
    as nuclear model for Myanmar
        67, 104
    as pariah state 64, 195, 202, 210,
        364
    as strategic threat to US 143, 239
    assassination attempt on South
        Korean President 62, 181–3
    cargo shipments to Myanmar 43,
        62, 88, 100, 101, 187
    claims about ties with Myanmar
        61–4
    claims of military technology
        assistance to Myanmar 43, 63,
        70, 87, 89, 101, 105, 148,
        175, 187, 239, 258, 291, 297
    claims of nuclear assistance to
        Myanmar 4, 43, 44, 45, 62,
        63, 64, 65, 66, 67, 68, 71,
        101, 103–4, 107–8, 134–6,
        138, 143, 148, 175, 176, 187,
        297
    defence ties with Myanmar 101,
        143, 145, 187, 188, 292, 301,
        305
    growing ties with Myanmar 44,
        48, 68, 80, 183
    international concern over ties
        with Myanmar 44
    international criticism of 64
    labelled rogue regime by US 22
    military infrastructure expertise
        45, 63
    military infrastructure in
        Myanmar 45, 61–2, 105, 174
    multilateral dialogue with 50

Myanmar delegation visits to 43,
     89
Myanmar exports to 63
Myanmar severs relations with
     62, 182
Myanmar's promise to sever ties
     with 161, 162, 175, 183, 185,
     186, 237, 238–9, 240, 375
Myanmar's ties with 4, 66, 100,
     123, 133–6, 148, 160, 171,
     183, 202
nuclear conspiracy with Myanmar
     and Iran 43–6
nuclear proliferation 44, 71
nuclear status 44
philately 282
prohibition of arms exports from
     88, 100, 108, 238, 240
prohibition of defence links with
     145, 148, 161
restoration of diplomatic relations
     with Myanmar 44, 89
scope of activity in Myanmar 5
UN sanctions on 195
UNSC Resolution 1718 (2006)
     100, 101, 238, 240
UNSC Resolution 1874 (2009)
     88, 100, 101, 195, 238, 240
US call for regime change 34
US claims of links with Myanmar
     22, 66, 99
US claims of WMD program 44,
     105, 176
US concern over ties with
     Myanmar 68, 102, 106, 108,
     135, 136, 160, 179, 187, 195,
     237–41, 259
US criticism of 34, 66
US sanctions against 143
Norway 103, 284
nuclear nonproliferation 160, 179
Burma's support for 44
Burmese obligations 45, 135, 161,
     238, 259

see also Non-Proliferation Treaty;
     nuclear proliferation
nuclear proliferation 67
by Burma 106
by North Korea 71
fears of 131, 171
Myanmar's opposition to 44
US–Myanmar discussions over
     101, 196
see also Non-Proliferation Treaty;
     nuclear nonproliferation;
     nuclear weapons
nuclear reactor, claims about 62, 64,
     104, 108
nuclear research, Myanmar's program
     of 70, 138, 161, 175, 179, 186,
     259
nuclear weapons
     and ASEAN 148
     India as nuclear power 143
     North Korean proliferation 44, 71
     North Korean status 44
     Pakistan nuclear program 72
     Southeast Asia as nuclear weapon–
          free zone 148
     Thailand, rumours of Burmese
          nuclear program 43, 45
     see also Non-Proliferation Treaty;
          nuclear nonproliferation;
          nuclear proliferation
nuclear weapons, Myanmar
     activist claims of 48, 62, 67, 105
     aspirations for 64, 66, 67, 88,
          103–6, 107, 108, 136, 137,
          139, 145, 259, 375
     assurances to US on 179, 185
     Australia and Myanmar's nuclear
          status 87
     Barack Obama on rumours of 195
     Bush administration's silence on
          claims of 67
     claims in US Congress 67, 136,
          187

claims of component supply from North Korea 62, 63, 88, 101, 143, 160
claims of development of 5, 43, 45, 46, 61, 297
claims of North Korean assistance with 4, 43, 44, 45, 64, 65, 66, 67, 68, 71, 103–4, 107–8, 134–6, 138, 148, 175, 176, 187, 297
clandestine infrastructure claims 63
debates about 61, 133–6, 137
defectors' claims of 65
doubts about capability 90, 104, 105
fears about Myanmar's development of 4, 87
IISS dossier on claims 69–72
imports of dual-use equipment 89, 104
lack of evidence of 70, 105, 107, 134, 187
media claims of 65–8, 103–6, 107–8, 123–4, 134, 138–40, 295
missile warheads 89
motivation for 64, 70
North Korea as model for 67, 104
conspiracy with North Korea and Iran 43–7
Obama administration on 67, 195
Obama administration on rumours of 43, 46
Pakistan assistance to 45, 105
research 104
Russian technology 43, 44–5, 64, 70, 71, 138
scepticism about claims of 5
status 258, 259
suspicions of 67
Tatmadaw's capability 104
UK claims about 45, 87
US concern about 68, 187

US dismissal of claims about 64, 238
US failure to address claims about 173–6, 259
US response to rumours of 64, 65–8, 69, 72, 87, 106, 135–6, 160, 175, 238, 258–9
numerology 73, 74, 76
see also astrology; feng shui; magic; occult; superstition; yadaya

Obama administration
and Myanmar nuclear rumours 43, 46
critics of 83, 93, 186, 188, 300
embrace of ASEAN 82
engagement with Asia 160
Myanmar policy 172, 177, 306
Myanmar policy review 47, 49, 50, 51, 67, 79, 170
'pragmatic engagement' policy 4, 79–83, 93, 99, 186, 194, 300
relations with Myanmar 166, 177
sanctions against Myanmar 51–2, 170, 178, 187
see also United States
Obama, Barack 135, 172, 237, 289
and Aung San Suu Kyi 193, 195, 327
and military ties with Myanmar 195
and Myanmar nuclear rumours 195
and Myanmar sanctions 51–2, 239, 407
executive order 187, 239
Myanmar policy 102, 172, 196
Myanmar policy critics 93, 99, 100, 407
Myanmar policy review 51
Nobel Peace Prize 193, 204
on Muammar Gaddafi 141
'pragmatic engagement' policy 4, 79, 80, 83, 93, 99, 194

takes office 47, 48, 67
visit to Myanmar 193–6, 202,
210, 237, 238, 239, 244, 258
occult 73, 75, 76
see also astrology; *feng shui*; magic;
numerology; superstition;
yadaya
Office of the Chief of Military
Security Affairs (OCMSA) 459
Organisation for the Prohibition
of Chemical Weapons 301
Orwell, George 110, 329
Ostergaard, Anders 125

Pakistan 58, 476
and China 368
arms sales to Myanmar 96, 293,
462
defence ties with Myanmar 292,
293
nuclear assistance to Myanmar
45, 105
nuclear program 72
Rohingyas in 190, 217, 449
Pakokku 298
Panglong Agreement (1947) 416
Panthay 216
Pantoja-Hidalgo, Cristina 398
Parker, Clive 111
Parsons, Alf 396
Pashu (Malay Muslims) 216
Pathi 216
Patumanonda, Teerawat 426
Pauk 298
Pedersen, Morten 116, 449
People's Police Force (PPF) 356,
386–7
Perlez, Jane 327
philately 281–5, 414, 416, 471–4
Philippines, the 266, 452
Pilger, John 124
plutonium 70, 71
Poland 26, 96

police
Aviation 332, 357
border 332, 386, 437
Highway 357
Maritime 332, 467, 468, 469,
470
Tourist 332, 357
see also Australian Federal
Police; Bureau of Special
Investigations; Indian Imperial
Police; Myanmar Police Force
(MPF)
postage stamps, *see* philately
Powell, Colin 34
prodemocracy movement 32, 33, 38,
158, 233, 345
see also 'Saffron Revolution'
prodemocracy uprising (1988) 283,
307, 397, 414, 445
activists' use of pseudonyms
during 111
and fracturing of opposition
movement 38
as genesis of Burma-watching
137, 297
as genesis of films about 123, 124
as genesis of scholarly attention to
Myanmar 4, 369–70
as prompt to international
attention 130, 198, 390
as turning point in relations with
UN 304
Aung San Suu Kyi's rise to
prominence during 320, 397,
415
Australian condemnation of
response to 429
calls for invasion in response to 32
diplomatic isolation after 80
easing of punitive measures 186
entrenched power of military after
91, 92
expansion of military after 25, 27,
171, 292, 293

failure of 33, 150
hopes for change after 36
image of Myanmar after 171
lack of international attention to
14, 142
numbers killed 50
prompts fear of invasion 19–20,
21, 23, 90
sanctions/embargoes after 13, 96,
150, 171, 208, 429
Tatmadaw's response to xxi, 19,
21, 38, 90, 208, 387, 429
propaganda 59, 90, 112, 125, 192,
223, 282, 320, 337, 431
Putin, Vladimir 203
Pyidaungsu Hluttaw (Union
Assembly) xxvi
Pyitthu Hluttaw (House of
Representatives) xxvi
Pyongyang, *see* North Korea

Queen Victoria 281

Rajapaksa, Mahinda 75
Rakhine (Arakan) State xxi, 472, 476
and Buddhist extremists 433
Arakan Rohingya Salvation Army
attacks in 406, 431, 437, 400,
440, 450, 476
'area clearance operations' in 3,
445, 453, 473, 475, 477
communal violence in 190, 191,
199, 209, 215
focus of resources on 433
government 450
human rights abuses in 219, 433,
447, 462
Kamans in 216
land reallocation to Buddhists 440
Muslim migration to 192
'people who believe in Islam in'
402, 473
plan to expel Rohingyas from
440, 441

religious violence in 191, 192,
215, 219, 223, 232, 268, 450
Rohingyas in 216, 218, 431, 447,
450
security operations in 199, 406,
407, 433, 437–8, 446, 458,
464, 476
see also Arakan Army; Arakan
Rohingya Salvation Army;
Arakan State; Arakanese
Rambo 29–32
Rangoon (Yangon) 88, 101, 192, 193
AFP office in 245
anti-Indian riots 218
as administrative capital xxii
as location for foreign embassies
80, 396, 398, 401
assassination attempt on South
Korean president in 62, 181–3
attacks on Aung San Suu Kyi in
350
Aung San Suu Kyi's home in 53,
55, 322
Australian Embassy in 1n.1, 191,
288, 380, 395, 401, 425
Bangladeshi Embassy in 217
Barack Obama's visit to 193–4
bombings (2005) 266, 267
City Hall 344, 351
demonstrations in 343–6, 351,
352
media 298
Mughal emperor in 57
name change xxi, 272
restoration of Australian defence
attaché to 244, 295, 425
Rohingyas in 216
rumour mill 232, 338, 343
Shwedagon Pagoda 58
transfer of capital from 75
UK defence attaché in 244
UMP marches on 386
US Embassy in 402

withdrawal of Australian defence
attaché from 208, 425
see also Yangon
Rangoon University 194
Ratnagiri 58
Reagan, Ronald 76
Red Cross, *see* International
Committee of the Red Cross;
Myanmar Red Cross
religion, *see* Buddhism; Christianity;
Hindus; Islam; Muslims
Renouf, Alan 395
Republic of Korea (ROK) 181
see also South Korea
'responsibility to protect' doctrine
(R2P) 17, 21, 22, 32, 141, 143
Rice, Condoleezza 22, 35, 130
Rice, Susan 67
Ride, Edwin 396
Robertson, Tim 327, 329
Robespierre, Norman 111
rockets 63, 139, 299
see also missiles
Rohingya crisis 5, 431, 433, 434,
435, 437–41, 446, 449, 452–3,
463
resistance to solution 189, 190,
432, 433, 435, 441, 448
Rohingyas
activism by 218
and European Union 403, 441
and Indonesia 435
'area clearance operations' against
3, 4, 432, 438, 445, 461, 473,
475, 477
as largest group of Muslims in
Myanmar 216
as minority population 178, 325,
326
attempts to link to terrorism
218–19, 438
Aung San Suu Kyi denies status
of 190, 474, 476
Aung San Suu Kyi's lack of action
on 6, 325, 328, 406, 419,
420, 422, 423, 431, 435
Aung San Suu Kyi's prohibition
of use of 'Rohingya' 402–3,
473, 476
Australian humanitarian intake
of 191
Australian position on 189–92,
290, 403
Burmese attitudes to 190, 192,
408, 421, 432, 433, 440, 441,
448, 477
deaths of 190, 218, 432
denial of citizenship 190, 440, 473
denial of international recognition
189
denial of recognition 189, 399,
402–3, 471, 473, 474
discrimination against 190, 217,
264, 305, 328, 408, 439
displacement of 190, 218, 439,
440, 445
'ethnic cleansing' of 4, 440, 451,
470, 473
genocide against 422, 432, 451,
475–6
human rights abuses against 5–6,
178, 247, 325, 326, 419, 432,
438, 440, 446, 447
in India 439
in Pakistan 190, 217, 449
insurgents 431, 434, 439, 450
international activism for 189,
190, 202, 209
international concern about 4,
178, 189, 362, 408, 421, 422,
433, 435, 440, 461–2, 464,
465, 470
in Thailand 190, 439
land given to Buddhists 440
links to terrorism 268, 449–53
MPF operations against 432

Muslim countries' concern about
189, 439, 452, 462
no right of return 190
numbers of 189, 216, 218, 432,
448, 450, 451, 465, 476
opposition to violence 218, 450
origins 217, 473
plan to drive out of Myanmar
437, 440
plight as cause for international
terrorism 268, 439, 450, 452
pogroms against 190, 218, 448
recruitment by terrorists 449–53
refugees in Bangladesh 190, 191,
218, 432, 435, 437, 440, 445,
448, 450–1, 453, 465, 476
self-identification as 216, 403, 431
state violence against 202, 209,
218, 247, 290, 406, 431–3,
437, 439, 445, 447, 464
statelessness of 406, 420, 431, 451
status of 190, 403, 406, 471, 473,
474, 476, 477
violence against 218, 233, 432,
440, 446, 481
see also Arakan Rohingya Salvation
Army; Islam; Muslims
Roosevelt, Franklin Delano 76
Ros-Lehtinen, Ileana 187
Rowland, John 395
Royal Australian Navy (RAN) 295,
425
Royal Thai Army (RTA) 426, 427,
428, 429
Rudd, Kevin 102, 273, 361, 362
rule of law, see law—rule of
Rumsfeld, Donald 130, 131
Russia 5n.12, 70, 481
arms sales to Myanmar 26, 96,
174, 258, 292, 293, 374, 462,
464
defence ties with Myanmar 175,
375, 464

nuclear technology 43, 44–5, 64,
70, 71, 138
protection of Myanmar at UN 4,
464
relations with Myanmar 14, 48,
80, 284
see also Soviet Union
Ryckmans, Pierre 109

'Saffron Revolution' (2007) 22, 39,
111, 114, 414
brutality of military response to
25, 27, 48
Buddhist monks' participation in
13, 27, 39, 212
'citizen journalists' during 125
crushing of 39, 114
diplomatic response to 14
examination of 114, 125
impact on military rank and file
25, 27, 50
international publicity 14
lack of international punitive
measures 14
limits of international influence 13
militia involvement in 233, 250
MPF response to 27, 199
prompts questioning of 'active
pacifism' 39
sanctions
after prodemocracy uprising
(1988) 13, 96, 150, 171, 208,
429
against Tatmadaw 240, 433
ASEAN rules out 14, 96
Aung San Suu Kyi calls for
international 230, 261–4,
276, 309, 310, 311–12, 326
Barack Obama and 51–2, 239,
407
by European Union on Myanmar
14, 80, 96, 463
by UN on Myanmar 62, 461

by US on Myanmar 14, 21, 33, 35, 48, 51–2, 80, 81, 82, 143, 159, 170, 186, 187, 194, 241, 263, 407
Hillary Clinton on 48, 49
Obama administration and 51–2, 170, 178, 187
UN on North Korea 195
US on North Korea 143
see also arms—embargoes
Saudi Arabia 190, 441
Saw Maung 59
Scott, J.G. 110
security forces, *see* Myanmar Police Force; *Tatmadaw*
Serbia 96, 174
Shan xxiv, 165, 186, 213, 299, 328, 471
Shan State 407, 458, 472
Shu Maung xxiv, 110
see also Ne Win
Shwe Mann 230, 310, 312
Shwedagon Pagoda 58, 59, 269
Shwepyithar Industrial Zone 351, 352
Siam (Thailand) 426, 427
Singapore 45, 62, 76, 83, 132, 146, 201, 266, 356, 452
as ASEAN chair 14
defence links with Myanmar 174, 258
Sittwe 218
SLORC, *see* State Law and Order Restoration Council
Slovakia 96
Smith, Stephen 95
South Asia 189, 216, 439, 449, 451, 452
South Korea 62, 96, 181–83
Southeast Asia 451, 480
and nuclear weapons 64, 69–70
as nuclear weapon–free zone 148
military forces in 26, 198, 294
Muslim populations in 215, 439, 452

Southeast Asian Games 267
Soviet Union 282, 398
see also Russia
SPDC, *see* State Peace and Development Council
Special Branch (SB) xxiii, 198, 357, 386, 388, 459
see also Myanmar Police Force
Spender, Jean 396
Sri Lanka 75, 368
St Petersburg 293
Stalin, Joseph 203
Stallone, Sylvester 29, 30, 31, 32
stamps, *see* philately
State Law and Order Restoration Council (SLORC) xxv, 25, 316, 317, 427, 429
State Peace and Development Council (SPDC) xxv, 25, 27, 47, 48, 49, 50, 174, 176, 284
State Secrets Act (1923) 298
Steinberg, David 32, 35, 118, 143, 320
Steinberg, Jim 48
Stern, Ricki 125
Straits Times 201
Stuart, Francis 396
Subcommittee on East Asian and Pacific Affairs (US) 239
Subcontinent, the 216
see also South Asia
submarines 5, 63, 291–5, 375, 469
Foxtrot class 292
Kilo class 293
Sang-O class 292
Yugo class 292
Suharto 75
Sukarno 75
Sun Yat Sen 416
Sundberg, Annie 125
Supayalat 58
superstition 73–7, 80, 213, 222
see also astrology; *feng shui*; magic; numerology; occult; *yadaya*

Suzuki, Takashi 398
Swan Arshin/Swan Ah Shin (SAS)
    (militia) 233, 350, 351
    see also Myanmar Police Force
Sydney Morning Herald 65, 66, 380
Syria 34, 44, 66, 71

T'ang National Liberation Army 407
Taiwan 174, 258, 416
Taliban 268
tanks 376
    MBT-2000 374
    T-72 374
Tanner, Lindsay 138
Tatmadaw xxv, 18, 36, 90, 214, 468
    accountability of 244, 253, 445,
        446, 447, 461
    and 1988 prodemocracy uprising
        xxi, 19, 21, 38, 208, 429
    and Aung San 414, 415, 478
    and Border Guard Forces 252
    and MPF 197, 198, 200, 312,
        332, 385–8
    and peacekeeping 303
    and PPF 387
    and Swan Arshin 350, 351
    and territorial defence 26, 385
    and UMP 386
    and WMD 186, 297–9, 375
    anti-China faction in 152
    'area clearance operations' 3, 4,
        432, 438, 445, 461, 473, 475,
        477
    arms acquisitions 3, 26, 96, 97,
        373, 374, 376, 461, 462
    arms embargo against 95, 244
    as apparatus of state 3, 198, 209,
        210, 229, 255, 408
    as central political institution 3,
        209, 210, 229, 255, 305, 377,
        387, 406, 408
    assistance from India 463
    Aung San Suu Kyi's challenge to
        262, 277, 310, 311, 421
    Aung San Suu Kyi's lack of
        control over 405, 408, 423,
        432, 438, 459
    Aung San Suu Kyi's relations with
        228, 230, 277, 309, 310, 328,
        408, 420, 459
    Aung San Suu Kyi's support of 3,
        230, 310, 478
    Australian contact with 245–6,
        429
    Australian training of 207–8, 210
    autonomy of 3, 230, 406, 420
    capability 26, 95, 293, 373
    chain of command xxiii, 446,
        447, 457, 459, 469
    coalition with Aung San Suu Kyi
        311, 477
    commitment to 'disciplined
        democracy' 2, 40, 310, 311,
        389
    commitment to three 'national
        causes' 252, 312, 434
    complicity in anti-Muslim
        violence 190, 234, 351
    conscripts 26
    consolidation of power 171, 435
    constitutional protection of xxvi,
        156, 229, 252–3, 310, 312,
        328, 387, 391, 408, 420, 432
    constraints on power of 254, 392
    control of 118, 241
    control of government xxv, 5,
        115, 116, 118, 210, 251, 277,
        312, 328
    corruption 37, 125, 209, 253,
        385, 388
    counterinsurgency operations 26,
        27, 147–8, 152, 198, 247,
        276, 376, 386, 407, 408–9,
        426, 427
    creation of SLORC xxv, 25
    defectors from 134
    depiction in *Rambo* 29–31
    desertions from 26

diffusion of power 117, 121, 200, 349

diminution of 25, 26, 229, 254, 351, 448

discipline within 25, 27, 28, 50, 120, 143, 446, 447

doctrine 15, 167, 306, 373, 434, 447, 458

domination of politics 247, 255, 262

expansion of 22, 25, 26, 374, 464–5

external engagement with 209, 244, 248, 262, 313, 433, 464, 470

failure to constrain power of 408

fear of foreign invasion 21, 22, 23

funding 178, 229, 253, 294, 377, 387, 464

guardianship role 27, 40, 229, 253, 434, 441

hardliners within 118, 161, 224, 313, 434

human rights abuses by 4, 209, 247, 305, 445, 447, 464, 476

image of 209, 433, 478

in operation 125

in parliament xxvi, 40, 92, 156, 254, 311, 312, 373, 377, 420

insurgent attacks against 431–2, 438

intelligence apparatus xxiii, 198, 312, 457–8, 459, 460

international condemnation of 252, 429, 461, 464, 470

intervention in state affairs 252, 254, 313, 408

keeping Aung San Suu Kyi from presidency xxvi, 2, 156, 227–30, 252, 264, 300–13, 326, 363, 392

lack of women in 356

leadership of 15, 115, 200, 209, 230, 240, 311, 313, 392, 407, 433, 441

loosening grip of 200, 229

loyalty of 15, 25–8, 120, 142, 199, 294, 388

modernisation of 22, 25, 292, 294, 374, 377, 385, 433

monopoly of force 386

mutineers 386

nomenclature xxiii, 211

nuclear capability 104

off-budget revenue 253, 387

operations against Rohingyas 4, 5, 190, 247, 431–3, 437, 441, 445, 447, 464

opposition to democratic reform 253, 267, 313, 435

order of battle 3, 374

peace agreements with ethnic groups 3, 5, 152, 267, 305, 326, 362, 364, 376, 406, 407, 416, 421–2, 434

potential for coup by 251–2, 254, 408

power of 116, 119, 224, 313, 373, 376–7, 387, 392, 406

professionalisation of 244, 248, 249, 373, 374, 433

public information about 25, 298, 339–40, 374, 446

rank and file 15, 27, 209, 229, 253, 312

relations with China 96, 209, 248

response to Cyclone Nargis 19, 27

restructure of 26, 117, 385

retaking of power (1988) xxiii, xxv, 19, 21, 25, 38, 170, 283, 349, 414, 427

retreat from politics 2, 121, 229, 244, 262, 312, 363, 377, 385, 389–90, 458

role in liberalisation 209, 305–6, 363, 393

sanctions against 240, 433

seizure of power (1962) xxv, 2

size of 26, 27, 198, 373, 374

strategy 251, 390, 437, 438, 441
submarine acquisition 291–2
support for Aung San Suu Kyi
    228, 229–30
support for coastguard 467–9
support for democratic reform
    212, 264, 305–6, 307, 312,
    377, 389–92
suspicion of Aung San Suu Kyi
    224, 312
threats to 15, 253, 310
use of child soldiers 26, 305
use of terror 447
Western assistance to 209, 241,
    243, 244, 247, 248, 306, 317,
    433
willingness to use force 15, 27
see also Bureau of Special
    Investigations; Military
    Intelligence; Military
    Intelligence Service; Myanmar
    Air Force; Myanmar Navy;
    Myanmar Police Force; Swan
    Arshin
Taung Tha Army 233
Taylor, Robert 392, 421, 457
Tenet, George 131
terrorism
    and Nobel Peace Prize 203
    anti-Muslim sentiment as cause of
        268, 269
    as excuse for military operations
        437, 438, 476
    attacks in Myanmar 265–6, 439,
        452, 453
    attempts to link Rohingyas to
        218–19, 438
    Aung San Suu Kyi's warnings
        about 452
    Burmese Muslims turning to 269
    coastguard responsibility for 468
    counterproductivity of 269
    counterterrorism 269
    difficulty of sustaining 269

exiles' support for 38
international 269, 434, 437, 452
Rohingyas' links to 268, 449–53
Rohingyas' plight as cause for
    268, 439, 450, 452
threat of 449–53
terrorists
    adoption of tactics 266
    recruitment of Rohingyas by 268,
        449–53
    regime opponents labelled as 267
    see also extremists; individual
        group names; jihadists
Thailand 33–4, 113, 356
    activists in 75, 266
    Burmese exile groups in 38
    companies' defence assistance
        to Myanmar 258
    Exercise Cobra Gold 210, 244
    George W. Bush's visit to 33–6
    king 90
    relations with Myanmar 427
    Rohingyas in 190, 439
    rumours of Burmese nuclear
        program 43, 45
    US strategic interest in 90
    see also Royal Thai Army; Siam
Thailand–Myanmar border 1, 318,
    426–9, 468
    activists along 124
    Karen 29, 31, 317
    refugees crossing 31, 34, 427
    weapons on 88
Than Shwe 15, 59, 73, 75, 76, 117,
    118, 121, 166, 171, 284, 319
Thanbyuzayat 426
The Age 65–6
The Australian 66, 67
The Diplomat 327
The Interpreter 1, 4, 6, 8, 65, 68, 145,
    170, 173, 287, 309, 327, 399,
    413, 479–81
The Irrawaddy (magazine) 111
The Lady (2011 film) 213, 320

The New York Times 327
The Times 327
Thein Htay 237, 240, 241
Thibaw Min, King 58
Thirty Comrades 110
three 'national causes' 252, 312, 434
Three Pagodas Pass 1, 425–29
TIME (magazine) 202, 203, 327
Tin Maung Maung Than 146
Tokyo 266
Tom Lantos Block Burmese JADE (Junta's Anti-Democratic Efforts) Act (JADE Act) (US) 46, 49, 68, 135, 173, 174, 176, 257, 259
Tonkin, Derek 240, 274, 289
Toungoo 218
Tourist Police 332, 357
Treaty of Amity and Cooperation 82
Turnbull, Malcolm 401
Turnell, Sean 364

U Nu 74, 76, 283, 284, 386
U Thant 284, 303
U Wirathu 233
Ukraine 26, 96, 174, 375, 463, 464
undemocratic 92, 143, 170, 305
Union Assembly, see *Pyidaungsu Hluttaw*
Union Constabulary 386
Union Military Police (UMP) 386
Union Solidarity and Development Party (USDP) xxv, 156, 212, 228, 230, 234, 254
Union Solidarity Development Association (USDA) 350
United Kingdom (UK) 125, 156, 222, 228, 281, 293, 317, 318, 320, 356, 364, 415
    activism against engagement with Myanmar 313
    and claims of Myanmar nuclear program 45, 87
    and Cyclone Nargis 22, 48
    and use of Burma/Myanmar name 272, 274, 399
    anti-British sentiment in Burma 58
    arms embargo against Myanmar 95
    British Empire 281
    Burmese independence from xxi, 74, 207, 272, 315, 414, 427, 472
    call for action on Myanmar 130
    colonial rule of Burma 110, 217, 245, 272, 316, 356
    colonisation of India 57, 316
    conquest of Burma xxii, 58, 59, 110, 216, 473
    criticism of Myanmar election laws 91
    defence ties with Myanmar 243, 244, 245, 295
    media 39, 57, 124
    opposition to military regime 202, 399
    philately 281, 474
    Thein Sein visit to 202, 244
United Nations (UN) 14, 29, 131, 190, 402
    and Geneva Protocol 316
    and philately 283, 284
    claims of 'ethnic cleansing'/ genocide 4, 422, 432, 438, 451, 462, 470, 473
    criticism of Myanmar in 22, 283, 304, 435
    development assistance 304, 332
    fact-finding missions 304, 475–6
    failure of 36
    interdiction of exports 101
    lack of action on Myanmar 36
    Myanmar's distrust of 21, 22, 304
    on use of Burma/Myanmar name xxii, 272, 289, 379
    peacekeeping, Myanmar's involvement in 303–7, 358
    refugee aid 218
    relations with Myanmar 303, 304

sanctions/embargoes 62, 461
Secretary-General 39, 142, 284,
    303, 304, 406, 432, 435
Special Envoy 304
Special Rapporteur on Burma
    142, 304
United Nations Children's Fund
    (UNICEF) 332, 398
United Nations General Assembly
    39, 142
United Nations High Commissioner
    for Refugees (UNHCR) 189, 332
United Nations Human Rights
    Council 14, 141, 446, 475–6
United Nations Observation Group
    in the Lebanon (UNOGIL) 303
United Nations Office on Drugs and
    Crime 245, 332, 359
United Nations Operation in the
    Congo (ONUC) 303
United Nations Postal Administration
    284
United Nations Security Council
    (UNSC) 22, 96, 141
    and Libya 141–2
    China and Russia's protection of
        Myanmar at 4, 96, 122, 150,
        464
    compliance with resolutions of
        101, 161, 162, 179, 240, 241
    Myanmar's resolution violations
        101, 102, 108, 148, 160, 187,
        188, 305
    North Korean resolution
        violations 145, 160, 187, 305
    presidential statement on
        Myanmar 14
    Resolution 1718 (2006) 100, 101,
        238, 240
    Resolution 1874 (2009) 88, 100,
        101, 195, 238, 240
    US actions on 34, 44–5, 67
United States (US) xxv, 29, 30, 32,
    76, 130–1, 358, 398, 470, 480
    alliance with Australia 208

and ASEAN 82, 195
and Cyclone Nargis 22, 35, 48
and Iran 44, 66
and Iraq 22, 66
and Myanmar elections 99, 178
and Myanmar nuclear program
    rumours 64, 65–8, 69, 72, 87,
    106, 135–6, 160, 175, 238,
    258–9
and Myanmar's missile acquisition
    88, 89, 160, 161, 175, 187,
    238, 239, 241, 258
and Myanmar's submarine
    acquisition 293
and nonproliferation 45, 135,
    179, 196, 238
and North Korea 22, 44, 66
and Rohingya crisis 440–1, 476
and Syria 44, 66
arms embargo 96, 100–1, 108,
    135–6
Congress 46, 49, 50, 67, 68, 133,
    135, 136, 172, 173, 176, 186,
    188, 238, 241, 258, 306, 407
congressional committees 176
criticism of Aung San Suu Kyi 407
criticism of Myanmar election
    laws 91, 93
demand for regime change 34, 130
desire for civilian government in
    Myanmar 19, 81
formal 'designation' of actors 237,
    239–40
House of Representatives 100
House of Representatives
    Committee on Foreign Affairs
    177–9
intelligence agencies 66–7, 176
invasion of Afghanistan 34
invasion of Iraq 34
invitation for Thein Sein to visit
    202
labels Myanmar 'outpost of
    tyranny' 22, 34, 35, 48

lack of influence on Myanmar 33,
35, 80, 93, 99, 306
military presence 20
military ties with Myanmar 195,
210, 241, 243–8, 295, 334
Myanmar as threat to foreign
policy of 34, 239
Myanmar as threat to national
security of 34, 239, 179, 195,
239
Myanmar policy 36, 135, 143–4,
153, 222, 240, 364
Myanmar policy failure 33, 35,
100, 172, 194, 263
Myanmar policy review 47–50,
51, 54, 67, 79, 170
Myanmar's assurances to on
nuclear weapons 179, 185
Myanmar's fears of military
intervention by 20, 21–3, 35,
36, 43, 48, 63, 90, 102, 376
on Myanmar's chemical weapons
capability 299–300
on UN Security Council 34,
44–5, 67, 96
opposition to Myanmar as
ASEAN chair 146, 148
Pacific forces 88
pivot to Asia 194
'pragmatic engagement' policy
4, 79–83, 93, 99–100, 172,
177–9, 186, 194, 306
recognition of NLD government
34
relations with Asia 34
relations with Myanmar 50, 81,
102, 153, 159–62, 172, 176,
177–9, 193–6, 237, 313,
367–71
sanctions against Myanmar 14,
21, 33, 35, 48, 51–2, 80, 81,
82, 143, 159, 170, 186, 187,
194, 241, 263, 407
Senate 100, 136, 248

Senate Committee on Foreign
Relations 49, 136, 239
special envoy to Burma 133, 173
Special National Security
Intelligence Estimate 299
State Department 45, 89, 135,
160, 169n.1, 173–6, 176,
185, 187, 238–40, 244, 257,
258, 259, 289, 350, 476
State Department Office for
Mainland Southeast Asia 49
strategic competition with China
160, 194
Treasury Department 237, 240
Treaty of Amity and Cooperation
82
use of Burma/Myanmar name
272, 274, 289, 399, 401, 402
see also Bush administration;
Obama administration
United States Agency for
International Development
(USAID) 338
United States Institute of Peace 245,
448
United States Navy 20, 21, 22, 62, 88
Unity Journal 298, 300
Universal Postal Union 281
uranium 44, 45, 71, 104
USDA, see Union Solidarity
Development Association
USDP, see Union Solidarity and
Development Party

vehicles
military 376
unmanned 374, 462
Vietnam 26, 148, 188, 292, 464
vigilantes 346, 349–53, 432
see also 'auxiliaries'; militias; Swan
Arshin

Waller, Keith 395
war 29, 74, 123, 167
Anglo-Burmese 217

crimes 202, 253
First War of Independence 57
Great Mutiny 57
Iraq 46
of independence, Bangladesh 217
on Korean Peninsula 6, 183
proxy 440
rape as weapon of 447
see also Cold War; crimes against
humanity; World War II
war, civil
against Karens 29, 31
in Kachin State 209, 223
war, guerilla 38, 152, 156, 252, 266
against KIA 152
Washington, DC 79, 133, 135,
169n.1, 238, 407
Watt, Alan 395
weapons 5, 90, 186, 297–301,
375, 376
antisubmarine 292
political 139
psychological 88
strategic 102, 103, 106
see also arms; artillery; ballistic
missiles; biological weapons;
chemical weapons; gunboat;
helicopters; helicopter
gunships; missiles; nuclear
weapons; rockets; tanks
Webb, Jim 143
Webster, Jonathan 322
West, the
attacks against 481
Myanmar as target of criticism
by 18
Myanmar's distrust of 48, 304,
313
Myanmar's relations with 4, 172,
207, 209, 243, 247
punitive measures against
Myanmar 170, 208, 313, 429,
433
superstition in 76

Western
bias 73
commentators 7, 370
criticism of Myanmar 304, 364
engagement with Myanmar 172,
207, 243, 247, 248, 333, 397,
398, 433
governments 46, 144, 289
hypocrisy 143
intelligence 67
media 76, 107, 299
missionaries 29
music 320, 322, 323
ostracism of Myanmar 150, 369
personal names xxiv
policy on Myanmar 171, 248, 368
politicians 130, 221, 224
relations with Aung San Suu Kyi
171, 221, 224, 415
-style democracy 364
support for democracy 36, 76
use of Burma/Myanmar name 7,
289, 399
White Paper, *see* Defence White Paper
Williams, Evan 124
Wilson, Trevor 395, 397, 398
Woodard, Garry xviii, 396
Woolcott, Richard 395
World Bank 122
World Economic Forum 172
World War II 216, 244, 426

yadaya 74
see also astrology; *feng shui*;
magic; numerology; occult;
superstition
Yamethin 218
Yangon (Rangoon)
as administrative capital xxii, 427
Aung San museum in 415
Aung San Suu Kyi's house in 53,
414
Australian defence attaché in 244,
295, 425

Australian Embassy in 1n.1, 191,
    288, 380, 395, 428
Australian–Myanmar Strategic
    Dialogue in 425
MIS headquarters 429
name change xxi, 272
rumour mill 385
see also Rangoon
Yeoh, Michelle 320
Yettaw, John 53, 54, 55
Yunnan 153, 216

Zarganar 111
Zerbadee 216
Zimbabwe 34

www.ingramcontent.com/pod-product-compliance
Lightning Source LLC
Chambersburg PA
CBHW051442270326
41932CB00035B/3378